prévert vous parle...

à

Jeanne Varney Pleasants
en témoignage d'admiration
et d'affection

a. b.
d. n.

prévert vous parle...

18 *poèmes*
choisis et commentés
par

ANDRÉE BERGENS
Carleton University

DAVID NOAKES
New York University

PRENTICE-HALL, INC. *Englewood Cliffs, New Jersey*

Prentice-Hall International, Inc., *London*
Prentice-Hall of Australia, Pty. Ltd., *Sydney*
Prentice-Hall of Canada, Ltd., *Toronto*
Prentice-Hall of India Private Ltd., *New Delhi*
Prentice-Hall of Japan, Inc., *Tokyo*

Library of Congress Catalog Card No.: 68-10016

Current printing (last digit)

10   9   8   7   6   5   4   3

Printed in the United States of America

preface

The guiding principle of all sound teaching methods is to arouse and sustain the student's interest, for people do well only what they enjoy doing. When students are no longer children, this principle requires that their starting language study at an elementary level not be used as an excuse for treating them intellectually at the same level. Experience shows that the best and surest way of exciting young people's interest is by using simple and short texts of recognized literary value, presented in such a way as to let them express themselves from the very beginning in language that is authentically French instead of in insipid sentences fabricated to illustrate theoretical rules of grammar.

Jacques Prévert seems to us to be the ideal author for a reader at this level. His poetry combines in equal measure literary value, intellectual and emotional appeal, simplicity and directness of expression. Students get a feeling of achievement by mastering interesting texts in the "new" language at an early stage.

Our selection of poems has been made with pedagogical as well as literary considerations in mind and is based on many years of experience with such poems both in the classroom and in the language laboratory. Although the first five offer relatively little difficulty and may well be studied first, neither they nor the following ones have to be taken up in the order given.

Let us explain briefly the six sections into which the study of each poem is divided.

PREMIÈRE PARTIE
lecture du poème

With the text in front of him so that pronunciation can be associated with spelling, the student listens to the poem. It is necessary that Prévert be read aloud, for sounds, rhythms, stress, intonation, emphasis, and tone are elements which bring out the meaning and the value of his poetry.

On the tapes provided for use in the language laboratory there are three readings: (A) the entire poem; (B) the poem broken into thought-groups, each of which is followed by a pause during which the student repeats and records; (C) the entire poem without breaks. All three readings are at normal speed. The student's repeating the poem in (B) also serves as a drill on stress and intonation. The sign / . . . / is used throughout the book to indicate a pause during which the student should repeat what he has just heard.

DEUXIÈME PARTIE
étude du texte

Before turning to the questions included under this heading, the student will have followed up his aural introduction to the poem by making sure he thoroughly understands it. For this purpose, he will find on the left-hand page facing the text, under the heading "Notes explicatives," explanations in French of words and expressions whose specific use in the poem requires special attention. The basic meanings of all words used, whether by Prévert or by us (except for those occurring only in the phonetic exercises), will be found in the French-English vocabulary at the end.

The questions in «Etude du texte,» varying in number and for the most part factual, are designed to be a means of simple and direct exploration of the poem, leading in many cases to an «explication de texte»—a study of the text that will bring out the author's themes or thoughts and the various stylistic devices he uses to express them.

Oral preparation of the questions should be assigned as homework. The instructor may choose those that best fit his class's needs and ability. They are intended for classroom use, with the teacher acting as a constant guide, for their pedagogical value depends on a general discussion made possible by various personal interpretations.

TROISIÈME PARTIE
phonétique

These exercises, intended for use by the student in the language laboratory with the script before his eyes, are of two kinds:

I. *Contrastes.* These "contrasts" between English and French words let the student hear the differences between apparently similar sounds (especially regarding diphthongs). An American voice pronounces the English word and a French speaker the contrasting French one. This is repeated three times. Then the French word is repeated three times by the French speaker, and the student repeats it three times afterwards during the ensuing pause.

II. *Oppositions.* These "oppositions" let the student learn how to distinguish between pairs of French vowel sounds that seem at first almost or completely identical. Each pair of words or phrases is followed by a pause during which the student repeats. Then the pair is repeated one final time by the French speaker.

The eighteen sections of phonetic exercises have been designed to cover the entire range of sounds used in the French language. A special index at the end of the book provides a table of these phonemes with key words and page references.

QUATRIÈME PARTIE
exercices

Exercises of various types back up particular aspects of vocabulary and patterns found in each poem. The explanations given do not constitute a methodical study of grammar and are not meant to substitute for the student's regular textbook.

Most of them are oral, although a few are in writing. Some which are based only on repetition will also serve as drills on stress and intonation (as in section I). A special index at the end of the book provides page references for the various points treated.

We have deliberately avoided translations and compositions, for at this stage both are dangerous in that they encourage students to think in English and therefore use patterns of their own language.

CINQUIÈME PARTIE
compréhension

On the tapes provided for laboratory use, a brief passage containing some of the vocabulary of the poem is read twice at normal speed. Then five questions based on the passage are asked (each is asked twice). The student writes a very short answer in French (one or two words) merely to show that he has understood the question.

SIXIÈME PARTIE
dictée

Dictations play a very important part in language learning. The laboratory is their ideal location, for it enables the teacher to use his classroom time for more appropriate subjects.

A short paragraph is based on material the student is already familiar with, but in a new presentation. He writes it on his answer sheet and turns it in for correction at the end of the laboratory session.

*   *   *

We recommend that work on each assignment be divided into two parts for laboratory purposes. Sections I and III («Lecture du poème» and «Phonétique») of the poem to which the student is being introduced will be combined with sections IV, V, and VI («Exercices,» «Compréhension,» and «Dictée») of the poem previously studied. With this in mind, the tapes to be used with each poem have been divided into two parts and can be used in any order the instructor chooses.

A. B.

D. N.

contents

prévert vous parle...

quelques mots sur jacques prévert

Voici tout d'abord une présentation «bio-bibliographique» succincte de la vie et des principaux ouvrages de l'auteur:

1900, 4 fév.	Naissance de Jacques Prévert à Neuilly-sur-Seine.
1915	Il quitte l'école et commence à gagner sa vie en faisant divers métiers.
1920	Service militaire en France, puis en Turquie (armée d'occupation). A son retour, il habite rue du Château avec le peintre Yves Tanguy et Marcel Duhamel.
1925	Rencontre avec les surréalistes qui, bientôt, fréquenteront la rue du Château (Breton, Aragon, Péret, Desnos, Leiris, Queneau, etc.).
1930	Les premiers textes de Prévert apparaissent dans différentes revues.
1932–1936	Il travaille avec la troupe théâtrale du «Groupe Octobre». Il écrit des pièces pour elle et les interprète également. Pendant cette période, il écrit les scénarios de ses premiers films et ses chansons commencent à être chantées; il continue à écrire des poèmes.
1937	*Drôle de drame,* film avec Marcel Carné.
1938	Séjour d'un an aux Etats-Unis. *Quai des brumes,* film avec M. Carné.
1939	*Le Jour se lève,* film avec M. Carné.

1

1942	*Les Visiteurs du soir,* film avec M. Carné et P. Laroche.
1943	*Les Enfants du paradis,* film avec M. Carné.
1945	*Les Portes de la nuit,* film avec M. Carné. *Aubervilliers,* film avec Eli Lotar.
1946	*Paroles,* 1ère éd. collection de textes de Jacques Prévert avec une couverture de Brassaï. Ed. du Point du Jour, Coll. «Le Calligraphe». (Suivie de nombreuses rééditions dans les années qui suivent.) *Histoires,* en collaboration avec André Verdet (Le Pré aux Clercs). *Voyage-surprise,* film avec son frère Pierre Prévert. Naissance de sa fille Michèle.
1947	*Contes pour enfants pas sages* (Le Pré aux Clercs). *Paroles,* nouvelle édition revue et augmentée (Le Point du Jour).
1951	*Spectacle* (Le Point du Jour-N.R.F.).
1952	*Lettres des Iles Baladar* (Le Point du Jour-N.R.F.). *Guignol* (Lausanne, La Guilde du Livre).
1955	*La Pluie et le beau temps* (Le Point du Jour-N.R.F.) Il quitte Saint-Paul-de-Vence où il habitait depuis 1948 avec sa femme et sa fille et s'installe définitivement à Paris.
1957	Exposition de ses collages à la Galerie Adrien Maeght. *Images,* présentées par René Bertelé (Adrien Maeght).
1963	*Histoires,* nouvelle édition (Le Point du Jour-N.R.F.).
1966	*Fatras,* avec 55 collages de l'auteur (Le Point du Jour-N.R.F.).

Il semble que la poésie ait toujours été considérée comme une forme littéraire réservée à une élite intellectuelle seule capable de l'apprécier. Or, voici que dépassant les cercles spécialisés, Jacques Prévert atteint le grand public, le conquiert et sa soudaine célébrité vient remettre en question une conception admise de longue date.

Ce phénomène a lieu en 1946 quand l'éditeur René Bertelé réunit les poèmes écrits par Prévert depuis une quinzaine d'années et les publie en recueil sous le titre *Paroles*. Le succès est immédiat, le nom du poète sur toutes les lèvres.

Ce succès est compréhensible. Il s'agit d'une poésie spontanée et sincère qui traite de sujets familiers—émotions, faits-divers, événements—et les exprime d'une manière simple et directe avec des mots de tous les jours. Il faut encore y ajouter un extraordinaire don d'invention verbale et une verve jaillissante qui renouvellent constamment l'expression. Car Prévert a le sens de la communication. Rien ne peut mieux le caractériser que le titre même de son recueil. En effet, il parle plutôt qu'il n'écrit. C'est donc une erreur que de lire du Prévert seulement avec les yeux, il faut qu'il soit lu à haute voix ou récité.

On comprend alors mieux ce qu'il a à dire. Il a d'ailleurs beaucoup à dire sur ce qu'il aime et, surtout, sur ce qu'il n'aime pas. Qu'aime-t-il? Tout ce qui est beau, simple, naturel—le soleil, les fleurs, les oiseaux, les enfants, l'amour—et il s'indigne contre tout ce qui constitue un obstacle à la vie, à la liberté, au bonheur. Il dit alors leur fait à ceux qui en sont responsables et il n'y va pas par quatre chemins, il le dit avec véhémence, parfois avec violence. Attitude nécessaire car pour être entendu, il ne faut pas s'exprimer en demi-teinte. Au contraire, il faut parler fort et répéter souvent la même chose. Le langage parlé s'accommode très bien de la répétition.

Comment peut-on situer Prévert dans la littérature française contemporaine? Il est un fait qu'il y occupe une place importante car il apporte quelque chose de nouveau. Prévert «poète» emprunte à Prévert «homme de cinéma» certaines de ses techniques et fait subir au langage des transformations profondes qui le renouvellent tout en lui conservant son apparence habituelle. C'est ce travail de rénovation et de rajeunissement qui, joint à l'utilisation de thèmes familiers exprimés en langage parlé, donne à cette poésie populaire sa véritable originalité.

I

le jardin

le jardin: Il s'agit ici du parc mentionné dans le poème.

2 **Ne sauraient:** Ne pourraient (*formes conditionnelles de* savoir *et* pouvoir; *forme négative spéciale, voir p. 13, exercice II, B*).

3 **dire:** exprimer, expliquer

5 **tu m'as embrassé:** tu m'as donné un baiser (Embrasser *est très rarement employé dans le sens de serrer dans ses bras.*)

6 **je t'ai embrassée:** *Sur l'emploi du participe passé avec* te, *voir p. 117, exercice B, 2.*

8 **parc Montsouris:** jardin public situé dans le sud de Paris

le jardin

Des milliers et des milliers d'années
Ne sauraient suffire
Pour dire
La petite seconde d'éternité
Où tu m'as embrassé
Où je t'ai embrassée
Un matin dans la lumière de l'hiver
Au parc Montsouris à Paris
A Paris
Sur la terre
La terre qui est un astre.

Paroles

PREMIÈRE PARTIE

lecture du poème

A. PREMIÈRE LECTURE SANS PAUSES

B. DEUXIÈME LECTURE AVEC PAUSES

le jardin

Des milliers et des milliers d'années / . . . /
Ne sauraient suffire / . . . /
Pour dire
La petite seconde d'éternité / . . . /
5   Où tu m'as embrassé / . . . /
Où je t'ai embrassée / . . . /
Un matin dans la lumière de l'hiver / . . . /
Au parc Montsouris à Paris / . . . /
A Paris
10   Sur la terre / . . . /
La terre qui est un astre. / . . . /

C. TROISIÈME LECTURE SANS PAUSES

DEUXIÈME PARTIE

étude du texte

1. Où se déroule cette scène?
2. En quelle saison?
3. A quel moment de la journée?
4. Combien y a-t-il de personnages?
5. Utilisez votre imagination et décrivez les amoureux.
6. Le mot «seconde» opposé au mot «éternité» forme un contraste intéressant. Pourquoi?
7. Pensez-vous que l'expression «petite seconde» ajoute à la valeur du contraste? Exposez votre point de vue.
8. Essayez d'expliquer pourquoi Prévert semble donner plus d'importance à l'intensité qu'à la durée.
9. Indiquez plusieurs adjectifs pour caractériser «la lumière de l'hiver».
10. Si la terre est une planète et le soleil un astre, pourquoi le poète dit-il: «La terre qui est un astre»?
11. Pouvez-vous indiquer ce que représente la progression suivante dans les quatre derniers vers: parc Montsouris, Paris, terre, astre?
12. Qu'est-ce que l'auteur a voulu glorifier dans ce poème?

TROISIÈME PARTIE

phonétique

I. CONTRASTES

[i]	[e]
sea / si	may / mes
sea / si	may / mes
sea / si	may / mes
si, si, si / . . . /	mes, mes, mes / . . . /
lee / lit	eight / étiez
lee / lit	eight / étiez
lee / lit	eight / étiez
lit, lit, lit / . . . /	étiez, étiez, étiez / . . . /
cream / crime	Kay / quai
cream / crime	Kay / quai
cream / crime	Kay / quai
crime, crime, crime / . . . /	quai, quai, quai / . . . /
ship / chipe	prey / pré
ship / chipe	prey / pré
ship / chipe	prey / pré
chipe, chipe, chipe / . . . /	pré, pré, pré / . . . /
humid / humide	baby / bébé
humid / humide	baby / bébé
humid / humide	baby / bébé
humide, humide, humide / . . . /	bébé, bébé, bébé / . . . /

II. OPPOSITIONS [i] [e]

y / eh . . . y / eh
dis / des . . . dis / des
ci / ces . . . ci / ces
si / ses . . . si / ses
bis / bée . . . bis / bée
qui / quai . . . qui / quai
gui / gai . . . gui / gai
gît / j'ai . . . gît / j'ai
fit / fée . . . fit / fée
mis / mes . . . mis / mes
ni / nez . . . ni / nez
lit / les . . . lit / les
riz / ré . . . riz / ré

assis / assez . . . assis / assez
gâchis / gâcher . . . gâchis / gâcher
ami / aimé . . . ami / aimé

paradis / parader . . . paradis / parader
c'est Paris / séparer . . . c'est Paris / séparer
atterri / atterré . . . atterri / atterré

Des génies . . . Des génies
L'éternité. . . . L'éternité
Il est irrité. . . . Il est irrité.
J'ai critiqué ses idées. . . . J'ai critiqué ses idées.
Des milliers et des milliers   Des milliers et des milliers
d'années . . . d'années
Cécile évite de répéter   Cécile évite de répéter
des clichés. . . . des clichés.

QUATRIÈME PARTIE

exercices

I. VOCABULAIRE

A. **An** et **année**

1. **An** s'emploie avec les adjectifs cardinaux. (*Exception:* dans l'expression **tous les ans.**)

Remplacez les tirets par le mot qui convient:

(*a*) Un siècle a une durée de cent ——.

(*b*) Ces amoureux ont dix-neuf ——.

(*c*) Tous les ——, ils reviennent en pèlerinage au parc Montsouris.

2. **Année** s'emploie avec les adjectifs ordinaux et les expressions indéterminées de quantité et de durée.

Remplacez les tirets par le mot qui convient:

(*a*) Ils sont dans leur vingtième ——.

(*b*) Ils se sont connus il y a plusieurs ——.

(*c*) Chaque ——, ils reviennent en pèlerinage au parc Montsouris.

B. **Où** a parfois une valeur temporelle.

Répétez les phrases suivantes:

(*a*) La petite seconde d'éternité **où** je t'ai embrassée. / ... /

(*b*) Au moment **où** ils s'embrassent, la terre devient un astre. / ... /

(*c*) Ils ont eu le coup de foudre au moment **où** ils se sont vus. / . . . /

II. GRAMMAIRE

A. Article indéfini; forme pluriel **des**

(*Notez:* La forme pluriel de l'article indéfini n'existe pas en anglais.)

Répétez les phrases suivantes en substituant les mots indiqués:

(*a*) Il y a **des** [amoureux] au parc Montsouris.
fleurs / arbres / passants / enfants

(*b*) **Des** [milliers] et **des** [milliers] d'années représentent **des** millions d'heures.
centaines / douzaines / milliards / dizaines

(*c*) Les amoureux se sont connus chez **des** [amis].
parents / compatriotes / voisins / cousins

B. Forme négative de certains verbes

Après **savoir, pouvoir, oser, cesser,** on n'utilise pas toujours la seconde partie de la négation (**pas**).

Répétez les phrases suivantes en substituant les verbes indiqués:

(*a*) Ils **ne** sauraient [penser (à)] tout.
parler (de) / se souvenir (de) / se rappeler / s'intéresser (à)

(*b*) Les amoureux **n'**ont pu [se marier] jeudi dernier.
se parler / aller en voyage / déménager / dîner

(*c*) Les enfants **n'**osent [parler].
jouer / sortir / faire du bruit / aller au jardin

(*d*) Les oiseaux **ne** cessent de [chanter].
manger / voler d'une place à l'autre / nourrir leurs petits / sautiller

CINQUIÈME PARTIE

compréhension (laboratoire)

SIXIÈME PARTIE

dictée (laboratoire)

II

déjeuner du matin

1 **mis**: *participe passé de* mettre

6 **café au lait**: café dans lequel on a mis du lait (*Sur l'emploi de la préposition* à, *voir p. 25, exercice I, A.*)

9 **bu**: *participe passé de* boire

10 **a reposé**: a posé de nouveau

11 **Sans . . . parler**: *Sur l'emploi de l'infinitif, voir p. 242, exercice II, A.*

14 **a fait des ronds**: a formé des cercles

25 **pleuvait**: *imparfait de* pleuvoir; *forme impersonnelle*

déjeuner du matin

Il a mis le café
Dans la tasse
Il a mis le lait
Dans la tasse de café
5   Il a mis le sucre
Dans le café au lait
Avec la petite cuiller
Il a tourné
Il a bu le café au lait
10 Et il a reposé la tasse
Sans me parler
Il a allumé
Une cigarette
Il a fait des ronds
15 Avec la fumée
Il a mis les cendres
Dans le cendrier
Sans me parler
Sans me regarder
20 Il s'est levé
Il a mis
Son chapeau sur sa tête
Il a mis
Son manteau de pluie
25 Parce qu'il pleuvait
Et il est parti
Sous la pluie
Sans une parole

Sans me regarder
30   Et moi j'ai pris
Ma tête dans ma main
Et j'ai pleuré.

Paroles

PREMIÈRE PARTIE

lecture du poème

A. PREMIÈRE LECTURE SANS PAUSES

B. DEUXIÈME LECTURE AVEC PAUSES

déjeuner du matin

Il a mis le café
Dans la tasse / . . . /
Il a mis le lait
Dans la tasse de café / . . . /
5   Il a mis le sucre
Dans le café au lait / . . . /
Avec la petite cuiller
Il a tourné / . . . /
Il a bu le café au lait / . . . /
10   Et il a reposé la tasse
Sans me parler / . . . /
Il a allumé
Une cigarette / . . . /
Il a fait des ronds
15   Avec la fumée / . . . /
Il a mis les cendres
Dans le cendrier / . . . /
Sans me parler / . . . /
Sans me regarder / . . . /
20   Il s'est levé / . . . /

Il a mis
Son chapeau sur sa tête / . . . /
Il a mis
Son manteau de pluie
25 Parce qu'il pleuvait / . . . /
Et il est parti
Sous la pluie / . . . /
Sans une parole / . . . /
Sans me regarder / . . . /
30 Et moi j'ai pris
Ma tête dans ma main / . . . /
Et j'ai pleuré. / . . . /

C. TROISIÈME LECTURE SANS PAUSES

DEUXIÈME PARTIE

étude du texte

1. Où se passe la scène?
2. Combien y a-t-il de personnages?
3. Qui est-ce qui raconte la scène?
4. A quel moment se passe-t-elle?
5. Combien y a-t-il de parties dans le poème?
6. Dans les premières parties décrivez les gestes de l'homme.
7. L'auteur ne donne pas de noms aux personnages et les désigne par des pronoms. Essayez d'expliquer pourquoi.
8. En dépit du caractère vague des personnages, on les voit vivre devant nos yeux. Pourquoi?

9. Pouvez-vous montrer comment toute l'attention est concentrée sur un seul personnage?

10. Quelle est l'attitude de l'homme envers la femme? Indiquez des expressions qui reviennent plusieurs fois et qui montrent cette attitude.

11. Quels gestes de l'homme montrent qu'il n'est pas pressé de partir?

12. Comment la femme montre-t-elle ses sentiments?

13. En plus du silence, y a-t-il un élément extérieur qui renforce la tristesse de la scène?

14. Les verbes sont-ils tous au même temps?

15. Le style est très simple. Pouvez-vous indiquer quelques phrases qui montrent cette simplicité?

16. Peut-on dire que la scène est: (a) normale?
                                    (b) tragique?
                                    (c) triste?
                                    (d) dramatique?
                                    (e) habituelle?

Choisissez l'adjectif qui vous semble le mieux convenir à la situation et dites pourquoi vous l'avez choisi.

17. Les deux personnages ne se parlent pas. Ont-ils les mêmes raisons de ne pas se parler?

18. Il peut y avoir différentes causes à leur désaccord. Essayez d'en imaginer deux.

19. Quelle est votre réaction à l'attitude de l'homme dans ce poème?

TROISIÈME PARTIE

phonétique

I. CONTRASTES

[e]	[ɛ]
day / des	day / dais
day / des	day / dais
day / des	day / dais
des, des, des / . . . /	dais, dais, dais / . . . /
grey / gré	Ben / benne
grey / gré	Ben / benne
grey / gré	Ben / benne
gré, gré, gré / . . . /	benne, benne, benne / . . . /
neigh / nez	pain / peine
neigh / nez	pain / peine
neigh / nez	pain / peine
nez, nez, nez / . . . /	peine, peine, peine / . . . /
to say / tousser	a tray / attrait
to say / tousser	a tray / attrait
to say / tousser	a tray / attrait
tousser, tousser, tousser / . . . /	attrait, attrait, attrait / . . . /

II. OPPOSITIONS   [e] [ɛ]

et / est . . . et / est
quai / qu'est . . . quai / qu'est
ces / c'est . . . ces / c'est
ses / sait . . . ses / sait
tes / taie . . . tes / taie
des / dais . . . des / dais
bée / baie . . . bée / baie
fée / fait . . . fée / fait
mes / mais . . . mes / mais
nez / naît . . . nez / naît
j'ai / jet . . . j'ai / jet
les / lait . . . les / lait
ré / raie . . . ré / raie

parler / parlait . . . parler / parlait
pleurer / pleurait . . . pleurer / pleurait
tourner / tournait . . . tourner / tournait

allumer / allumait . . . allumer / allumait
déjeuner / déjeunait . . . déjeuner / déjeunait
regarder / regardait . . . regarder / regardait

Elle a aimé ce café au lait. . . . Elle a aimé ce café au lait.
La tête penchée, Hélène   La tête penchée, Hélène
pleurait. . . . pleurait.
Il était allé acheter des   Il était allé acheter des
cigarettes américaines. . . . cigarettes américaines.
Renée a apporté les sept paires   Renée a apporté les sept paires
de souliers qu'elle devait   de souliers qu'elle devait
envoyer à sa mère. . . . envoyer à sa mère.

QUATRIÈME PARTIE

exercices

I. VOCABULAIRE

A. La préposition **à** sert à dénoter une caractéristique.

Répétez les phrases suivantes:

(*a*) L'étudiant a bu du café **au** lait. | . . . |
(*b*) La petite fille a demandé une glace **à** la vanille. | . . . |
(*c*) Le garçon a mangé un éclair **au** chocolat. | . . . |
(*d*) L'homme a commandé une soupe **à** l'oignon. | . . . |
(*e*) La femme a repris du gâteau **au** café. | . . . |

II. GRAMMAIRE

A. Le passé composé

1. Avec l'auxiliaire **avoir**

Répétez les phrases suivantes:

(*a*) Il **a mis** le café dans la tasse. | . . . |
(*b*) Il **a bu** le café au lait. | . . . |
(*c*) Il **a allumé** une cigarette. | . . . |

2. Avec l'auxiliaire **être**

Répétez les phrases suivantes:

(*a*) Il **est parti** sous la pluie. / . . . /

(*b*) Il **est resté** sans parler. / . . . /

(*c*) Il **est allé** acheter des cigarettes. / . . . /

3. Verbes pronominaux (toujours avec l'auxiliaire **être**)

Répétez les phrases suivantes:

(*a*) Il s'**est assis** sans me regarder. / . . . /

(*b*) Il s'**est levé** sans me parler. / . . . /

(*c*) Il s'**est promené** sous la pluie. / . . . /

B. Exercices de substitution

Répétez les phrases suivantes en substituant les mots indiqués:

(*a*) L'homme [a allumé] une cigarette.
a fumé / a demandé / a offert / a pris

Mettez les phrases suivantes à la forme interrogative:

(*b*) [Le garçon] a mis le café dans la tasse.
Le garçon a-t-il mis le café dans la tasse?
l'étudiant / la petite fille / l'homme / la femme

Mettez les phrases suivantes à la forme négative:

(*c*) L'étudiant a bu [le café au lait].
L'étudiant n'a pas bu le café au lait.
le thé glacé / la bière blonde / l'eau minérale / le vin
blanc

Notez: Le passé composé est un temps qui indique des actions
qui ont eu lieu à un moment déterminé dans le passé. Vous
avez vu que chacun des verbes du poème et des exercices
indique clairement chaque action.

CINQUIÈME PARTIE

compréhension (laboratoire)

SIXIÈME PARTIE

dictée (laboratoire)

III

pour toi mon amour

[1] **marché aux oiseaux:** *Sur l'emploi de la préposition à, voir p. 25, exercice I, A.*

pour toi mon amour

Je suis allé au marché aux oiseaux
Et j'ai acheté des oiseaux
Pour toi
mon amour
5   Je suis allé au marché aux fleurs
Et j'ai acheté des fleurs
Pour toi
mon amour
Je suis allé au marché à la ferraille
10   Et j'ai acheté des chaînes
De lourdes chaînes
Pour toi
mon amour
Et puis je suis allé au marché aux esclaves
15   Et je t'ai cherchée
Mais je ne t'ai pas trouvée
mon amour

Paroles

PREMIÈRE PARTIE

lecture du poème

A. PREMIÈRE LECTURE SANS PAUSES

B. DEUXIÈME LECTURE AVEC PAUSES

pour toi mon amour

Je suis allé au marché aux oiseaux / . . . /
Et j'ai acheté des oiseaux / . . . /
Pour toi
mon amour / . . . /
5   Je suis allé au marché aux fleurs / . . . /
Et j'ai acheté des fleurs / . . . /
Pour toi
mon amour / . . . /
Je suis allé au marché à la ferraille / . . . /
10   Et j'ai acheté des chaînes / . . . /
De lourdes chaînes / . . . /
Pour toi
mon amour / . . . /
Et puis je suis allé au marché aux esclaves / . . . /
15   Et je t'ai cherchée / . . . /
Mais je ne t'ai pas trouvée
mon amour / . . . /

C. TROISIÈME LECTURE SANS PAUSES

DEUXIÈME PARTIE

étude du texte

1. A qui le poème est-il adressé?
2. Qui est-ce qui parle?
3. Combien y a-t-il de parties dans le poème?
4. Décrivez le décor de chacune des parties.
5. Ce poème est basé sur le procédé de la répétition. Etudiez:
   - (a) les éléments fixes et les éléments variables de chaque partie;
   - (b) la variante dans la dernière partie.
6. Quel est le leitmotiv du poème?
7. Pourquoi l'homme utilise-t-il le tutoiement?
8. Pourquoi achète-t-il d'abord des oiseaux et des fleurs?
9. Pourquoi achète-t-il ensuite des chaînes?
10. Pourquoi choisit-il de «lourdes» chaînes?
11. Pourquoi n'achète-t-il rien au marché aux esclaves?
12. A votre avis, que va-t-il faire maintenant des fleurs, des oiseaux et des chaînes qu'il a achetés?
13. Que pensez-vous de l'expression «Pour toi mon amour» dans la première et la deuxième partie?
14. Quelle est votre réaction lorsqu'elle est répétée pour la troisième fois?
15. Quelle est votre réaction à la lecture des deux derniers vers?
16. Etes-vous sensible à leur ironie? Dites pourquoi.
17. Comment l'auteur réussit-il à créer un climat d'ironie alors que les éléments de chaque partie sont presque les mêmes?
18. Le lyrisme et l'ironie sont deux éléments de nature opposée. Essayez de dire pourquoi ils ne peuvent coexister dans une même œuvre.
19. En dépit de son titre, s'agit-il d'un poème d'amour?

TROISIÈME PARTIE

phonétique

I. CONTRASTES:

[ɛ]	[a]
bay / baie	lack / lac
bay / baie	lack / lac
bay / baie	lack / lac
baie, baie, baie / . . . /	lac, lac, lac / . . . /
pen / peine	pat / patte
pen / peine	pat / patte
pen / peine	pat / patte
peine, peine, peine / . . . /	patte, patte, patte / . . . /
gain / gaîne	salad / salade
gain / gaîne	salad / salade
gain / gaîne	salad / salade
gaîne, gaîne, gaîne / . . . /	salade, salade, salade / . . . /
array / arrêt	Barbara / Barbara
array / arrêt	Barbara / Barbara
array / arrêt	Barbara / Barbara
arrêt, arrêt, arrêt / . . . /	Barbara, Barbara, Barbara / . . . /

II. OPPOSITIONS [ɛ] [a]

est / a . . . est / a
qu'est / qu'a . . . qu'est / qu'a
c'est / ça . . . c'est / ça
sait / sa . . . sait / sa
taie / ta . . . taie / ta
mais / ma . . . mais / ma
naît / n'a . . . naît / n'a
lait / la . . . lait / la
raie / rat . . . raie / rat
baie / bat . . . baie / bat
fait / fa . . . fait / fa
vais / va . . . vais / va
rouet / rat . . . rouet / rat
jouet / joie . . . jouet / joie

allait / alla . . . allait / alla
trouvait / trouva . . . trouvait / trouva
cherchait / chercha . . . cherchait / chercha

C'est cela même. . . . C'est cela même.
La belle Hélène . . . La belle Hélène
Sa marraine s'appelle Marcelle. . . . Sa marraine s'appelle Marcelle.
La reine serra le bras du roi. . . . La reine serra le bras du roi.
Barbara la traîna par sa chaîne. . . . Barbara la traîna par sa chaîne.
Adèle aime la vieille ferraille. . . . Adèle aime la vieille ferraille.
Elle allait au marché aux   Elle allait au marché aux
esclaves. . . . esclaves.

QUATRIÈME PARTIE

exercices

I. GRAMMAIRE

A. Article indéfini au pluriel

Des est remplacé par **de** quand l'adjectif précède le nom.

Répétez les phrases suivantes en remplaçant successivement les compléments d'objet direct:

(*a*) Le poète a acheté **des** chaînes. / . . . /
　　　　　　　　　　　de lourdes chaînes. / . . . /
　　　　　　　　　　　des chaînes pesantes. / . . . /
　　　　　　　　　　　de lourdes chaînes rouillées. / . . . /

(*b*) Il a vu **des** fleurs. / . . . /
　　　　　　de belles fleurs. / . . . /
　　　　　　des fleurs jaunes. / . . . /
　　　　　　de petites fleurs rouges. / . . . /

(*c*) Il a admiré **des** oiseaux. / . . . /
　　　　　　　　de nombreux oiseaux. / . . . /
　　　　　　　　des oiseaux magnifiques. / . . . /
　　　　　　　　de beaux oiseaux exotiques. / . . . /

B. Pronoms personnels toniques après une préposition

Répétez les phrases suivantes en substituant les mots indiqués:

(*a*) Jacqueline est venue [vers] moi.
　　　avec / chez / devant / près de

(*b*) Philippe a fait comme [toi].
　　　elle / lui / nous / vous

(*c*) Jean a agi [contre eux].
       selon vous / sans moi / sur toi / avant elles

Reprenez les exercices précédents en mettant les verbes au présent.

CINQUIÈME PARTIE

compréhension (laboratoire)

SIXIÈME PARTIE

dictée (laboratoire)

IV

l'addition

l'addition: la somme à payer dans un restaurant ou un café

2 **vous avez:** vous avez pris

3 **un veau, un petit pois, etc.:** une portion de veau, de petits pois, d'asperges, de fromage avec du beurre, d'amandes vertes
4 **café-filtre:** tasse de café préparée avec un filtre
4 **un téléphone:** une communication téléphonique

6 **C'est ça même:** C'est exact

l'addition

LE CLIENT

Garçon, l'addition!

LE GARÇON

Voilà. (*Il sort son crayon et note.*) Vous avez . . . deux œufs durs, un veau, un petit pois, une asperge, un fromage avec beurre, une amande verte, un café filtre, un téléphone.

LE CLIENT

Et puis des cigarettes!

LE GARÇON
(*Il commence à compter.*)

C'est ça même . . . des cigarettes . . .
. . . Alors ça fait . . .

LE CLIENT

N'insistez pas, mon ami, c'est inutile, vous ne réussirez jamais.

LE GARÇON

! ! !

LE CLIENT

On ne vous a donc pas appris à l'école que c'est ma-thé-ma-ti-que-ment impossible d'additionner des choses d'espèce différente!

[12] **Enfin, tout de même**: *exclamations d'impatience*

[14] **un veau avec des cigarettes**: *Il serait préférable de dire «un veau et des cigarettes».*

[17] **Légion d'honneur**: ordre français pour récompenser des services civils et militaires; **grand officier**: grade élevé dans cet ordre
[17] **pendant que vous y êtes**: pendant que vous êtes en train de faire cela
[20] **ça ne donnerait rien**: cela ne donnerait aucun résultat (*jeu de mots basé sur* donner un pourboire)

à titre gracieux: sans payer

LE GARÇON

! ! !

LE CLIENT
(*élevant la voix*)

Enfin, tout de même, de qui se moque-t-on?...Il faut réellement être insensé pour oser essayer de tenter d'«additionner» un
veau avec des cigarettes, des cigarettes avec un café filtre, un café
filtre avec une amande verte et des œufs durs avec des petits pois,
des petits pois avec un téléphone...Pourquoi pas un petit pois
avec un grand officier de la Légion d'honneur, pendant que vous y
êtes! (*Il se lève.*)

Non, mon ami, croyez-moi, n'insistez pas, ne vous fatiguez pas,
ça ne donnerait rien, vous entendez, rien, absolument rien...pas
même le pourboire!

(*Et il sort en emportant le rond de serviette à titre gracieux.*)

Histoires

PREMIÈRE PARTIE

lecture du poème

A. PREMIÈRE LECTURE SANS PAUSES

B. DEUXIÈME LECTURE AVEC PAUSES

l'addition

LE CLIENT

Garçon, l'addition! / . . . /

LE GARÇON

Voilà. Vous avez . . . / . . . / deux œufs durs, un veau, un petit
pois, / . . . / une asperge, un fromage avec beurre, / . . . / une
amande verte, un café filtre, un téléphone. / . . . /

LE CLIENT

Et puis des cigarettes! / . . . /

LE GARÇON

C'est ça même . . . / . . . / des cigarettes . . . / . . . /
. . . Alors ça fait . . . / . . . /

LE CLIENT

N'insistez pas, mon ami, / . . . / c'est inutile, vous ne réussirez
jamais. / . . . /

LE GARÇON

! ! !

LE CLIENT

On ne vous a donc pas appris à l'école / . . . / que c'est ma-thé-ma-ti-que-ment impossible / . . . / d'additionner des choses d'espèce différente! / . . . /

LE GARÇON

! ! !

LE CLIENT

Enfin, tout de même, de qui se moque-t-on? . . . / . . . / Il faut réellement être insensé / . . . / pour oser essayer / . . . / de tenter d'«additionner» / . . . / un veau avec des cigarettes, / . . . / des cigarettes avec un café filtre, / . . . / un café filtre avec une amande verte / . . . / et des œufs durs avec des petits pois, / . . . / des petits pois avec un téléphone . . . / . . . / Pourquoi pas un petit pois / . . . / avec un grand officier de la Légion d'honneur, / . . . / pendant que vous y êtes! / . . . /

Non, mon ami, croyez-moi, / . . . / n'insistez pas, / . . . / ne vous fatiguez pas, / . . . / ça ne donnerait rien, / . . . / vous entendez, / . . . / rien, absolument rien . . . / . . . / pas même le pourboire! / . . . /

C. TROISIÈME LECTURE SANS PAUSES

DEUXIÈME PARTIE

étude du texte

1. Où se passe la scène?
2. Combien y a-t-il de personnages? Qui sont ces personnages?
3. Le menu choisi par le client montre qu'il s'agit d'un déjeuner. Indiquez les différences entre un déjeuner en France et un déjeuner aux Etats-Unis.
4. Expliquez pourquoi le client a raison quand il dit qu'on ne peut pas additionner un veau et des cigarettes, etc.
5. Expliquez comment on peut faire une addition avec des articles de nature différente.
6. Aimez-vous les plats choisis par le client? Discutez son choix.
7. Imaginez que vous êtes en France. Commandez un repas dont vous allez payer l'addition.
8. Imaginez que vous êtes en France. Commandez un repas dont l'addition sera payée par quelqu'un de très riche.
9. Donnez le nom de deux fameux plats français.
10. Donnez le nom de trois vins français réputés—un rouge, un blanc, un champagne.

TROISIÈME PARTIE

phonétique

I. CONTRASTES

[a]	[*a*]
page / page	pale / pâle
page / page	pale / pâle
page / page	pale / pâle
page, page, page / . . . /	pâle, pâle, pâle / . . . /
ball / bal	bat / bas
ball / bal	bat / bas
ball / bal	bat / bas
bal, bal, bal / . . . /	bas, bas, bas / . . . /
bar / barre	grace / grâce
bar / barre	grace / grâce
bar / barre	grace / grâce
barre, barre, barre / . . . /	grâce, grâce, grâce / . . . /
sad / Sade	grass / grasse
sad / Sade	grass / grasse
sad / Sade	grass / grasse
Sade, Sade, Sade / . . . /	grasse, grasse, grasse / . . . /
alarm / une larme	pastry / pâtisserie
alarm / une larme	pastry / pâtisserie
alarm / une larme	pastry / pâtisserie
une larme, une larme, une larme / . . . /	pâtisserie, pâtisserie, pâtisserie / . . . /

a trap / attrape	alas / hélas
a trap / attrape	alas / hélas
a trap / attrape	alas / hélas
attrape, attrape, attrape / . . . /	hélas, hélas, hélas / . . . /

II. OPPOSITIONS [a] [ɑ]

a / ah . . . a / ah
Anne / âne . . . Anne / âne
halles / hâle . . . halles / hâle
pal / pâle . . . pal / pâle
ta / tas . . . ta / tas
tache / tâche . . . tache / tâche
qu'a / cas . . . qu'a / cas
bat / bas . . . bat / bas
bal / Bâle . . . bal / Bâle
chat / chas . . . chat / chas
chasse / châsse . . . chasse / châsse
Charles / châle . . . Charles / châle
mal / mâle . . . mal / mâle
ami / âme . . . ami / âme
lame / l'âme . . . lame / l'âme

Va là-bas. . . . Va là-bas.
Papa est las. . . . Papa est las.
Sacha ne boit pas. . . . Sacha ne boit pas.
Le diable et son sabbat . . . Le diable et son sabbat
Anna se hâte vers le canal. . . . Anna se hâte vers le canal.
Hélas! Le chat avala la pâte. . . . Hélas! Le chat avala la pâte.
Le roi va à la chasse dans   Le roi va à la chasse dans
le bois. . . . le bois.

QUATRIÈME PARTIE

exercices

I. GRAMMAIRE

A. Différentes formes de l'article partitif

Répétez les phrases suivantes en substituant les mots indiqués:

(*a*) Garçon, donnez-moi **du** [café].
  vin / sel / fromage / thé / sucre
(*b*) Avez-vous **de la** [bière] ?
  crème / confiture / salade / viande / glace
(*c*) Apportez-moi **de l'**[eau], je vous prie.
  huile / ail / ananas / orangeade / oie
(*d*) Je voudrais **des** [cigarettes françaises].
  dattes / amandes vertes / légumes / fruits / gâteaux
(*e*) Non, merci, je ne veux pas **de** [café].
  cigarettes / viande / orangeade / légumes /
  amandes vertes

Notez: Le verbe **aimer** n'est pas suivi du partitif.

Aimez-vous [**le** tabac américain] ?

Répétez la question et répondez négativement en substituant les mots indiqués:

Non, je n'aime pas **le** tabac américain.
veau / champagne / crème fouettée / dattes / fromage

Répétez les deux phrases suivantes en substituant les mots indiqués:

(*a*) Avez-vous [**du** veau] ? Aimez-vous [**le** veau] ?
  asperges / fromage / petits pois / viande / œufs durs

(*b*) Nous n'avons pas **de** [veau]. Nous n'aimons pas [**le** veau].

asperges / fromage / petits pois / viande / œufs durs

B. Remarques orthographiques sur certains verbes du premier groupe (infinitif en -**er**)

1. Infinitif en -**ger**

Le **g** se change en **ge** devant **a** et **o** pour garder le même son qu'à l'infinitif.

Répétez les formes verbales suivantes en substituant les verbes indiqués:

je mange, nous mangeons
je mangeais, nous mangeâmes
juger / rager / songer / nager / s'affliger

2. Infinitif en -**cer**

On met une cédille sous le **c** (**ç**) devant **a** et **o** pour garder le même son qu'à l'infinitif.

je commence, nous commençons
il commença, en commençant
lancer / avancer / placer / tracer / rincer

3. Infinitif en -**oyer**, -**uyer** et -**ayer**

L'**y** se change en **i** devant un **e** muet.

j'emploie, nous balayons,
vous employez, ils essuient
tutoyer / essayer / s'ennuyer / rudoyer / payer

Notez: Dans les verbes en -**ayer** on peut employer **y** ou **i**. Les deux formes suivantes sont correctes:

Le monde se paye sa tête.
Le monde se paie sa tête.

CINQUIÈME PARTIE

compréhension (laboratoire)

SIXIÈME PARTIE

dictée (laboratoire)

V

chanson des escargots

qui

vont à l'enterrement

2 **s'en vont :** se rendent, vont

4 **crêpe :** Le crêpe est une étoffe noire que l'on porte lorsqu'on est en deuil.

5 **dans le noir :** (*a*) dans l'obscurité; (*b*) allusion au noir de la tenue de deuil; (*c*) *être dans le noir*—ne pas savoir où l'on est

15 **prenez la peine de vous asseoir :** asseyez-vous, je vous prie

17 **bière :** (*a*) breuvage; (*b*) cercueil

18 **Si le cœur vous en dit :** Si vous en avez envie

22 **Vous verrez du pays :** Vous vous instruirez en voyageant

24 **C'est moi qui vous le dis :** Vous pouvez me croire

chanson des escargots qui vont à l'enterrement

A l'enterrement d'une feuille morte
Deux escargots s'en vont
Ils ont la coquille noire
Du crêpe autour des cornes
5   Ils s'en vont dans le noir
Un très beau soir d'automne
Hélas quand ils arrivent
C'est déjà le printemps
Les feuilles qui étaient mortes
10 Sont toutes ressuscitées
Et les deux escargots
Sont très désappointés
Mais voilà le soleil
Le soleil qui leur dit
15 Prenez prenez la peine
La peine de vous asseoir
Prenez un verre de bière
Si le cœur vous en dit
Prenez si ça vous plaît
20 L'autocar pour Paris
Il partira ce soir
Vous verrez du pays
Mais ne prenez pas le deuil
C'est moi qui vous le dis
25 Ça noircit le blanc de l'œil

[33] **Se mettent à:** Commencent à

[34] **à tue-tête:** de toutes les forces de leur voix

[37] **Et tout le monde de boire:** *infinitif de narration,*
voir p. 64, exercice II, A

[42] **S'en retournent:** Rentrent

[48] **La lune veille sur eux:** Un proverbe français
dit qu'«il y a un dieu pour les ivrognes.»

Et puis ça enlaidit
Les histoires de cercueils
C'est triste et pas joli
Reprenez vos couleurs
30   Les couleurs de la vie
Alors toutes les bêtes
Les arbres et les plantes
Se mettent à chanter
A chanter à tue-tête
35   La vraie chanson vivante
La chanson de l'été
Et tout le monde de boire
Tout le monde de trinquer
C'est un très joli soir
40   Un joli soir d'été
Et les deux escargots
S'en retournent chez eux
Ils s'en vont très émus
Ils s'en vont très heureux
45   Comme ils ont beaucoup bu
Ils titubent un p'tit peu
Mais là-haut dans le ciel
La lune veille sur eux.

Paroles

PREMIÈRE PARTIE

lecture du poème

A. PREMIÈRE LECTURE SANS PAUSES

B. DEUXIÈME LECTURE AVEC PAUSES

chanson des escargots
qui
vont à l'enterrement

A l'enterrement d'une feuille morte
Deux escargots s'en vont / . . . /
Ils ont la coquille noire / . . . /
Du crêpe autour des cornes / . . . /
5   Ils s'en vont dans le noir / . . . /
Un très beau soir d'automne / . . . /
Hélas quand ils arrivent
C'est déjà le printemps / . . . /
Les feuilles qui étaient mortes
10   Sont toutes ressuscitées / . . . /
Et les deux escargots
Sont très désappointés / . . . /
Mais voilà le soleil / . . . /
Le soleil qui leur dit / . . . /
15   Prenez prenez la peine
La peine de vous asseoir / . . . /
Prenez un verre de bière

Si le cœur vous en dit / . . . /
Prenez si ça vous plaît
20   L'autocar pour Paris / . . . /
Il partira ce soir / . . . /
Vous verrez du pays / . . . /
Mais ne prenez pas le deuil / . . . /
C'est moi qui vous le dis / . . . /
25   Ça noircit le blanc de l'œil / . . . /
Et puis ça enlaidit / . . . /
Les histoires de cercueils
C'est triste et pas joli / . . . /
Reprenez vos couleurs / . . . /
30   Les couleurs de la vie / . . . /
Alors toutes les bêtes / . . . /
Les arbres et les plantes
Se mettent à chanter / . . . /
A chanter à tue-tête
35   La vraie chanson vivante / . . . /
La chanson de l'été / . . . /
Et tout le monde de boire / . . . /
Tout le monde de trinquer / . . . /
C'est un très joli soir / . . . /
40   Un joli soir d'été / . . . /
Et les deux escargots
S'en retournent chez eux / . . . /
Ils s'en vont très émus / . . . /
Ils s'en vont très heureux / . . . /
45   Comme ils ont beaucoup bu / . . . /
Ils titubent un p'tit peu / . . . /
Mais là-haut dans le ciel / . . . /
La lune veille sur eux. / . . . /

C. TROISIÈME LECTURE SANS PAUSES

DEUXIÈME PARTIE

étude du texte

1. Qui va à l'enterrement?
2. Qui va-t-on enterrer?
3. Que pensez-vous de l'idée d'un enterrement individuel pour chaque feuille morte?
4. Comment sont vêtus les escargots? Pourquoi?
5. L'auteur prête un comportement humain aux escargots. Montrez en quoi le procédé est amusant.
6. Quand les escargots partent-ils?
7. Quand arrivent-ils?
8. La feuille est morte en automne et ils arrivent au printemps. Pourquoi?
9. Pourquoi les escargots sont-ils très désappointés?
10. Qui les accueille à leur arrivée?
11. Comment sont-ils accueillis?
12. Le soleil est-il généralement considéré comme un ami des escargots? Justifiez votre réponse.
13. Pouvez-vous énumérer les conseils que leur donne le soleil?
14. Quel est celui qui vous semble le plus important?
15. Pourquoi les bêtes, les arbres et les plantes se mettent-ils à chanter?
16. En raison des circonstances, quelle décision les escargots prennent-ils?
17. Qu'est-ce que les escargots font avant de partir qui les rend «émus et heureux»?
18. Ne trouvez-vous pas que l'image d'un escargot «titubant» est inattendue et amusante? Expliquez pourquoi.
19. Bien que le poème ait un titre funèbre, le trouvez-vous triste? Justifiez votre opinion.
20. Relevez tous les termes qui se rapportent à un enterrement.

TROISIÈME PARTIE

phonétique

I. CONTRASTES

[ɑ]

hat / hâte
hat / hâte
hat / hâte
hâte, hâte, hâte / . . . /

mall / mâle
mall / mâle
mall / mâle
mâle, mâle, mâle / . . . /

pal / pâle
pal / pâle
pal / pâle
pâle, pâle, pâle / . . . /

paw / pas
paw / pas
paw / pas
pas, pas, pas / . . . /

[ɔ]	[o]
Rome / Rome	bow / beau
Rome / Rome	bow / beau
Rome / Rome	bow / beau
Rome, Rome, Rome / . . . /	beau, beau, beau / . . . /

tone / tonne	grow / gros
tone / tonne	grow / gros
tone / tonne	grow / gros
tonne, tonne, tonne / . . . /	gros, gros, gros / . . . /
more / mort	row / rôt
more / mort	row / rôt
more / mort	row / rôt
mort, mort, mort / . . . /	rôt, rôt, rôt / . . . /
autumn / automne	assault / assaut
autumn / automne	assault / assaut
autumn / automne	assault / assaut
automne, automne, automne / . . . /	assaut, assaut, assaut / . . . /

II. OPPOSITIONS   [ɑ] [ɔ] [o]

âme / homme / ohm . . . âme / homme / ohm
casse / cosse / Causse . . . casse / cosse / Causse
tas / toc / tôt . . . tas / toc / tôt
pâle / Paul / pôle . . . pâle / Paul / pôle
lasse / l'os / l'eau . . . lasse / l'os / l'eau
Bâle / bol / Baule . . . Bâle / bol / Baule
mâle / molle / môle . . . mâle / molle / môle
noix / nonne / nos . . . noix / nonne / nos
basse / bosse / Beauce . . . basse / bosse / Beauce
roi / roc / rôt . . . roi / roc / rôt
las / l'or / l'eau . . . las / l'or / l'eau

L'homme est pâle. . . . L'homme est pâle.
Le roi est mort. . . . Le roi est mort.
Oh! les beaux gâteaux . . . Oh! les beaux gâteaux
Ce porto est trop fort. . . . Ce porto est trop fort.
Paul est haut comme trois   Paul est haut comme trois
pommes. . . . pommes.

L'hôte casse des noix et des os. . . .	L'hôte casse des noix et des os.
Faust a vendu son âme au diable. . . .	Faust a vendu son âme au diable.
Homère est l'auteur de l'*Odyssée*. . . .	Homère est l'auteur de l'*Odyssée*.

QUATRIÈME PARTIE

exercices

I. VOCABULAIRE

A. Expressions courantes avec le verbe **prendre**

> **prendre** le deuil
> **prendre** un verre
> **prendre** l'autocar
> **prendre** la peine (de)

Faites une phrase avec chacune des expressions ci-dessus; vous mettrez le verbe **prendre**:

(*a*) au présent
(*b*) à l'imparfait
(*c*) au futur
(*d*) au passé composé
(*e*) au conditionnel présent (avec une proposition subordonnée commençant par **si**)

II. GRAMMAIRE

A. **Se mettre** + **à** + verbe à l'infinitif

Répétez les phrases suivantes:

(*a*) Le soleil **se met à** parler aux escargots. / . . . /
(*b*) Les bêtes et les plantes **se mettent à** chanter. / . . . /
(*c*) Les escargots **se mettent à** boire avec leurs nouveaux amis. / . . . /

Reprenez le même exercice en mettant les verbes au passé composé.

B. Infinitif de narration

Cette forme verbale correspond au «présent historique» et donne une certaine rapidité au récit. (Elle est rarement employée en français moderne.)

Répétez les phrases suivantes:

(*a*) Et tout le monde **de boire** / . . . /
(*b*) Tout le monde **de trinquer** / . . . /
(*c*) Et au printemps les feuilles **de ressusciter** / . . . /
(*d*) Et les escargots **de se dépêcher** / . . . /

Reprenez le même exercice en remplaçant l'infinitif de narration par **se mettre à** *(au temps présent).*

CINQUIÈME PARTIE

compréhension (laboratoire)

SIXIÈME PARTIE

dictée (laboratoire)

VI

barbara

2 **Brest:** port militaire de Bretagne, détruit par les bombardements pendant la deuxième guerre mondiale
2 **sans cesse:** sans s'arrêter
4 **épanouie:** montrant ta joie

8 **je t'ai croisée:** je t'ai rencontrée venant dans le sens opposé
8 **rue de Siam:** rue principale de Brest
10 **de même:** de la même manière

15 **quand même:** malgré tout

17 **s'abritait:** se mettait à l'abri (de la pluie)

24 **ne m'en veux pas:** *en vouloir* (*à quelqu'un*)—souhaiter du mal (à quelqu'un)
24 **je te tutoie:** *tutoyer*—employer *tu, te, toi* au lieu de *vous;* marque de familiarité
26 **je ne les ai vus qu'une fois:** je les ai vus seulement une fois (*Sur l'emploi de* ne . . . que, *voir p. 77, exercice I, A.*)
27 **s'aiment:** *S'aimer* indique un amour réciproque.

barbara

Rappelle-toi Barbara
Il pleuvait sans cesse sur Brest ce jour-là
Et tu marchais souriante
Epanouie ravie ruisselante
5   Sous la pluie
Rappelle-toi Barbara
Il pleuvait sans cesse sur Brest
Et je t'ai croisée rue de Siam
Tu souriais
10   Et moi je souriais de même
Rappelle-toi Barbara
Toi que je ne connaissais pas
Toi qui ne me connaissais pas
Rappelle-toi
15   Rappelle-toi quand même ce jour-là
N'oublie pas
Un homme sous un porche s'abritait
Et il a crié ton nom
Barbara
20   Et tu as couru vers lui sous la pluie
Ruisselante ravie épanouie
Et tu t'es jetée dans ses bras
Rappelle-toi cela Barbara
Et ne m'en veux pas si je te tutoie
25   Je dis tu à tous ceux que j'aime
Même si je ne les ai vus qu'une seule fois
Je dis tu à tous ceux qui s'aiment
Même si je ne les connais pas

³⁵ **arsenal**: ici indique l'endroit où sont construits, réparés ou armés les navires de guerre (*naval dockyard* plutôt qu'*arsenal*)
³⁶ **Ouessant**: petite île près de Brest

³⁸ **connerie**: *expression vulgaire qui désigne une très grosse bêtise et quelquefois une erreur*
³⁹ **Qu'es-tu devenue**: *A la forme interrogative, le verbe* devenir *a parfois le sens* «*what has become of (someone)?*»

⁴⁴ **disparu**: *Un disparu se dit d'une personne dont on constate l'absence mais dont on ne peut établir le décès.*
⁴⁴ **ou bien**: *même sens que* ou

⁵³ **Qui crèvent comme des chiens**: *crever*—mourir (en parlant des animaux). *L'expression* «les nuages crèvent» *signifie* il pleut.
⁵⁵ **au fil de l'eau**: emportés par le courant

Rappelle-toi Barbara
30   N'oublie pas
Cette pluie sage et heureuse
Sur ton visage heureux
Sur cette ville heureuse
Cette pluie sur la mer
35   Sur l'arsenal
Sur le bateau d'Ouessant
Oh Barbara
Quelle connerie la guerre
Qu'es-tu devenue maintenant
40   Sous cette pluie de fer
De feu d'acier de sang
Et celui qui te serrait dans ses bras
Amoureusement
Est-il mort disparu ou bien encore vivant
45   Oh Barbara
Il pleut sans cesse sur Brest
Comme il pleuvait avant
Mais ce n'est plus pareil et tout est abîmé
C'est une pluie de deuil terrible et désolée
50   Ce n'est même plus l'orage
De fer d'acier de sang
Tout simplement des nuages
Qui crèvent comme des chiens
Des chiens qui disparaissent
55   Au fil de l'eau sur Brest
Et vont pourrir au loin
Au loin très loin de Brest
Dont il ne reste rien.

Paroles

PREMIÈRE PARTIE

lecture du poème

A. PREMIÈRE LECTURE SANS PAUSES

B. DEUXIÈME LECTURE AVEC PAUSES

barbara

Rappelle-toi Barbara / . . . /
Il pleuvait sans cesse sur Brest ce jour-là / . . . /
Et tu marchais souriante / . . . /
Epanouie ravie ruisselante
5   Sous la pluie / . . . /
Rappelle-toi Barbara / . . . /
Il pleuvait sans cesse sur Brest / . . . /
Et je t'ai croisée rue de Siam / . . . /
Tu souriais
10 Et moi je souriais de même / . . . /
Rappelle-toi Barbara / . . . /
Toi que je ne connaissais pas / . . . /
Toi qui ne me connaissais pas / . . . /
Rappelle-toi
15 Rappelle-toi quand même ce jour-là / . . . /
N'oublie pas / . . . /
Un homme sous un porche s'abritait / . . . /
Et il a crié ton nom
Barbara / . . . /

20 Et tu as couru vers lui sous la pluie / . . . /
Ruisselante ravie épanouie / . . . /
Et tu t'es jetée dans ses bras / . . . /
Rappelle-toi cela Barbara / . . . /
Et ne m'en veux pas si je te tutoie / . . . /
25 Je dis tu à tous ceux que j'aime / . . . /
Même si je ne les ai vus qu'une seule fois / . . . /
Je dis tu à tous ceux qui s'aiment / . . . /
Même si je ne les connais pas / . . . /
Rappelle-toi Barbara / . . . /
30 N'oublie pas
Cette pluie sage et heureuse / . . . /
Sur ton visage heureux / . . . /
Sur cette ville heureuse / . . . /
Cette pluie sur la mer / . . . /
35 Sur l'arsenal / . . . /
Sur le bateau d'Ouessant / . . . /
Oh Barbara / . . . /
Quelle connerie la guerre / . . . /
Qu'es-tu devenue maintenant
40 Sous cette pluie de fer / . . . /
De feu d'acier de sang / . . . /
Et celui qui te serrait dans ses bras
Amoureusement / . . . /
Est-il mort disparu ou bien encore vivant / . . . /
45 Oh Barbara / . . . /
Il pleut sans cesse sur Brest / . . . /
Comme il pleuvait avant / . . . /
Mais ce n'est plus pareil et tout est abîmé / . . . /
C'est une pluie de deuil terrible et désolée / . . . /
50 Ce n'est même plus l'orage
De fer d'acier de sang / . . . /
Tout simplement des nuages / . . . /
Qui crèvent comme des chiens / . . . /
Des chiens qui disparaissent

55   Au fil de l'eau sur Brest / . . . /
        Et vont pourrir au loin / . . . /
        Au loin très loin de Brest
        Dont il ne reste rien. / . . . /

C. TROISIÈME LECTURE SANS PAUSES

DEUXIÈME PARTIE

étude du texte

1. Où se déroule l'histoire?
2. Que savez-vous de Brest? Son climat? Sa position stratégique?
3. Qui parle?
4. Qui est Barbara?
5. Comment le poète l'a-t-il connue?
6. Comment sait-il qu'elle s'appelle Barbara?
7. Pourquoi Barbara semble-t-elle si heureuse sous la pluie?
8. Pourquoi le poète sourit-il lui aussi?
9. Pourquoi tutoie-t-il Barbara?
10. Quels sont les gens qu'il tutoie?
11. Pourquoi le poète recommande-t-il tellement à Barbara de se rappeler ce jour-là, de ne surtout pas l'oublier?
12. Quel est le leitmotiv du poème?
13. Le poème se déroule à des époques différentes. Combien y en a-t-il?
14. Décrivez historiquement chacune d'elles.
15. Dans la première période la pluie constitue-t-elle un élément de tristesse?
16. Vous comprenez maintenant pourquoi Prévert dit que Barbara est «ruisselante, épanouie, souriante». Que pensez-vous de ce choix d'adjectifs?

17. De quel genre de pluie s'agit-il dans la deuxième période?
18. Comment pouvez-vous caractériser la pluie dans la troisième période?
19. Qu'est-ce que Prévert attaque dans ce poème?
20. Citez des passages où il montre que Barbara et Brest ont un destin commun.
21. Qu'est-ce que Barbara symbolise?

TROISIÈME PARTIE

phonétique

I. CONTRASTES

[o]	[u]
dough / dos	shoe / chou
dough / dos	shoe / chou
dough / dos	shoe / chou
dos, dos, dos / . . . /	chou, chou, chou / . . . /
bow / beau	new / nous
bow / beau	new / nous
bow / beau	new / nous
beau, beau, beau / . . . /	nous, nous, nous / . . . /
rose / rose	rue / roue
rose / rose	rue / roue
rose / rose	rue / roue
rose, rose, rose / . . . /	roue, roue, roue / . . . /
toll / tôle	to / toux
toll / tôle	to / toux
toll / tôle	to / toux
tôle, tôle, tôle / . . . /	toux, toux, toux / . . . /

go / Goth   cool / coule
go / Goth   cool / coule
go / Goth   cool / coule
Goth, Goth, Goth / . . . /   coule, coule, coule / . . . /

hello / allô   part two / partout
hello / allô   part two / partout
hello / allô   part two / partout
allô, allô, allô / . . . /   partout, partout, partout / . . . /

II. OPPOSITIONS [o] [u]

oh / ou . . . oh / ou
haut / houx . . . haut / houx
peau / pou . . . peau / pou
beau / bout . . . beau / bout
sceau / saoul . . . sceau / saoul
chaud / chou . . . chaud / chou
vos / vous . . . vos / vous
l'eau / loup . . . l'eau / loup
tôt / tout . . . tôt / tout
dos / doux . . . dos / doux
Goth / goût . . . Goth / goût
faux / fou . . . faux / fou
sot / sous . . . sot / sous
rôt / roux . . . rôt / roux
mot / mou . . . mot / mou
trop / trou . . . trop / trou
broc / brou . . . broc / brou
les eaux / les zoos . . . les eaux / les zoos

L'eau bout . . . L'eau bout
Douze roses rouges . . . Douze roses rouges
La poule au pot . . . La poule au pot
Elle sourit toujours. . . . Elle sourit toujours.

Pour toi, mon amour . . . Pour toi, mon amour
Souviens-toi, n'oublie pas. . . . Souviens-toi, n'oublie pas.
Il y a beaucoup d'autos sur   Il y a beaucoup d'autos sur
    la route. . . . la route.
Où pouvez-vous trouver Claude?   Où pouvez-vous trouver Claude?
    A Toulouse. . . . A Toulouse.

QUATRIÈME PARTIE

exercices

I. VOCABULAIRE

A. La locution **ne . . . que** signifie **seulement** et marque une restriction.

> Je **ne** les ai vus **qu'**une fois.
> Je les ai vus **seulement** une fois.

Répétez les phrases suivantes en remplaçant **ne . . . que** *par* **seulement**:

(*a*) Le poète **ne** tutoie **que** les gens qu'il aime.
(*b*) Barbara **ne** s'intéressait **qu'**à son amour.
(*c*) Ce jour-là, il **n'**avait plu **que** sur Brest.
(*d*) L'amoureux de Barbara **ne** voyait **qu'**elle.

Répétez les phrases suivantes en remplaçant **seulement** *par* **ne . . . que**:

(*a*) Le poète a vu Barbara **seulement** dans la rue de Siam.
(*b*) Quand il fait vilain, il pleut **seulement** sur les côtes de Bretagne.
(*c*) La guerre apporte **seulement** des douleurs et des misères.

(*d*) Les gens lisent **seulement** les livres qui les intéressent.

(*e*) Ces voyageurs ont visité Brest **seulement** une fois.

II. GRAMMAIRE

A. L'impératif (forme affirmative)

1. Verbes ordinaires (non pronominaux)

Les formes de l'impératif sont généralement identiques à celles de l'indicatif. (*Exception:* La deuxième personne du singulier des verbes en **-er** prend un **s** uniquement devant **y** et **en.**)

Répétez les phrases suivantes en substituant les mots indiqués:

(*a*) **Songe** aux jours heureux [d'avant-guerre].

(*b*) **Evoquons** les jours heureux [d'avant-guerre].

(*c*) **Pensez** aux jours heureux [d'avant-guerre].
des vacances / de notre enfance / des années de collège / de la lune de miel

2. Verbes pronominaux

Avec les verbes ordinaires à l'impératif, il n'y a pas de pronom sujet, mais les verbes pronominaux sont suivis du pronom personnel (forme tonique).

(*a*) **Rappelle-toi** [ces jours heureux].

(*b*) **Remémorons-nous** [ces jours heureux].

(*c*) **Souvenez-vous** de [ces jours heureux].
cette belle promenade / ce voyage intéressant / cette chanson nostalgique / ce paysage de montagne

Notez: Il ne faut pas confondre les verbes pronominaux à l'impératif (donc suivis d'un pronom) avec les verbes ordinaires à la forme interrogative:

Evoquons-nous les jours heureux d'avant-guerre?
Pensez-vous aux jours heureux d'avant-guerre?

B. L'impératif (forme négative)

1. Verbes ordinaires (non pronominaux)

(*a*) [**Ne regrette pas**] les jours heureux d'avant-guerre.
oublier / penser (à) / songer (à) / évoquer

2. Verbes pronominaux

(*a*) Demain, [**ne te réveille pas**] trop tard.
se lever / se coucher / s'habiller / s'endormir

Notez: A la forme négative, on emploie **te** au lieu de **toi**:

Réveille-**toi** de bonne heure.
Ne te réveille **pas** de bonne heure.

Reprendre l'exercice précédent en mettant le verbe à la forme affirmative et en remplaçant **trop tard** *par* **de bonne heure**.

CINQUIÈME PARTIE

compréhension (laboratoire)

SIXIÈME PARTIE

dictée (laboratoire)

VII

la grasse matinée

la grasse matinée: *faire la grasse matinée*—profiter de ce que l'on ne travaille pas pour rester au lit le matin; *dans le texte, simplement* ne pas travailler

5 **la tête:** l'expression de son visage

8 **la glace:** la vitre de la devanture d'un magasin
8 **grand magasin:** un magasin de grande dimension (*ne pas confondre avec* les grands magasins: «*department stores*»)
9 **couleur de poussière:** *expression qui a la valeur d'un adjectif*
11 **Potin:** nom d'une importante maison d'épicerie à succursales multiples
12 **s'en fout:** ne s'en inquiète pas (*expression populaire*)
13 **y:** à sa tête

17 **sauce de vinaigre:** sauce à la vinaigrette

18 **n'importe quoi:** une chose quelconque

22 **le monde:** la société
22 **se paye sa tête:** se moque de lui (*expression familière*) (*S'écrit aussi* paie; *voir p. 50, exercice I, B*)
23 **il ne peut rien:** il ne peut rien faire

26 **cela fait trois jours qu'il n'a pas mangé:** il n'a pas mangé depuis trois jours (*voir p. 92, exercice II, A*)
27 **il a beau se répéter:** il se répète en vain (*voir p. 91, exercice I, A*)

la grasse matinée

Il est terrible
le petit bruit de l'œuf dur cassé sur un comptoir d'étain
il est terrible ce bruit
quand il remue dans la mémoire de l'homme qui a faim
5   elle est terrible aussi la tête de l'homme
la tête de l'homme qui a faim
quand il se regarde à six heures du matin
dans la glace du grand magasin
une tête couleur de poussière
10   ce n'est pas sa tête pourtant qu'il regarde
dans la vitrine de chez Potin
il s'en fout de sa tête l'homme
il n'y pense pas
il songe
15   il imagine une autre tête
une tête de veau par exemple
avec une sauce de vinaigre
ou une tête de n'importe quoi qui se mange
et il remue doucement la mâchoire
20   doucement
et il grince des dents doucement
car le monde se paye sa tête
et il ne peut rien contre ce monde
et il compte sur ses doigts un deux trois
25   un deux trois
cela fait trois jours qu'il n'a pas mangé
et il a beau se répéter depuis trois jours
Ça ne peut pas durer
ça dure
30   trois jours

37 **flics :** agents de police (*pop.*)

39 **que de :** quel grand nombre de
39 **malheureuses :** de peu de valeur
40 **bistro :** café populaire. *S'écrit aussi* bistrot.

47 **café-crème :** café au lait

48 **café arrosé rhum :** café dans lequel on verse du rhum

51 **café-crime :** *effet stylistique basé sur* café-crème

53 **en plein jour :** pendant la journée

56 **soit :** c'est-à-dire

trois nuits
sans manger
et derrière ces vitres
ces pâtés ces bouteilles ces conserves
35 poissons morts protégés par les boîtes
boîtes protégées par les vitres
vitres protégées par les flics
flics protégés par la crainte
que de barricades pour six malheureuses sardines . . .
40 Un peu plus loin le bistro
café-crème et croissants chauds
l'homme titube
et dans l'intérieur de sa tête
un brouillard de mots
45 un brouillard de mots
sardines à manger
œuf dur café-crème
café arrosé rhum
café-crème
50 café crème
café-crime arrosé sang! . . .
Un homme très estimé dans son quartier
a été égorgé en plein jour
l'assassin le vagabond lui a volé
55 deux francs
soit un café arrosé
zéro franc soixante-dix
deux tartines beurrées
et vingt-cinq centimes pour le pourboire du garçon

60 Il est terrible
le petit bruit de l'œuf dur cassé sur un comptoir d'étain
il est terrible ce bruit
quand il remue dans la mémoire de l'homme qui a faim.

Paroles

PREMIÈRE PARTIE

lecture du poème

A. PREMIÈRE LECTURE SANS PAUSES

B. DEUXIÈME LECTURE SANS PAUSES

la grasse matinée

Il est terrible
le petit bruit de l'œuf dur cassé sur un comptoir d'étain / . . . /
il est terrible ce bruit / . . . /
quand il remue dans la mémoire de l'homme qui a faim / . . . /
5   elle est terrible aussi la tête de l'homme / . . . /
la tête de l'homme qui a faim / . . . /
quand il se regarde à six heures du matin
dans la glace du grand magasin / . . . /
une tête couleur de poussière / . . . /
10   ce n'est pas sa tête pourtant qu'il regarde
dans la vitrine de chez Potin / . . . /
il s'en fout de sa tête l'homme / . . . /
il n'y pense pas / . . . /
il songe / . . . /
15   il imagine une autre tête / . . . /
une tête de veau par exemple
avec une sauce de vinaigre / . . . /
ou une tête de n'importe quoi qui se mange / . . . /
et il remue doucement la mâchoire / . . . /
20   doucement / . . . /

et il grince des dents doucement / . . . /
car le monde se paye sa tête / . . . /
et il ne peut rien contre ce monde / . . . /
et il compte sur ses doigts un deux trois / . . . /
25   un deux trois / . . . /
cela fait trois jours qu'il n'a pas mangé / . . . /
et il a beau se répéter depuis trois jours / . . . /
Ça ne peut pas durer / . . . /
ça dure / . . . /
30   trois jours
trois nuits
sans manger / . . . /
et derrière ces vitres / . . . /
ces pâtés ces bouteilles ces conserves / . . . /
35   poissons morts protégés par les boîtes / . . . /
boîtes protégées par les vitres / . . . /
vitres protégées par les flics / . . . /
flics protégés par la crainte / . . . /
que de barricades pour six malheureuses sardines . . . / . . . /
40   Un peu plus loin le bistro / . . . /
café-crème et croissants chauds / . . . /
l'homme titube / . . . /
et dans l'intérieur de sa tête / . . . /
un brouillard de mots / . . . /
45   un brouillard de mots / . . . /
sardines à manger / . . . /
œuf dur café-crème / . . . /
café arrosé rhum / . . . /
café-crème / . . . /
50   café-crème / . . . /
café-crime arrosé sang! . . . / . . . /
Un homme très estimé dans son quartier / . . . /
a été égorgé en plein jour / . . . /
l'assassin le vagabond lui a volé
55   deux francs / . . . /

soit un café arrosé / . . . /
zéro franc soixante-dix / . . . /
deux tartines beurrées / . . . /
et vingt-cinq centimes pour le pourboire du garçon / . . . /

60   Il est terrible
le petit bruit de l'œuf dur cassé sur un comptoir d'étain / . . . /
il est terrible ce bruit / . . . /
quand il remue dans la mémoire de l'homme qui a faim. / . . . /

C. TROISIÈME LECTURE SANS PAUSES

DEUXIÈME PARTIE

étude du texte

1. Combien y a-t-il de parties dans le poème ? Décrivez-les.
2. Elles sont de longueurs inégales. Essayez d'expliquer pourquoi.
3. Décrivez le personnage, spécialement d'un point de vue social.
4. Pourquoi l'homme a-t-il une tête «couleur de poussière» ?
5. Avez-vous déjà vu des gens qui avaient la tête «couleur de poussière» ?
   Dans quelles circonstances ?
6. Imaginez plusieurs raisons pour lesquelles l'homme a faim.
7. L'homme ne titube pas uniquement parce qu'il a faim. Indiquez
   d'autres possibilités.
8. L'auteur dit que l'homme a «un brouillard de mots» dans la tête.
   Expliquez cette image.
9. Pourquoi l'homme commet-il son crime en plein jour, sans se cacher ?
10. Trouvez-vous que le crime est justifié par tout ce que l'auteur nous
    a appris dans la première partie ?

11. Qu'est-ce que Prévert veut dire quand il écrit que «le monde se paye la tête de l'homme»? (N'oubliez pas qu'en France, on guillotine les condamnés à mort.)

12. Pourquoi l'assassin n'a-t-il pris que deux francs? Que compte-t-il faire?

13. L'auteur cherche-t-il à minimiser le crime en limitant la somme volée à deux francs?

14. Pourquoi le bruit d'un œuf dur cassé sur un comptoir d'étain est-il si douloureux pour l'homme qui a faim?

15. Etudiez la progression aux vers 35-39 et expliquez les différentes sortes de protection dont il s'agit.

16. Pourquoi l'auteur a-t-il donné ce titre au poème?

17. La tête de veau à la vinaigrette est un plat que l'on mange souvent en France. Quelle serait votre réaction si l'on vous en servait?

TROISIÈME PARTIE

phonétique

I. CONTRASTES

[œ]	[ø]
purr / peur	blur / bleu
purr / peur	blur / bleu
purr / peur	blur / bleu
peur, peur, peur / . . . /	bleu, bleu, bleu / . . . /
gull / gueule	but / bœufs
gull / gueule	but / bœufs
gull / gueule	but / bœufs
gueule, gueule, gueule / . . . /	bœufs, bœufs, bœufs / . . . /

her / heure	feud / feu
her / heure	feud / feu
her / heure	feud / feu
heure, heure, heure / ... /	feu, feu, feu / ... /
buff / bœuf	pew / pieu
buff / bœuf	pew / pieu
buff / bœuf	pew / pieu
bœuf, bœuf, bœuf / ... /	pieu, pieu, pieu / ... /
sir / sœur	cue / queue
sir / sœur	cue / queue
sir / sœur	cue / queue
sœur, sœur, sœur / ... /	queue, queue, queue / ... /
enough / un œuf	hurry / heureux
enough / un œuf	hurry / heureux
enough / un œuf	hurry / heureux
un œuf, un œuf, un œuf / ... /	heureux, heureux, heureux / ... /

II. OPPOSITIONS [œ] [ø]

heure / eux ... heure / eux
sœur / ceux ... sœur / ceux
cœur / qu'eux ... cœur / qu'eux
gueule / gueux ... gueule / gueux
deuil / deux ... deuil / deux
peur / peu ... peur / peu
bœuf / bœufs ... bœuf / bœufs
veuille / vœux ... veuille / vœux
jeune / jeu ... jeune / jeu
feuille / feu ... feuille / feu
meurt / meut ... meurt / meut
lieur / lieue ... lieur / lieue
un œil / un nœud ... un œil / un nœud
fumeur / fumeux ... fumeur / fumeux

horreur / heureux . . . horreur / heureux
meilleur / mielleux . . . meilleur / mielleux

Deux feuilles . . . Deux feuilles
Le feu meurt. . . . Le feu meurt.
Leurs deux sœurs pleurent. . . . Leurs deux sœurs pleurent.
A la queue leu leu . . . A la queue leu leu
Heureux ceux qui n'ont pas   Heureux ceux qui n'ont pas
peur. . . . peur.
Ils veulent du beurre avec   Ils veulent du beurre avec
leurs œufs. . . . leurs œufs.
D'heure en heure, le vieux   D'heure en heure, le vieux
monsieur va mieux. . . . monsieur va mieux.

QUATRIÈME PARTIE

exercices

I. VOCABULAIRE

A. **Avoir beau** + infinitif

(s'emploie toujours à la forme affirmative)

Répétez les phrases suivantes en substituant les mots indiqués:

(*a*) L'homme **a beau** [se répéter] que ça ne peut pas durer,
ça dure depuis trois jours.
croire / se convaincre / comprendre / savoir / décider /
dire

(*b*) J'**aurai beau** [insister], Philippe fera ce qui lui plaira.
intervenir / crier / (me) désoler / (lui) donner des
conseils / (le) critiquer / (lui) parler / (me) plaindre

B. **Penser à . . .** (penser de façon générale)

(*a*) L'homme **pense-t-il** [**aux** pâtés] dans la vitrine?
bouteilles de vin / conserves de poissons / boîtes de
sardines / croissants chauds / œufs durs

Penser de . . . (porter un jugement, une évaluation)

(*b*) Qu'est-ce que vous **pensez de** [cet homme]?
son crime / ses souffrances / ce vol / sa vie malheureuse
/ le bruit de l'œuf dur pour quelqu'un qui a faim

II. GRAMMAIRE

A. Expressions de temps

Dans chacune des phrases suivantes, substituez les mots indiqués:

(*a*) L'homme ne [mange] pas **depuis** trois jours.
(*b*) **Voilà** trois jours **que** l'homme ne [mange] pas.
(*c*) **Il y a** trois jours **que** l'homme ne [mange] pas.
(*d*) **Cela fait** trois jours **que** l'homme ne [mange] pas.
boire / travailler / se laver / se raser / sortir

(*a*) Philippe [n'a pas écrit] **depuis** une semaine.
(*b*) **Voilà** une semaine **que** Philippe [n'a pas écrit].
(*c*) **Il y a** une semaine **que** Philippe [n'a pas écrit].
(*d*) **Cela fait** une semaine **que** Philippe [n'a pas écrit].
téléphoner / se reposer / donner de ses nouvelles / aller
en ville / faire une promenade / sortir

B. **Chez** pour les personnes; **à** pour les lieux

Mettez les phrases suivantes à la forme interrogative:

(*a*) Jean achète des boîtes de sardines **chez** Potin.
Jean achète des boîtes de sardines **à** l'épicerie.

(*b*) Jacqueline va chercher sa viande **chez** le boucher sur
la place.

Jacqueline va chercher sa viande **à** la boucherie sur **la** place.

(*c*) Catherine prend son pain **chez** le boulanger du coin.
Catherine prend son pain **à** la boulangerie du coin.

C. L'adverbe de quantité **que** employé dans une exclamation correspond à l'anglais *how, how many, how much.*

Répétez les phrases suivantes:

(*a*) **Que** de barricades pour six malheureuses sardines!
/ . . . /
(*b*) **Que** ce bruit de l'œuf dur cassé est pénible pour celui qui a faim! / . . . /
(*c*) **Que** cet homme doit être malheureux! / . . . /
(*d*) **Que** de sang pour rien! / . . . /
(*e*) **Que** cette histoire est douloureuse à entendre! / . . . /

CINQUIÈME PARTIE

compréhension (*laboratoire*)

SIXIÈME PARTIE

dictée (*laboratoire*)

VIII

page d'écriture

page d'écriture : exercice d'écriture

[3] **huit et huit font seize :** huit et huit égalent seize

[4] **le maître :** l'instituteur (écoles primaires)

[8] **voilà l'oiseau-lyre qui passe :** Voilà *marque l'apparition soudaine de l'oiseau.*
[8] **oiseau-lyre :** oiseau dont la queue est en forme de lyre

[24–25] **qu'est-ce qu'ils font ? Ils ne font rien :** *jeu de mots basé sur le verbe* faire *(ne rien faire—«to be idle»)*

[27] **de toute façon :** quoi qu'il arrive

page d'écriture

Deux et deux quatre
quatre et quatre huit
huit et huit font seize . . .
Répétez! dit le maître
5   Deux et deux quatre
quatre et quatre huit
huit et huit font seize.
Mais voilà l'oiseau-lyre
qui passe dans le ciel
10   l'enfant le voit
l'enfant l'entend
l'enfant l'appelle:
Sauve-moi
joue avec moi
15   oiseau!
Alors l'oiseau descend
et joue avec l'enfant
Deux et deux quatre . . .
Répétez! dit le maître
20   et l'enfant joue
l'oiseau joue avec lui . . .
Quatre et quatre huit
huit et huit font seize
et seize et seize qu'est-ce qu'ils font?
25   Ils ne font rien seize et seize
et surtout pas trente-deux
de toute façon
et ils s'en vont.

37 fichent le camp: s'en vont (*expression populaire*)

38 ne font ni une ni deux: s'en vont rapidement (*expression familière*). *Jeu de mots basé sur* un et un qui ne font «ni une ni deux»

39 un à un: l'un après l'autre

43 Quand vous aurez fini de faire le pitre!: Arrêtez de faire le pitre. **Faire le pitre:** se comporter comme un clown

52 porte-plume: *jeu de mots* (*l'oiseau porte des plumes*; **porte-plume:** «*penholder*»)

Et l'enfant a caché l'oiseau
30 dans son pupitre
et tous les enfants
entendent sa chanson
et tous les enfants
entendent la musique
35 et huit et huit à leur tour s'en vont
et quatre et quatre et deux et deux
à leur tour fichent le camp
et un et un ne font ni une ni deux
un à un s'en vont également.
40 Et l'oiseau-lyre joue
et l'enfant chante
et le professeur crie:
Quand vous aurez fini de faire le pitre!
Mais tous les autres enfants
45 écoutent la musique
et les murs de la classe
s'écroulent tranquillement.
Et les vitres redeviennent sable
l'encre redevient eau
50 les pupitres redeviennent arbres
la craie redevient falaise
le porte-plume redevient oiseau.

Paroles

PREMIÈRE PARTIE

lecture du poème

A. PREMIÈRE LECTURE SANS PAUSES

B. DEUXIÈME LECTURE AVEC PAUSES

page d'écriture

Deux et deux quatre / . . . /
quatre et quatre huit / . . . /
huit et huit font seize . . . / . . . /
Répétez! dit le maître / . . . /
5   Deux et deux quatre / . . . /
quatre et quatre huit / . . . /
huit et huit font seize. / . . . /
Mais voilà l'oiseau-lyre
qui passe dans le ciel / . . . /
10   l'enfant le voit / . . . /
l'enfant l'entend / . . . /
l'enfant l'appelle: / . . . /
Sauve-moi / . . . /
joue avec moi
15   oiseau! / . . . /
Alors l'oiseau descend
et joue avec l'enfant / . . . /
Deux et deux quatre . . . / . . . /
Répétez! dit le maître / . . . /
20   et l'enfant joue / . . . /

l'oiseau joue avec lui . . . / . . . /
Quatre et quatre huit / . . . /
huit et huit font seize / . . . /
et seize et seize qu'est-ce qu'ils font? / . . . /
25   Ils ne font rien seize et seize / . . . /
et surtout pas trente-deux
de toute façon / . . . /
et ils s'en vont. / . . . /
Et l'enfant a caché l'oiseau
30   dans son pupitre / . . . /
et tous les enfants
entendent sa chanson / . . . /
et tous les enfants
entendent la musique / . . . /
35   et huit et huit à leur tour s'en vont / . . . /
et quatre et quatre et deux et deux / . . . /
à leur tour fichent le camp / . . . /
et un et un ne font ni une ni deux / . . . /
un à un s'en vont également. / . . . /
40   Et l'oiseau-lyre joue
et l'enfant chante / . . . /
et le professeur crie: / . . . /
Quand vous aurez fini de faire le pitre! / . . . /
Mais tous les autres enfants
45   écoutent la musique / . . . /
et les murs de la classe
s'écroulent tranquillement. / . . . /
Et les vitres redeviennent sable / . . . /
l'encre redevient eau / . . . /
50   les pupitres redeviennent arbres / . . . /
la craie redevient falaise / . . . /
le porte-plume redevient oiseau. / . . . /

C. TROISIÈME LECTURE SANS PAUSES

DEUXIÈME PARTIE

étude du texte

1. Où se passe la scène?
2. Quel cours le professeur est-il en train d'enseigner?
3. D'après ce qu'il enseigne, quel est l'âge des enfants?
4. Pourquoi le poète a-t-il choisi un oiseau-lyre?
5. A votre avis, y a-t-il vraiment un oiseau dans la classe? Expliquez votre point de vue.
6. Pourquoi l'enfant le voit-il?
7. Pourquoi le professeur ne peut-il pas le voir?
8. Si Prévert était dans la classe, le verrait-il? Expliquez pourquoi.
9. Pourquoi l'enfant demande-t-il à l'oiseau de le sauver?
10. De quoi veut-il être sauvé?
11. Que fait l'oiseau pour sauver l'enfant?
12. L'auteur déclare que «seize et seize ne font rien et surtout pas trente-deux». En quoi cette déclaration est-elle révélatrice de la personnalité de Prévert?
13. Qu'est-ce que l'enfant a fait de l'oiseau?
14. En raison de ce qui se passe, que font les chiffres? Expliquez pourquoi ils se comportent ainsi.
15. Quelle est l'attitude du professeur devant sa classe? Est-ce qu'elle vous surprend? Expliquez pourquoi.
16. Qu'arrive-t-il aux murs de la classe?
17. Qu'arrive-t-il aux objets qui se trouvent dans la classe?
18. Pourquoi les vitres redeviennent-elles sable?
19. Pourquoi l'encre redevient-elle eau?
20. Pourquoi les pupitres redeviennent-ils arbres?
21. Pourquoi la craie redevient-elle falaise?
22. Expliquez le jeu de mots «le porte-plume redevient oiseau».
23. Pour apprendre à ses élèves à faire des additions, le professeur leur

fait répéter les chiffres et leurs sommes. Que pensez-vous de la répétition comme méthode pédagogique?

TROISIÈME PARTIE

phonétique

I. CONTRASTES

[y]

cube / cube
cube / cube
cube / cube
cube, cube, cube / . . . /

but / but
but / but
but / but
but, but, but / . . . /

jury / jury
jury / jury
jury / jury
jury, jury, jury / . . . /

structure / structure
structure / structure
structure / structure
structure, structure, structure / . . . /

new / nue
new / nue
new / nue
nue, nue, nue / . . . /

due / dû
due / dû
due / dû
dû, dû, dû / . . . /

review / revue
review / revue
review / revue
revue, revue, revue / . . . /

culture / culture
culture / culture
culture / culture
culture, culture, culture / . . . /

scripture / écriture
scripture / écriture
scripture / écriture
écriture, écriture, écriture / . . . /

II. OPPOSITIONS   [y] [i]

hure / ire . . . hure / ire
tu / t'y . . . tu / t'y
du / dit . . . du / dit
dune / dîne . . . dune / dîne
dur / dire . . . dur / dire
fût / fit . . . fût / fit
vue / vie . . . vue / vie
su / si . . . su / si
sur / sire . . . sur / sire
mue / mis . . . mue / mis
nu / ni . . . nu / ni
lu / lit . . . lu / lit
pure / pire . . . pure / pire
plus / pli . . . plus / pli
buse / bise . . . buse / bise

rue / rit . . . rue / rit
rude / ride . . . rude / ride
cru / cri . . . cru / cri
truc / trique . . . truc / trique

Une plume . . . Une plume
Sur le mur . . . Sur le mur
Ce lit est dur. . . . Ce lit est dur.
Jules a des scrupules. . . . Jules a des scrupules.
Lucie est sûre de lui. . . . Lucie est sûre de lui.
La musique de Lulli . . . La musique de Lulli
Au su et au vu du juge . . . Au su et au vu du juge
Si! Suzy a bu du jus   Si! Suzy a bu du jus
de prunes. . . . de prunes.

QUATRIÈME PARTIE

exercices

I. VOCABULAIRE

A. **Jouer de** . . . (instruments de musique)

Jouer à . . . (sports ou activité)

Remplacez les tirets par la préposition qui convient:

(*a*) Mes amis jouent ———— bridge.
(*b*) Le roi joue ———— échecs.
(*c*) Les enfants jouent ———— balle.
(*d*) Les étudiants américains jouent ———— football.
(*e*) La jeune fille joue ———— harpe.
(*f*) Philippe joue ———— piano.

(*g*) Je joue —— tennis.
(*h*) Louis Armstrong joue —— trompette.

II. GRAMMAIRE

A. Pronoms compléments directs d'objet

Répétez la question, en substituant les mots indiqués, et répondez affirmativement:

(*a*) L'enfant voit-il [**l'oiseau**]? Oui, il [**le**] voit.
la fleur / les tableaux / l'image / le professeur

Répétez la question, en substituant les mots indiqués, et répondez négativement:

(*b*) Est-ce que l'enfant entend [**l'oiseau**]? Non, il ne [**l'**] entend pas.
le bruit des voitures / la radio / les cris des autres enfants / le chant de l'oiseau

Répétez la question et répondez affirmativement:

(*c*) L'enfant appelle-t-il [**l'oiseau**]? Oui, il [**l'**]appelle.
sa mère / ses amis / Philippe au téléphone / ses cousines

B. Pronoms compléments indirects d'objet avec préposition

Répétez la question, en substituant les mots indiqués, et répondez négativement:

(*a*) L'enfant joue-t-il **avec** [**l'oiseau**]? Non, il ne joue pas **avec** [**lui**].
son chien / ses petits amis / les petites filles / sa cousine

Répétez la question, en substituant les mots indiqués, et répondez affirmativement:

(*b*) Est-ce que Claude [est triste] **sans l'oiseau**? Oui, il [est triste] **sans lui**.

s'ennuyer / se sentir seul / être malheureux / pouvoir vivre

Répétez la question et répondez affirmativement:

(*c*) L'oiseau a-t-il chanté **pour [l'enfant]**? Oui, il a chanté **pour [lui]**.

votre amie Marie / leurs parents / les trois jeunes filles / tous les élèves

C. Futur antérieur

1. Ce temps indique une action qui sera accomplie à un moment déterminé du futur.

   Répétez les phrases suivantes en substituant les mots indiqués:

   (*a*) Les enfants joueront quand le professeur [**aura fini** de parler].

   quitter la classe / rentrer chez lui / finir son explication / terminer la leçon / partir déjeuner

2. Expression idiomatique avec le verbe **finir**

   Employée au futur antérieur à la deuxième personne, elle équivaut à un impératif.

   (*a*) Quand vous **aurez fini** [de faire le pitre]!
   de dire des bêtises / d'agir comme un enfant / de déranger les gens qui travaillent / de taquiner le chien / d'ennuyer tout le monde

CINQUIÈME PARTIE

compréhension (laboratoire)

SIXIÈME PARTIE

dictée (laboratoire)

IX

le message

1 quelqu'un: *pronom indéfini dont la forme masculine sert pour les deux genres. Au pluriel*: quelques-uns (*masc.*) *et* quelques-unes (*fém.*)

3 la chaise où: la chaise sur laquelle

11 la rivière où: la rivière dans laquelle

12 l'hôpital où: l'hôpital dans lequel

le message

La porte que quelqu'un a ouverte
La porte que quelqu'un a refermée
La chaise où quelqu'un s'est assis
Le chat que quelqu'un a caressé
5   Le fruit que quelqu'un a mordu
La lettre que quelqu'un a lue
La chaise que quelqu'un a renversée
La porte que quelqu'un a ouverte
La route où quelqu'un court encore
10   Le bois que quelqu'un traverse
La rivière où quelqu'un se jette
L'hôpital où quelqu'un est mort.

Paroles

PREMIÈRE PARTIE

lecture du poème

A. PREMIÈRE LECTURE SANS PAUSES

B. DEUXIÈME LECTURE AVEC PAUSES

le message

La porte que quelqu'un a ouverte / . . . /
La porte que quelqu'un a refermée / . . . /
La chaise où quelqu'un s'est assis / . . . /
Le chat que quelqu'un a caressé / . . . /
5   Le fruit que quelqu'un a mordu / . . . /
La lettre que quelqu'un a lue / . . . /
La chaise que quelqu'un a renversée / . . . /
La porte que quelqu'un a ouverte / . . . /
La route où quelqu'un court encore / . . . /
10   Le bois que quelqu'un traverse / . . . /
La rivière où quelqu'un se jette / . . . /
L'hôpital où quelqu'un est mort. / . . . /

C. TROISIÈME LECTURE SANS PAUSES

DEUXIÈME PARTIE

étude du texte

1. Combien y a-t-il de parties dans le poème? Indiquez-les.
2. Où se déroule la première partie?
3. Quels sont les éléments du décor suggérés successivement par les cinq premiers vers?
4. Peut-on dire que l'atmosphère créée par ces cinq premiers vers est:
   - (a) familière?
   - (b) désinvolte?
   - (c) monotone?
   - (d) incroyable?
   - (e) paisible?

   Choisissez l'adjectif qui convient le mieux à la situation et expliquez pourquoi vous l'avez choisi.
5. Le personnage désigné par le pronom indéfini «quelqu'un» est-il un homme ou une femme? Exposez votre point de vue.
6. Quel est le vers qui fait repartir l'action?
7. Indiquez le changement d'atmosphère après la lecture de la lettre.
8. En étudiant les temps des verbes, montrez comment l'auteur réussit, sans rien changer à la structure de chaque vers, à:
   - (a) donner une impression d'accélération;
   - (b) renforcer l'intensité dramatique.
9. Le poème présente une certaine ambiguïté, d'où deux interprétations possibles: (a) il n'y a qu'un personnage (un homme ou une femme);
   (b) il y a deux personnages (un homme et une femme).

   Discutez ces deux interprétations.
10. Indiquez ce qui, dans le poème, rend la deuxième interprétation possible.
11. Essayez d'imaginer le contenu de la lettre.
12. Etudiez la symétrie parfaite du poème (nombre de vers dans chaque partie, etc.).

13. Le poème est basé sur le procédé de la répétition. Etudiez:
    (a) la structure de chaque vers;
    (b) les éléments fixes;
    (c) les éléments variables.

14. Bien que le poème soit très court, pensez-vous qu'on puisse le présenter comme «une tragédie en douze vers»? Exposez votre point de vue.

15. Avez-vous été surpris par le dénouement brutal? Exprimez votre réaction.

TROISIÈME PARTIE

phonétique

I. CONTRASTES

[ɛ̃]	[œ̃]
main / main	dun / d'un
main / main	dun / d'un
main / main	dun / d'un
main, main, main / . . . /	d'un, d'un, d'un / . . . /
fin / faim	lung / l'un
fin / faim	lung / l'un
fin / faim	lung / l'un
faim, faim, faim / . . . /	l'un, l'un, l'un / . . . /
vein / vingt	brunch / brun
vein / vingt	brunch / brun
vein / vingt	brunch / brun
vingt, vingt, vingt / . . . /	brun, brun, brun / . . . /

simple / simple	humble / humble
simple / simple	humble / humble
simple / simple	humble / humble
simple, simple, simple / . . . /	humble, humble, humble / . . . /

rince / rince	defunct / défunt
rince / rince	defunct / défunt
rince / rince	defunct / défunt
rince, rince, rince / . . . /	défunt, défunt, défunt / . . . /

indistinct / indistinct	commune / commun
indistinct / indistinct	commune / commun
indistinct / indistinct	commune / commun
indistinct, indistinct, indistinct / . . . /	commun, commun, commun / . . . /

II. OPPOSITIONS   [ɛ̃] [œ̃]

Ain / un . . . Ain / un
daim / d'un . . . daim / d'un
main / Meung . . . main / Meung
lin / l'un . . . lin / l'un
brin / brun . . . brin / brun
Alain / alun . . . Alain / alun

Rien à craindre . . . Rien à craindre
Lundi prochain . . . Lundi prochain
Un fin parfum . . . Un fin parfum
Le marin est brun. . . . Le marin est brun.
Martin a un chien. . . . Martin a un chien.
Le défunt était importun   Le défunt était importun
et commun. . . . et commun.
En vain, ce coquin feint   En vain, ce coquin feint
d'être un humble saint. . . . d'être un humble saint.
Le train pour Verdun part   Le train pour Verdun part
à cinq heures vingt et un. . . . à cinq heures vingt et un.

QUATRIÈME PARTIE

exercices

I. GRAMMAIRE

A. Pronoms relatifs

1. Sujet: **qui** (pour les personnes et pour les choses)

   Répétez les phrases suivantes en substituant les mots indiqués:

   (*a*) La porte **qui** est [ouverte] est celle de la salle à manger.
   fermée / peinte en rouge / entrebâillée / en acajou /
   verrouillée

2. Complément d'objet direct: **que** (pour les personnes et
   pour les choses)

   (*a*) La porte **que** j'ai [ouverte] est celle de la salle à manger.
   fermée / peinte en jaune / entr'ouverte / poussée /
   fermée à clé

3. Complément d'objet indirect: préposition + **qui** (pour
   les personnes); préposition + **lequel, etc.** (pour les choses)

   (*a*) Voilà [l'enfant] **à qui** j'ai parlé.
   le médecin / la femme / les amis / les étudiantes /
   Philippe
   (*b*) Voici [le mur] **devant lequel** j'ai arrêté ma voiture.
   le parc / les arbres / le magasin / les maisons / la porte
   du garage

   Notez: **où** est l'équivalent de **dans lequel**, de **sur lequel**,
   etc.

La chaise **où** je suis assis est ancienne.

La chaise **sur laquelle** je suis assis est ancienne.

Répétez les phrases suivantes en employant la préposition et le pronom relatif qui conviennent à la place de **où**:

(*a*) L'hôpital **où** il est mort est à quatre kilomètres de la ville.

(*b*) Les routes **où** nous roulons sont bordées de chênes.

(*c*) Le cercueil **où** l'oiseau est couché est en paille.

(*d*) La maison **où** nous habitons est près de la rivière.

B. Accord du participe passé

1. Participe passé avec **être**

Le participe passé s'accorde avec le sujet.

Répétez les phrases suivantes en substituant les mots indiqués:

(*a*) La lettre a été [lue].
déchirée / envoyée / reçue / tapée à la machine / écrite à la main

(*b*) [La chaise] était renversée.
le verre / les meubles / les bouteilles / les tables / la lampe

2. Participe passé avec **avoir**

Le participe passé s'accorde avec le complément d'objet direct si celui-ci est placé avant le verbe, sinon il reste invariable.

Notez: En français, le complément d'objet direct est généralement placé *après* le verbe sauf dans le cas des pronoms et de certaines phrases interrogatives.

Répétez les phrases suivantes:

(*a*) J'ai lu ces lettres. Je les ai lues. / . . . /

(*b*) Il a ouvert la porte. Il l'a ouverte. / . . . /

(*c*) Les enfants ont mangé les fruits. Il les ont mangés. / . . . /

Répétez les phrases suivantes en substituant les mots indiqués:

(*d*) Quelle porte avez-vous [ouverte]?
fermée / peinte / changée / remplacée / entr'ouverte

(*e*) Quelles lettres ont-ils [lues]?
quels livres / quels documents / quelles histoires /
quelles annonces / quels journaux

*Remplacez les tirets par les participes passés des verbes; faites
l'accord si c'est nécessaire:*

(*f*) La femme est ——————— (arriver) à la maison.
Elle a ——————— (regarder) le chat. Ensuite, elle
a ——————— (fermer) la porte. Les lettres qu'elle
a ——————— (lire) sont ——————— (tomber) par
terre. Elle les a ——————— (ramasser) et les a
——————— (placer) sur la table.

3. Verbes pronominaux avec **être**

Bien que l'auxiliaire soit **être,** le participe passé s'accorde
avec le complément d'objet direct si celui-ci précède le
verbe.

Répétez les exemples suivants:

(*a*) Elle s'est lavée. / . . . /
(Il y a accord parce que le complément d'objet direct
précède le verbe.)

(*b*) Elle s'est lavé les mains. / . . . /
(Le participe passé est invariable parce que le complément d'objet direct **les mains** est placé après le verbe.)

(*c*) Elle se les est lavées. / . . . /
(Il y a accord parce que le complément d'objet direct
les précède le verbe.)

Reprenez les formes précédentes en utilisant les phrases suivantes:

(*a*) se masser le cuir chevelu
(*b*) se laver la tête
(*c*) se couper les cheveux
(*d*) se vernir les ongles

CINQUIÈME PARTIE

compréhension (laboratoire)

SIXIÈME PARTIE

dictée (laboratoire)

X

les derniers

sacrements

les derniers sacrements: rites administrés par l'Eglise catholique à un mourant

1 **grandes eaux de la misère:** Grandes eaux *se dit en parlant de jeux d'eau de fontaines. Le rapprochement des termes* «noyé» *et* «grandes eaux de la misère» *permet ici un effet stylistique.*

1 **misère:** pauvreté et malheur

2 **horriblement:** *adverbe qui a perdu de sa force dans la conversation courante mais qui a ici toute sa valeur*

4 **un mourant:** quelqu'un en train de mourir

7 **veilleuse:** mèche flottant sur une couche d'huile, qu'on allume la nuit

20 **Il y a le feu:** La chambre est en feu

24 **Rien d'autre:** *Voir p. 242, exercice II, B.*

les derniers sacrements

Noyé dans les grandes eaux de la misère
Qui suintent horriblement
Le long des murs de sa chambre sordide
Un mourant
5   Livide abandonné et condamné
Aperçoit
Dans l'ombre de la veilleuse
Promenée et bercée par le vent
Contre le mur suintant
10   Une lueur vivante et merveilleuse
La flamme heureuse des yeux aimés
Et il entend
Distinctement
En mourant
15   Dans l'éclatant silence de la chambre mortuaire
Les plus douces paroles de l'amour retrouvé
Dites par la voix même de la femme tant aimée
Et la chambre un instant s'éclaire
Comme jamais palais ne fut éclairé
20   Il y a le feu
Disent les voisins
Ils se précipitent
Et ne voient rien
Rien d'autre qu'un homme seul
25   Couché dans des draps sales
Et souriant
Malgré le vent d'hiver
Qui entre dans la chambre

[31] **Cassés ... par le temps:** *Il s'agit des fenêtres
d'une vieille maison qui tombe en ruines.*

Par les carreaux cassés
30   Cassés par la misère
Et par le temps.

Histoires

PREMIÈRE PARTIE

lecture du poème

A. PREMIÈRE LECTURE SANS PAUSES

B. DEUXIÈME LECTURE AVEC PAUSES

les derniers sacrements

Noyé dans les grandes eaux de la misère / . . . /
Qui suintent horriblement / . . . /
Le long des murs de sa chambre sordide / . . . /
Un mourant / . . . /
5   Livide abandonné et condamné / . . . /
Aperçoit
Dans l'ombre de la veilleuse / . . . /
Promenée et bercée par le vent
Contre le mur suintant / . . . /
10   Une lueur vivante et merveilleuse / . . . /
La flamme heureuse des yeux aimés / . . . /
Et il entend
Distinctement
En mourant / . . . /
15   Dans l'éclatant silence de la chambre mortuaire / . . . /
Les plus douces paroles de l'amour retrouvé / . . . /
Dites par la voix même de la femme tant aimée / . . . /
Et la chambre un instant s'éclaire / . . . /
Comme jamais palais ne fut éclairé / . . . /
20   Il y a le feu

Disent les voisins / . . . /
Ils se précipitent
Et ne voient rien / . . . /
Rien d'autre qu'un homme seul / . . . /
25 Couché dans des draps sales / . . . /
Et souriant / . . . /
Malgré le vent d'hiver
Qui entre dans la chambre / . . . /
Par les carreaux cassés / . . . /
30 Cassés par la misère
Et par le temps. / . . . /

C. TROISIÈME LECTURE SANS PAUSES

DEUXIÈME PARTIE

étude du texte

1. Où se déroule l'histoire?

2. A quel moment? Le jour ou la nuit? Citez la phrase qui nous l'apprend.

3. En quelle saison?

4. Décrivez la chambre où l'homme est couché.

5. Décrivez l'état dans lequel l'homme se trouve.

6. Quel âge lui donnez-vous? Justifiez votre point de vue.

7. Au vers 5, l'auteur emploie les adjectifs «livide abandonné condamné» qui caractérisent des états de nature différente. Commentez ces adjectifs et essayez d'expliquer pourquoi Prévert les a rapprochés.

8. Relevez tous les termes utilisés par l'auteur pour créer une atmosphère de malheur.

9. Qu'est-ce que le mourant aperçoit tout d'abord?

10. Pourquoi a-t-il cette vision?

11. Ensuite, qu'entend-il?

12. Pourquoi a-t-il cette hallucination auditive?

13. Commentez le contraste des mots dans l'expression «l'éclatant silence».

14. On peut admettre l'hallucination visuelle d'un mourant. Mais que peut-on dire des voisins qui croient qu'il y a le feu dans la chambre de l'homme? (N'oubliez pas que l'ambiguïté est un élément cher à Prévert.)

15. Lorsqu'ils se précipitent chez lui, est-ce par curiosité ou pour l'aider? Expliquez quels sont leurs véritables motifs.

16. Pourquoi le mourant sourit-il?

17. Etudiez le rapprochement «chambre-palais».

18. Si ce poème a provoqué en vous une certaine émotion, essayez de la décrire.

19. Pourquoi Prévert utilise-t-il un titre religieux pour un poème qui ne l'est pas?

20. Quel sens peut-on alors donner au titre «Les derniers sacrements»?

TROISIÈME PARTIE

phonétique

I. CONTRASTES

[ã]

dent / dent
dent / dent
dent / dent
dent, dent, dent / . . . /

plan / plan
plan / plan
plan / plan
plan, plan, plan / . . . /

tan / taon
tan / taon
tan / taon
taon, taon, taon / . . . /

ban / banc
ban / banc
ban / banc
banc, banc, banc / . . . /

lance / lance
lance / lance
lance / lance
lance, lance, lance / . . . /

flank / flanc
flank / flanc
flank / flanc
flanc, flanc, flanc / . . . /

tremble / tremble
tremble / tremble
tremble / tremble
tremble, tremble, tremble / . . . /

lamp / lampe
lamp / lampe
lamp / lampe
lampe, lampe, lampe / . . . /

champion / champion
champion / champion
champion / champion
champion, champion, champion / . . . /

entrance / en transe
entrance / en transe
entrance / en transe
en transe, en transe, en transe / . . . /

enchantment / enchantement
enchantment / enchantement
enchantment / enchantement
enchantement, enchantement, enchantement / . . . /

II. OPPOSITIONS   [ɛ̃] [ã]

Ain / en . . . Ain / en
saint / sang . . . saint / sang
teint / temps . . . teint / temps
daim / dent . . . daim / dent
Quint / camp . . . Quint / camp
gain /gant . . . gain / gant
pin / pend . . . pin / pend

bain / banc . . . bain / banc
faim / fend . . . faim / fend
vin / vend . . . vin / vend
main / ment . . . main / ment
nain / n'en . . . nain / n'en
lin / lent . . . lin / lent
Alain / allant . . . Alain / allant
lien / liant . . . lien / liant

En avant . . . En avant
Le chant des anges . . . Le chant des anges
Blanche a trente ans. . . . Blanche a trente ans.
Jean danse en cadence. . . . Jean danse en cadence.
Cet enfant mange lentement. . . . Cet enfant mange lentement.
Roland avance en rampant. . . . Roland avance en rampant.
Les branches tremblent   Les branches tremblent
dans le vent. . . . dans le vent.
Dans l'éclatant silence   Dans l'éclatant silence
de la chambre . . . de la chambre
Il entend distinctement   Il entend distinctement
en mourant. . . . en mourant.

QUATRIÈME PARTIE

exercices

I. VOCABULAIRE

A. Le participe présent (forme verbale en **-ant**) sert à former un certain nombre de noms.

Exemples: un mourant (mourir)
une mendiante (mendier)

des croyants (croire)
des débutantes (débuter)

Formez les noms qui correspondent aux verbes suivants et faites une phrase avec chacun d'eux:

| gagner | occuper | passer |
| revenir | partir | commander |

II. GRAMMAIRE

A. Inversion verbe-sujet dans les propositions incises

Répétez les phrases suivantes en substituant les mots indiqués:

(*a*) Il y a le feu, [**disent**] les voisins.
déclarer / affirmer / s'écrier / expliquer / s'exclamer

Répétez cet exercice en mettant le verbe d'abord à l'imparfait, ensuite au passé composé.

Servez-vous du modèle ci-dessous pour construire les phrases suivantes avec une proposition incise:

Les voisins disent qu'il y a le feu dans la chambre.
Il y a le feu dans la chambre, **disent les voisins.**

(*a*) Une femme annonce que l'homme est mort seul.
(*b*) Une voisine déclare qu'il a le visage souriant.
(*c*) Un jeune garçon explique que les carreaux sont cassés.
(*d*) Le mourant pense qu'il entend la voix aimée.

B. Différentes positions de la locution négative **ne ... pas**

Elles varient selon le temps et le mode du verbe employé.

1. Temps simples

Ne précède toujours le verbe et les pronoms compléments d'objet.

Pas est placé après le verbe et, dans une phrase interrogative, après le pronom sujet.

Répétez les phrases suivantes en étudiant attentivement la position de la locution négative:

(*a*) Je **ne** parle **pas**. / ... /
(*b*) **Ne** parlez **pas**. / ... /
(*c*) Je **ne** vous parle **pas**. / ... /
(*d*) **Ne** parle-t-il **pas**? / ... /
(*e*) Il **ne** veut **pas** parler. / ... /
(*f*) Tu **ne** te dépêches **pas**. / ... /

2. Temps composés

Même règle que plus haut, mais elle s'applique à l'auxiliaire.

(*a*) Je **n'**ai **pas** parlé. / ... /
(*b*) Je **ne** vous ai **pas** parlé. / ... /
(*c*) **N'**a-t-il **pas** parlé? / ... /
(*d*) Il **n'**a **pas** voulu parler. / ... /
(*e*) Tu **ne** t'es **pas** dépêché. / ... /

3. Les deux parties de la locution précèdent le verbe quand celui-ci est à l'infinitif.

Répétez la phrase suivante en substituant les verbes indiqués:

(*a*) Attendre, **ne pas** [se décourager].
s'impatienter / se lasser / se désoler / s'inquiéter

Notez: Les autres locutions négatives employées le plus fréquemment sont:

> **ne ... plus**
> **ne ... point** (s'emploie rarement en français moderne)
> **ne ... jamais**
> **ne ... guère**
> **ne ... rien**
> **ne ... personne**

(Aux temps composés, **personne** suit le participe passé. *Exemple:* Hier, je **n'**ai vu **personne**.)

CINQUIÈME PARTIE

compréhension (laboratoire)

SIXIÈME PARTIE

dictée (laboratoire)

XI

rien à craindre

rien à craindre : Il n'y a rien à craindre

4 **bien morts :** complètement morts

7-8 **On ne peut, ils ne peuvent :** *forme négative spéciale, voir p. 13, exercice II, B.*
8 **se sauver :** fuir, s'échapper

12 **un entourage de fer :** *Dans les cimetières français il y a généralement une sorte de grille autour des tombes.*
13 **lits-cages :** lits pliants ; *ici Prévert fait allusion aux barreaux des lits d'enfants.*
14 **en bas âge :** très jeunes

17 **Sait-on jamais :** *expression courante qui exprime le doute*

22 **Se dégager :** Se rendre libre

26 **Horreur et catacombes :** *exclamation destinée à marquer l'horreur de la situation*

28 **Vous voyez cela d'ici :** Comme vous pouvez le voir, le constater

rien à craindre

Ne craignez rien
Gens honnêtes et exemplaires
Il n'y a pas de danger
Vos morts sont bien morts
5   Vos morts sont bien gardés
Il n'y a rien à craindre
On ne peut vous les prendre
Ils ne peuvent se sauver
Il y a des gardiens dans les cimetières
10 Et puis
Tout autour des tombes
Il y a un entourage de fer
Comme autour des lits-cages
Où dorment les enfants en bas âge
15 Et c'est une précaution sage
Dans son dernier sommeil
Sait-on jamais
Le mort pourrait rêver encore
Rêver qu'il est vivant
20 Rêver qu'il n'est plus mort
Et secouant ses draps de pierre
Se dégager
Et se pencher
Et tomber de la tombe
25 Comme un enfant du lit
Horreur et catacombes
Retomber dans la vie
Vous voyez cela d'ici

29 **Tout serait remis en question :** Il faudrait reconsidérer tout

31 **succession :** héritage

32 **braves :** honnêtes et bons

38 **Il n'y aura jamais plus à revenir là-dessus :** On ne sera jamais plus obligé de reprendre cette chose en considération (*Sur l'emploi de* **avoir à,** *voir p. 147, exercice I, F.*)
38 **là-dessus :** sur cela

41 **chrysanthèmes :** fleurs d'automne généralement associées à la Toussaint, fête des morts qui tombe le 1er novembre

42 **vaquer :** s'appliquer

44 **éternels regrets :** *variation de la formule* regrets éternels *utilisée dans les annonces nécrologiques*

Tout serait remis en question
30   L'affection et la désolation
Et la succession
Rassurez-vous braves gens
Honnêtes et exemplaires
Vos morts ne reviendront pas
35   S'amuser sur la terre
Les larmes ont été versées une fois pour toutes
Et il n'y aura pas
Il n'y aura jamais plus à revenir là-dessus
Et rien dans le cimetière
40   Ne sera saccagé
Les pots de chrysanthèmes resteront à leur place
Et vous pourrez vaquer en toute tranquillité
L'arrosoir à la main devant le mausolée
Aux doux labeurs champêtres des éternels regrets.

Histoires

PREMIÈRE PARTIE

lecture du poème

A. PREMIÈRE LECTURE SANS PAUSES

B. DEUXIÈME LECTURE AVEC PAUSES

rien à craindre

Ne craignez rien
Gens honnêtes et exemplaires / . . . /
Il n'y a pas de danger / . . . /
Vos morts sont bien morts / . . . /
5   Vos morts sont bien gardés / . . . /
Il n'y a rien à craindre / . . . /
On ne peut vous les prendre / . . . /
Ils ne peuvent se sauver / . . . /
Il y a des gardiens dans les cimetières / . . . /
10   Et puis
Tout autour des tombes / . . . /
Il y a un entourage de fer / . . . /
Comme autour des lits-cages
Où dorment les enfants en bas âge / . . . /
15   Et c'est une précaution sage / . . . /
Dans son dernier sommeil / . . . /
Sait-on jamais / . . . /
Le mort pourrait rêver encore / . . . /
Rêver qu'il est vivant / . . . /
20   Rêver qu'il n'est plus mort / . . . /

Et secouant ses draps de pierre / . . . /
Se dégager
Et se pencher / . . . /
Et tomber de la tombe
25 Comme un enfant du lit / . . . /
Horreur et catacombes / . . . /
Retomber dans la vie / . . . /
Vous voyez cela d'ici / . . . /
Tout serait remis en question / . . . /
30 L'affection et la désolation
Et la succession / . . . /
Rassurez-vous braves gens
Honnêtes et exemplaires / . . . /
Vos morts ne reviendront pas
35 S'amuser sur la terre / . . . /
Les larmes ont été versées une fois pour toutes / . . . /
Et il n'y aura pas / . . . /
Il n'y aura jamais plus à revenir là-dessus / . . . /
Et rien dans le cimetière
40 Ne sera saccagé / . . . /
Les pots de chrysanthèmes resteront à leur place / . . . /
Et vous pourrez vaquer en toute tranquillité / . . . /
L'arrosoir à la main devant le mausolée / . . . /
Aux doux labeurs champêtres des éternels regrets. / . . . /

C. TROISIÈME LECTURE SANS PAUSES

DEUXIÈME PARTIE

étude du texte

1. A qui l'auteur s'adresse-t-il?
2. De quoi les «gens honnêtes et exemplaires» ont-ils peur?
3. Indiquez quelques précautions prises pour empêcher le retour des morts.
4. Les gardiens dans les cimetières «gardent»-ils vraiment les morts? A quoi servent-ils?
5. Pourquoi les «gens honnêtes et exemplaires» craignent-ils le retour des morts?
6. Qu'arriverait-il s'ils revenaient? Décrivez les conséquences de leur retour s'il fallait remettre en question: (a) l'affection;
   (b) la désolation;
   (c) la succession.
7. Des trois éléments précédents, quel est celui qui vous semble le plus important? Expliquez pourquoi.
8. Les «gens honnêtes et exemplaires» sont-ils vraiment honnêtes et exemplaires? Expliquez ces deux adjectifs et essayez de montrer l'ironie de ce jugement.
9. L'auteur utilise fréquemment les mots «sommeil» et «lits». Pourquoi?
10. Relevez tous les termes qui s'y rattachent plus ou moins.
11. Essayez d'imaginer les rêves que font les morts.
12. Quelles sortes de jugement pourraient-ils porter sur les vivants?
13. De quelle façon les vivants craignent-ils que les morts manifestent leur mécontentement?
14. Comme en réalité les vivants n'ont rien à craindre des morts, comment expliquez-vous leur comportement et leur attitude?
15. Les vivants sont-ils (a) détachés?
    (b) hypocrites?
    (c) sincères?

      (d) distraits?

      (e) conformistes?

Choisissez deux adjectifs qui s'adaptent à la situation et justifiez votre choix.

TROISIÈME PARTIE

phonétique

I. CONTRASTES

[õ]

on / on
on / on
on / on
on, on, on / . . . /

ton / ton
ton / ton
ton / ton
ton, ton, ton / . . . /

found / fond
found / fond
found / fond
fond, fond, fond / . . . /

count / comte
count / comte
count / comte
comte, comte, comte / . . . /

bomb / bombe
bomb / bombe
bomb / bombe
bombe, bombe, bombe / . . . /

prompt / prompt
prompt / prompt
prompt / prompt
prompt, prompt, prompt / . . . /

function / fonction
function / fonction
function / fonction
fonction, fonction, fonction / . . . /

conjunction / conjonction
conjunction / conjonction
conjunction / conjonction
conjonction, conjonction, conjonction / . . . /

The sound is long / Le son est long
The sound is long / Le son est long
The sound is long / Le son est long
Le son est long, Le son est long, Le son est long / . . . /

The emotion is profound / L'émotion est profonde
The emotion is profound / L'émotion est profonde
The emotion is profound / L'émotion est profonde
L'émotion est profonde, L'émotion est profonde, L'émotion est profonde / . . . /

II. OPPOSITIONS   [ō] [ã]

on / an . . . on / an
son / sans . . . son / sans
qu'on / camp . . . qu'on / camp
gond / gant . . . gond / gant
ton / temps . . . ton / temps
dont / dent . . . dont / dent

bon / banc . . . bon / banc
blond / blanc . . . blond / blanc
pont / pend . . . pont / pend
plomb / plan . . . plomb / plan
jonc / Jean . . . jonc / Jean
mon / ment . . . mon / ment
non / n'en . . . non / n'en
rond / rang . . . rond / rang
long / lent . . . long / lent
ombre / ambre . . . ombre / ambre
compagne / campagne . . . compagne / campagne
tondre / tendre . . . tondre / tendre
fronce / France . . . fronce / France
concert / cancer . . . concert / cancer

QUATRIÈME PARTIE

exercices

I. GRAMMAIRE

A. Exercice sur la locution **il y a**

D'après le contexte des phrases suivantes, remplacez les tirets par le verbe au temps qui convient:

(*a*) Aujourd'hui, **il y** ———— peu de monde dans les rues parce qu'il pleut.

(*b*) Hier soir, **il y** ———— beaucoup de monde au cinéma.

(*c*) Quand l'acteur entra en scène, **il y** ———— de nombreux applaudissements.

(*d*) Demain, **il y** ———— certainement beaucoup de monde à la conférence du Professeur Bergeret.

(*e*) S'il faisait beau, **il y** ———— beaucoup plus de monde
à la plage.

(*f*) Bien qu'**il y** ———— peu de monde dans la salle, les
acteurs jouent remarquablement.

(*g*) Hier matin, **il y** ———— un grave accident juste
devant chez moi.

(*h*) On nous avait dit qu'après ce terrible orage, **il y**
———— de graves inondations.

(*i*) Même s'il n'est pas élu, **il y** ———— beaucoup de gens
qui auront montré leur intérêt pour ce candidat.

(*j*) S'il avait fait beau, **il y** ———— beaucoup plus de
monde dans les rues.

(*k*) Je crains qu'hier **il n'y** ———— un accident grave à ce
croisement.

B. Quand deux verbes sont employés ensemble, le deuxième est
généralement à l'infinitif.

1. Certains verbes sont suivis directement de l'infinitif. **Aimer,
pouvoir, vouloir, espérer, aller,** etc., ne sont pas suivis
d'une préposition.

Notez: Les verbes de perception ne sont jamais suivis
d'une préposition.

Répétez les phrases suivantes en substituant les verbes indiqués:

(*a*) Le mort [**pourrait**] rêver qu'il est vivant.
aimer / vouloir / oser / paraître / aller

(*b*) Les enfants [**regardent**] passer les voitures.
écouter / voir / entendre

C. **Rien** + **à** + verbe à l'infinitif

(*a*) Il n'y a **rien à** [craindre].
voir / faire / espérer / redouter / dire

D. **Quelque chose** + **à** + verbe à l'infinitif

(*a*) Nous avions **quelque chose à** [terminer].
expliquer / envoyer / finir / étudier / discuter

E. La construction **à** + verbe à l'infinitif s'emploie également après un nom, et le verbe qui précède la préposition **à** est généralement **avoir**.

(*a*) Philippe **a** des lettres **à** [écrire].
relire / envoyer / mettre à la poste / dicter à la secrétaire / taper à la machine

F. **Avoir à** + verbe à l'infinitif marque une obligation et est employé à la place de **devoir**.

(*a*) Je n'ai pas pu sortir hier soir, j'**ai eu à** [faire mes devoirs].
lire ce livre pour demain / apprendre ce poème / réparer ma voiture / chercher des amis à l'aéroport / cirer les parquets

Notez: Le participe passé du verbe **devoir** est **dû**.
(Les formes **due, dus, dues** ne prennent pas d'accent circonflexe.)

CINQUIÈME PARTIE

compréhension (laboratoire)

SIXIÈME PARTIE

dictée (laboratoire)

XII

le chat et l'oiseau

¹ **désolé**: affligé; adjectif qui se rapporte à *village*

⁵ **à moitié**: en partie

¹⁰ **funérailles**: enterrement (toujours au pluriel; généralement employé lorsqu'il s'agit de quelqu'un d'important)

¹⁶ **fasse**: présent du subjonctif de *faire,* a ici le sens d'un conditionnel; **faire de la peine**: causer du chagrin
¹⁸ **tout entier**: entièrement

²² **là-bas**: au bout du monde
²³ **en**: de là-bas

²⁶ **Il ne faut jamais faire les choses à moitié**: Ce vers est un proverbe français

le chat et l'oiseau

Un village écoute désolé
Le chant d'un oiseau blessé
C'est le seul oiseau du village
Et c'est le seul chat du village
5 Qui l'a à moitié dévoré
Et l'oiseau cesse de chanter
Le chat cesse de ronronner
Et de se lécher le museau
Et le village fait à l'oiseau
10 De merveilleuses funérailles
Et le chat qui est invité
Marche derrière le petit cercueil de paille
Où l'oiseau mort est allongé
Porté par une petite fille
15 Qui n'arrête pas de pleurer
Si j'avais su que cela te fasse tant de peine
Lui dit le chat
Je l'aurais mangé tout entier
Et puis je t'aurais raconté
20 Que je l'avais vu s'envoler
S'envoler jusqu'au bout du monde
Là-bas où c'est tellement loin
Que jamais on n'en revient
Tu aurais eu moins de chagrin
25 Simplement de la tristesse et des regrets

Il ne faut jamais faire les choses à moitié.

Histoires

151

PREMIÈRE PARTIE

lecture du poème

A. PREMIÈRE LECTURE SANS PAUSES

B. DEUXIÈME LECTURE AVEC PAUSES

le chat et l'oiseau

Un village écoute désolé / . . . /
Le chant d'un oiseau blessé / . . . /
C'est le seul oiseau du village / . . . /
Et c'est le seul chat du village
5   Qui l'a à moitié dévoré / . . . /
Et l'oiseau cesse de chanter / . . . /
Le chat cesse de ronronner / . . . /
Et de se lécher le museau / . . . /
Et le village fait à l'oiseau / . . . /
10 De merveilleuses funérailles / . . . /
Et le chat qui est invité / . . . /
Marche derrière le petit cercueil de paille / . . . /
Où l'oiseau mort est allongé / . . . /
Porté par une petite fille
15 Qui n'arrête pas de pleurer / . . . /
Si j'avais su que cela te fasse tant de peine / . . . /
Lui dit le chat / . . . /
Je l'aurais mangé tout entier / . . . /
Et puis je t'aurais raconté / . . . /
20 Que je l'avais vu s'envoler / . . . /
S'envoler jusqu'au bout du monde / . . . /

Là-bas où c'est tellement loin / . . . /
Que jamais on n'en revient / . . . /
Tu aurais eu moins de chagrin / . . . /
25 Simplement de la tristesse et des regrets / . . . /

Il ne faut jamais faire les choses à moitié. / . . . /

C. TROISIÈME LECTURE SANS PAUSES

DEUXIÈME PARTIE

étude du texte

1. Pourquoi le village est-il désolé?
2. Qu'est-ce qui est arrivé à l'oiseau?
3. Pourquoi les gens du village aiment-ils tellement l'oiseau?
4. Même blessé, l'oiseau chante. Pourquoi cesse-t-il bientôt de chanter?
5. Pourquoi le chat cesse-t-il de ronronner et de se lécher le museau?
6. On ne fait généralement pas de «merveilleuses funérailles» à un oiseau. Pourquoi est-ce différent ici?
7. Qu'arrive-t-il habituellement quand un oiseau meurt?
8. Pourquoi les gens du village ont-ils placé l'oiseau dans un petit cercueil de paille plutôt que dans un petit cercueil de bois?
9. Qu'est-ce qui montre que les gens du village ne savent pas qui a tué l'oiseau?
10. S'ils avaient su la vérité, qu'auraient-ils fait au chat?
11. Quel est le personnage qui symbolise le chagrin du village?
12. Comment la petite fille manifeste-t-elle son chagrin?
13. Pourquoi le poète a-t-il choisi ce personnage? Indiquez au moins deux raisons.

14. On pourrait croire que le chat est peiné par le chagrin de la petite fille. Montrez quels sont ses sentiments en vous servant de ses propres paroles.

15. La petite fille peut-elle ou ne peut-elle pas croire ce que lui dit le chat? Etudiez les deux possibilités.

16. Pourquoi la petite fille aurait-elle eu moins de chagrin si l'oiseau avait simplement disparu?

17. Quel nom donne-t-on à cette région mystérieuse située au bout du monde et d'où l'on ne revient jamais?

18. Que pensez-vous des regrets du chat et de la conclusion en forme de proverbe?

19. Commentez ce proverbe (*a*) dans son sens général;
                          (*b*) dans ce cas particulier.

20. Au lieu d'appeler «Le chat et l'oiseau» un poème, pourrait-on lui donner un autre nom?

21. «Le chat et l'oiseau» vous rappelle-t-il des œuvres du même genre écrites par un poète classique français du 17ème siècle? Qui est ce poète?

TROISIÈME PARTIE

phonétique

I. CONTRASTES

semi-voyelle [j]

bay / baille
bay / baille
bay / baille
baille, baille, baille / . . . /

veil / veille
veil / veille
veil / veille
veille, veille, veille / . . . /

pie / paille
pie / paille
pie / paille
paille, paille, paille / . . . /

piece / pièce
piece / pièce
piece / pièce
pièce, pièce, pièce / . . . /

dew / douille
dew / douille
dew / douille
douille, douille, douille / . . . /

anti / entier
anti / entier
anti / entier
entier, entier, entier / . . . /

royal / royal
royal / royal
royal / royal
royal, royal, royal / . . . /

pioneer / pionnier
pioneer / pionnier
pioneer / pionnier
pionnier, pionnier, pionnier / . . . /

prayer / prière
prayer / prière
prayer / prière
prière, prière, prière / . . . /

motion / moitié
motion / moitié
motion / moitié
moitié, moitié, moitié / . . . /

funeral / funérailles
funeral / funérailles
funeral / funérailles
funérailles, funérailles, funérailles / . . . /

II. EXERCICES SUR LA SEMI-VOYELLE [j]

air / hier . . . air / hier
Seine / sienne . . . Seine / sienne
sans / sciant . . . sans / sciant
saint / sien . . . saint / sien
sel / ciel . . . sel / ciel
qui / quille . . . qui / quille
quai / quiet . . . quai / quiet
teint / tien . . . teint / tien
d'idées / Didier . . . d'idées / Didier
père / Pierre . . . père / Pierre
pré / prier . . . pré / prier
pont / pion . . . pont / pion
baie / biais . . . baie / biais
bain / bien . . . bain / bien
fer / fier . . . fer / fier
vin / viens . . . vin / viens
rein / rien . . . rein / rien
roule / rouille . . . roule / rouille
lait / liait . . . lait / liait
long / lion . . . long / lion
lent / liant . . . lent / liant
il a / il y a . . . il a / il y a
allé / allié . . . allé / allié
voulez / vouliez . . . voulez / vouliez
portons / portions . . . portons / portions

Viens à pied. . . . Viens à pied.
Le vieux piano . . . Le vieux piano

Un cercueil de paille . . . Un cercueil de paille
Le soleil brille dans le ciel. . . . Le soleil brille dans le ciel.
La fillette a pitié du chien. . . . La fillette a pitié du chien.
Le vieux monsieur ne se   Le vieux monsieur ne se
souvient de rien. . . . souvient de rien.
Daniel vient de plier sa   Daniel vient de plier sa
serviette. . . . serviette.
Pierre travaille dans une   Pierre travaille dans une
société financière. . . . société financière.
Combien y a-t-il de pièces . . . Combien y a-t-il de pièces
dans cette collection? . . . dans cette collection?
Julien a oublié la moitié   Julien a oublié la moitié
de sa prière. . . . de sa prière.

QUATRIÈME PARTIE

exercices

I. GRAMMAIRE

A. Proposition (clause) introduite par **si**

1. Proposition subordonnée introduite par **si**: présent de l'indicatif

Proposition principale: futur

Si le village **aime** l'oiseau, il **sera** désolé de sa mort.
Si le village **aime** l'oiseau, **sera**-t-il désolé de sa mort?

Mettez les phrases suivantes à la forme interrogative:

(*a*) **Si** le chat **mange** l'oiseau, il **perdra** un ami sincère.

(*b*) **Si** la petite fille **apprend** qui a tué l'oiseau, elle **aura** beaucoup de chagrin.

2. Proposition subordonnée introduite par **si**: imparfait de l'indicatif

Proposition principale: présent du conditionnel

(*a*) **Si** le chat **aimait** l'oiseau, il **serait** vraiment son ami.
(*b*) **Si** la petite fille **savait** la vérité, elle ne **parlerait** plus au chat.
(*c*) **Si** les gens du village **connaissaient** le coupable, ils le **puniraient** sévèrement.

3. Proposition subordonnée introduite par **si**: plus-que-parfait de l'indicatif

Proposition principale: passé du conditionnel

(*a*) **Si** j'**avais su** que cela te fasse tant de peine, je l'**aurais mangé** tout entier.
(*b*) **Si** je l'**avais mangé** tout entier, tu **aurais eu** moins de peine.
(*c*) **Si** l'oiseau **s'était envolé** au loin, tu **aurais été** moins malheureuse.

Notez: **Si** n'est jamais suivi du futur ni du conditionnel sauf quand il a le sens de *whether*.

B. **Il** (**elle**) **est** ou **c'est** devant un nom (profession, activité, religion, nationalité)

1. On emploie **il est** (ou **elle est**) quand le nom est seul.

(Le verbe peut être à n'importe quel temps.)

Répétez les phrases suivantes en substituant les mots indiqués:

(*a*) **Il est** [avocat].
(*b*) **Elle était** [étudiante].
(*c*) **Il avait été** [médecin].

secrétaire / professeur / Français / catholique / infirmier

Notez: Le nom n'est jamais précédé d'un article comme en anglais (*he is a lawyer, she is a student, he is a doctor*).

2. On emploie **c'est** quand le nom n'est pas seul (quand il est qualifié).

> **C'est** un avocat.
> **C'est** un avocat célèbre.
> **C'est** un bon avocat.

Répétez les phrases suivantes en substituant les mots indiqués:

(*a*) **C'est** une étudiante [française].
fameux / intelligent / consciencieux / de talent / exceptionnel

(*b*) **C'est** un [excellent] médecin.
bon / grand / vieux / ancien / brave

3. Exercice d'application

Remplacez les tirets par **il est** *ou* **c'est** *selon le cas:*

(*a*) —— professeur.
(*b*) —— un bon professeur.
(*c*) —— un professeur français.
(*d*) —— professeur depuis cinq ans.
(*e*) —— un médecin en qui j'ai confiance.
(*f*) —— un avocat qui a beaucoup de talent.
(*g*) —— avocat à Paris.
(*h*) —— un avocat qui est aussi critique littéraire.
(*i*) —— étudiant à la Sorbonne.

C. Verbe + **à** ou **de** + verbe à l'infinitif

Il y a des verbes qui sont toujours suivis d'une préposition; **à** et **de** sont les prépositions le plus souvent employées.

1. Voici quelques verbes qui sont toujours suivis de la préposition **à** + verbe à l'infinitif.

Répétez les phrases suivantes en substituant les verbes indiqués:

(*a*) Il y a longtemps que Philippe [apprend] **à** parler anglais.

réussir / persister / parvenir / arriver / s'appliquer

Répétez le même exercice en mettant les verbes à l'imparfait.

2. Voici maintenant quelques verbes qui sont toujours suivis de la préposition **de** + verbe à l'infinitif.

(*a*) L'oiseau [cesse] **de** chanter.
      arrêter / finir / s'efforcer / essayer / se dépêcher
(*b*) La petite fille [n'arrête pas] **de** pleurer.
      craindre / regretter / cesser / finir / s'empêcher

Notez: En francais comme en anglais, il n'y a pas de règle qui indique quelles sont les prépositions qui suivent certains verbes. La seule façon de les apprendre est de construire des phrases et de les répéter aussi souvent que possible.

CINQUIÈME PARTIE

compréhension (laboratoire)

SIXIÈME PARTIE

dictée (laboratoire)

XIII

l'expédition

expédition : (a) excursion ou action militaire; (b) action de faire disparaître; (c) action d'envoyer

2 **musée du Louvre :** ancienne résidence royale à Paris, aujourd'hui un des plus riches musées du monde

10 **sur de l'ouate :** sur du coton (hydrophile)

14 **ferme-boîte :** mot inventé par l'auteur pour former un contraste amusant avec *ouvre-boîte*

17 **En évidence :** Placée de façon à attirer l'attention

24 **cargo boat :** *boat* est prononcé ici à la française de façon à imiter le son de *boîte*

l'expédition

Un homme avec une boîte
Entre au musée du Louvre
Et s'assoit sur un banc
Examinant la boîte
5 Attentivement
Puis il ouvre la boîte
Avec un ouvre-boîte
Et place soigneusement
Très sûr de lui
10 Et sur de l'ouate
L'ouvre-boîte
Dans la boîte
Et refermant la boîte
Avec un ferme-boîte
15 Il pose la boîte
Délicatement
En évidence
Sur le banc
Et s'en va tranquillement
20 En souriant
Et en boitant
Gagne les rues de la Seine
Où l'attend
Un gros cargo boat
25 Tout blanc
Et tout en gravissant les marches de fer
De la passerelle du commandant
En boitant

Et en boitant / . . . /
Gagne les rues de la Seine / . . . /
Où l'attend
Un gros cargo boat
25 Tout blanc / . . . /
Et tout en gravissant les marches de fer / . . . /
De la passerelle du commandant / . . . /
En boitant / . . . /
Il examine le ferme-boîte
30 En souriant / . . . /
Et puis il le jette à la Seine / . . . /
A l'instant même / . . . /
Le navire disparaît
Instantanément. / . . . /

C. TROISIÈME LECTURE SANS PAUSES

DEUXIÈME PARTIE

étude du texte

1. Combien y a-t-il de parties dans le poème? Indiquez-les.
2. Où se passe le début du poème?
3. Quel climat l'auteur cherche-t-il à créer quand, dès les premiers vers, il attire l'attention du lecteur sur la boîte?
4. Que fait l'homme dès qu'il est entré au musée?
5. Que fait-on généralement dans un musée?
6. L'attitude de l'homme ne vous semble-t-elle pas étrange? Expliquez pourquoi.

7. L'homme se livre à une série d'actions avec la boîte. Décrivez-les.

8. Il pose la boîte délicatement près de lui. Pourquoi cet adverbe indique-t-il quelque chose d'inquiétant?

9. Cependant, on peut se demander pourquoi il la pose «en évidence» sur le banc. Comment interprétez-vous ce geste?

10. Dans cette atmosphère de «suspense», essayez d'imaginer un rapport entre cette boîte mystérieuse et le musée du Louvre.

11. L'auteur ne dit rien de l'homme. Est-ce que c'est:

    (*a*) un saboteur?

    (*b*) un collectionneur?

    (*c*) un vandale?

    (*d*) un mystificateur?

    (*e*) un marin?

    (*f*) un espion?

Etudiez chacune de ces possibilités et indiquez celle qui s'applique le mieux à la situation.

12. Prévert dit que l'homme «s'en va tranquillement en souriant». Cette attitude est-elle conforme à la possibilité que vous venez de choisir? Pourquoi?

13. Quand l'homme quitte le musée, où va-t-il?

14. Que fait-il ensuite?

15. Montrez comment ce poème est «une mise en boîte». («Une mise en boîte», dérivée de «mettre quelqu'un en boîte», est une expression assez courante en français parlé. On ne peut pas en donner une traduction littérale. Le mieux qu'on puisse faire est de combiner le sens des deux expressions suivantes: (a) *to pull someone's leg*; (b) *to say something with tongue in cheek*.)

TROISIÈME PARTIE

phonétique

I. CONTRASTES

[w]	[ɥ]
we / oui	quiz / cuise
we / oui	quiz / cuise
we / oui	quiz / cuise
oui, oui, oui / . . . /	cuise, cuise, cuise / . . . /
what / ouate	suite / suite
what / ouate	suite / suite
what / ouate	suite / suite
ouate, ouate, ouate / . . . /	suite, suite, suite / . . . /
boy / bois	swear / suaire
boy / bois	swear / suaire
boy / bois	swear / suaire
bois, bois, bois / . . . /	suaire, suaire, suaire / . . . /
Lewis / Louis	swan / suant
Lewis / Louis	swan / suant
Lewis / Louis	swan / suant
Louis, Louis, Louis / . . . /	suant, suant, suant / . . . /
loin / loin	Louis / lui
loin / loin	Louis / lui
loin / loin	Louis / lui
loin, loin, loin / . . . /	lui, lui, lui / . . . /

poignant / poignant   cruel / cruel
poignant / poignant   cruel / cruel
poignant / poignant   cruel / cruel
poignant, poignant, poignant / . . . /   cruel, cruel, cruel / . . . /

II. OPPOSITIONS   [w] [ɥ]

pois / puis . . . pois / puis
toile / tuile . . . toile / tuile
quoi / cuit . . . quoi / cuit
couard / cuir . . . couard / cuir
bois / buis . . . bois / buis
bouée / buée . . . bouée / buée
brois / bruit . . . brois / bruit
doit / d'huile . . . doit / d'huile
fois / fuis . . . fois / fuis
froid / fruit . . . froid / fruit
sois / suis . . . sois / suis
moi / muet . . . moi / muet
nouer / nuée . . . nouer / nuée
noix / nuit . . . noix / nuit
noir / nuire . . . noir / nuire
roi / rua . . . roi / rua
roué / ruer . . . roué / ruer
Louis / lui . . . Louis / lui
Loire / luire . . . Loire / luire
l'alouette / la luette . . . l'alouette / la luette
tatoué / t'a tué . . . tatoué / t'a tué

Les pois cuisent. . . . Les pois cuisent.
Au coin d'un bois . . . Au coin d'un bois
Je suis épuisé. . . . Je suis épuisé.
Ces bois sont noirs la nuit. . . . Ces bois sont noirs la nuit.
Quoi, tu bois du jus de   Quoi, tu bois du jus de
fruit froid ? . . . fruit froid ?

Aujourd'hui c'est le huit juillet. . . .	Aujourd'hui c'est le huit juillet.
Louis a mis de l'ouate dans la boîte. . . .	Louis a mis de l'ouate dans la boîte.
Le bruit de la pluie au loin dans la nuit . . .	Le bruit de la pluie au loin dans la nuit
Louise a ensuite conduit la voiture noire. . . .	Louise a ensuite conduit la voiture noire.

QUATRIÈME PARTIE

exercices

I. ORTHOGRAPHE

A. Les accents

En français, les accents sont très importants. Dans les exemples suivants, ils ne modifient pas la prononciation mais ils changent le sens des mots.

Répétez les phrases suivantes en mettant les verbes à l'imparfait:

(*a*) L'homme est assis **sur** un banc.
Il est **sûr** de faire quelque chose d'important.

(*b*) L'homme est-il un simple visiteur **ou** un criminel?
Où a-t-il posé la boîte?

(*c*) L'homme a mis **du** coton dans la boîte.
Il a **dû** employer un outil pour ouvrir la boîte.

(*d*) L'homme **a** beaucoup de patience.
Il est **à** Paris depuis deux jours.

(*e*) L'homme **boite** depuis son accident.
L'homme a remis l'outil dans la **boîte**.

II. GRAMMAIRE

A. Les adverbes

    1. Formation des adverbes

    La plupart des adverbes sont formés en ajoutant **-ment** au féminin singulier des adjectifs ou au masculin quand il est terminé par une voyelle.

        attentive → attentive**ment**
        tranquille → tranquille**ment**
        instantané → instantané**ment**

    Notez: Méfiez-vous de la forme **vite** qui ne prend jamais **-ment.**

    Formez les adverbes à partir des adjectifs suivants:

        (*a*) grand   (*c*) fin   (*e*) rapide
        (*b*) simple   (*d*) horrible (*f*) délicat

    2. Position des adverbes

    Temps simples
    L'adverbe suit généralement le verbe.

    Répétez les phrases suivantes en mettant les verbes à l'imparfait:

    (*a*) L'homme examine attentivement la boîte.
    (*b*) Il place soigneusement l'ouvre-boîte dans la boîte.
    (*c*) Il s'en va tranquillement en souriant.
    Temps composés.
    L'adverbe précède le participe passé.

    Reprenez l'exercice précédent en mettant les verbes au plus-que-parfait.

B. **En** + participe présent

    Après une préposition, le verbe est toujours à l'infinitif.
    Exception: **En** est toujours suivi du participe présent (gerund).

(*Attention*! Méfiez-vous de la construction anglaise, préposition + participe en **-ing**.)

Répétez la phrase suivante en substituant les formes indiquées:

L'homme part [en souriant].

en boitant / en courant / en riant / en pleurant / en
s'indignant

C. Pluriel des noms composés

1. Adjectif + nom;
nom + nom

Les adjectifs et les noms prennent généralement la marque
du pluriel.

un grand-père, des grands-pères
un wagon-restaurant, des wagons-restaurants

2. Mot invariable + nom;
verbe + nom

Seul le nom prend la marque du pluriel:
un contre-ordre, des contre-ordres
un tire-bouchon, des tire-bouchons

Notez: Le nom est au pluriel s'il peut avoir un sens pluriel.
un abat-jour, des abat-jour (abattent le jour)
un couvre-lit, des couvre-lits (couvrent des lits)

Mettez les noms suivants au pluriel:

(*a*) une arrière-garde, des ――― ―――
(*b*) un prie-dieu, des ――― ―――
(*c*) un ouvre-boîte, des ――― ―――
(*d*) une basse-cour, des ――― ―――
(*e*) un wagon-lit, des ――― ―――
(*f*) un porte-monnaie, des ――― ―――
(*g*) un vice-président, des ――― ―――
(*h*) un après-midi, des ――― ―――
(*i*) une demi-heure, des ――― ―――

CINQUIÈME PARTIE

compréhension (laboratoire)

SIXIÈME PARTIE

dictée (laboratoire)

XIV

par le temps qui court!

Par le temps qui court: (a) signifie en ce moment, à cette époque-ci; (b) c'est également une allusion au passage du temps

26 **actuellement:** à cette époque-ci

par le temps qui court!

Il faudrait trouver l'historien
le sociologue le philosophe le pédagogue le métaphysicien
    qui aurait
logiquement
simplement
5   scientifiquement
économiquement
vu
prédit
entrevu
10   ou aperçu
HISTORIQUEMENT
En 1750 ce qui se passerait en 1780
En 1780 ce qui se passerait en 1793
En 1793 ce qui se passerait en 1815
15   En 1815 ce qui se passerait en 1830
En 1830 ce qui se passerait en 1848
En 1848 ce qui se passerait en 1870
En 1870 ce qui se passerait en 1871
En 1871 ce qui se passerait en 1900
20   En 1900 ce qui se passerait en 1914
En 1914 ce qui se passerait en 1918
En 1918 ce qui se passerait en 1936
En 1936 ce qui se passerait en 1940
En 1940 ce qui se passerait en 1944
25   En 1944 ce qui se passera en 1970 et 11

Et ceci simplement concernant une des régions où beaucoup
    parmi nous vivent actuellement.

Spectacle

PREMIÈRE PARTIE

lecture du poème

A. PREMIÈRE LECTURE SANS PAUSES

B. DEUXIÈME LECTURE AVEC PAUSES

par le temps qui court!

Il faudrait trouver l'historien / . . . /
le sociologue le philosophe / . . . / le pédagogue le méta-
    physicien / . . . / qui aurait
logiquement / . . . /
simplement / . . . /
5 scientifiquement / . . . /
économiquement / . . . /
vu
prédit
entrevu
10 ou aperçu / . . . /
HISTORIQUEMENT / . . . /

En 1750 ce qui se passerait en 1780 / . . . /
En 1780 ce qui se passerait en 1793 / . . . /
En 1793 ce qui se passerait en 1815 / . . . /
15 En 1815 ce qui se passerait en 1830 / . . . /
En 1830 ce qui se passerait en 1848 / . . . /
En 1848 ce qui se passerait en 1870 / . . . /
En 1870 ce qui se passerait en 1871 / . . . /
En 1871 ce qui se passerait en 1900 / . . . /

20   En 1900 ce qui se passerait en 1914 / . . . /

        En 1914 ce qui se passerait en 1918 / . . . /

        En 1918 ce qui se passerait en 1936 / . . . /

        En 1936 ce qui se passerait en 1940 / . . . /

        En 1940 ce qui se passerait en 1944 / . . . /

25   En 1944 ce qui se passera en 1970 et 11 / . . . /

        Et ceci simplement concernant une des régions / . . . / où
beaucoup parmi nous vivent actuellement. / . . . /

C. TROISIÈME LECTURE SANS PAUSES

DEUXIÈME PARTIE

étude du texte

1. Combien y a-t-il de parties dans le poème? Indiquez-les.

2. En quoi l'activité d'un historien diffère-t-elle de celle d'un sociologue?
   Comparez de la même façon les activités des cinq individus mentionnés par l'auteur.

3. Quel est celui qui vous semble le plus apte à faire une bonne prédiction?

4. Quel est celui qui ferait la moins bonne prédiction? Pourquoi?

5. Pourquoi est-il difficile de faire des prédictions de ce genre?

6. A quel temps sont les verbes de la première partie? Citez-les.

7. Vous remarquerez que la série de verbes est au singulier. Essayez de dire pourquoi.

8. Parmi les dates du 18ème siècle, choisissez celle qui correspond à la mort d'un personnage important. Qui est ce personnage? Dans quelles circonstances est-il mort?

9. Indiquez les dates qui, au 19ème siècle, sont celles:

    (*a*) d'une abdication. Laquelle?

    (*b*) d'une révolution. Laquelle?

    (*c*) d'une guerre. Laquelle?

10. Au 20ème siècle, donnez les dates qui se rapportent à des événements d'importance mondiale et dites quelques mots sur chacun.

11. Sauf la première et la dernière, toutes les dates du poème ont chacune deux fonctions. Indiquez ces fonctions et donnez deux exemples.

12. Quelle remarque pouvez-vous faire à propos de la dernière date choisie par Prévert, 1970 et 11?

13. A quel pays l'auteur fait-il allusion à la fin du poème?

14. Des deux interprétations possibles du titre, indiquez celle qui vous semble la plus significative. Dites pourquoi.

TROISIÈME PARTIE

phonétique

I. CONTRASTES

[r]

A. Position initiale

risk / risque	rate / rate
risk / risque	rate / rate
risk / risque	rate / rate
risque, risque, risque / . . . /	rate, rate, rate / . . . /
rue / rue	roll / rôle
rue / rue	roll / rôle
rue / rue	roll / rôle
rue, rue, rue / . . . /	rôle, rôle, rôle / . . . /

read / raide   rose / rose
read / raide   rose / rose
read / raide   rose / rose
raide, raide, raide / . . . /   rose, rose, rose / . . . /

B. Position intermédiaire

rare / rare   terrible / terrible
rare / rare   terrible / terrible
rare / rare   terrible / terrible
rare, rare, rare / . . . /   terrible, terrible, terrible / . . . /

serious / sérieux   portrait / portrait
serious / sérieux   portrait / portrait
serious / sérieux   portrait / portrait
sérieux, sérieux, sérieux / . . . / portrait, portrait, portrait / . . . /

grave / grave   pearl / perle
grave / grave   pearl / perle
grave / grave   pearl / perle
grave, grave, grave / . . . /   perle, perle, perle / . . . /

C. Position finale

fare / faire   tear / terre
fare / faire   tear / terre
fare / faire   tear / terre
faire, faire, faire / . . . /   terre, terre, terre / . . . /

far / phare   letter / lettre
far / phare   letter / lettre
far / phare   letter / lettre
phare, phare, phare / . . . /   lettre, lettre, lettre / . . . /

four / fort   scripture / écriture
four / fort   scripture / écriture
four / fort   scripture / écriture
fort, fort, fort / . . . /   écriture, écriture, écriture / . . . /

II. EXERCICES SUR LA CONSONNE [r]

a / art / arme . . . a / art / arme
cas / car / carte . . . cas / car / carte
paie / perd / perle . . . paie / perd / perle
pas / part / parle . . . pas / part / parle
pot / port / porte . . . pot / port / porte
pou / pour / ourle . . . pou / pour / ourle
la / lard / larme . . . la / lard / larme
fait / fer / ferme . . . fait / fer / ferme
mot / mort / morte . . . mot / mort / morte

rat . . . rat
ré . . . ré
riz . . . riz
rôt . . . rôt
roux . . . roux
rend . . . rend
rond . . . rond
rein . . . rein

Hier soir . . . Hier soir
Trois rats morts . . . Trois rats morts
Lire et écrire . . . Lire et écrire
Être ou ne pas être . . . Être ou ne pas être
Leur mère part pour Paris. . . . Leur mère part pour Paris.
Qui pourrait prévoir et prédire? . . . Qui pourrait prévoir et prédire?
Robert ira voir son professeur. . . . Robert ira voir son professeur.
Au restaurant, Marc prend du   Au restaurant, Marc prend du
raisin noir. . . . raisin noir.
Le frère de Pierre arrivera vers   Le frère de Pierre arrivera vers
quatre heures. . . . quatre heures.

QUATRIÈME PARTIE

exercices

I. GRAMMAIRE

Les Adjectifs numéraux

A. Adjectifs cardinaux

Ils indiquent le nombre.

1. Ils sont simples ou composés.

Répétez les phrases suivantes:

(*a*) deux enfants; quatre hommes; cinq femmes / . . . /

(*b*) vingt-deux enfants; cinquante-quatre hommes; quatre-vingt-cinq femmes / . . . /

Notez: Quand ils sont composés, chaque nombre est séparé par un trait d'union (quand le nombre est inférieur à cent), sauf quand **et** est employé.

vingt **et** un livres (mais dix-neuf livres; vingt-deux livres)
trente **et** un étudiants
quarante **et** un étages, etc. . . .

2. Ils sont généralement invariables.

Exceptions:

un, une

un concerto, trois concertos
une sonate, cinq sonates

vingt et **cent**

Ils prennent un **s** quand ils sont précédés d'un nombre.

trois cents francs; sept cents kilomètres; quatre-vingts centimes

Ils sont invariables quand ils sont suivis d'un nombre.

trois cent cinquante francs; sept cent vingt-cinq kilomètres; quatre-vingt-cinq centimes

Ecrivez en lettres les nombres suivants:

800; 970; 558; 685
21; 94; 674; 200

3. Ils sont généralement placés avant le nom.

Répétez les phrases suivantes:

(*a*) dix pommes; douze enfants; quatre philosophes / . . . /
(*b*) dix-sept oiseaux; quarante-deux sociologues; trente et un poètes / . . . /

Exception:

L'adjectif cardinal est placé après les noms de souverains (en anglais, on emploie l'adjectif ordinal).

Henri IV; Louis XIV

4. **Cent** et **mille** ne sont jamais précédés par **un.**

cent kilomètres (*one hundred kilometers*);
mille francs (*one thousand francs*)

mais trois cents kilomètres; dix mille francs

B. Adjectifs ordinaux

Ils indiquent l'ordre, le rang.

1. Ils sont formés en ajoutant **-ième** à l'adjectif cardinal.

deux, deuxième
trois, troisième

Répétez les phrases suivantes:

(*a*) C'est la deuxième fois que je vais dans la lune. / . . . /

(*b*) Mars est le troisième mois de l'année. / . . . /

2. Quand l'adjectif cardinal se termine par un **e** muet, celui-ci disparaît.

> quatre, quatrième / onze, onzième / quatorze, quatorzième

(*a*) Les Durand habitent au quatrième étage. / . . . /
(*b*) Il a gagné le tournoi de tennis pour la onzième fois. / . . . /
(*c*) Il vient de finir son quatorzième livre. / . . . /

Exceptions:

> **premier, première** pour **un, une**

(*a*) Philippe est le premier de sa classe. / . . . /
(*d*) C'est la première fois que nous allons en Californie. /. . ./

mais l'on dit vingt et unième, deux cent unième, etc. / . . . /

3. **Second**(**e**) remplace deuxième quand il s'agit d'une série de deux unités.

> La première fois, c'était remarquable; la deuxième et la troisième fois, c'était ennuyeux.
> Sa seconde tentative a été un fiasco, il s'est arrêté ensuite.

C. Nombres collectifs

Ils ont un sens approximatif. On les forme en ajoutant **-aine** à certains adjectifs cardinaux.

Répétez les principaux nombres collectifs suivants:

(*a*) une huitaine / . . . /
(*b*) une dizaine / . . . /
(*c*) une douzaine / . . . /
(*d*) une quinzaine / . . . /
(*e*) une vingtaine / . . . /
(*f*) une trentaine / . . . / (etc.)
(*g*) une centaine / . . . /
(*h*) un millier / . . . /

D. Quelques problèmes de prononciation

  1. On prononce la consonne finale d'un adjectif cardinal

    1. quand il est seul:

      Répétez les phrases suivantes:

        (*a*) Combien avez-vous d'enfants? Cin**q**. / . . . /

    2. devant une voyelle ou un **h** muet:

        (*a*) Troi**s a**mis / . . . /, trois personnes / . . . /
        (*b*) Si**x h**ommes / . . . /, six livres / . . . /

    3. devant un nom de mois (même si celui-ci commence par une consonne):

        (*a*) Le hui**t** mars / . . . /
        (*b*) le dix-sept septembre / . . . /

  2. Le **t** de **vingt** est prononcé de 22 à 29 mais il n'est pas prononcé de 82 à 89.

    Répétez ces deux séries de nombres:

    (*a*) vingt-deux (etc.) / . . . /
    (*b*) quatre-vingt-deux (etc.) / . . . /

  3. Le **t** de **cent** n'est jamais prononcé devant **un, une.**

    Répétez les phrases suivantes:

    (*a*) Cent une personnes ont pris le train aujourd'hui. / . . . /
    (*b*) Cette robe coûte cent un francs. / . . . /

  4. On ne fait jamais de liaison devant **huit, onze** et leurs dérivés.

    (*a*) les huit arbres / . . . /
    (*b*) les onze enfants Durand / . . . /

CINQUIÈME PARTIE

compréhension (laboratoire)

SIXIÈME PARTIE

dictée (laboratoire)

XV

tout s'en allait...

Tout s'en allait: Tout s'en allait en morceaux, rien ne tenait plus

[5] **hommes de paille:** Un *homme de paille* est celui qui sert de prête-nom dans une opération. Expression prise ici dans un sens littéral: hommes qui flambent facilement parce qu'ils sont en paille

[8] **blêmes de savoir:** blêmes parce qu'ils savaient

[24] **suant sang et eau:** *suer sang et eau*—se donner une peine extrême. Ici, l'expression est prise au sens propre.

[25] **gaz éclaté:** les conduites de gaz avaient éclaté

[26] **plaies et bosses:** *rêver de plaies et bosses*—rêver d'aventures, de querelles

tout s'en allait...

Il y avait de faibles femmes
et puis des femmes faciles
et des femmes fatales
qui pleuraient hurlaient sanglotaient
5   devant des hommes de paille
qui flambaient
Des enfants perdus couraient dans des ruines de rues
tout blêmes de savoir qu'ils ne se retrouveraient jamais plus
Et des chefs de famille
10 qui ne reconnaissaient plus le plancher du plafond
voletaient d'un étage à l'autre
dans une pluie de paillassons de suspensions de petites cuil-
        lers et de plumes d'édredon
Tout s'en allait
La ville s'écroulait
15 grouillait
s'émiettait
en tournant sur elle-même
sans même avoir l'air de bouger
Des cochons noirs aveuglés
20 dans la soudaine obscurité
d'une porcherie modèle désaffectée
galopaient
La ville s'en allait
suant sang et eau
25 gaz éclaté
Ceux qui n'avaient rêvé que plaies et bosses
se réveillaient

²⁹ **peignes et brosses:** allitération avec **plaies et bosses.** De plus, Prévert fait un rapprochement intéressant avec **décapités,** indiquant que ceux-ci n'ont que faire de peignes et de brosses.

³¹ **une noce:** les mariés, la famille et les invités
³¹ **toute noire:** carbonisée
³¹ **sur pied:** debout

³⁵ **torréfié:** grillé (terme généralement employé pour le café)
³⁵ **terrifié:** allitération avec le mot précédent et en rapport avec la situation

³⁷ **hommage de guerre:** jeu de mots sur *dommages de guerre*

³⁸ **jeux de reconstruction:** jeu de mots sur *jeux de construction*

³⁹ **profits et pertes:** argent gagné ou perdu d'une façon imprévue, faisant l'objet d'un compte spécial (*terme commercial*)

⁴⁰ **bois et charbons:** inscription qui, autrefois, indiquait que l'on pouvait acheter du bois et du charbon dans certains débits de boissons. Prévert utilise cette expression à cause du mot *charbon*

⁴¹ **carré:** espace carré devant une maison; **dernier carré:** autrefois formation en carré permettant de faire face à l'ennemi sur quatre côtés à la fois; ultime tentative de défense sur le champ de bataille quand tout est perdu (*expression militaire*)

⁴⁶ **faisait corps-grillé avec:** *faire corps avec*— adhérer à

décapités
ayant perdu peignes et brosses
30   et autres petites mondanités
Une noce toute noire morte sur pied
depuis le garçon d'honneur jusqu'aux mariés
gardait un équilibre de cendre figée
devant un photographe
35   torréfié terrifié
Nouvelles ruines toutes neuves
hommage de guerre
jeux de reconstruction
profits et pertes
40   bois et charbons
Sur le dernier carré d'une maison ouvrière
une omelette abandonnée
pendait comme un vieux linge
sur une verrière brisée
45   et dans les miettes d'un vieux lit calciné mêlées à la sciure
       grise d'un buffet volatilisé
la viande humaine faisait corps-grillé avec la viande à manger

Dans les coulisses du progrès
des hommes intègres poursuivaient intégralement la désinté-
       gration progressive de la matière vivante
désemparée.

La Pluie et le beau temps

PREMIÈRE PARTIE

lecture du poème

A. PREMIÈRE LECTURE SANS PAUSES

B. DEUXIÈME LECTURE AVEC PAUSES

tout s'en allait...

Il y avait de faibles femmes / . . . /
et puis des femmes faciles / . . . /
et des femmes fatales / . . . /
qui pleuraient hurlaient sanglotaient / . . . /
5   devant des hommes de paille
qui flambaient / . . . /
Des enfants perdus couraient dans des ruines de rues / . . . /
tout blêmes de savoir qu'ils ne se retrouveraient jamais
      plus / . . . /
Et des chefs de famille / . . . /
10   qui ne reconnaissaient plus le plancher du plafond / . . . /
voletaient d'un étage à l'autre / . . . /
dans une pluie de paillassons de suspensions / . . . / de petites
      cuillers et de plumes d'édredon / . . . /
Tout s'en allait / . . . /
La ville s'écroulait / . . . /
15   grouillait
s'émiettait
en tournant sur elle-même / . . . /
sans même avoir l'air de bouger / . . . /
Des cochons noirs aveuglés / . . . /
20   dans la soudaine obscurité / . . . /

d'une porcherie modèle désaffectée
galopaient / . . . /
La ville s'en allait / . . . /
suant sang et eau / . . . /
25 gaz éclaté / . . . /
Ceux qui n'avaient rêvé que plaies et bosses / . . . /
se réveillaient
décapités / . . . /
ayant perdu peignes et brosses / . . . /
30 et autres petites mondanités / . . . /
Une noce toute noire morte sur pied / . . . /
depuis le garçon d'honneur jusqu'aux mariés / . . . /
gardait un équilibre de cendre figée / . . . /
devant un photographe / . . . /
35 torréfié terrifié / . . . /
Nouvelles ruines toutes neuves / . . . /
hommage de guerre / . . . /
jeux de reconstruction / . . . /
profits et pertes / . . . /
40 bois et charbons / . . . /
Sur le dernier carré d'une maison ouvrière / . . . /
une omelette abandonnée / . . . /
pendait comme un vieux linge / . . . /
sur une verrière brisée / . . . /
45 et dans les miettes d'un vieux lit calciné / . . . / mêlées à la
        sciure grise d'un buffet volatilisé / . . . /
la viande humaine faisait corps-grillé / . . . / avec la viande à
        manger / . . . /

Dans les coulisses du progrès / . . . /
des hommes intègres poursuivaient intégralement / . . . / la
        désintégration progressive / . . . / de la matière vivante
désemparée. / . . . /

C. TROISIÈME LECTURE SANS PAUSES

DEUXIÈME PARTIE

étude du texte

1. Où se déroule la scène?
2. Qu'est-ce qui se passe?
3. Que font les femmes?
4. Décrivez les trois types de femmes dont il s'agit. (Remarquez les allitérations qui ont une influence sur le choix des adjectifs.)
5. Qu'est-ce qui arrive aux hommes?
6. Que font les enfants?
7. Pourquoi sont-ils perdus?
8. Que signifie «une pluie de paillassons de suspensions», etc.?
9. Décrivez le phénomène de destruction de la ville.
10. Qu'est-ce qui arrive aux animaux?
11. Peut-on se réveiller décapité? Montrez ce que la situation a d'improbable.
12. Qu'est-ce qui est arrivé à la noce et au photographe?
13. Montrez le rapport entre la soudaineté de la catastrophe et le tableau de la noce présenté par Prévert.
14. Il est rare de voir une omelette accrochée à une verrière. Qu'est-ce qui s'est passé?
15. Est-ce un phénomène naturel qui s'est abattu sur la ville? De quelle sorte de désastre s'agit-il plutôt?
16. Est-ce que cela ne vous rappelle pas un événement historique? Lequel? Où? Quand?
17. Les trois derniers vers montrent des hommes en train de travailler. Quel genre de travail font-ils?
18. Comparez les mots «intègres», «intégralement» et «désintégration».
19. Qu'est-ce que l'auteur veut montrer dans ce poème?

TROISIÈME PARTIE

phonétique

I. CONTRASTES

[1]

A. Position intermédiaire

alley / aller	balloon / ballon
alley / aller	balloon / ballon
alley / aller	balloon / ballon
aller, aller, aller / . . . /	ballon, ballon, ballon / . . . /

illegal / illégal	ballet / ballet
illegal / illégal	ballet / ballet
illegal / illégal	ballet / ballet
illégal, illégal, illégal / . . . /	ballet, ballet, ballet / . . . /

B. En groupes de consonnes inséparables

feeble / faible	angle / angle
feeble / faible	angle / angle
feeble / faible	angle / angle
faible, faible, faible / . . . /	angle, angle, angle / . . . /

sniffle / siffle
sniffle / siffle
sniffle / siffle
siffle, siffle, siffle / . . . /

oracle / oracle   disciple / disciple
oracle / oracle   disciple / disciple
oracle / oracle   disciple / disciple
oracle, oracle, oracle / . . . /   disciple, disciple, disciple / . . . /

C. Position finale

sell / sel   bill / bile
sell / sel   bill / bile
sell / sel   bill / bile
sel, sel, sel / . . . /   bile, bile, bile / . . . /

veal / ville   bull / boule
veal / ville   bull / boule
veal / ville   bull / boule
ville, ville, ville / . . . /   boule, boule, boule / . . . /

bell / belle   fatal / fatal
bell / belle   fatal / fatal
bell / belle   fatal / fatal
belle, belle, belle / . . . /   fatal, fatal, fatal / . . . /

sale / salle   facile / facile
sale / salle   facile / facile
sale / salle   facile / facile
salle, salle, salle / . . . /   facile, facile, facile / . . . /

II. EXERCICES SUR LA CONSONNE [l]

a / halles . . . a / halles
haie / aile . . . haie / aile
paix / pelle . . . paix / pelle
pou / poule . . . pou / poule
qu'a / cale . . . qu'a / cale
cou / coule . . . cou / coule

baie / belle . . . baie / belle
bat / balle . . . bat / balle
boue / boule . . . boue / boule
bu / bulle . . . bu / bulle
dais / d'elle . . . dais / d'elle
goût / goule . . . goût / goule
taie / telle . . . taie / telle
tu / tulle . . . tu / tulle
qui / qu'il . . . qui / qu'il
qu'est / qu'elle . . . qu'est / qu'elle
mit / mille . . . mit / mille
mais / mêle . . . mais / mêle
ma / malle . . . ma / malle
mou / moule . . . mou / moule
nu / nul . . . nu / nul
fit / fil . . . fit / fil
fou / foule . . . fou / foule
si / s'il . . . si / s'il
vit / ville . . . vit / ville
va / val . . . va / val
jais / gel . . . jais / gel
roue / roule . . . roue / roule
sait / sel . . . sait / sel
se / seul . . . se / seul
aura / oral . . . aura / oral
rêvait / révèle . . . rêvait / révèle

Elle est folle. . . . Elle est folle.
Quelle belle ville! . . . Quelle belle ville!
Les boules roulent seules. . . . Les boules roulent seules.
Adèle est belle. . . . Adèle est belle.
La salle est tranquille. . . . La salle est tranquille.
Elle s'appelle Marcelle. . . . Elle s'appelle Marcelle.
La foule a ses idoles. . . . La foule a ses idoles.
Elle allait allumer la lampe. . . . Elle allait allumer la lampe.
Cette pilule est facile à avaler. . . . Cette pilule est facile à avaler.
La nouvelle élève lance la   La nouvelle élève lance la
balle à Lili. . . . balle à Lili.

QUATRIÈME PARTIE

exercices

I. GRAMMAIRE

A. Le pronom indéfini **tout**

1. Au singulier, **tout** est toujours au masculin; il a le sens neutre de **toute chose.**

Répétez les phrases suivantes en substituant les mots indiqués:

(*a*) **Tout** [s'en allait].
s'écrouler / flamber / brûler / s'émietter / se désintégrer

Reprenez le même exercice en mettant les verbes au présent.

2. Au pluriel, il est masculin **tous** ou féminin **toutes.**

(*a*) **Tous** les [animaux] galopaient dans les rues.
cheval / cochon / chien / chat / mouton

(*b*) **Toutes** les femmes [pleuraient].
hurler / sangloter / crier / courir / être pris de panique

Reprenez les deux exercices précédents en mettant les verbes au passé composé.

Notez: Au masculin pluriel, l'adjectif indéfini et le pronom indéfini ont la même forme, **tous,** mais leur prononciation est différente.

Tous les étudiants s'intéressent à la politique.
(Quand **tous** est adjectif, le **s** n'est pas prononcé.)

les étudiants s'intéressent-ils à la politique? Oui,
tous.

(Quand **tous** est pronom, le **s** est prononcé.)

B. L'imparfait

Vous avez vu que le passé composé est employé quand il
s'agit d'une action qui a eu lieu dans le passé à un moment
déterminé. L'imparfait a deux usages principaux:

1. Il sert à décrire des états et des actions dans le passé.

Répétez les phrases suivantes:

(*a*) Des femmes pleuraient, hurlaient, sanglotaient. / . . . /
(*b*) Des hommes de paille flambaient. / . . . /
(*c*) Des enfants perdus couraient. / . . . /
(*d*) La ville s'écroulait, grouillait, s'émiettait. / . . . /

Reprenez les phrases précédentes et mettez-les à la forme inter-
rogative en utilisant la locution **est-ce que** *. . . ; ensuite mettez*
ces phrases au présent.

2. Il sert à marquer la répétition d'une action dans le passé.

Répétez les phrases suivantes:

(*a*) Quand Catherine était à Paris, elle allait souvent à la
Comédie française. / . . . /
(*b*) Pendant les vacances, nous nous levions tous les matins
à six heures. / . . . /
(*c*) Il pleuvait chaque fois que je voulais faire une promenade. / . . . /
(*d*) Les étudiants travaillaient deux fois par semaine au
laboratoire. / . . . /

Reprenez les phrases précédentes et mettez-les à la forme négative.
Ensuite, mettez ces phrases au présent.

CINQUIÈME PARTIE

compréhension (laboratoire)

SIXIÈME PARTIE

dictée (laboratoire)

XVI

l'accent grave

L'accent grave: (a) signe qui se place au-dessus d'une voyelle comme dans le mot *père;* (b) ton sérieux ou solennel. Ici, le mot *grave* indique toute l'importance qu'il faut accorder à ce signe de ponctuation

2 **Hein ... Quoi ... Pardon ...:**   interjections exprimant à la fois surprise et incompréhension

5 **vous êtes ... dans les nuages:** vous pensez à autre chose, vous êtes ailleurs

7 **Suffit:** Cela suffit
7 **Pas tant de manières:** Ne faites pas tant de manières, ne rendez pas les choses plus difficiles
7 **conjuguez-moi:** Dans cette expression, le pronom *moi* ne sert qu'à renforcer l'impératif

11 **Bien:** Oui

l'accent grave

LE PROFESSEUR

Élève Hamlet!

L'ÉLÈVE HAMLET
(*sursautant*)

... Hein ... Quoi ... Pardon ... Qu'est-ce qui se
passe ... Qu'est-ce qu'il y a ... Qu'est-ce que c'est? ...

LE PROFESSEUR
(*mécontent*)

Vous ne pouvez pas répondre «présent» comme tout le
monde? Pas possible, vous êtes encore dans les nuages.

L'ÉLÈVE HAMLET

Être ou ne pas être dans les nuages!

LE PROFESSEUR

Suffit. Pas tant de manières. Et conjuguez-moi le verbe
être, comme tout le monde, c'est tout ce que je vous demande.

L'ÉLÈVE HAMLET

To be ...

LE PROFESSEUR

En français, s'il vout plaît, comme tout le monde.

L'ÉLÈVE HAMLET

Bien, monsieur. (*Il conjugue:*)
Je suis ou je ne suis pas

16 **vous . . . n'y êtes pas :** vous ne comprenez pas,
vous vous trompez

17 **C'est exact :** C'est vrai

19 **dans le fond :** en réalité
19 **hein :** n'est-ce pas ?

Tu es ou tu n'es pas
Il est ou il n'est pas
15 Nous sommes ou nous ne sommes pas . . .

LE PROFESSEUR
(*excessivement mécontent*)

Mais c'est vous qui n'y êtes pas, mon pauvre ami!

L'ÉLÈVE HAMLET

C'est exact, monsieur le professeur,
Je suis «où» je ne suis pas
Et, dans le fond, hein, à la réflexion,
20 Être «où» ne pas être
C'est peut-être aussi la question.

Paroles

PREMIÈRE PARTIE

lecture du poème

A. PREMIÈRE LECTURE SANS PAUSES

B. DEUXIÈME LECTURE AVEC PAUSES

l'accent grave

LE PROFESSEUR

Élève Hamlet! / . . . /

L'ÉLÈVE HAMLET

. . . Hein . . . Quoi . . . Pardon . . . / . . . / Qu'est-ce qui
se passe . . . / . . . / Qu'est-ce qu'il y a . . . / . . . / Qu'est-ce
que c'est ? / . . . /

LE PROFESSEUR

5 Vous ne pouvez pas répondre «présent» / . . . / comme
tout le monde? / . . . / Pas possible, / . . . / vous êtes
encore dans les nuages. / . . . /

L'ÉLÈVE HAMLET

Être ou ne pas être dans les nuages! / . . . /

LE PROFESSEUR

Suffit. Pas tant de manières. / . . . / Et conjuguez-moi le
10 verbe être, / . . . / comme tout le monde, / . . . / c'est tout
ce que je vous demande. / . . . /

L'ÉLÈVE HAMLET

To be ... / ... /

LE PROFESSEUR

En français, s'il vous plaît, / ... / comme tout
le monde. / ... /

L'ÉLÈVE HAMLET

15   Bien, monsieur. / ... /
Je suis ou je ne suis pas / ... /
Tu es ou tu n'es pas / ... /
Il est ou il n'est pas / ... /
Nous sommes ou nous ne sommes pas ... / ... /

LE PROFESSEUR

20   Mais c'est vous qui n'y êtes pas, mon pauvre ami! / ... /

L'ÉLÈVE HAMLET

C'est exact, monsieur le professeur, / ... /
Je suis «où» je ne suis pas / ... /
Et dans le fond, hein, à la réflexion, / ... /
Être «où» ne pas être / ... /
25   C'est peut-être aussi la question. / ... /

C. TROISIÈME LECTURE SANS PAUSES

DEUXIÈME PARTIE

étude du texte

1. Où se passe la scène?
2. Pourquoi le professeur prononce-t-il le nom de l'élève Hamlet?
3. Pourquoi l'élève Hamlet sursaute-t-il quand il entend son nom?
4. Qu'est-ce qu'il aurait dû répondre pour faire comme tout le monde?
5. Pourquoi ne répond-il pas comme tout le monde?
6. Quel verbe français le professeur est-il en train d'enseigner?
7. Pourquoi Prévert a-t-il appelé cet élève Hamlet?
8. Pourquoi l'élève Hamlet conjugue-t-il ce verbe en anglais?
9. Pourquoi le conjugue-t-il à la forme affirmative et à la forme négative?
10. Conjuguez le verbe *être* au passé composé à la forme affirmative et à la forme négative.
11. Quelle est la différence entre «ou» et «où»? Indiquez ce que ces mots représentent grammaticalement et faites une phrase avec chacun.
12. Vous comprenez maintenant pourquoi Prévert a intitulé ce poème «L'accent grave». Commentez ce titre.
13. Choisissez l'une des deux interprétations de l'expression «d'accent grave» et expliquez votre choix.
14. Essayez d'expliquer le jeu de mots dans la phrase «Mais c'est vous qui n'y êtes pas».
15. Montrez comment ce pronom adverbial «y» amène un nouveau jeu de mots avec «où» dans la phrase suivante.
16. Quelle est l'expression favorite du professeur?
17. D'après cette expression, quel est le trait de caractère prédominant chez le professeur?

TROISIÈME PARTIE

phonétique

I. CONTRASTES

[p] [t] [k] [b] [d] [g]

A. Position initiale

Paul / Paul	ball / balle
Paul / Paul	ball / balle
Paul / Paul	ball / balle
Paul, Paul, Paul / . . . /	balle, balle, balle / . . . /
ton / tonne	diner / dîner
ton / tonne	diner / dîner
ton /tonne	diner / dîner
tonne, tonne, tonne / . . . /	dîner, dîner, dîner / . . . /
college / collège	guard / garde
college / collège	guard / garde
college / collège	guard / garde
collège, collège, collège / . . . /	garde, garde, garde / . . . /

B. Position finale

type / type	barb / barbe
type / type	barb / barbe
type / type	barb / barbe
type, type, type / . . . /	barbe, barbe, barbe / . . . /

meat / mite   hard / hardes
meat / mite   hard / hardes
meat / mite   hard / hardes
mite, mite, mite / . . . /   hardes, hardes, hardes / . . . /

civic / civique   bag / bague
civic / civique   bag / bague
civic / civique   bag / bague
civique, civique, civique / . . . /   bague, bague, bague / . . . /

II. EXERCICES SUR LES CONSONNES [p] [t] [k] [b] [d] [g]

cou / coupe . . . cou / coupe
camp / campe . . . camp / campe
petit / petite . . . petit / petite
rat / rate . . . rat / rate
saint / cinq . . . saint / cinq
la / lac . . . la / lac
bon / bombe . . . bon / bombe
Jean / jambe . . . Jean / jambe
rond / ronde . . . rond / ronde
marchand / marchande . . . marchand / marchande
long / longue . . . long / longue
hareng / harangue . . . hareng / harangue

Paul ne part pas pour Paris   Paul ne part pas pour Paris
parce qu'il pleut. . . . parce qu'il pleut.
Ton thé t'a-t-il tenté à table? . . . Ton thé t'a-t-il tenté à table?
Le cousin de Colette, qui a une   Le cousin de Colette, qui a une
cravate de couleur comme   cravate de couleur comme
Claude, connaît le collège de   Claude, connaît le collège de
Québec au Canada. . . . Québec au Canada.
Bernard a bien bu la bonne   Bernard a bien bu la bonne
bière blonde. . . . bière blonde.
Daniel et Alfred demandent de   Daniel et Alfred demandent de

la dinde pour le dîner   la dinde pour le dîner
de mardi. . . . de mardi.
Le grand garçon garde la grosse   Le grand garçon garde la grosse
voiture grise dans le garage   voiture grise dans le garage
à gauche de la gare. . . . à gauche de la gare.

QUATRIÈME PARTIE

exercices

I. GRAMMAIRE

A. Pronoms interrogatifs

1. Personnes

1. Sujet

Répétez les phrases suivantes en substituant les mots indiqués:

Forme longue (*a*) **Qui est-ce qui** vient de [passer] ?
Forme courte (*b*) **Qui** vient de [passer] ?
téléphoner / partir / parler / faire du bruit

Complément d'objet direct

Forme longue (*a*) **Qui** **est-ce** **que** vous avez vu
[passer] ?
Forme courte (*b*) **Qui** avez-vous vu [passer] ?
monter en voiture / traverser la rue / acheter des fleurs /
promener son chien

2. Choses
Sujet

Forme longue (*a*) **Qu'est-ce qui** [fait ce bruit] ?

Forme courte (*b*) (Il n'y a pas de forme courte qui
corresponde à **qu'est-ce qui.**)

arriver / provoquer ce dérangement / se passer / être à
l'origine de cette rumeur

Complément d'objet direct

Forme longue (*a*) **Qu'est-ce que** vous avez [dit] ?
Forme courte (*b*) **Qu'**avez-vous [dit] ?
suggérer / insinuer / déclarer / raconter

B. Pronoms adverbiaux employés comme adverbes de lieux

En et **Y**

1. **En** signifie *de cet endroit, de là,* toujours avec des verbes de
mouvement.

(*a*) Quand êtes-vous allé chez Catherine ? J'**en** [viens]
justement.
sortir / arriver / revenir / repartir

2. **Y** signifie *là, à cet endroit.*

(*a*) Pensez-vous aller bientôt à Paris ? Oui, je vais **y** [aller]
cet été.
habiter / passer deux jours / séjourner / rester trois
semaines

C. Pronoms relatifs sans antécédents

Ce qui, Ce que

Ils se réfèrent à une idée non exprimée.

1. Sujet

Répétez la phrase suivante en substituant les mots indiqués:

(*a*) **Ce qui** arrive à l'élève Hamlet est [incroyable].
étonnant / imprévu / incompréhensible / peu clair

Reprenez cet exercice en mettant le premier verbe au passé composé.

2. Complément d'objet direct

(*a*) **Ce que** [demande] le professeur est simple, faites comme tout le monde.
ordonner / réclamer / indiquer / répéter

Reprenez cet exercice en mettant les verbes à l'imparfait.

CINQUIÈME PARTIE

compréhension (laboratoire)

SIXIÈME PARTIE

dictée (laboratoire)

XVII

maintenant

j'ai grandi

1 **Enfant:** Quand j'étais enfant

3 **fou rire:** rire prolongé qu'on ne peut contenir

9 **je n'avais rien d'autre que d'être vivant:** la seule chose que j'avais était d'être vivant

13 **faisais semblant:** feignais

24 **à prendre ou à laisser:** expression qui signifie accepter une chose telle qu'elle est ou y renoncer

25—26 **J'étais ... sans mentalité:** J'avais l'esprit libre, ouvert à tout

28 **me tenir compagnie:** rester avec moi

maintenant j'ai grandi

Enfant
j'ai vécu drôlement
le fou rire tous les jours
le fou rire vraiment
et puis une tristesse tellement triste
quelquefois les deux en même temps
Alors je me croyais désespéré
Tout simplement je n'avais pas d'espoir
je n'avais rien d'autre que d'être vivant
j'étais intact
j'étais content
et j'étais triste
mais jamais je ne faisais semblant
Je connaissais le geste pour rester vivant
Secouer la tête
pour dire non
secouer la tête
pour ne pas laisser entrer les idées des gens
Secouer la tête pour dire non
et sourire pour dire oui
oui aux choses et aux êtres
aux êtres et aux choses à regarder à caresser
à aimer
à prendre ou à laisser
J'étais comme j'étais
sans mentalité
Et quand j'avais besoin d'idées
pour me tenir compagnie

[38] **je leur ris . . . au nez :** je m'en moque

[43] **au coin d'un bois :** cliché qui désigne un lieu idéal pour une embuscade

[46] **je leur coupe l'appétit :** je leur enlève l'envie de manger

        je les appelais
30   Et elles venaient
        et je disais oui à celles qui me plaisaient
        les autres je les jetais

        Maintenant j'ai grandi
        les idées aussi
35   mais ce sont toujours de grandes idées
        de belles idées
        d'idéales idées
        Et je leur ris toujours au nez
        Mais elles m'attendent
40   pour se venger
        et me manger
        un jour où je serai très fatigué
        Mais moi au coin d'un bois
        je les attends aussi
45   et je leur tranche la gorge
        je leur coupe l'appétit.

                        La Pluie et le beau temps

PREMIÈRE PARTIE

lecture du poème

A. PREMIÈRE LECTURE SANS PAUSES

B. DEUXIÈME LECTURE AVEC PAUSES

maintenant j'ai grandi

Enfant
j'ai vécu drôlement / . . . /
le fou rire tous les jours / . . . /
le fou rire vraiment / . . . /
5   et puis une tristesse tellement triste / . . . /
quelquefois les deux en même temps / . . . /
Alors je me croyais désespéré / . . . /
Tout simplement je n'avais pas d'espoir / . . . /
je n'avais rien d'autre que d'être vivant / . . . /
10   j'étais intact / . . . /
j'étais content / . . . /
et j'étais triste / . . . /
mais jamais je ne faisais semblant / . . . /
Je connaissais le geste pour rester vivant / . . . /
15   Secouer la tête
pour dire non / . . . /
secouer la tête
pour ne pas laisser entrer les idées des gens / . . . /
Secouer la tête pour dire non / . . . /
20   et sourire pour dire oui / . . . /

oui aux choses et aux êtres / . . . /
aux êtres et aux choses à regarder / . . . / à caresser
à aimer / . . . /
à prendre ou à laisser / . . . /
25   J'étais comme j'étais / . . . /
sans mentalité / . . . /
Et quand j'avais besoin d'idées
pour me tenir compagnie / . . . /
je les appelais / . . . /
30   Et elles venaient / . . . /
et je disais oui à celles qui me plaisaient / . . . /
les autres je les jetais / . . . /

Maintenant j'ai grandi / . . . /
les idées aussi / . . . /
35   mais ce sont toujours de grandes idées / . . . /
de belles idées / . . . /
d'idéales idées / . . . /
Et je leur ris toujours au nez / . . . /
Mais elles m'attendent
40   pour se venger / . . . /
et me manger / . . . /
un jour où je serai très fatigué / . . . /
Mais moi au coin d'un bois / . . . /
je les attends aussi / . . . /
45   et je leur tranche la gorge / . . . /
je leur coupe l'appétit. / . . . /

C. TROISIÈME LECTURE SANS PAUSES

DEUXIÈME PARTIE

étude du texte

1. Combien y a-t-il de parties dans ce poème? Décrivez-les.

2. A quoi est consacrée la première partie?

3. La seconde partie est en apparence différente de la première. Montrez en quoi elle lui ressemble.

4. Décrivez les deux dispositions extrêmes dans lesquelles se trouvait l'enfant.

5. Quelle est la différence entre «être désespéré» et «être sans espoir»?

6. Croyez-vous qu'un état de fou rire et de grande tristesse puissent coexister? Essayez de donner un exemple tiré de votre expérience.

7. Quel est le geste suggéré par Prévert «pour rester vivant»? Commentez ce geste.

8. Pourquoi ne faut-il pas «laisser entrer» les idées des gens? Quel danger représentent-elles aux yeux de l'auteur?

9. De quelle façon faut-il dire «oui» aux choses? Que pensez-vous de cette attitude?

10. L'enfant recherche parfois la compagnie d'idées. Donnez quelques exemples d'idées qui, à votre avis, peuvent lui plaire.

11. Au début de la seconde partie, quel est l'adverbe qui indique que l'attitude de Prévert est la même qu'autrefois? Montrez l'importance de cet adverbe.

12. Quelle est l'attitude présente de l'auteur envers les idées? Expliquez son agressivité.

13. Quelle est l'attitude des idées envers lui?

14. Le poète donne aux idées un comportement humain. Indiquez quelques-unes de leur actions humaines.

15. Pourquoi les idées attendent-elles que l'auteur soit fatigué pour se venger?

16. Que compte-t-il faire pour se protéger?

17. Quand un auteur évoque ses jeunes années, il prête généralement à

l'enfant qu'il était ses pensées d'adulte. Pensez-vous que ce soit le cas dans ce poème? Indiquez votre point de vue.

TROISIÈME PARTIE

phonétique

I. CONTRASTES

[f] [s] [ʃ]

[v] [z] [ʒ]

A. Position initiale   *B.* Position finale

fair / faire	tough / touffe
fair / faire	tough / touffe
fair / faire	tough / touffe
faire, faire, faire / . . . /	touffe, touffe, touffe / . . . /
set / sept	vice / vice
set / sept	vice / vice
set / sept	vice / vice
sept, sept, sept / . . . /	vice, vice, vice / . . . /
shack / chaque	mesh / mêche
shack / chaque	mesh / mêche
shack / chaque	mesh / mêche
chaque, chaque, chaque / . . . /	mêche, mêche, mêche / . . . /
very / varie	rave / rave
very / varie	rave / rave
very / varie	rave / rave
varie, varie, varie / . . . /	rave, rave, rave / . . . /

zeal / zèle   chase / chaise
zeal / zèle   chase / chaise
zeal / zèle   chase / chaise
zèle, zèle, zèle / . . . /   chaise, chaise, chaise / . . . /

gem / j'aime   page / page
gem / j'aime   page / page
gem / j'aime   page / page
j'aime, j'aime, j'aime / . . , /   page, page, page / . . . /

chimney / cheminée
chimney / cheminée
chimney / cheminée
cheminée, cheminée, cheminée / . . . /

II. EXERCICES
SUR LES CONSONNES [f] [v] [ʃ] [s] [z] [ʒ]

œufs / œuf . . . œufs / œuf
bœufs / bœuf . . . bœufs / bœuf
nœud / neuf . . . nœud / neuf

vie / vive . . . vie / vive
mot / mauve . . . mot / mauve
loup / louve . . . loup / louve

frais / fraîche . . . frais / fraîche
au bout / la bouche . . . au bout / la bouche
blanc / blanche . . . blanc / blanche

ni / Nice . . . ni / Nice
pas / passe . . . pas / passe
sot / sauce . . . sot / sauce

mauvais / mauvaise . . . mauvais / mauvaise
pot / pose . . . pot / pose
heureux / heureuse . . . heureux / heureuse

roue / rouge . . . roue / rouge
ment / mange . . . ment / mange
Oran / orange . . . Oran / orange

Son frère a fait frire un œuf très frais. . . .	Son frère a fait frire un œuf très frais.
Où vont-ils vendre vos nouveaux livres ? . . .	Où vont-ils vendre vos nouveaux livres ?
Cette émotion silencieuse est sentie avec satisfaction par sa sœur. . . .	Cette émotion silencieuse est sentie avec satisfaction par sa sœur.
«Treize, quatorze, quinze», disent Suzanne et Zoé assises sur des chaises grises et roses. . . .	«Treize, quatorze, quinze», disent Suzanne et Zoé assises sur des chaises grises et roses.
Dimanche, ce cher Charles va acheter un cheval et un chien. . . .	Dimanche, ce cher Charles va acheter un cheval et un chien.
Jean et le jeune Georges ne mangent jamais d'oranges. . . .	Jean et le jeune Georges ne mangent jamais d'oranges.

QUATRIÈME PARTIE

exercices

I. GRAMMAIRE

A. L'imparfait, le passé composé

Remplacez chaque tiret par le verbe entre parenthèses au temps qui convient (imparfait ou passé composé):

Quand Prévert ——— (être) enfant, il ————— (vivre) de façon curieuse. Il y ——— (avoir) des jours où il ——— (être) très gai, d'autres jours où il ——— ——— (se sentir) très triste. Parfois, il ——— (rire) et il ——— (pleurer) à la fois. C'——— (être) parce qu'il n'avait pas d'espoir. Pour rester vivant, il ——— (faire) toujours le même geste, il —————

(secouer) la tête, il ———— (dire) «non» aux idées des gens. Pour lui, les idées des gens ———————— (représenter) des idées préconçues, des clichés, des superstititions. Pour dire «oui», il ——————— (sourire) et, alors, il ———————— (être) heureux. En grandissant, le poète ———————— (rester) le même, et il ——————— (conserver) son attitude d'autrefois.

B. Position des pronoms personnels

   1. Temps simples et temps composés

   Le pronom personnel est toujours placé avant le verbe.

   Répétez les phrases suivantes en remplacant les mots indiqués par le pronom convenable:

   (*a*) L'enfant appelait [les idées].
        L'enfant [les] appelait.
   (*b*) L'enfant avait appelé [les idées].
        L'enfant [les] avait appelées.

        ses amis / sa cousine Jacqueline / les oiseaux / son chien

   2. Verbe + infinitif

   Le pronom personnel précède l'infinitif.

   Répétez les phrases suivantes en substituant les mots indiqués:

   (*a*) Il veut leur [trancher la gorge].
   (*b*) Il avait voulu leur [trancher la gorge].
        couper l'appétit / arracher les yeux / faire peur / faire du mal

   Reprenez les deux exercices précédents en mettant les phrases:
   (a) à la forme interrogative (b) à la forme négative

   3. Impératif

   A la forme affirmative le pronom personnel est placé *après* le verbe.

   Répétez la phrase suivante en remplaçant les mots indiqués par le pronom convenable:

(*a*) Appelez [les idées].
Appelez-[les].
vos amis / votre mère / votre frère / vos chiens

A la forme négative le pronom personnel est placé *avant* le verbe.

Répétez la phrase suivante en remplaçant les mots indiqués par le pronom convenable:

(*b*) Ne répétez pas [ces idées fausses].
Ne [les] répétez pas.
ce bruit / cette nouvelle affreuse / les histoires de la famille / leurs mensonges

Notez: A l'impératif il n'y a jamais de pronom sujet.

XVIII

pour faire le portrait

d'un oiseau

1 **Peindre:** Cet infinitif a le sens d'un impératif impersonnel. Il s'agit ici d'une série de conseils analogues à ceux d'une recette de cuisine

4 **quelque chose de joli:** *Voir p. 242, exercice II, B*

14 **sans ... dire:** *Voir p. 16, note 11*

17 **aussi bien:** indique une seconde possibilité
17 **mettre:** employer (une certaine quantité de temps)
17 **de longues années:** de nombreuses années (*Voir p. 36, exercice I, A*)

21 **s'il le faut:** si c'est nécessaire

24 **réussite:** résultat satisfaisant

pour faire le portrait
d'un oiseau

Peindre d'abord une cage
Avec une porte ouverte
peindre ensuite
quelque chose de joli
5   quelque chose de simple
quelque chose de beau
quelque chose d'utile
pour l'oiseau
placer ensuite la toile contre un arbre
10   dans un jardin
dans un bois
ou dans une forêt
se cacher derrière l'arbre
sans rien dire
15   sans bouger . . .
Parfois l'oiseau arrive vite
mais il peut aussi bien mettre de longues années
avant de se décider
Ne pas se décourager
20   attendre
attendre s'il le faut pendant des années
la vitesse ou la lenteur de l'arrivée de l'oiseau
n'ayant aucun rapport
avec la réussite du tableau
25   Quand l'oiseau arrive
s'il arrive

42 **mauvais signe:** mauvais présage

observer le plus profond silence
attendre que l'oiseau entre dans la cage
et quand il est entré
30 fermer doucement la porte avec le pinceau
puis
effacer un à un tous les barreaux
en ayant soin de ne toucher aucune des plumes de l'oiseau
Faire ensuite le portrait de l'arbre
35 en choisissant la plus belle de ses branches
pour l'oiseau
peindre aussi le vert feuillage et la fraîcheur du vent
la poussière du soleil
et le bruit des bêtes de l'herbe dans la chaleur de l'été
40 et puis attendre que l'oiseau se décide à chanter
Si l'oiseau ne chante pas
c'est mauvais signe
signe que le tableau est mauvais
mais s'il chante c'est bon signe
45 signe que vous pouvez signer
Alors vous arrachez tout doucement
une des plumes de l'oiseau
et vous écrivez votre nom dans un coin du tableau.

Paroles

PREMIÈRE PARTIE

lecture du poème

A. PREMIÈRE LECTURE SANS PAUSES

B. DEUXIÈME LECTURE AVEC PAUSES

pour faire le portrait
d'un oiseau

Peindre d'abord une cage / . . . /
Avec une porte ouverte / . . . /
peindre ensuite
quelque chose de joli / . . . /
5   quelque chose de simple / . . . /
quelque chose de beau / . . . /
quelque chose d'utile
pour l'oiseau / . . . /
placer ensuite la toile contre un arbre / . . . /
10   dans un jardin / . . . /
dans un bois / . . . /
ou dans une forêt / . . . /
se cacher derrière l'arbre / . . . /
sans rien dire / . . . /
15   sans bouger . . . / . . . /
Parfois l'oiseau arrive vite / . . . /
mais il peut aussi bien mettre de longues années / . . . /
avant de se décider / . . . /
Ne pas se décourager / . . . /

20 attendre / . . . /
attendre s'il le faut pendant des années / . . . /
la vitesse ou la lenteur de l'arrivée de l'oiseau / . . . /
n'ayant aucun rapport
avec la réussite du tableau / . . . /
25 Quand l'oiseau arrive / . . . /
s'il arrive / . . . /
observer le plus profond silence / . . . /
attendre que l'oiseau entre dans la cage / . . . /
et quand il est entré / . . . /
30 fermer doucement la porte avec le pinceau / . . . /
puis
effacer un à un tous les barreaux / . . . /
en ayant soin de ne toucher aucune des plumes de l'oiseau
/ . . . /
Faire ensuite le portrait de l'arbre / . . . /
35 en choisissant la plus belle de ses branches
pour l'oiseau / . . . /
peindre aussi le vert feuillage / . . . / et la fraîcheur du vent
/ . . . /
la poussière du soleil / . . . /
et le bruit des bêtes de l'herbe / . . . / dans la chaleur de
l'été / . . . /
40 et puis attendre que l'oiseau se décide à chanter / . . . /
Si l'oiseau ne chante pas / . . . /
c'est mauvais signe / . . . /
signe que le tableau est mauvais / . . . /
mais s'il chante c'est bon signe / . . . /
45 signe que vous pouvez signer / . . . /
Alors vous arrachez tout doucement
une des plumes de l'oiseau / . . . . /
et vous écrivez votre nom dans un coin du tableau. / . . . /

C. TROISIÈME LECTURE SANS PAUSES

DEUXIÈME PARTIE

étude du texte

1. A qui l'auteur s'adresse-t-il?
2. Où se passe la scène?
3. Quelles différences y a-t-il entre un jardin, un bois et une forêt?
4. Pourquoi faut-il peindre une cage avec la porte ouverte?
5. Quand on voit une cage dont la porte est ouverte, qu'est-ce que cela signifie généralement?
6. Donnez un exemple de quelque chose de joli, de simple, de beau et d'utile pour l'oiseau.
7. Pourquoi faut-il placer la cage contre un arbre?
8. Pourquoi le peintre doit-il se cacher derrière cet arbre?
9. Quelle doit être l'attitude du peintre quand la toile est placée contre l'arbre?
10. Pourquoi Prévert conseille-t-il d'effacer les barreaux quand l'oiseau est entré dans la cage?
11. Connaissez-vous des endroits où il y a des barreaux aux fenêtres? Donnez deux exemples.
12. Pourquoi ne faut-il pas toucher aux plumes de l'oiseau quand on efface les barreaux?
13. On peut peindre «le vert feuillage», mais comment peindre «la fraîcheur du vent» et «le bruit des bêtes dans la chaleur de l'été»?
14. Pourquoi le poète pense-t-il que l'oiseau viendra?
15. Si l'oiseau ne chante pas, pourquoi est-ce signe que le tableau est mauvais?
16. Est-il possible d'arracher «tout doucement» une plume à un oiseau vivant? Qu'arriverait-il en pareil cas?
17. Relevez tous les sens du mot «signe».
18. Qu'est-ce qu'un cygne?

TROISIÈME PARTIE

phonétique

I. CONTRASTES

[m]

Marie / Marie
Marie / Marie
Marie / Marie
Marie, Marie, Marie / . . . /

rim / rime
rim / rime
rim / rime
rime, rime, rime / . . . /

esteem / estime
esteem / estime
esteem / estime
estime, estime, estime / . . . /

mummy / momie
mummy / momie
mummy / momie
momie, momie, momie / . . . /

[n]

nun / nonne
nun / nonne
nun / nonne
nonne, nonne, nonne / . . . /

vain / vaine
vain / vaine
vain / vaine
vaine, vaine, vaine / . . . /

rein / reine
rein / reine
rein / reine
reine, reine, reine / . . . /

quinine / quinine
quinine / quinine
quinine / quinine
quinine, quinine, quinine / . . . /

[ɲ]

sing / signe
sing / signe
sing / signe
signe, signe, signe / . . . /

sang / saigne

sang / saigne

sang / saigne

saigne, saigne, saigne / . . . /

dignity / dignité

dignity / dignité

dignity / dignité

dignité, dignité, dignité / . . . /

magnetism / magnétisme

magnetism / magnétisme

magnetism / magnétisme

magnétisme, magnétisme, magnétisme / . . . /

II. EXERCICES

[m]	[n]
a / âme . . . a / âme	a / Anne . . . a / Anne
oh / homme . . . oh / homme	paix / peine . . . paix / peine
hue / hume . . . hue / hume	pas / panne . . . pas / panne
taie / thème . . . taie / thème	t'a / tanne . . . t'a / tanne
beau / baume . . . beau / baume	tôt / tonne . . . tôt / tonne
fa / femme . . . fa / femme	qu'a / canne . . . qu'a / canne
sait / sème . . . sait / sème	fa / fane . . . fa / fane
mais / même . . . mais / même	va / vanne . . . va / vanne
riz / rime . . . riz / rime	mis / mine . . . mis / mine
la / lame . . . la / lame	n'est / naine . . . n'est / naine

[ɲ]

art / hargne . . . art / hargne

paix / peigne . . . paix / peigne

pas / pagne . . . pas / pagne

qu'a / cagne . . . qu'a / cagne

baie / baigne . . . baie / baigne

                    bat / bagne . . . bat / bagne
                    dit / digne . . . dit / digne
                    sait / saigne . . . sait / saigne
                    si / cygne . . . si / cygne
                    lit / ligne . . . lit / ligne

                    Mignonne . . . Mignonne
                    Une aumône . . . Une aumône
               Ma mère et moi . . . Ma mère et moi
    J'aime ces moments de calme. . . . J'aime ces moments de calme.
          Agnès soigne sa ligne. . . . Agnès soigne sa ligne.
       La dignité de l'homme . . . La dignité de l'homme
    La cane et le cygne se baignent. . . . La cane et le cygne se baignent.
       C'est signe que vous pouvez   C'est signe que vous pouvez
                    signer. . . . signer.

QUATRIÈME PARTIE

exercices

I. VOCABULAIRE

A. Le verbe **mettre** a plusieurs sens; ici, il signifie: *employer une quantité de temps pour faire quelque chose.*

Remplacez les tirets par le verbe **mettre** *au temps qui convient:*

(*a*) La terre ————— vingt-quatre heures pour tourner autour du soleil.

(*b*) L'oiseau peut ————— de longues années avant de se décider à venir.

(*c*) Demain, s'il ne pleut pas, Philippe ————— environ une demi-heure pour aller chez Claude.

(*d*) Jean a ————— trois ans pour écrire son dernier livre.

II. GRAMMAIRE

A. **Sans** + l'infinitif remplace la forme négative.

Remplacez la forme négative par **sans** + *l'infinitif:*

(*a*) Le peintre ne [bouge] pas. Le peintre reste sans [bouger].
s'impatienter / remuer / s'inquiéter / parler / faire de
bruit

(*Voir* Déjeuner du matin, *p.* 16, *note 11.*)

B. **Quelque chose** + **de** + adjectif;
rien + **de** + adjectif

Répétez les phrases suivantes en substituant les mots indiqués:

(*a*) Peignez quelque chose de [joli].
simple / beau / agréable / autre / intéressant
(*b*) Aujourd'hui, nous n'avons rien vu de [nouveau].
inquiétant / beau / passionnant / autre / sensationnel

Notez: L'adjectif est toujours au masculin singulier.

C. Un emploi de l'infinitif

L'infinitif peut indiquer un ordre (comme l'impératif), une
indication, un avis.

*Répétez les phrases suivantes en substituant pour chaque exemple
les verbes indiqués:*

(*a*) [Prendre] une toile et la [placer] contre un arbre.
peindre, poser / regarder, laisser / soulever, accrocher /
acheter, fixer

Au négatif, **ne . . . pas** précède l'infinitif.

(*b*) Ne pas [se décourager], [attendre] silencieusement.
bouger, patienter / parler, espérer / toucher aux plumes

de l'oiseau, être adroit / faire mal à l'oiseau, être attentif
/ oublier de signer, être fier

CINQUIÈME PARTIE

compréhension (laboratoire)

SIXIÈME PARTIE

dictée (laboratoire)

vocabulaire

This vocabulary defines words only as they are used in the book but includes virtually every French word except for those found only in phonetic exercises and the most elementary "function words" such as articles and pronouns. Since cognates and "twins" have been used wherever possible in the text, even the beginner will probably not have to look up the meaning of most words. However, it is part of sound vocabulary-building habits for students to be able to verify at any time the exact form (spelling, gender, etc.) of all expressions they have encountered. It is hoped that the completeness of this vocabulary will encourage them to do so.

abréviations :

adj.	adjective	[N]	noun appears here
adv.	adverb	*pl.*	plural
cond.	conditional	*pop.*	popular, vulgar
conj.	conjunction	*p. p.*	past participle
f.	feminine noun	*pres.*	present
fut.	future	*ps. p.*	present participle
fig.	figurative	*sj.*	subjunctive
[I]	infinitive appears here	[V]	verb appears here
m.	masculine noun		

A

à at, to, in, into, for, with, on, upon
abandonné, -e abandoned
abat-jour *m.* lampshade
abattre to fell, lower
   s'— to fall, come (sweep) down
abdication *f.* abdication
abîmé, -e spoiled
abord : d'— first, at first
   tout d'— first of all
abri *m.* shelter, cover
   se mettre à l'— to take shelter
s'abriter to take shelter, shelter oneself
absolument absolutely
acajou *m.* mahogany
accélération *f.* acceleration
accent *m.* accent
accepter to accept
s'accommoder de to permit, allow
accomplir to accomplish, complete
accord *m.* agreement
accorder to accord, give
   s'— to agree
accrocher to hook, hang up
accueillir to greet, welcome
acheter to buy
acier *m.* steel
acteur *m.* actor
action *f.* action
activité *f.* activity
actuellement now, at present, currently
s'adapter to apply
addition *f.* bill, check
additionner to add
adjectif *m.* adjective
admettre to admit, accept
administrer to administer
admirer to admire
admis *p. p.* of **admettre**
adresser to address, direct
   s'— to address, speak
adroit, -e skillful, clever, crafty
adulte *m.* or *f.* adult
adverbe *m.* adverb
adverbial, -e adverbial
aéroport *m.* airport
affection *f.* affection
affirmatif, -ive affirmative

affirmativement affirmatively
affirmer to affirm
affligé, -e afflicted
s'affliger to grieve
âge *m.* age
   en bas — very young
agent *m.* agent
   — de police policeman
agir to act
   il s'agit de it is a question of, it's
     about, it concerns
agréable agreeable, pleasant
agressivité *f.* aggressiveness
aider to aid, help
ail *m.* garlic
ailleurs elsewhere
   d'— moreover, for that matter
aimer to love, like
ainsi thus, so
air : avoir l'— de to seem to
ait *sj.* of **avoir**
ajouter to add
aller to go
   ne pas y — par quatre chemins to
     get right to the point, not to beat
     about the bush
   s'en — to go away, leave
allitération *f.* alliteration
allongé, -e lying, stretched out
allumer to light
allusion *f.* allusion, reference
   faire — to refer
alors then, in that case
   — que when
amande *f.* almond
ambiguïté *f.* ambiguity
amener to bring, introduce
américain, -e American
ami *m.* friend
amour *m.* love
amoureusement lovingly, passionately
amoureux *m.* lover, sweetheart
amusant, -e funny, amusing
an *m.* year
analogue analogous, similar
ananas *m.* pineapple
ancien, -enne old, former
anglais *m.* English (language)
anglais, -e English
animal *m.* animal
année *f.* year

annonce *f.* announcement, advertisement
— **nécrologique** obituary
annoncer to announce
antécédent *m.* antecedent
antérieur, -e : futur — future perfect
apercevoir to perceive, see, catch sight of
aperçu *p. p.* of **apercevoir**
apparaître to appear
apparence *f.* appearance
en — apparently
apparition *f.* appearance
appeler to call
s'— to be called, named
elle s'appelle ... her name is ...
appétit *m.* appetite
couper l'— to spoil one's appetite
applaudissement *m.* applause
s'appliquer à to apply oneself to, work at
apporter to bring
apprendre to learn, teach, show, tell
— **à quelqu'un** to teach someone
approximatif, -ive approximate
après after
d'— according to, judging by
après-midi *m.* afternoon
apte apt, qualified
arbre *m.* tree
argent *m.* money
armée *f.* army
armer to arm
arracher to tear out, pull out
arrêter to stop
s'— to stop
arrière-garde *f.* rear guard
arrivée *f.* arrival
arriver to happen
quoi qu'il arrive whatever happens
arroser to water
café arrosé rhum coffee laced with rum
arrosoir *m.* sprinkler, watering can
arsenal *m.* naval dockyard
article *m.* article
asperge *f.* asparagus
assassin *m.* assassin
s'asseoir to sit down
assis *p. p.* of **asseoir**
assis, -e seated

associer à to associate with
astre *m.* star
atmosphère *f.* atmosphere
attaquer to attack
atteindre to reach
attendre to wait (for)
attentif, -ive attentive
attention *f.* attention
attentivement attentively
attirer to attract
attitude *f.* attitude, pose
aucun, -e : ne [V] **aucun** not any, none
au-dessus (de) over, above
auditif, -ive auditory
augmenté, -e enlarged
aujourd'hui today
aurai *fut.* of **avoir**
aussi also
— **bien** just as well
auteur *m.* author
autocar *m.* streetcar
automne *m.* autumn
autour (de) around
autre other
— **chose** something else
rien d'— nothing else
autrefois formerly
auxiliaire *m.* auxiliary
avancer to advance, move forward
avant (de) before
avant-guerre *m.* pre-war period
d'— pre-war (*adj.*)
avec with
aventure *f.* adventure
aveugler to blind
avis *m.* opinion, (piece of) advice
à votre — in your opinion
avocat *m.* lawyer
avoir to have
— **l'air de** to seem to
— **beau faire quelque chose** to do something in vain
— **besoin de** to need
— **envie de** to want (to)
— **lieu** to take place
n'— **que faire de** not to know what to do with, have no use for
— **raison** to be right
— **soin** to be careful, take care
il y a there is, there are

il y a trois jours que . . . It's been three days since . . . , . . . for three days
ayant *ps. p.* of **avoir**

B

baiser *m.* kiss
balayer to sweep
balle *f.* ball
banc *m.* bench
barreau *m.* bar
barricade *f.* barricade
bas, basse low
 en bas âge very young
baser to base
basse-cour *f.* farmyard
bataille *f.* battle
bateau *m.* boat, ship
beau, belle beautiful, fine
 avoir beau faire quelque chose to do something in vain
 faire beau to be fine, fair (weather)
beaucoup a great deal, a lot
 — de many, much
bercer to rock
besoin *m.* need
 avoir — de to need
bête *f.* beast, animal
bêtise *f.* stupidity, absurdity, blunder
beurre *m.* butter
bien well, completely, indeed, all right
 aussi — just as well
 ou — or (else)
bien que although
bientôt soon
bière *f.* beer
bistro *m.* pub, sort of café, bar
blanc *m.* white (of the eye)
blanc, blanche white
blême pale
blesser to hurt, wound
blond, -e blond, light, pale
boire to drink
bois *m.* wood, woods
boisson *f.* beverage, drink
 débit de boissons tavern, pub
boîte *f.* box, can
boiter to limp
bombardement *m.* bombing, bombardment

bon, bonne good
 de bonne heure early
bonheur *m.* happiness
bordé, -e bordered, lined
bosse *f.* bump
boucher *m.* butcher
boucherie *f.* butcher shop
bouger to move
boulanger *m.* baker
boulangerie *f.* bakery
bout *m.* end
bouteille *f.* bottle
branche *f.* branch
bras *m.* arm
brave good, honest, worthy
Bretagne *f.* Brittany
breuvage *m.* drink, beverage
bridge *m.* bridge
brisé, -e broken
brosse *f.* brush
brouillard *m.* fog
bruit *m.* noise
brûler to burn
brume *f.* fog, mist
brutal, -e brutal
bu *p. p.* of **boire**
buffet *m.* sideboard

C

ça (contraction of **cela**) that, it
 C'est — même That's right
cacher to hide, cover up
café *m.* café, coffee
 café-crème coffee with milk
cage *f.* cage
calciner to burn, char
Californie *f.* California
calligraphe *m.* calligrapher
camp *m.*: **ficher le —** to leave, get out (*pop.*)
candidat *m.* candidate
capable capable, able
car for, because
caractère *m.* character, nature
caractériser to characterize
caractéristique *f.* characteristic, salient feature
carboniser to carbonize, char
cardinal, -e cardinal

caresser to caress
carré *m.* square, yard
carré, -e square
carreau *m.* window pane
cas *m.* case
  en pareil — in such cases
  selon le — as the case may be
casser to break
catacombes *f. pl.* catacombs
catastrophe *f.* catastrophe
catholique catholic
cause *f.* cause, reason
  à — de because of
causer to cause
ce, cet, cette, ces this, that, these, those
  — [N]-là that (those) [N]
  ce qui what
  ce que what, the fact that
ceci this
cédille *f.* cedilla
cela that
  — fait trois jours que . . . It's been three days since . . . , . . . for three days
célèbre famous, celebrated
célébrité *f.* celebrity, fame
celles the ones, those
celui, celle the one
  —-ci the latter
cendre *f.* ash(es)
cendrier *m.* ashtray
cent (a, one) hundred
centaine *f.* (about a) hundred
centime *m.* centime (one 100th part of a franc)
cependant however
cercle *m.* circle, ring
cercueil *m.* coffin
certain, -e some, certain
certainement certainly
cesse *f.* cease, ceasing
cesser to cease, stop
c'est-à-dire that is to say
ceux the ones, those
chacun, -e each
chagrin *m.* grief, sorrow
chaîne *f.* chain
chaise *f.* chair
chaleur *f.* heat
chambre *f.* room, bedroom
champ *m.* field, ground

champagne *m.* champagne
champêtre rustic, pastoral
changement *m.* change
changer to change
  se — to change, be changed
chanson *f.* song
chant *m.* song, singing
chanter to sing
chapeau *m.* hat
chaque each, every
charbon *m.* charcoal, coal
chat *m.* cat
chaud, -e warm, hot
chef *m.* chief, head
chemin *m.* road
  ne pas y aller par quatre —s to get right to the point, not to beat about the bush
chêne *m.* oak
cher, chère dear
chercher to seek, look for, search for, go and get (meet, fetch)
  — à [I] to try to [I]
cheval *m.* horse
chevelu, -e hairy
  cuir — scalp
cheveux *m. pl.* hair
chez at *or* to the home *or* business of; in, with
  — eux to (at) their home
  — Potin at Potin's (store)
chien *m.* dog
chiffre *m.* number
chocolat *m.* chocolate
choisir to choose
choix *m.* choice
chose *f.* thing
  autre — something else
chrysanthème *m.* chrysanthemum
ci-dessous below
ci-dessus above
ciel *m.* sky
cigarette *f.* cigarette
cimetière *m.* cemetery
cinéma *m.* cinema, movies
cinq five
cinquante fifty
cinquième fifth
circonflexe circumflex
circonstance *f.* circumstance
cirer to wax

citer to cite, quote
civil, -e civil, civic
clair, -e clear
clairement clearly
classe *f.* class, classroom
classique classical
clé *f.* key
    fermer à — to lock
clerc *m.* clerk, scholar
cliché *m.* stock phrase
client *m.* customer, client
climat *m.* climate
clown *m.* clown
cochon *m.* pig
cœur *m.* heart
    si le — vous en dit if you feel like it
coexister to coexist
coin *m.* corner, retired spot
    du — corner (*adj.*)
collaboration *f.* collaboration
collage *m.* collage
collectif, -ive collective
collection *f.* collection
collectionneur *m.* collector
collège *m.* college, school
combien how many, how much
combiner to combine
commandant *m.* commanding officer, captain
commander to order
comme as, like, since
commencer to begin
comment how, what
commenter to comment on
commercial, -e commercial
commettre to commit
commun, -e common
communication *f.* communication
    — téléphonique phone call
compagnie *f.* company
    me tenir — to bear me company
compatriote *m.* compatriot, fellow countryman
complément *m.* complement
    — d'objet object
complètement completely
comportement *m.* behavior
se comporter to behave
composé, -e compound
compréhensible comprehensible

compréhension *f.* comprehension, understanding
comprendre to understand
compte *m.* account
compter to count, reckon, plan, expect
comptoir *m.* counter, bar
concentrer to concentrate
concernant concerning
concerto *m.* concerto
conclusion *f.* conclusion, ending
condamné *m.* convict
    — à mort convict under sentence of death
condamner to condemn
conditionnel *m.* conditional
conditionnel, -elle conditional
conduite *f.* pipe
conférence *f.* lecture
confiance *f.* confidence
confiture *f.* jam, preserves
confondre to confuse
conforme à consistent with
conformiste conformist
conjuguer to conjugate
connaître to know, be acquainted with
    il l'a connue he met her
    ils se sont connus they met
connerie *f.* nonsense, stupidity, colossal blunder (*pop.*)
connu *p. p.* of **connaître**
conquérir to conquer, win over
consacrer to devote
consciencieux, -euse conscientious
conseil *m.* (piece of) advice
conseiller to advise, recommend
    — de faire quelque chose to advise that one do something, that something be done
conséquence *f.* consequence
conserve *f.* preserve, canned food
conserver to keep, retain
considération *f.* consideration, account
considérer to consider
consonne *f.* consonant
constamment constantly
constater to note, observe, ascertain, state
constituer to constitute
construction *f.* construction, building
construire to construct, build

conte *m.* story, tale
contemporain, -e contemporary
contenir to control, restrain
content, -e glad, happy
contenu *m.* contents
contexte *m.* context
contraire : au — on the contrary
contraste *m.* contrast
contre against
contre-ordre *m.* counter-order, counter-mand
convaincre to convince
convenable appropriate, correct
convenir to suit, be suitable
coquille *f.* shell
corne *f.* horn, feeler
corps *m.* body
  faire — avec to stick to
correct, -e correct
correspondre to correspond
côte *f.* coast
côté *m.* side
coton *m.* cotton
couche *f.* layer
couché, -e lying (down)
coucher to lay down
  se — to go to bed
couleur *f.* color
  — de poussière dust-colored
coulisse *f.* wings (of a theater)
  dans les — behind the scenes
coup *m.* : **avoir le — de foudre** to fall in love at first sight
coupable *m.* culprit, guilty person
couper to cut
  — l'appétit to spoil one's appetite
courant *m.* current
courant, -e ordinary, in current use
courir to run
cours *m.* course, class
court, -e short
cousin *m.*, **cousine** *f.* cousin
coûter to cost
couverture *f.* cover
couvre-lit *m.* bedspread
craie *f.* chalk
craindre to fear
crainte *f.* fear
crayon *m.* pencil
créer to create

crème *f.* cream
  café-crème coffee with milk
crêpe *m.* crape
crever to burst, (of animals) die
cri *m.* shout, cry
crier to shout
crime *m.* crime
criminel *m.* criminal
critique *m.* critic
critiquer to criticize
croire to believe, think
croisement *m.* intersection
croiser [N] to meet [N] coming in the opposite direction
croissant *m.* crescent roll
croyant *m.* believer
cuiller *f.* spoon
cuir *m.* leather
  — chevelu scalp
cuisine *f.* kitchen, cooking
  livre de — cookbook
curieux, -euse curious
  de façon curieuse in a curious way
curiosité *f.* curiosity
cygne *m.* swan

D

d'abord first, at first
d'ailleurs moreover, for that matter
danger *m.* danger
dans in, into, to
d'après according to, judging by
date *f.* date
  de longue — of long standing
datte *f.* date (fruit)
de of, by, from, about, with
débit *m.* store, shop
  — de boissons tavern, pub
debout standing
début *m.* beginning
débutante *f.* debutante
débuter to begin
décapiter to decapitate, behead
décès *m.* death
déchirer to tear
décider to decide
  se — to make up one's mind
décision *f.* decision

prendre une — to make a decision
déclarer to declare, state
décor *m.* setting, background
se décourager to lose heart, be discouraged
décrire to describe
défense *f.* defense
définitivement definitively, for good
se dégager to free oneself, escape
déjà already
déjeuner *m.* lunch
  — du matin breakfast
déjeuner to have lunch
délicatement delicately
demain tomorrow
demander to ask
  se — to wonder
déménager to move
demi-heure *f.* half-hour
demi-teinte *f.* half-tone
  en — in subtle hues
dénoter to denote, indicate
dénouement *m.* outcome, ending
dent *f.* tooth
  grincer des dents to gnash one's teeth
dépasser to go beyond
se dépêcher to hurry
dépit *m.*: **en — de** in spite of
depuis since, for
dérangement *m.* disturbance
déranger to disturb
dérivé *m.* derivative
dériver to derive
dernier, -ière last
se dérouler to take place
derrière behind
dès from, as early as
  — que as soon as
désaccord *m.* dissension, disagreement, clash of interests
désaffecté, -e no longer in use
désappointé, -e disappointed
désastre *m.* disaster
descendre to descend, come down
description *f.* description
désemparé, -e disabled, in distress
désespéré, -e desperate, in despair
désigner to indicate, designate
désintégration *f.* disintegration

se désintégrer to disintegrate
désinvolte detached, offhand
désolation *f.* desolation, grief
désolé, -e desolate, devastated, grieved, disconsolate
se désoler to be grieved
destin *m.* destiny
destiner to intend, mean
destruction *f.* destruction
détaché, -e detached, unconcerned
déterminé, -e specific, fixed
déterminer to determine
détruire to destroy
deuil *m.* mourning
  prendre le — to go into mourning
deux two
  ne faire ni une ni — to waste no time
deuxième second
devant in front of
devanture *f.* front, window
devenir to become
  Qu'es-tu devenue? What has become of you?
devoir *m.* duty, exercise, homework
devoir to have to, should, ought, must, owe
dévorer to devour
dictée *f.* dictation
dicter to dictate
dieu *m.* god
différent, -e different, various
difficile difficult
dimension *f.* dimension, size
dîner to dine, have dinner
dire to tell, say, express
  se — to be said
  — son fait à quelqu'un to give someone a piece of one's mind
direct, -e direct
directement directly
discuter to discuss
disparaître to disappear
disparu *m.* missing person
disposition *f.* disposition, frame of mind
distinctement distinctly
distrait, -e absent-minded, inattentive, listless
dit *p. p.* of **dire**
divers, -e diverse, various
dix ten

dix-neuf nineteen
dix-sept seventeen
dizaine *f.* about ten, half a score
document *m.* document
dommage *m.* damage, loss
don *m.* gift
donc therefore, then
donner to give, provide, furnish, attribute
dont of which, whose
d'où from which, whence
doucement softly, gently
douleur *f.* suffering, pain, sorrow
douloureux, -euse painful, distressing
doute *m.* doubt
doux, douce sweet
douzaine *f.* dozen
douze twelve
dramatique dramatic
drame *m.* drama
drap *m.* sheet
drôle funny, droll
drôlement strangely, oddly, in a funny way
dû *p. p.* of **devoir**
dur, -e hard
  œuf dur hard-boiled egg
durée *f.* duration, length of time
durer to last

E

eau *f.* water
  au fil de l'— with the stream
s'échapper to escape
échecs *m. pl.* chess
éclairer to light, illuminate
  s'— to light up
éclatant, -e loud, dazzling
éclater to burst
école *f.* school
économiquement economically
écouter to listen
s'écrier to cry out, shout, exclaim
écrire to write
  s'— to be written
écrit, -e written
  — à la main handwritten
écriture *f.* handwriting

s'écrouler to crumble, collapse, fall in
éditeur *m.* publisher
édition *f.* edition
édredon *m.* eiderdown
effacer to erase
effet *m.* effect
  en — indeed
s'efforcer to strive, try
également also, equally
égaler to equal
église *f.* church
égorger to slit the throat of
élément *m.* element
élève *m.* or *f.* pupil, student
élevé, -e high
élever to raise, rear
élire to elect
élite *f.* elite
élu *p. p.* of **élire**
embrasser to kiss
embuscade *f.* ambush
s'émietter to crumble (away)
émotion *f.* emotion
empêcher to prevent
  s'— to refrain
emploi *m.* use
employer to use
  s'— to be used
emporter to carry away
emprunter à to borrow from
en in, into, to, at, of, on
  en (+*ps. p.*) by, while
en from there, of it, of them
  s'— aller to go away, leave
  — vouloir à quelqu'un to bear someone ill will, a grudge
encore still, again
encre *f.* ink
s'endormir to fall asleep
endroit *m.* place
enfance *f.* childhood
enfant *m.* or *f.* child
enfin at last, finally, really!, come now!
enlaidir to disfigure, make ugly
enlever to remove, take away
ennemi *m.* enemy
s'ennuyer to be bored
ennuyeux, -euse tedious, boring
enseigner to teach
ensemble together

ensuite then, afterwards, next
entendre to hear, understand
enterrement *m.* burial, interment, funeral
entier, -ière entire, whole
  le manger tout entier to eat it completely, eat all of it
entièrement entirely, completely
entourage *m.* wire fence, fencing
entre between
entrebâillé, -e ajar, half-opened
entrer (dans, à [N]) to enter ([N])
entrevoir to catch a glimpse of, have an inkling of
entrevu *p. p.* of **entrevoir**
entrouvert, -e ajar
énumérer to enumerate
envers toward
envie *f.* desire
  avoir — (de) to want
  si vous en avez — if you want to, if you feel like it
environ about, approximately
s'envoler to fly away
envoyer to send
épanoui, -e beaming
épicerie *f.* groceries, grocery store
époque *f.* period, time
équilibre *m.* equilibrium
équivalent *m.* equivalent
équivaloir to be equivalent
erreur *f.* mistake
escargot *m.* snail
esclave *m.* or *f.* slave
espace *m.* space
espèce *f.* kind, sort
  d'— différente of different kinds
espérer to hope
espion *m.* spy
espoir *m.* hope
esprit *m.* mind
  — libre open mind
essayer to try
essuyer to wipe
estimer to respect, esteem
et and
établir to establish, verify
étage *m.* story, floor
étain *m.* tin
état *m.* state
Etats-Unis *m. pl.* United States

été *m.* summer
été *p. p.* of **être**
éternel, -elle eternal
éternité *f.* eternity
étoffe *f.* material, cloth
étonnant, -e surprising
étonner to surprise
étrange strange
être *m.* being
être to be
  — en train de faire quelque chose to be engaged in (busy) doing something
  pendant que vous y êtes while you are about it
  vous n'y êtes pas you don't understand
étude *f.* study
étudiant *m.,* **étudiante** *f.* student
étudier to study
eu *p. p.* of **avoir**
évaluation *f.* evaluation
événement *m.* event
évidence *f.*: **en —** in a conspicuous position
évoquer to evoke
exact, -e exact, correct, right
examiner to examine
excellent, -e excellent
exception *f.* exception
excessivement excessively
exclamation *f.* exclamation
s'exclamer to exclaim
excursion *f.* excursion, raid
exemplaire exemplary
exemple *m.* example
  par — for example
exercice *m.* exercise
exister to exist, be
exotique exotic
expédition *f.* expedition, dispatch, shipment
expérience *f.* experience
expliquer to explain
exposer to expose, state
exposition *f.* exhibition, show
expression *f.* expression, phrase
exprimer to express
extérieur, -e exterior, outside, external
extraordinaire extraordinary
extrême extreme

F

face *f.*: **faire — à** to face, confront
facile easy
  femme — woman of easy virtue
facilement easily
façon *f.* way, manner
  de — à so as to
  de — curieuse in a curious way
  de la même — in the same way
  de toute — in any case
faible feeble, weak
faim *f.* hunger
  avoir — to be hungry
faire to make, do, cause, form
  — allusion to refer
  — beau to be fine, fair (weather)
  — corps avec to stick to
  — divers métiers to engage in various occupations
  — face à to face, confront
  — des funérailles to give a funeral
  — la grasse matinée to sleep late, lie in bed all morning
  — (du) mal à to hurt
  — de la peine à to grieve
  — peur à to frighten
  — le pitre to clown (around)
  — une promenade to take a walk
  — un rêve to have a dream
  — semblant to pretend
  — vilain to be nasty (weather)
  cela fait trois jours que . . . It's been three days since . . . , . . . for three days
  ne — ni une ni deux to waste no time
fait *m.* fact, act, deed
  dire son — à quelqu'un to give someone a piece of one's mind
fait-divers *m.* news item
falaise *f.* cliff
falloir to be necessary
fameux, -euse famous, renowned
familiarité *f.* familiarity
familier, -ière familiar
famille *f.* family
fasse *sj.* of **faire**
fatal, -e fatal

femme fatale siren, vamp
fatigué, -e tired
se fatiguer to tire oneself out
fatras *m.* jumble, hotchpotch
faudrait *cond.* of **falloir**
faut: **il faut** it is necessary
favori, -ite favorite
feindre to feign, pretend
féminin *m.* feminine gender
féminin, -e feminine
femme *f.* woman
  — facile woman of easy virtue
  — fatale siren, vamp
fenêtre *f.* window
fer *m.* iron
fera *fut.* of **faire**
fermer to close
  — à clé to lock
ferraille *f.* old iron, scrap iron
fête *f.* feast day, holiday
feu *m.* fire
  il y a le — it's on fire!, there's a fire there!
feuillage *m.* foliage
feuille *f.* leaf
fiasco *m.* fiasco
ficher: **le camp —** to leave, get out (*pop*).
fier, fière proud
figé, -e congealed, set
fil *m.* thread
  au — de l'eau with the stream
fille *f.* daughter, girl
  jeune — girl
film *m.* film
filtre *m.* filter
fin, -e fine, small, delicate
final, -e final
finir to finish
fixe fixed
fixer to fix, fasten
flamber to flame, blaze
flamme *f.* flame
fleur *f.* flower
flic *m.* policeman, cop (*pop.*)
flotter to float
fois *f.* time
  une — once
  à la — at the same time
folle *f.* of **fou**
fonction *f.* function
fond *m.* bottom

au —, dans le — fundamentally,
   after all
font *pres.* of faire
huit et huit — seize eight and eight
   are sixteen
fontaine *f.* fountain
football *m.* football, soccer
force *f.* strength, force
formation *f.* formation
forme *f.* form
   en — de in the form of a
former to form, make
formule *f.* formula, phrase
fort: parler — to speak loud(ly)
fou, folle mad, crazy
   fou rire uncontrollable laughter
foudre *f.* thunderbolt, lightning
   avoir le coup de — to fall in love at
      first sight
fouetté, -e whipped
foutre: il s'en fout he doesn't care,
   give a damn (*pop.*)
fraîcheur *f.* coolness
franc *m.* franc (money)
Français *m.* Frenchman
français *m.* French (language)
français, -e French
   à la française in the French way
fréquemment frequently
fréquenter to frequent, visit frequently
frère *m.* brother
froid, -e cold
fromage *m.* cheese
fruit *m.* fruit
fuir to flee, run away
fumée *f.* smoke
fumer to smoke
funèbre funereal
funérailles *f. pl.* funeral
   faire des — to give a funeral
fut *passé simple* of être
futur *m.* future (tense)

G

gagner to earn, reach, arrive at, win
gai, -e gay
galerie *f.* gallery
galoper to gallop
garage *m.* garage

garçon *m.* boy, waiter
   — d'honneur best man
garder to keep, preserve, guard, protect
gardien *m.* guardian, keeper
gâteau *m.* cake
gaz *m.* gas
général, -e general
généralement generally
genre *m.* kind
gens *m. pl.* people
geste *m.* gesture, movement
glace *f.* glass, mirror, ice cream
glacé, -e iced
glorifier to glorify
gorge *f.* throat
gracieux, -euse: à titre — gratis, free
   of charge
grade *m.* grade, rank
grammaire *f.* grammar
grammaticalement grammatically
grand, -e big, large, tall, great, high
grand-père *m.* grandfather
grandir to grow up
gras, grasse fat
   faire la grasse matinée to sleep late,
      lie in bed all morning
grave serious, grave
gravir to climb
grille *f.* grill, railing
grillé, -e grilled, burned
grincer to grate, grind
   — des dents to gnash one's teeth
gris, -e gray
gros, grosse big
grouiller to teem, swarm
groupe *m.* group
guère: ne [V] — hardly, scarcely, barely, not much
guerre *f.* war
guignol *m.* Punch; Punch and Judy
   show
guilde *f.* guild
guillotiner to guillotine

H

(* indicates aspirate *h*)
s'habiller to get dressed
habiter to live, dwell
habituel, -elle usual

habituellement usually
hallucination *f.* hallucination
*****harpe** *f.* harp
*****haut, -e** high
  à haute voix aloud
*****haut** *adv.* high (up)
  plus — above
*****hein** eh?, what?
hélas alas!
herbe *f.* grass
héritage *m.* inheritance, heritage
heure *f.* hour
  de bonne — early
  à six —s at six o'clock
heureux, -euse happy
hier yesterday
  — soir last night
histoire *f.* story, tale
historien *m.* historian
historique historic(al)
historiquement historically
hiver *m.* winter
hommage *m.* homage, tribute
homme *m.* man
honnête honest, respectable, honorable
honneur *m.* honor
  garçon d'— best man
hôpital *m.* hospital
horreur *f.* horror
horriblement horribly, horrifyingly
huile *f.* oil
*****huit** eight
*****huitaine** *f.* (about) eight
humain, -e human
*****hurler** to howl, yell
hydrophile absorbent
hypocrite hypocritical

I

ici here
idéal, -e ideal
idée *f.* idea
identique identical
idiomatique idiomatic
île *f.* island
image *f.* picture, image
imagination *f.* imagination
imaginer to imagine
imiter to imitate

immédiat, -e immediate
imparfait *m.* imperfect
impatience *f.* impatience
s'impatienter to lose patience, be impatient
impératif *m.* imperative
impersonnel, -elle impersonal
importance *f.* importance
important, -e important
importer: n'importe quoi anything, no matter what
  à n'importe quel temps in any tense
impression *f.* impression
imprévu, -e unexpected, unforeseen
improbable improbable
  ce que la situation a d'— the improbable aspect of the situation
inattendu, -e unexpected
incise: proposition — interpolated clause
incompréhensible incomprehensible
incompréhension *f.* incomprehension
incroyable incredible, unbelievable
indéfini, -e indefinite
indéterminé, -e indefinite
indicatif *m.* indicative
indication *f.* indication, instruction
s'indigner to become or be indignant
indiquer to show, indicate
indirect, -e indirect
individu *m.* individual
individuel, -elle individual
inégal, -e unequal
inférieur, -e inferior, lower, below
infinitif *m.* infinitive
infirmier *m.* hospital attendant, male nurse
influence *f.* influence
inondation *f.* flood
inquiétant, -e disturbing, alarming
s'inquiéter to be concerned, worry
inscription *f.* inscription, sign
insensé, -e mad, insane
insinuer to insinuate
insister to insist
s'installer to settle, take up one's abode
instant *m.* moment, instant
instantané, -e instant
instantanément instantly
instituteur *m.* teacher
instruire to instruct

s'— to improve one's mind
instrument *m.* instrument
intact, -e intact
intégralement completely, fully
intègre honest, upright
intellectuel, -elle intellectual
intelligent, -e intelligent
intensité *f.* intensity
intéressant, -e interesting
s'intéresser à to be interested in, take
  an interest in
intérêt *m.* interest
intérieur *m.* inside, interior
interjection *f.* interjection
interprétation *f.* interpretation
interpréter to interpret
interrogatif, -ive interrogative
intervenir to intervene
intituler to entitle, call
inutile useless
invariable invariable
inventer to invent
invention *f.* invention, inventiveness
inversion *f.* inversion
invité *m.* guest
ironie *f.* irony
ivrogne *m.* drunkard

J

jaillissant, -e gushing, springing
jamais ever, never
  ne [V] — never
jardin *m.* garden
jaune yellow
jeter to throw (away)
jeu *m.* play, game
  — **de mots** play on words, pun
jeudi *m.* Thursday
jeune young
  — **fille** girl
joie *f.* joy
joint à added to
joli, -e pretty
jouer to play, act
jour *m.* day, daylight
  en plein — in broad daylight
  tous les —s every day
journée *f.* day, daytime
jugement *m.* judgment, opinion

  porter un — to form a judgment
juger to judge
juillet *m.* July
jusque until
juste just, right
justement precisely, just
justifier to justify

K

kilomètre *m.* kilometer

L

là there
  ce [N] — that
  — **bas** yonder, over (out) there
  — **dessus** on that, to that
  — **haut** up there
labeur *m.* labor
laboratoire *m.* laboratory
laisser to let, leave
  à prendre ou à — take it or leave it
lait *m.* milk
lampe *f.* lamp
lancer to throw
langage *m.* language
laquelle which?, which one?
larme *f.* tear
se lasser to grow tired
laver to wash
lécher to lick
leçon *f.* lesson
lecteur *m.* reader
lecture *f.* reading
légion *f.* legion
légume *m.* vegetable
leitmotiv *m.* leitmotif
lenteur *f.* slowness
lequel, laquelle, lesquels, lesquelles
  which, which (one, ones)?
lettre *f.* letter
se lever to stand up, get up
  le jour se lève day is breaking
lèvre *f.* lip
liaison *f.* liaison (sounding of final
  consonant before initial vowel sound)
liberté *f.* liberty, freedom
libre free

esprit — open mind
lieu *m*. place
  au — de instead of
  avoir — to take place
limiter to limit
linge *m*. linen, cloth
  un vieux — a piece of old cloth, rag
lire to read
lit *m*. bed
  au — in bed
littéraire literary
littéral, -e literal
littérature *f*. literature
livide livid
livre *m*. book
  — de cuisine cookbook
se livrer à to devote oneself to, indulge in, give oneself over to
locution *f*. expression, phrase
logiquement logically
loin far
  au — far away
  plus — farther
long, longue long
  le long de along
longtemps (for) a long time
longueur *f*. length
lorsque when
lourd, -e heavy
lu *p. p.* of **lire**
lueur *f*. gleam, glimmer
lumière *f*. light
lune *f*. moon
  — de miel honeymoon
lyre *f*. lyre
lyrisme *m*. lyricism

M

machine *f*.: **taper à la —** to type
mâchoire *f*. jaw
magasin *m*. store, shop
magnifique magnificent, splendid
main *f*. hand
  écrit(e) à la — handwritten
maintenant now
mais but
maison *f*. house
  — d'épicerie grocery store
maître *m*. teacher

mal *m*. harm, evil
  faire (du) — à to hurt
malgré despite
malheur *m*. misfortune, unhappiness
malheureux, -euse unhappy, sad, miserable, paltry, wretched
manger to eat
  qui se mange which is (can be) eaten
  salle à — dining room
manière *f*. way, manner
  de la même — in the same way
manifester to manifest
manteau *m*. coat
marche *f*. step
marché *m*. market
marcher to walk
marié *m*. bridegroom
  les —s bride and bridegroom
se marier to marry, get married
marin *m*. sailor
marque *f*. mark, sign
marquer to mark
mars *m*. March
masculin *m*. masculine gender
masculin, -e masculine
masser to massage
mathématiquement mathematically
matière *f*. matter
matin *m*. morning
  le — in the morning, all morning
matinée *f*. morning
  faire la grasse — to sleep late, lie in bed all morning
mausolée *m*. mausoleum
mauvais, -e bad
mèche *f*. wick
mécontent, -e discontented, displeased
mécontentement *m*. dissatisfaction, displeasure
médecin *m*. doctor, physician
se méfier to distrust, be suspicious
  méfiez-vous beware
mêler to mix
même even, very, same
  C'est ça — That's right
  de — in the same way
  de — que just as
  quand — even so, even though, nevertheless
  tout de — really!, come now!

mémoire *f.* memory
mendiant *m.,* **mendiante** *f.* beggar
mendier to beg
mentalité *f.* mentality, turn of mind
mentionner to mention
mer *f.* sea
mère *f.* mother
merveilleux, -euse marvelous
métaphysicien *m.* metaphysician
méthode *f.* method
métier *m.* trade, profession
  faire divers —s to engage in various
    occupations
mettre to put, place, take
  — à la poste to mail
  se — à to begin
  se — à l'abri to take shelter
meuble *m.* piece of furniture
  les —s (the) furniture
miel *m.* honey
  lune de — honeymoon
miette *f.* crumb, piece
mieux better
  le — best
militaire military
mille (a, one) thousand
milliard *m.* billion
millier *m.* (about a) thousand
million *m.* million
minéral, -e mineral
minimiser to minimize
mis *p. p.* of **mettre**
mise *f.* placing, putting
misère *f.* misery, poverty, misfortune
mode *m.* mood, mode
modèle *m.* model
modèle model, exemplary
moderne modern
modifier to modify
moins less
  le — least
mois *m.* month
moitié *f.* half
  à — half, by halves
moment *m.* moment, time
  en ce — at the moment, now
mondanités *f. pl.* worldly vanities
monde *m.* world, people, society
  tout le — everybody
mondial, -e world-wide
  guerre mondiale world war

monotone monotonous
montagne *f.* mountain
monter to mount, get into
montrer to show, indicate
se moquer de to laugh at, make fun of
morceau *m.* piece
mordre to bite
mort *m.* dead person
  les —s the dead
mort *f.* death
  condamné à — convict under sen-
    tence of death
mort, -e dead
mortuaire mortuary
  chambre — death chamber or room
mot *m.* word
  jeu de mots play on words, pun
motif *m.* motive
mourant *m.* dying man
mourir to die
mouton *m.* sheep
mouvement *m.* movement, motion
muet, muette mute
multiple multiple, many
mur *m.* wall
museau *m.* muzzle, snout
musée *m.* museum
musique *f.* music
mystérieux, -euse mysterious
mystificateur *m.* hoaxer, mystifier

N

nager to swim
naissance *f.* birth
narration *f.* narration, narrative
nationalité *f.* nationality
nature *f.* nature, kind, character
  de — différente (opposée) of different
    (opposite) kinds
naturel, -elle natural
navire *m.* ship, vessel, boat
nécessaire necessary
nécrologique necrological
  annonce — obituary
négatif, -ive negative
négation *f.* negation, negative
négativement negatively, in the negative
neuf nine

neuf, neuve new
neutre neuter
nez *m.* nose
    je leur ris au — I laugh in their face
noce *f.* wedding, wedding party
noir *m.* darkness, dark
noir, -e black
noircir to blacken, darken
nom *m.* name, noun
nombre *m.* number
nombreux, -euse numerous
non no
normal, -e normal
nostalgique nostalgic
noter to note, jot down
nourrir to feed
nouveau, nouvelle new
nouvelle *f.* news
    donner de ses —s let one hear from
      him
noyer to drown
nuage *m.* cloud
nuit *f.* night
    la — at night

O

objet *m.* object
obligation *f.* obligation
obligé, -e obliged, bound
obscurité *f.* darkness
observer to observe
obstacle *m.* obstacle
occupation *f.* occupation
occuper to occupy
octobre *m.* October
œil *m.* eye
œuf *m.* egg
œuvre *f.* work
offert *p. p.* of **offrir**
officier *m.* officer
offrir to offer
oie *f.* goose
oignon *m.* onion
oiseau *m.* bird
oiseau-lyre *m.* lyre bird
ombre *f.* shadow
omelette *f.* omelet
on (or **l'on**) one, people, they
ongle *m.* fingernail

onze eleven
onzième eleventh
opération *f.* operation, transaction
opinion *f.* opinion
opposé, -e opposite
opposer to oppose, contrast
or now (*conj.*, often untranslatable)
orage *m.* storm
orangeade *f.* orangeade
ordinaire ordinary
ordinal, -e ordinal
ordonner to order, command, direct
ordre *m.* order, command
originalité *f.* originality
origine *f.* origin
orthographe *f.* spelling
orthographique orthographical
oser to dare
ou or
où where, when, at which, in which
    d'— from where, whence
ouate *f.* wadding, absorbent cotton
oublier to forget
oui yes
outil *m.* tool
ouvert, -e open
ouvrage *m.* work
ouvre-boîte *m.* can opener
ouvrier, -ière working-man's (*adj.*)
ouvrir to open

P

paillasson *m.* (door)mat
paille *f.* straw
    en — of straw
    homme de — dummy
paisible peaceful
palais *m.* palace
panique *f.* panic
    pris de — panic-stricken
par by, through
    deux fois — semaine twice a week
paradis *m.* paradise
paraître to seem
parc *m.* park
parce que because
pardon *m.* pardon
pareil, pareille alike, similar, such
    en pareil cas in such cases

ce n'est plus pareil it is no longer the same
parent *m.* relative
  parents *pl.* relatives, parents
parenthèse *f.* parenthesis
parfois sometimes
parlé, -e spoken
parler to speak
parmi among
parole *f.* word
parquet *m.* floor
participe *m.* participle
partie *f.* part
partir to leave, depart
partitif, -ive partitive
parvenir to succeed
passage *m.* passage, passing
passant *m.* passer-by
passé *m.* past
passé, -e past
passer to pass, spend
  se — to take place
passerelle *f.* gangway
passionnant, -e entrancing, thrilling
pâté *m.* pâté (meat paste)
patience *f.* patience
patienter to be patient, exercise patience
pauvre poor
pauvreté *f.* poverty
payer to pay
pays *m.* country, countryside
paysage *m.* scenery, landscape
pédagogique pedagogical
pédagogue *m.* pedagogue
peigne *m.* comb
peindre to paint
peine *f.* grief, trouble, pains
  prenez la — de [I] pray [I], please [I]
peiné, -e pained, grieved, distressed
peint, -e painted
peintre *m.* painter
pèlerinage *m.* pilgrimage
  en — on a pilgrimage
se pencher to lean
pendant for, during
  — que while
pendre to hang
pénible painful, distressing
pensée *f.* thought
penser (à) to think (of)
perception *f.* perception

perdre to lose
père *m.* father
période *f.* period
permettre to permit
  permettant de making it possible to
persister to persist
personnage *m.* character, person
personnalité *f.* personality
personne *f.* person
personnel, -elle personal
perte *f.* loss
  profits et —s profit and loss
pesant, -e heavy
petit, -e small, little
petits *m. pl.* the young (of animals)
peu (de) little, few, not very
  un — somewhat
peur *f.* fear
  avoir — to be afraid
  faire — à to frighten
peut, peuvent *pres.* of **pouvoir**
phénomène *m.* phenomenon
philosophe *m.* philosopher
phonétique *f.* phonetics
photographe *m.* photographer
phrase *f.* sentence
piano *m.* piano
pièce *f.* play
pied *m.* foot
  sur — afoot, standing
pierre *f.* stone
pinceau *m.* paint brush
pitre *m.* clown
  faire le — to clown (around)
place *f.* place, square
  à la — de instead of
placer to place
plafond *m.* ceiling
plage *f.* beach
plaie *f.* wound
se plaindre to complain
plaire to please
  s'il vous plaît please
plancher *m.* floor
planète *f.* planet
plat *m.* dish
plein, -e full
  en plein jour in broad daylight
pleurer to cry
pleuvoir to rain
  il pleuvait it was raining

pliant, -e folding
plu *p. p.* of **pleuvoir**
pluie *f.* rain
plume *f.* feather
plupart *f.* majority
  la — des [N] most [N]
pluriel *m.* plural
pluriel, -elle plural
plus (de) more
  de — moreover
  en — de in addition to
  ne [V] **—** no longer
plusieurs several
plus-que-parfait *m.* pluperfect
plutôt rather
  il parle — qu'il n'écrit he speaks
  rather than writes
poème *m.* poem
poésie *f.* poetry
poète *m.* poet
point *m.* point
  — de vue viewpoint
  — du jour daybreak
point: ne [V] **—** not (at all)
pois *m.* pea
  petit — green pea
poisson *m.* fish
police *f.* police force
  agent de — policeman
politique *f.* politics
pomme *f.* apple
ponctuation *f.* punctuation
populaire popular, vulgar, intended for
  or used by common people
porche *m.* porch
porcherie *f.* pigsty
port *m.* port
porte *f.* door, gate
porte-monnaie *m.* purse
porte-plume *m.* penholder
porter to wear, bear, carry
  — un jugement to form a judgment
portion *f.* portion, serving
poser to place
position *f.* position
possibilité *f.* possibility
possible possible
poste *f.* post (office)
  mettre à la — to mail
pot *m.* pot
pour for, (in order) to

pourboire *m.* tip
pourquoi why
pourraient *cond.* of **pouvoir**
pourrez *fut.* of **pouvoir**
pourrir to decay, rot
poursuivre to pursue, continue
pourtant however
pousser to push
poussière *f.* dust
  couleur de — dust-colored
pouvoir to be able, can, may
pré *m.* meadow
précaution *f.* precaution
précedent, -e preceding, previous
précéder to precede
se précipiter to rush up
préconçu, -e preconceived
prédiction *f.* prediction
prédire to predict, foretell
prédit *p. p.* of **prédire**
prédominant, -e predominant
premier, -ière first
prendre to take, buy
  — une décision to make a decision
  — le deuil to go into mourning
  à — ou à laisser take it or leave it
  prenez la peine de [V] pray [V],
  please [V]
préparer to prepare
préposition *f.* preposition
présage *m.* presage, omen
près de near, close to
présent *m.* present
présent, -e present
présentation *f.* presentation
présenter to present
presque nearly, almost
pressé, -e hurried, in a hurry
prête-nom *m.* figurehead, dummy, man
  of straw
prêter to lend, attribute
prie-dieu *m.* kneeling-chair, prayer stool
prier to beg, ask
  je vous prie please
primaire primary
principal, -e principal
printemps *m.* spring
pris *p. p.* of **prendre**
  — de panique panic-stricken
problème *m.* problem
procédé *m.* procedure, technique

professeur *m.* professor
profession *f.* profession
profit *m.* profit
  —s **et pertes** profit and loss
profiter to take advantage
profond, -e deep
progrès *m.* progress
progressif, -ive progressive, gradual
progression *f.* progression
prolongé, -e prolonged
promener to cast, project, walk, take
  for a walk
promenade *f.* walk
  faire une — to take a walk
pronom *m.* pronoun
pronominal, -e pronominal, reflexive
prononcer to pronounce
prononciation *f.* pronunciation
propos *m.*: **à — de** in connection with,
  apropos of
proposition *f.* clause
propre own, proper
  au sens — literally
protection *f.* protection
protéger to protect
proverbe *m.* proverb
provoquer to cause, arouse, provoke
pu *p. p.* of **pouvoir**
public *m.* public
  le grand — the general public
public, publique public
publier to publish
puis then, next
puisse, puissent *sj.* of **pouvoir**
punir to punish
pupitre *m.* desk

Q

quai *m.* quay, pier
qualifié, -e qualified, modified
quand when
  — même even so, even though,
  nevertheless
quantité *f.* quantity, amount
quarante forty
quartier *m.* neighborhood, district
quatorze fourteen
quatre four
quatre-vingts eighty

quatrième fourth
que whom, which, that, what, how, as
  ne [V] **—** only
  — de how much, how many
  n'avoir — faire de not to know what
  to do with, have no use for
quel, quelle what, which, what a, who
  à n'importe quel temps in any tense
quelconque any (whatever)
quelque some, any
quelque chose *m.* something
quelquefois sometimes
quelqu'un someone, somebody
querelle *f.* quarrel, dispute
qu'est-ce qui, qu'est-ce que what
question *f.* question
queue *f.* tail
qui who, whom
quinzaine *f.* (about) fifteen
quitter to leave
quoi what
  à — servent-ils ? What are they good
  for ? What purpose do they serve ?
  en — in what way
  n'importe — anything, no matter
  what
  — qu'il arrive whatever happens

R

raconter to tell, narrate
radio *f.* radio
rager to rage, be in a rage
raison *f.* reason
  avoir — to be right
  en — de on account of, owing to
rajeunissement *m.* rejuvenation
ramasser to pick up, gather
rang *m.* rank
rapidement rapidly
rapidité *f.* rapidity
rappeler to recall, remind
  se — to remember, recall, recollect
rapport *m.* connection, relation
  en — avec in keeping with
se rapporter to refer, relate, have
  reference
rapprochement *m.* juxtaposition
rapprocher to bring together, juxtapose
rare rare, uncommon

rarement rarely
se raser to shave
rassurer to reassure
   rassurez-vous set your mind at rest, feel reassured
se rattacher à to be connected with
ravi, -e enraptured, entranced, overjoyed
réaction *f.* reaction
réalité *f.* reality
recette *f.* recipe
recevoir to receive
rechercher to seek
réciproque reciprocal, mutual
récit *m.* story, account
réciter to recite
réclamer to call for
recommander to recommend
récompenser to recompense, reward
reconnaître to recognize, tell
reconsidérer to reconsider
reconstruction *f.* reconstruction
reçu *p. p.* of **recevoir**
recueil *m.* collection
redevenir to become again
redouter to fear, dread
réédition *f.* reissue, new edition
réellement really
se référer to refer
refermer to close again
réflexion *f.* reflection
   à la — on reflection, everything considered, when you come to think of it
regarder to look at
région *f.* region
règle *f.* rule
regret *m.* regret
regretter to regret
relatif, -ive relative
relever to pick out, point out
religieux, -euse religious
religion *f.* religion
relire to reread, read over
remarquable remarkable
remarquablement remarkably
remarque *f.* remark, observation
remarquer to remark, observe
se remémorer to remember
remettre to put back
   — en question to call in question again

remis *p. p.* of **remettre**
remplacer to substitute, replace
remuer to stir, move
rencontre *f.* meeting, encounter
rencontrer to meet
rendre to make
   se — to go
renforcer to reinforce
renoncer à to renounce, give up
renouveler to renew
rénovation *f.* renovation, renewal
rentrer to return, go home
renverser to overturn
réparer to repair
repartir to set out again, start again, leave again
repas *m.* meal
répéter to repeat
   se — to repeat to oneself
répétition *f.* repetition
répondre to answer
réponse *f.* answer
reposer to place again, put back down
   se — to rest
reprendre to take some more, take again, begin again, recover, regain, resume
représenter to represent
réputé, -e well-known
réservé, -e reserved, limited
résidence *f.* residence
responsable (de) responsible (for)
ressembler à to resemble
ressusciter to resuscitate, revive
restaurant *m.* restaurant
rester to stay, remain
   il reste there remains
restriction *f.* restriction
résultat *m.* result
retomber to fall again, fall back
retour *m.* return
s'en retourner to go back, return
retrouver to find again, rediscover
réunir to gather together
réussir à to succeed in
réussite *f.* success, successful result
se réveiller to awaken
révélateur, -trice revealing
revenir to return, come back, recur
rêver to dream
reviendront *fut.* of **revenir**

révolution *f.* revolution
revu, -e revised
revue *f.* review, magazine
rhum *m.* rum
  café arrosé — coffee laced with rum
riche rich
rien anything, nothing
  ne [V] — nothing, not anything
rincer to rinse
rire to laugh
  je leur ris au nez I laugh in their face
rire *m.* laughter
rite *m.* rite
rivière *f.* river, stream
robe *f.* dress
roi *m.* king
rond *m.* ring
ronronner to purr
rouge red
rouillé, -e rusty
rouler to drive, travel
royal, -e royal
rudoyer to bully, treat roughly
rue *f.* street
ruine *f.* ruin
ruisselant, -e dripping, streaming
rumeur *f.* rumor

S

sable *m.* sand
saboteur *m.* saboteur
saccager to ravage, despoil
sacrement *m.* rite, sacrament
sage good, gentle, wise, well-behaved
saison *f.* season
salade *f.* salad
sale dirty
salle *f.* room, hall, auditorium, theater
  — à manger dining room
sang *m.* blood
sangloter to sob
sans without
sardine *f.* sardine
satisfaisant, -e satisfactory, satisfying
sauce *f.* sauce, dressing
sauf except
sauraient *cond.* of **savoir**
sautiller to hop, skip
sauver to save
  se — to run away, escape, leave

savoir to know (how)
  ne sauraient . . . would not be able,
  could not
scénario *m.* scenario
scène *f.* scene, stage
scientifiquement scientifically
sciure *f.* sawdust
second, -e second
seconde *f.* second
secouer to shake
secrétaire *m.* or *f.* secretary
seize sixteen
séjour *m.* stay, sojourn
séjourner to stay, sojourn
sel *m.* salt
selon according to
  — le cas as the case may be
semaine *f.* week
semblant: faire — to pretend
sembler to seem, appear
sens *m.* sense, meaning
  au — propre literally
sensationnel, -elle sensational
sensible sensitive, responsive
sentiment *m.* sentiment, feeling
se sentir to feel
sept seven
septembre *m.* September
sera *fut.* of **être**
serait *cond.* of **être**
série *f.* series
sérieux, -euse serious
serrer to squeeze, hug
service *m.* service
serviette *f.* napkin
servir to serve, be used
  à quoi servent-ils ? What are they
  good for ? What purpose do they
  serve ?
seul, -e alone, only, single
seulement only
sévèrement severely
si if, so
siècle *m.* century
signe *m.* omen, sign, mark
signer to sign
significatif, -ive significant
signifier to mean
silence *m.* silence
silencieusement silently
simple simple
simplement simply, just, merely**

simplicité *f.* simplicity, plainness
sincère sincere
singulier *m.* singular
sinon if not, otherwise
situation *f.* situation
situer to situate, locate
six six
sixième sixth
social, -e social
société *f.* society
sociologue *m.* sociologist
soigneusement carefully
soin *m.* care
    avoir — to be careful, take care
soir *m.* evening
    hier — last night
soit (*pres. sj.* of être) say, that is
soixante sixty
soixante-dix seventy
soleil *m.* sun
solennel, -elle solemn
somme *f.* amount, sum
sommeil *m.* sleep
son *m.* sound
sonate *f.* sonata
songer to dream, think
sordide sordid, squalid
sorte *f.* kind, way, manner
sortir to go out, take out
soudain, -e sudden
soudaineté *f.* suddenness
souffrance *f.* suffering
souhaiter to wish
soulever to lift (up)
soupe *f.* soup
souriant, -e smiling
sourire to smile
sous under, beneath, below
se souvenir de to remember
souvent often
souverain *m.* sovereign
spécial, -e special
spécialement especially
spécialisé, -e specialized
spectacle *m.* spectacle, show
spontané, -e spontaneous
sport *m.* sport
stratégique strategic
structure *f.* structure
style *m.* style
stylistique stylistic
su *p. p.* of **savoir**

subir to undergo
subjonctif *m.* subjunctive
subordonné, -e subordinate
substituer to substitute
substitution *f.* substitution
succès *m.* success
succession *f.* inheritance
successivement successively, in succession, one after another
succinct, -e succinct
succursale *f.* branch (store)
sucre *m.* sugar
sud *m.* south, southern part
suer to sweat
suffire to be enough, suffice
suggérer to suggest
suinter to ooze, seep
suivant, -e following
suivre to follow
sujet *m.* subject
superstition *f.* superstition
sur on, upon, about
sûr, -e sure
surprendre to surprise
surprise *f.* surprise
surréaliste *m.* Surrealist
sursauter to start, give a jump
surtout especially, above all
suspension *f.* hanging lamp, chandelier
symboliser to symbolize
symétrie *f.* symmetry

T

tabac *m.* tobacco
tableau *m.* painting, picture
talent *m.* talent
    de — talented
tant (de) so much, so many, to such a degree
taper: — à la machine to type
taquiner to tease
tard late
tartine *f.* slice of bread (with jam or butter)
tasse *f.* cup
technique *f.* technique
tel, telle such
    telle qu'elle est as is
téléphone *m.* telephone, phone call
téléphoner to telephone

téléphonique telephone (*adj.*)
tellement so much, in such a way, to such a degree
temporel, -elle temporal
temps *m.* time, tense, weather
  à n'importe quel — in any tense
  en même — at the same time
tenir to hold together
  me — compagnie to bear me company
tennis *m.* tennis
tentative *f.* attempt
tenter to attempt
tenue *f.* dress, attire
terme *m.* term
terminer to finish
  se — to end
terre *f.* earth, ground
terrible terrible, frightful
terrifier to terrify
tête *f.* head, face, appearance
  se payer la — to make fun
  — de veau calf's head
texte *m.* text
thé *m.* tea
théâtral, -e theatrical
thème *m.* theme
tire-bouchon *m.* corkscrew
tirer to draw
tiret *m.* dash
titre *m.* title
  à — gracieux gratis, free of charge
tituber to totter, stagger
toile *f.* canvas
tombe *f.* tomb, grave
tomber to fall
ton *m.* tone
tonique tonic, stressed
  accent — stress
torréfier to roast
toucher to touch
  — à to interfere with, meddle with
toujours always, still
tour *m.* turn
tourner to stir, turn, revolve
tournoi *m.* tournament
Toussaint *f.* All Saints' Day (November 1)
tout, toute, tous, toutes all, every, complete
  tous les jours every day

tout le monde everybody
  de toute façon in any case
tout *adv.* quite, entirely, all
  — de même really!, come now!
  — en (+ *ps. p.*) while
tracer to trace
traduction *f.* translation
tragédie *f.* tragedy
tragique tragic
train *m.*: **être en — de faire quelque chose** to be engaged in (busy) doing something
trait *m.* trait
  — d'union hyphen
traiter to treat of, deal with
trancher to slit, cut
tranquille tranquil, quiet
tranquillement tranquilly, quietly
tranquillité *f.* tranquillity
transformation *f.* transformation
travail *m.* work
travailler to work
traverser to cross
trentaine *f.* (about) thirty
trente thirty
très very
trinquer to clink glasses
triste sad
tristesse *f.* sadness
trois three
troisième third
se tromper to be mistaken
trompette *f.* trumpet
troupe *f.* troop, company
trouver to find, think
  se — to be, be found, be situated
tuer to kill
tue-tête: à — at the top of one's voice
Turquie *f.* Turkey
tutoiement *m.* use of the familiar *tu* and *toi*
type *m.* type, kind

U

ultime ultimate, last
un, une one, a
  un à un one by one, one after the other
  ne faire ni une ni deux to waste no time

unième first (used only in compounds)
uniquement only
unité *f.* unit
usage *m.* use
utile useful
utilisation *f.* use
utiliser to use

V

vacances *f. pl.* holidays, vacation
vagabond *m.* vagabond, vagrant, tramp
vague vague, indefinite
vain, -e vain
vandale *m.* vandal
vanille *f.* vanilla
vaquer à to be occupied with, concern
  oneself with
variable variable, changing
variante *f.* variant
variation *f.* variation
varier to vary
veau *m.* veal
  tête de — calf's head
vécu *p. p.* of **vivre**
véhémence *f.* vehemence
veiller to watch
veilleuse *f.* night light
se venger to take one's revenge
venir to come
  — de [I] to have just [*p. p.*]
  venir [I] (often untranslatable)
vent *m.* wind
venu *p. p.* of **venir**
verbal, -e verbal
verbe *m.* verb
véritable true, real
vérité *f.* truth
vernir to varnish, polish, shine
verrait *cond.* of **voir**
verre *m.* glass
verrez *fut.* of **voir**
verrière *f.* glass awning
verrouillé, -e bolted, locked
vers *m.* verse
vers toward, to
verser to pour, shed
vert, -e green
verve *f.* verve
vêtu, -e dressed

viande *f.* meat
vice-président *m.* vice-president
vie *f.* life, livelihood
viendra *fut.* of **venir**
vieux, vieille old
vilain, -e nasty, unpleasant
  faire vilain to be nasty (weather)
village *m.* village
ville *f.* town, city
vin *m.* wine
vinaigre *m.* vinegar
vinaigrette *f.* vinegar dressing
  à la — with oil and vinegar
vingt twenty
vingtaine *f.* (about) twenty, a score
vingtième twentieth
violence *f.* violence
visage *m.* face
  il a le — souriant his face is smiling
vision *f.* vision
visiter to visit
visiteur *m.* visitor
visuel, -elle visual
vite quickly
vitesse *f.* speed
vitre *f.* window pane
vitrine *f.* store window
vivant *m.* living person
  les —s the living
vivant, -e alive, living
vivre to live
vocabulaire *m.* vocabulary
voici here is, here are
voilà there is, there are
  —! (in restaurant) Coming! Here I
  am! (often untranslatable)
  — trois jours que ... It's been three
  days since ..., ... for three days
voir to see
voisin *m.*, **voisine** *f.* neighbor
voiture *f.* car
voix *f.* voice
  à haute — aloud
vol *m.* theft
volatiliser to volatilize
voler to fly, steal
voleter to flutter, flit
voudrais *cond.* of **vouloir**
vouloir to want, wish
  en — à quelqu'un to bear someone
  ill will, a grudge

voulu *p. p.* of **vouloir**
voyage *m.* voyage, journey, trip
  aller en — to go on (take) a trip
voyager to travel
voyageur *m.* traveler
voyelle *f.* vowel
vrai, -e true
vraiment really, truly
vu *p. p.* of **voir**
vue *f.* view
  point de — viewpoint
vulgaire vulgar

W

wagon-lit *m.* sleeper, sleeping car
wagon-restaurant *m.* dining car

Y

y there
  il — a there is, there are
    il — a trois jours que ... It's been
    three days since ..., ... for three
    days
  pendant que vous — êtes while you
  are about it
  vous n'— êtes pas you don't understand
yeux (*pl.* of **œil**) eyes

Z

zéro *m.* zero

index de phonèmes

sons voyelles

[i]   lit, ici, Paris 11, 104

[e]   été, chez, parler, et, parlai, les 11, 24

[ɛ]   c'est, parlais, père, mer, terre 24, 35

[a]   tabac, la, par, bal, femme, Canada, ma, mal 35, 48

[ɑ]   pâle, bas, las, mât, mâle 48, 62

[ɔ]   orange, colle, robe, pomme 62

[o]   beau, chevaux, pot, sceau, 62, 76

[u]   vous, roue, houx, loup 76

[ɛ̃]   pain, fin, faim, vingt 115, 130

[õ]   on, long, bonjour 144

[ɑ̃]   enfant, en, dans, France 130, 144

[œ̃]   un, chacun 115

[y]   rue, vu, plus, eu 104

[œ]   heure, cœur, professeur 90

[ɸ]   deux, œufs, bleu, cheveux 90

[ə]   le, je, me, que, besoin, brusquement *voir p.* 90

semi-voyelles

[j]   hier, prière, travail, pierre 156

[w]   ouate, roi, oui, loi 170

[ɥ]   huit, pluie, depuis, cuisine 170

consonnes

[p]   père, typique, cap 212

[t]   thème, attaque, sept 212

[k]   car, accord, cinq 212

[b]   bateau, d'abord, jambe 212

[d]   dans, Adam, promenade 212

[g]   garçon, onguent, grégaire 212

[f]   force, affaire, fief 226

[v]   ville, avoir, sève 226

[ʃ]   chat, achat, fraîche 226

[s]   seul, assis, service 226

[z]   zèle, asile, fraise 226

[ʒ]   journal, agir, rage 226

[m]   mère, amour, même 240

[n]   nez, année, âne 240

[ɲ]   magnifique, campagne 240

[l]   lune, aller, foule 198

[r]   roux, arriver, alors 182

index

AMEN!
HALLELUJAH!
INSIGHTS INTO THE BOOK OF REVELATION

DALE WELLS

WESTBOW
PRESS®
A DIVISION OF THOMAS NELSON
& ZONDERVAN

NET Bible® copyright ©1996-2006 by Biblical Studies Press,
L.L.C. http://netbible.com All rights reserved

WestBow Press books may be ordered through booksellers or by contacting:

WestBow Press
A Division of Thomas Nelson & Zondervan
1663 Liberty Drive
Bloomington, IN 47403
www.westbowpress.com
1 (866) 928-1240

ISBN: 978-1-5127-6181-8 (sc)
ISBN: 978-1-5127-6182-5 (hc)
ISBN: 978-1-5127-6180-1 (e)

Library of Congress Control Number: 2016917763

Print information available on the last page.

WestBow Press rev. date: 10/28/2016

The twenty-four elders and the four living creatures threw themselves to the ground and worshiped God, who was seated on the throne, saying: "Amen! Hallelujah!
—Revelation 19:4

To my father, Weldon Wells, who instilled in me a love of preaching and teaching; Jack Miller and Dean Wiseman, who taught me to never stop thinking; Mike McCoy, who urged me to write what I was thinking, and who provided valuable insights as I wrote; and my wife, Mary, without whose love, support, and encouragement this book would never have been completed.

There is no greater drama in human record than the sight of a few Christians, scorned or oppressed by a succession of emperors, bearing all trials with a fierce tenacity, multiplying quietly, building order while their enemies generated chaos, fighting the sword with the word, brutality with hope, and at last defeating the strongest state that history has known. Caesar and Christ had met in the arena, and Christ had won.

—Will Durant, from *The Story of Civilization*

Contents

The Second Seven: Seven Seals (4:1–7:17)

The Third Seven : Seven Trumpets (8:1–11:19)

The Fourth Seven : Seven Visions of the Eternal Struggle (12:1–14:20)

Foreword

For years, every time I read Revelation, or heard someone teach on it, I came away with more questions than answers. Revelation's idioms and symbols seemed to belong to another era—a time I couldn't understand. In my experience, Revelation was a book many Christians argued about and few could agree on.

My view of Revelation at the time is best summed up in this little poem I wrote for this foreword.

Who's the antichrist? Many opined.

When's the return? I often whined.

Kingdoms, battles, and wars, Oh, My!

Understand it now, when written to them, why try?

Unsatisfactory opinions about Babylon and the identity of the antichrist dotted the landscape of my Christian world. News headlines sparked more books. Each new Christian book on Revelation convinced me I needed to focus on other parts of scripture, yet I had this nagging feeling the last book of the Bible was an indispensable part of the whole of scripture.

Things were about to change, and change they did.

My good friend and former colleague Dale Wells taught Revelation for a good number of weeks at his church. It was as if the Lord opened my mind to understand scripture just as Jesus did with the apostles. Dale energized and expanded my study of the Bible in ways I never imagined. Thanks to his teaching on Revelation, the many missing pieces of my scripture puzzle came together and questions began to be answered.

I suggested Dale put his teaching into written form so I could savor the richness of his perspectives rather than try to recall the breadth and depth of what I heard and saw on a screen. What you are about to read is my dream come true.

If you have any interest in the Bible, I highly recommend Dale's work on Revelation. You will not be disappointed.

—Hon. John M. McCoy (Ret.)

Preface

This book has been over fifty years in the making. To some it may seem a pitiful showing for so much time invested. But for me, it has been an exciting journey filled with all sorts of discoveries along the way.

It began in a little country church in Aquilla, Texas, where my dad taught and preached for almost thirty years. I sat in his classes on Revelation and listened to him teach the book as though it were a road map through history's timeline from the first century to the end of time.

Then, about forty years ago, I was introduced to Richard Rogers, who suggested that the best way to understand Revelation today was to first understand it in its first-century historical and cultural context. That made sense to me, and when I shared it with my dad, it made sense to him, too. Even though it was not consistent with the things he had previously believed and taught, he said he "would rather be right than consistent."

Start with the assumption that the last book of the Bible is exactly what it purports to be—a revelation, not a mystery. Add to that assumption the fact that it was written by a first-century author and that it was originally read by first-century readers who were expected to understand and obey the message it contained. Take into consideration their first-century frame of reference and the author's familiarity with the Old Testament. Wrap that all up in the popular "apocalyptic" literary genre of the first century, with its pervasive use of symbolism. That mixture of elements is what gave rise to Revelation. In order for twenty-first-century readers to properly understand it, we have to first look at it through first-century eyes. That is what this book attempts to do.

—Dale Wells

Prelude and Preliminaries

———◆———

THE CONTENT, CHARACTERISTICS, AND CONTEXT OF REVELATION (1:1–8)

Chapter 1

A BOOK TO BE UNDERSTOOD (1:1–3)

> The revelation of Jesus Christ, which God gave him to show his servants what must happen very soon. He made it clear by sending his angel to his servant John, who then testified to everything that he saw concerning the word of God and the testimony about Jesus Christ. Blessed is the one who reads the words of this prophecy aloud, and blessed are those who hear and obey the things written in it, because the time is near!
>
> —Revelation 1:1–3

God intended Revelation to be understood.

Does that surprise you?

It seems to many readers that there are almost as many interpretations of Revelation as there are commentaries on the book. There is so much confusion that many people have thrown their hands up in despair, convinced that the book is filled with deep, dark mysteries that we can never comprehend on this side of eternity.

The author of the book debunks that idea in his very first word. He affirms that the book is a "revelation." The Greek word *"apocalypsis"* means "an unveiling," "a revealing," or "a disclosure."

Its opposite is the Greek *"mysterion"* which is the basis for our word "mystery."

As you approach this book, keep in mind the essential difference between a "mystery," which is hidden, and a "revelation," which has been disclosed. The New Testament writers certainly knew the difference. Paul, for example, uses both words in one context in Ephesians 3:3–6, when he says that what had once been a "mystery" is now a "revelation": "... by revelation (*apocalypsis*) the divine secret (*mysterion*) was made known to me, as I wrote before briefly. When reading this, you will be able to understand my insight into this secret of Christ. Now this secret was not disclosed to people in former generations as it has now been revealed to his holy apostles and prophets by the Spirit, namely, that through the gospel the Gentiles are fellow heirs, fellow members of the body, and fellow partakers of the promise in Christ Jesus."

What was the mystery that had been revealed to Paul? It was one that his fellow Jews would never have suspected—that God intended all along for Gentiles to share with Jews in the salvation promised in the Messiah!

A mystery is not known until its meaning is revealed, but once revealed, it is no longer a mystery. In Revelation, a mystery was revealed so that it was no longer a mystery.

The mystery revealed in the book is called "the revelation of Jesus Christ" (Revelation 1:1). But what does that mean? It could mean "the revelation from Jesus Christ," or it could mean "the revelation about Jesus Christ." It appears to be both.

The book is clearly a message from Jesus. In Revelation 1:1 and 22:16, it is clear that Jesus has sent his angel to proclaim the message to John, so the message is clearly from Jesus.

But it is also a message *about* Jesus because he is central to the book's storyline. He is the High Priest who inspects the churches and reports his findings in Revelation 1–3; he is the Lamb of God who is worshipped in Revelation 5 and 6; he is the infant born to the woman and whose destiny is to rule over all the nations in Revelation 12; and he is the divine conqueror leading heaven's armies in Revelation 19.

The book begins with blessings on those who read, hear, and understand the prophecy. After John identifies the overall theme of the book, he pronounces a blessing on those who read, understand, and act on the message of the book. The word John uses in Revelation 1:3 is *"makarios"* (blessed). That is the same word Jesus used in setting out the beatitudes in Matthew 5:3–12.

Jesus gave the beatitudes to describe in broad strokes the character he expects of his followers. While none of us can claim to measure up fully to the character Jesus describes, none of us really thinks those character attributes are wholly unattainable.

Likewise, the blessings in Revelation are attached to things we can do. We may not do them perfectly, but we can do them to some degree.

"Blessed is the one who reads the words of this prophecy aloud, and blessed are those who hear and obey the things written in it, because the time is near!" (Revelation 1:3). The first blessing is pronounced on "the one who reads the words of this prophecy aloud." The Greek expression *"ho anaginooskon"* means "the one who reads aloud." This blessing suggests one person reading the message to an assembled congregation. But you don't have to know Greek to see that oral reading is in view because the very next blessing is pronounced on "those who hear." So it is clear that the reading John envisions is oral reading.

The second blessing is applied to "those who hear." The Greek word *"akouoo"* can mean "hear" or "understand," depending on how it is used in a particular context. When it is used with a noun in the genitive case, it means "hear." However, when it is used with a noun in the accusative case, as it is here, it means "understand."

There is a good example in the book of Acts that points out the difference between these two uses of *"akouoo"* as "hear" and as "understand." It is found in two accounts of Paul's experience on the road to Damascus.

In the King James Version, the two accounts seem contradictory.

> And the men ... hearing a voice ... (Acts 9:7 KJV)

> And they that were with me ... heard not the voice ...
> (Acts 22:9 KJV)

Which is it? Did they hear the voice, or did they not hear it? The answer is that both accounts are right. It is the translation in the King James Version that creates the apparent contradiction.

In Acts 9:7, "*akouoo*" is used with a noun in the genitive case, while in Acts 22:9, it is used with a noun in the accusative case. Modern translations clear up the apparent contradiction by properly applying the rules of Greek grammar.

> (Now the men who were traveling with him stood there speechless, because they heard the voice but saw no one.) (Acts 9:7)

> Those who were with me saw the light, but did not understand the voice of the one who was speaking to me. (Acts 22:9)

So when John wrote "Blessed are those who hear ..." in Revelation 1:3, which did he mean? In Revelation 1:3, "*akouoo*" is used with a noun in the accusative case, so it is clear he intended to convey that the message read orally would be understood by the hearers.

The third of John's blessings is decreed for "those who obey the things written in it." The Greek word "*terountes*" means "those who obey." It stands to reason that if God intended people to "understand" and "obey" the things written in Revelation, he must have written things that first-century readers could understand and they were capable of obeying. If that is the case, why is the book so misunderstood? The simple answer is that people misunderstand the book because of faulty assumptions they bring to the text, not because of what the text itself says.

Two Popular, but Flawed, Approaches to Revelation

Historicists

Some people view Revelation as a summary of history from the first century to the end of the world. They see the book as predicting an apostasy of the early church, the rise of the Catholic Church, the Protestant Reformation, and later developments in church history.

This view was predominant from the sixteenth through the nineteenth centuries. sixteenth-century proponents included Martin Luther, John Calvin, and other Protestant Reformers. Seventeenth-century adherents included Isaac Newton and Matthew Henry. Eighteenth-century teachers included Charles Wesley. Nineteenth-century writers included William Miller and Albert Barnes. Each found himself reapplying history to put himself in the last moments of time. For example, Charles Wesley predicted the end of the world would occur in 1794, and William Miller predicted it would occur on October 22, 1844.

Even in recent years, preachers have repeatedly calculated the date for the Second Coming of Christ, only to be proven wrong every time. For example, Harold Camping predicted the end of the world on September 6, 1994. Sixteen years later, he said it would occur on May 21, 2011. When that failed, he tried once more, promising it would happen on October 21, 2011. Since you're reading this text now, it is clear he was mistaken yet again.

Futurists

Many people believe Revelation deals almost exclusively with the end of time, which they inevitably place during their own lifetimes. This view did not have any popular support until the nineteenth century. It was first championed by John Nelson Darby, who is regarded as the Father of Dispensationalism. C. I. Scofield further popularized the notion of dispensationalism in the late nineteenth and early twentieth centuries.

This view really took hold after the creation of the modern state of Israel in May 1948. Since then, many writers have thought we are literally in the last moments of time. Popular modern writers who espouse this view include Hal Lindsey and Tim LaHaye. Hal Lindsey, for example, wrote, "The decade of the 1980s could very well be the last decade of history as we know it."[1] In the early 1990s, he stated that Christians should not plan to still be on earth by the year 2000.[2] Each author who has held this view has had to rewrite his view of Revelation repeatedly when time proved him wrong. Yet, in spite of the many failed predictions, this remains the most popular view of Revelation today. Something is fundamentally wrong with an approach that must rewrite its interpretation every time history disproves its predictions.

The Time Frame of Revelation Is Set by Two Phrases

"what must happen very soon"

> The revelation of Jesus Christ, which God gave him to show his servants what must happen very soon. (Revelation 1:1)

> Then the angel said to me, "… The Lord, the God of the spirits of the prophets, has sent his angel to show his servants what must happen soon." (Revelation 22:6)

The first expression is found at both ends of Revelation, like a pair of brackets encompassing everything in between. "What must happen very soon" is translated from the Greek *"dei genesthai en tachei,"* which means exactly that: "what must happen very soon." Some people assert that the expression "*en tachei*" means "certainly," but that is *certainly* not the case. The word "*tachos*" (which is the lexical form) means "quickly, at once, without delay," and it never meant anything else. Here are a few examples from the New Testament.

In Acts 22:17–18, Paul relates how the Lord told him in a vision to get out of Jerusalem because the people would not listen to him there. Without a doubt, in those circumstances, the Lord was not telling Paul that he should "certainly" get out of town, but rather that he should get out of town "quickly."

When Paul wrote to the Galatian Christians, he said he was astonished at how quickly they had abandoned the true gospel for a false one (Galatians 1:6–7). Paul was not saying they had "certainly" left the gospel; rather, he was amazed that they had abandoned it so "quickly."

Near the end of his life, Paul wanted Timothy to come see him in prison (2 Timothy 4:9). Time was of the essence. If Timothy delayed, Paul might already be dead. He wanted Timothy to come "quickly," while there was still time.

Here is one fundamental key to understanding Revelation. The first readers of Revelation understood that the fulfillment of its prophecy would be "soon"—from their point of view, not ours.

"the time is near!"

> Blessed is the one who reads the words of this prophecy aloud, and blessed are those who hear and obey the things written in it, because the time is near! (Revelation 1:3)

> Then he said to me, "Do not seal up the words of the prophecy contained in this book, because the time is near." (Revelation 22:10)

As with "what must happen very soon," so with "the time is

near." The expression stands like brackets at the beginning and end of the book, encompassing everything in between.

"The time is near" is translated from the Greek expression "*ho gar kairos engus*" (for the time is near). "*Engus*" literally means "in hand" or "within reach." This same expression, "the time is near," is used elsewhere by both Jesus and Paul.

According to Mark 1:14–15, Jesus's gospel began with the affirmation that "The time is fulfilled and the kingdom of God is near." In Romans 10:8–9, Paul affirms that "The word is near you, in your mouth and in your heart." And in Philippians 4:5, he insists that "The Lord is near!" No text uses "*engus*" in reference to something far away or remote. So those who were to "read," "hear," and "obey" the prophecy of Revelation in the first century would have expected nothing less than a fulfillment in the near future—from their perspective, not ours.

Revelation 1:1–3 gives three good reasons for interpreting Revelation in light of its time. First, it was a revelation to its readers, not a mystery. Second, it was intended to be read, understood, and acted on by those first-century Christians. Third, its time of fulfillment was "very soon" and "near" to their time.

Picture yourself as a Christian in Pergamum (Revelation 2:12–17). Antipas has been executed for his faith. You may be next! A messenger comes into the worship service carrying John's letter, and he wants to read it to the church. Do you want to know what to expect in two thousand years or so? No! You want to know if you're going to be alive tomorrow! And if not, what then? Was it worth it for Antipas to give up his life—or for you to give up yours—as a martyr? You don't care about twenty-first-century writers hypothesizing about some "end of the world" thousands of years in the future. You want to know what's going to happen to you in the short term, and what God is going to do about it.

Revelation is a message addressed to first-century Christians about those very concerns.

Amen!

Hallelujah!

Chapter 2

SYMBOLS AND OPPOSED PAIRS

We all know that all literature is not read alike. You don't read Elizabeth Barrett Browning the same way you read Edgar Allen Poe. You don't read William Shakespeare the same way you read Stephen King. You don't read a newspaper the same way you read poetry, or a biography the same way you read prophecy, or a history textbook the same way you read a math textbook. You read—and interpret—different genres of literature differently. Revelation is an example of the apocalyptic genre. It makes heavy use of symbols, and it uses imagery that was never intended to be taken literally. Yet the symbols and imagery was understood by the author and the original intended audience.

Imagine I were to tell you that yesterday, I had a vision in the form of a dream. I saw what looked like a living creature. It had four legs but it stood up on two, like a man. It had a prominent nose. It was brown with long ears. Then, in my dream, I saw another living creature. It looked like a bird without wings. It was blue and had two spindly legs with three toes on each foot. The first living creature sped toward the second creature, and at the last moment, the second living creature stepped aside and escaped certain death. Who are the two living creatures? Of course, they are Wile E. Coyote and the Road Runner.

You should read Revelation the same way you watch animation—making generous use of your imagination. Revelation includes mentions of a seven-headed dragon, a seven-headed beast, a lamb with seven horns and seven eyes, and a prostitute riding a monstrous beast, among other fantastic beings. Don't let the details distract you from the overall picture. Rather, allow the picture to grab your imagination, and you will understand the book!

Revelation uses symbols extensively. The meanings of some symbols are self-evident. Consider John's description of one like a son of man:

> And in the midst of the lampstands was one like a son of man. He was dressed in a robe extending down to his feet and he wore a wide golden belt around his chest. His head and hair were as white as wool, even as white as snow, and his eyes were like a fiery flame. His feet were like polished bronze refined in a furnace, and his voice was like the roar of many waters. He held seven stars in his right hand, and a sharp double-edged sword extended out of his mouth. His face shone like the sun shining at full strength. When I saw him I fell down at his feet as though I were dead, but he placed his right hand on me and said: "Do not be afraid! I am the first and the last, and the one who lives! I was dead, but look, now I am alive -- forever and ever -- and I hold the keys of death and of Hades! (Revelation 1:13–18)

This is clearly Jesus.

Consider the description of the Lion of the Tribe of Judah/ Lamb of God:

> Then one of the elders said to me, "Stop weeping! Look, the Lion of the tribe of Judah, the root of David, has conquered; thus he can open the scroll and its seven seals." Then I saw standing in the middle of the throne and of the four living creatures, and in

the middle of the elders, a Lamb that appeared to have been killed. He had seven horns and seven eyes, which are the seven spirits of God sent out into all the earth. (Revelation 5:5–6)

This has to be Jesus.

Consider the vignette about two witnesses:

These two have the power to close up the sky so that it does not rain during the time they are prophesying. They have power to turn the waters to blood and to strike the earth with every kind of plague whenever they want. (Revelation 11:6)

The men in the picture are clearly Elijah, who shut up the sky to keep it from raining, and Moses, who turned water to blood and inflicted plagues on Egypt.

A radiant woman gives birth to a unique child:

Then a great sign appeared in heaven: a woman clothed with the sun, and with the moon under her feet, and on her head was a crown of twelve stars. She was pregnant and was screaming in labor pains, struggling to give birth. Then another sign appeared in heaven: a huge red dragon that had seven heads and ten horns, and on its heads were seven diadem crowns. Now the dragon's tail swept away a third of the stars in heaven and hurled them to the earth. Then the dragon stood before the woman who was about to give birth, so that he might devour her child as soon as it was born. So the woman gave birth to a son, a male child, who is going to rule over all the nations with an iron rod. Her child was suddenly caught up to God and to his throne. (Revelation 12:1–5)

The woman is obviously Mary. The child is clearly Jesus.

A conquering king rides in on a white horse:

> Then I saw heaven opened and here came a white
> horse! The one riding it was called "Faithful" and
> "True," and with justice he judges and goes to war.
> His eyes are like a fiery flame and there are many
> diadem crowns on his head. He has a name written
> that no one knows except himself. He is dressed in
> clothing dipped in blood, and he is called the Word
> of God. The armies that are in heaven, dressed in
> white, clean, fine linen, were following him on white
> horses. From his mouth extends a sharp sword, so
> that with it he can strike the nations. He will rule
> them with an iron rod, and he stomps the winepress of
> the furious wrath of God, the All-Powerful. He has a
> name written on his clothing and on his thigh: "King
> of kings and Lord of lords." (Revelation 19:11–16)

This is clearly Jesus—the woman's son all grown up.

The text explains the less obvious symbols. What are the
stars and lampstands? The text gives us the answer.

> The mystery of the seven stars that you saw in my
> right hand and the seven golden lampstands is this:
> The seven stars are the angels of the seven churches
> and the seven lampstands are the seven churches.
> (Revelation 1:20)

Who is the dragon who tries to devour the child? Again, John
identifies him.

> So that huge dragon- the ancient serpent, the one
> called the devil and Satan, who deceives the whole
> world- was thrown down to the earth, and his angels
> along with him. (Revelation 12:9)

Who is the woman who rides the seven-headed beast? Inspiration identifies her.

> As for the woman you saw, she is the great city that has sovereignty over the kings of the earth. (Revelation 17:18)

> (This requires a mind that has wisdom.) The seven heads are seven mountains the woman sits on. They are also seven kings: five have fallen; one is, and the other has not yet come, but whenever he does come, he must remain for only a brief time. The beast that was, and is not, is himself an eighth king and yet is one of the seven, and is going to destruction. (Revelation 17:9–11)

Rome sat on seven hills and ruled the world—the woman is the city of Rome.

The woman is riding the sea beast that was introduced in Revelation 13. What is the sea beast?

> Then I saw a beast coming up out of the sea. It had ten horns and seven heads, and on its horns were ten diadem crowns, and on its heads a blasphemous name. Now the beast that I saw was like a leopard, but its feet were like a bear's, and its mouth was like a lion's mouth. The dragon gave the beast his power, his throne, and great authority to rule. One of the beast's heads appeared to have been killed, but the lethal wound had been healed. And the whole world followed the beast in amazement; they worshiped the dragon because he had given ruling authority to the beast, and they worshiped the beast too, saying: "Who is like the beast?" and "Who is able to make war against him?" The beast was given a mouth speaking proud words and blasphemies, and he was permitted to exercise ruling authority for forty-two months. So

the beast opened his mouth to blaspheme against
God -- to blaspheme both his name and his dwelling
place, that is, those who dwell in heaven. The beast
was permitted to go to war against the saints and
conquer them. He was given ruling authority over
every tribe, people, language, and nation, and all
those who live on the earth will worship the beast,
everyone whose name has not been written since the
foundation of the world in the book of life belonging
to the Lamb who was killed. (Revelation 13:1–8)

The woman is Rome. Rome rides atop the sea beast, which is
the Roman Empire. Revelation 13:2 goes a step further and tells
the reader that the Roman Empire receives its power from the
dragon, Satan, himself.

What is the earth beast?

Then I saw another beast coming up from the earth.
He had two horns like a lamb, but was speaking
like a dragon. He exercised all the ruling authority
of the first beast on his behalf, and made the earth
and those who inhabit it worship the first beast,
the one whose lethal wound had been healed. He
performed momentous signs, even making fire come
down from heaven in front of people and, by the signs
he was permitted to perform on behalf of the beast,
he deceived those who live on the earth. He told those
who live on the earth to make an image to the beast
who had been wounded by the sword, but still lived.
The second beast was empowered to give life to the
image of the first beast so that it could speak, and
could cause all those who did not worship the image of
the beast to be killed. He also caused everyone (small
and great, rich and poor, free and slave) to obtain a
mark on their right hand or on their forehead. Thus
no one was allowed to buy or sell things unless he
bore the mark of the beast -- that is, his name or his

number. This calls for wisdom: Let the one who has
insight calculate the beast's number, for it is man's
number, and his number is 666. (Revelation 13:11–18)

It looks like a lamb—a religious figure—but it speaks with
the dragon's voice. We know the dragon is Satan.

The earth beast forces people to worship the sea beast (the
Roman Empire and its kings) on pain of death. The earth beast
is also called the false prophet.

> Now the beast was seized, and along with him the false
> prophet who had performed the signs on his behalf --
> signs by which he deceived those who had received
> the mark of the beast and those who worshiped his
> image. Both of them were thrown alive into the lake
> of fire burning with sulfur. (Revelation 19:20)

The message is that Satan uses religion to promote his agenda.
The Roman Empire did exactly that. Emperor cults (*concilia*)
enforced worship of the emperors beginning near the end of the
first century.

The book of revelation is a puzzle to solve, not a mystery to
ignore. You start with what you know: the lamb is Jesus, the
dragon is Satan, the sea beast is the Roman Empire, the heads
are the emperors of Rome, the earth beast is the emperor cult,
and the wicked woman is the city of Rome. Once you get those
pieces in place, the picture starts to come together.

Here is Revelation for dummies: God rules! Jesus is Lord!
We win!

Opposed pairs of symbols are a feature of the book of revelation.
There are two lambs that stand opposed to one another in the
book. There is the Lamb of God (Revelation 5:6), and there is the
lamb that speaks with the voice of the dragon (Revelation 13:11).
Likewise, there are two women who are polar opposites. There
is the prostitute, who is judged (Revelation 19:1–2), and there is
the bride of the Lamb (Revelation 19:7). There are two who sit on

opposing thrones and claim absolute dominion. There is God, who sits on his throne (Revelation 4:2), and there is the beast, who sits on the dragon's throne (Revelation 13:2). The kings of the earth (Revelation 17:12) oppose the King of Kings (Revelation 19:16). And every person in Revelation wears a mark of ownership. Some wear the seal of God (Revelation 7:3), while others wear the mark of the beast (Revelation 13:16–17).

There are other pairs of opposites, but these should give you the idea. For every major good image, there is an evil counterpart. Keep that in mind as you study Revelation.

Amen!

Hallelujah!

Chapter 3

MAJOR SYMBOLIC NUMBERS AND THEIR OPPOSITES

As with the other images in Revelation, so with the numbers. The numbers were never intended to be taken literally, so we should not look for mathematical precision. Rather, the numbers stand as symbols of some very important concepts that permeate Revelation. In particular, two numbers, seven and twelve, stand out as symbols of key concepts. But two other numbers, three and one-half and six, are their sinister opposites in the book.

The number seven symbolizes God accomplishing his purpose. Seven occurs more often in Revelation than in the rest of the New Testament, and it occurs more often in Revelation than in any Old Testament book. As in Genesis 2:1–3, seven symbolizes God finishing his work: "The heavens and the earth were completed with everything that was in them. By the seventh day God finished the work that he had been doing, and he ceased on the seventh day all the work that he had been doing. God blessed the seventh day and made it holy because on it he ceased all the work that he had been doing in creation" (Genesis 2:1–3).

Prominent Sevens in Revelation

The first three chapters of Revelation develop seven letters to seven churches in seven cities in Asia Minor (Revelation 1:4, 11,

20). Even that set of sevens begins with the author's vision of "one like a son of man" walking among seven lampstands (1:12–13) holding seven stars (1:16).

In chapter 4, John sees seven torches before God's throne (4:5). These are the seven spirits who were the source of grace and peace at the very beginning of the message (1:4). In Revelation 5, a seven-horned, seven-eyed lamb opens a seven-sealed scroll (5:1–6).

Later in the book, God's judgments are announced by seven angels with seven trumpets (8:2–6). Seven thunders sound in chapter 10, but their message is not recorded (10:3–4).

At the midpoint of the book, there is a seven-headed dragon that wears seven diadems (12:3). There is also a seven-headed beast that comes up out of the sea (13:1).

Further into the book, a woman is seen riding a seven-headed beast (17:3). The seven heads correspond to seven mountains and seven kings (17:9). In chapter 15, seven angels administer God's judgments in the form of seven plagues (15:1, 6–8). These plagues are poured out on the earth from seven bowls containing God's wrath (16:1).

Those are some of the more prominent sevens in the book.

But wait; there's more!

Less Obvious Sevens in Revelation

Revelation includes seven recorded blessings (1:3; 14:13; 16:15; 19:9; 20:6; 22:7, 14). And like the Gospel of John, it contains seven "I am" sayings (1:8, 17, 18; 2:23; 21:6; 22:13, 16).

There are even more sevens that are easy to overlook. Seven kinds of people try to hide from God's wrath in Revelation 6:15–17. There are seven kinds of homage paid to the Lamb in Revelation 5:12. There are seven aspects of heaven's worship around God's throne in Revelation 7:11–12.

Whenever you see a seven in Revelation, you can rest assured that God is at work and that he *will* accomplish his purpose!

Three and One-Half

Three and one-half symbolizes Satan's attempt to thwart God's purpose. Three and one-half is the opposite of seven in Revelation. Seven is a symbol of God accomplishing his purpose. Three and one-half symbolizes a time of severe opposition by God's enemy. But as we shall see, it is also a time when God is still in control and when he continues to provide for his people.

The main use of this number is found in the phrase "three-and-one-half years." That same time frame is also described as "a time, times, and half-a-time," "forty-two months," and "1,260 days." Each of those descriptions views the same time frame from a different perspective.

Years ago I attended a rather unusual dinner theater performance. It was a murder mystery staged in a large multistory mansion, not on an ordinary stage. Action took place in the various rooms of the mansion simultaneously, and each person in attendance was assigned to follow one character. Your character might interact with one character in one room, run upstairs to interact with a second, and then run down the hall to interact with a third. Occasionally your character might end up in a room alone, engaging in a soliloquy. The result was that each observer saw the story from a different character's point of view. There was action that an observer might not see because his or her character was not involved. And even the action that he or she did see was flavored by the context of his or her other experiences in the play.

In a way, that is how these descriptions play out in Revelation. Each description looks at the scene from a different perspective.

But first we need to see the Old Testament background that shows that "three-and-one-half years" depicts a time of opposition to God. In Daniel 7, the prophet had a vision of four beasts rising out of the sea. The fourth beast was the sinister one. He would oppress God's people for "a time, times, and half a time" (Daniel 7:25). In the vision, this works out to three and one-half years, as follows: One year ("a time") plus two years ("times") plus six months ("half a time").

Three and one-half years was the length of time of oppression and provision for the prophet Elijah. It was the length of the drought during the reign of Ahab (James 5:17). But it was also the time when God made special provision for Elijah's survival (1 Kings 17:3–6).

As stated above, "three-and-one-half years" is also referred to in terms of "forty-two months" and "1,260 days." The composite picture comes from the process of sieges in the ancient world. In the first century, the time period contemporary with Revelation, invading armies measured sieges in terms of months. The Roman army would surround a city, cutting off its water and supplies. Then they would build siege works against the city walls. The outcome for a besieged city was certain. It would either be starved into surrender or it would ultimately be overrun. That is what happened during the Jewish-Roman War. Hostilities began in AD 66. Jerusalem fell forty-two months later, in AD 70.

"Three-and-one-half years" represents a time when Satan tries to stop God's work but God is still in control. Revelation 11 is a great example of this very thing. In the vision, Gentiles besiege God's city for forty-two months (11:1–2). During that same time, God's witnesses preach for 1,260 days (11:3). The beast kills God's witnesses, but after three and one-half days, God raises them from the dead and snatches them up to heaven, delivering them out of the enemy's reach (11:11–12). The point is that while Satan has the power of death, God has the power of life!

Invaders measure a siege in months because time is not critical to them. But inside the walls of the besieged city, survival is a day-by-day struggle. So protection and provision are expressed in days, not months. Who can think about that without remembering the prayer Jesus taught his disciples: "Give us today our daily bread" (Matthew 6:11).

From the perspective of the army, the city is trampled for forty-two months, but from the perspective of the witnesses in the city, God provides for them day by day for 1,260 days. This symbolism is also seen in Revelation 12, in the vision of the radiant woman and the dragon. In that chapter, "three-and-one-half years" is expressed as "1,260 days" and as "a time, times, and half a time." God cares for the woman for 1,260 days (12:6). During that same time, Satan tries to get at her for "a time, times, and half a time" (12:13–14). But Satan can't get to her, because God is protecting her. So, from the perspective of people who are suffering oppression, this time is expressed as "1,260 days." From the perspective of the oppressors, it is expressed as "forty-two months." But from God's heavenly perspective, it is just another "three-and-one-half years" that depicts Satan's never-ending effort to thwart God's work.

The good news for the reader of Revelation is that the outcome is always the same—God wins! God's seven always trumps Satan's "three-and-one-half."

Twelve

Twelve and its multiples (e.g., twenty-four, twelve thousand, and one hundred forty-four thousand) symbolize God's people. These are the second-most-prominent numbers in Revelation. They always identify the people who belong to God.

Twenty-four elders sit on thrones surrounding God's throne. "In a circle around the throne were twenty-four other thrones, and seated on those thrones were twenty-four elders ..." (Revelation 4:4). These elders are likely God's people under two covenants. The number twenty-four symbolizes both the twelve patriarchs of the Old Testament and the twelve apostles of the New Testament.

One hundred forty-four thousand people are marked with God's seal of approval.

> Now I heard the number of those who were marked
> with the seal, one hundred and forty-four thousand,
> sealed from all the tribes of the people of Israel: From

the tribe of Judah, twelve thousand were sealed, from the tribe of Reuben, twelve thousand, from the tribe of Gad, twelve thousand, from the tribe of Asher, twelve thousand, from the tribe of Naphtali, twelve thousand, from the tribe of Manasseh, twelve thousand, from the tribe of Simeon, twelve thousand, from the tribe of Levi, twelve thousand, from the tribe of Issachar, twelve thousand, from the tribe of Zebulun, twelve thousand, from the tribe of Joseph, twelve thousand, from the tribe of Benjamin, twelve thousand were sealed. (Revelation 7:4–8)

The number is not intended to be taken literally.

Excursus: The Symbolism of Numbers in the Bible

This is a convenient place for us to consider the symbolism of numbers in the Bible. For example, Jacob had twelve sons and Israel had twelve tribal land divisions, but they were not identical. Israel actually had thirteen tribes! It worked this way.

Jacob adopted Joseph's two sons in the place of their father (Genesis 48:5). So, instead of a single tribe of Joseph, Joseph's descendants created two tribes: Ephraim and Manasseh.

But when Israel arrived in the Promised Land, they awarded only twelve tribal land divisions. The Levites did not get a tribal land division. Rather, they were awarded towns and lands distributed within the other tribal territories (Numbers 35:2).

As another example, Jesus had twelve apostles, but in reality, he had thirteen. Of course, we are all aware that Judas was a traitor and his place was taken by Matthias (Acts 1:26). After that, God added Paul to make thirteen (Galatians 1:1; 2:7–9). Yet we always speak of the twelve apostles and the twelve tribes.

So how does Revelation come up with one hundred forty-four thousand if there were actually thirteen tribes? A look at the list of tribes in Revelation 7 shows that John gets to that number by leaving out the tribe of Dan.

The point of the text—that twelve thousand are redeemed out of each of the twelve tribes—is not that no one is redeemed from Dan, but that all of God's people are accounted for. The number is not intended to be literal. We shouldn't judge the Biblical writers for using numbers figuratively and not literally. To apocalyptic writers, numbers were symbols. They were not interested in mathematical accuracy but in the concepts represented by their symbolic use of numbers.

Here is another example from Jesus's genealogy, as recorded by Matthew: "So all the generations from Abraham to David are fourteen generations, and from David to the deportation to Babylon, fourteen generations, and from the deportation to Babylon to Christ, fourteen generations" (Matthew 1:17).

Matthew says there are three groups of fourteen generations in Jesus's genealogy, but the numbers don't add up. In the first group, you have to count both Abraham and David to get fourteen generations. In other words, you count the first and last names inclusively. The second group actually has sixteen names, so you have to exclude both the first and last names, David and Jeconiah, in order to reach fourteen. However, in the third group, you must include both the first and last names, Jeconiah and Jesus, in order to reach fourteen. So the third group must be counted inclusively, like the first group, but the second group must be counted differently than the first and third groups, in order to reach the threefold repetition of "fourteen generations."

But there are other problems with the accuracy of Matthew's genealogy. First, Matthew 1:8 says Joram was the father of Uzziah. This results in the omission of three names: Ahaziah, Joash, and Amaziah. The complete royal line at this point was Joram, Ahaziah, Joash, Amaziah, and Uzziah. Second, Matthew dropped Jehoiakim from the genealogy. Matthew 1:11 says Josiah was the father of Jeconiah. But the complete royal line at this point was Josiah, then Jehoiakim, who was replaced by Jehoiachin (aka Jeconiah). Third, Matthew 1:12 says Zerubbabel was Shealtiel's son. In reality, Zerubbabel was Shealtiel's nephew, the son of Shealtiel's brother, Pedaiah (1 Chronicles 3:19).

Why would Matthew make these changes and deletions? Because to ancient writers, numbers were not a matter of mathematical accuracy; rather, they represented important concepts.

In Matthew 1, the key is the name of David. Ancient alphabets were not like our modern alphabets. Hebrew and Greek alphabets consisted of characters that served dual purposes as letters and numerals. Thus *a* could be used as the numeral *1*, *b* could be used as the numeral *2*, etc. Ancient writers would sometimes encode words using a practice called gematria (Greek: *isopsephia*). They would take a name, assign the proper numerical values to each letter in that name, and then add up the values. The sum was the number of the name. Then they would use the sum to represent the name. By using the number instead of the name, initiates would know of whom they were speaking, while others would not. This is important to understanding the significance of the number 666 in Revelation 13:18. It is a gematria.

Archaeologists have discovered secular examples of gematria dating back to the first century. For example, archaeologists have discovered the following graffito on the walls of Pompeii's ruins: "I love her whose number is 545." Clearly the couple would know whom he was writing about. But no one else would, because any of a number of names would yield the gematrical sum. Thus 545 could be the number of any of several names.

A Roman inscription has been discovered that describes a man named Gaius (*Gaios*) as both holy (*hagios*) and good (*agathos*). Each of those three words has the same gematrical sum, calculated as follows:

Gaios = 3 + 1 + 10 + 70 + 200 = 284
(Ha)gios = 1 + 3 + 10 + 70 + 200 = 284
Aga(th)os =1 + 3 + 1 + 9 + 70 + 200 = 284

The three words are gematrically interchangeable, because 284 is the number of each of the words.

Gematria is the key to understanding the genealogy in Matthew 1. The name "David" consisted of three Hebrew letters—equivalent to our "DVD." *D* was the fourth letter of the Hebrew alphabet and *V* was the sixth letter. Ancient Hebrew had no vowels. The number of the name "David" is 14, calculated as follows:

D+V+D = 4+6+4 = 14

So Matthew lists fourteen names from Abraham to David, fourteen Davidic kings, and fourteen generations from the Davidic dynasty to Jesus. He does this because he wants the reader to see Jesus as the true Son of David.

Revelation follows an accepted practice of using numbers as symbols to represent concepts. In Revelation 12:1, the radiant woman wears a crown of twelve stars. Earlier we saw this woman as an idealized picture of Mary. But what about the twelve stars? Following the symbolism of numbers, it is easy to see that the twelve stars represent God's people—her crowning glory.

In Revelation 21:10–17, the number twelve dominates the description of the holy city, because this is the city where God's people live. It is a cube of twelve thousand stadia on each side, with twelve gates, secured by twelve angels, having walls 144 cubits thick. John's point is that the city has plenty of access (gates), plenty of room (dimensions), plenty of security (angels), and plenty of protection (walls).

The *New American Standard Bible* misses the point entirely. It calculates the dimensions literally and gives the length of each side as fifteen hundred miles. A cube that is fifteen hundred miles on each side would yield a volume 64 percent as large as the moon!

But the dimensions were *not* intended to be taken literally. Rather, they describe a city sufficient to house, provide for, and protect *all* of God's people. The use of "twelve" here follows its use in the rest of Revelation.

Six

Six stands in opposition to twelve. It depicts man's attempt to dispense with God. Twelve represents God's faithful people protected by him. Six represents man in rebellion against God.

Like Satan's attempts to stop God (three and one-half), man's rebellion against God always fails!

The most infamous use of six is that of the number of the beast in Revelation 13:18: "This calls for wisdom: Let the one who has insight calculate the beast's number, for it is man's number, and his number is 666." This is rebellion compounded. It is man's attempt to usurp God's throne.

The number 666 is a gematrical number that conceals a name. John and the original readers undoubtedly knew the name, but history quickly forgot it. As early as the second century, Irenaeus puzzled over the number, but he could not identify with any certainty the original name behind the number.

There are some possible names that make sense in light of the historical setting of Revelation. One possibility is the word "Latin" (*lateinos*). It would refer either to the city of Rome or the Roman Empire.

Lateinos = 30+1+300+5+10+50+70+200 = 666

A second possibility is "Titus" (*Teitan*). This was a common name used by the Flavian emperors in the second half of the first century. This makes sense, because many people believe that the immediate focus of Revelation was the persecution of Christians under Domitian.

Teitan = 300+5+10+300+1+50 = 666.

A third possibility is "Caesar Augustus" (*kaisarsebaston*). This was the imperial title that was taken as a part of the throne name of every Roman emperor in the first century, from Augustus through Domitian. The word literally means "worshipful Caesar," which would have been particularly offensive to Christians.

Kaisarsebaston = 20+1+10+200+1+100+200+5+2+1+6+70+ 50 = 666

However, there is a problem with this word as a possible solution. By the time of the first century, three ancient Greek letters had dropped out of use as letters, while being retained as numerals. One of those letters, *stigma*, had a value of six. So while "kaisarsebaston" was spelled with *sigma* (= 200) and *tau* (= 300) next to one another in the next-to-last syllable, when it was read orally, as Revelation was intended originally, it is possible that the hearers would still associate the "st" sound with the value of 6, thus yielding a gematrical number of 666.

As an interesting side note, eight represents resurrection and contrasts with six in other early writings. Early writers said Christians met on "the eighth day of the week, which is also the first," because of Jesus's resurrection. Also, in the second century, the Sibylline Oracles made a point of the fact that the number of the name "Jesus" (*Ieesous*) is 888.

The fact is that the one who is 666 can never measure up to the one who is 888!

Amen!

Hallelujah!

Chapter 4

LESS OBVIOUS SYMBOLIC NUMBERS

In addition to the major numbers that are key to understanding Revelation, five other symbolic numbers grace the pages of the Apocalypse.

One-Third

One-third symbolizes God's restraint in judgment.

> The first angel blew his trumpet, and there was hail and fire mixed with blood, and it was thrown at the earth so that a third of the earth was burned up, a third of the trees were burned up, and all the green grass was burned up. Then the second angel blew his trumpet, and something like a great mountain of burning fire was thrown into the sea. A third of the sea became blood, and a third of the creatures living in the sea died, and a third of the ships were completely destroyed. Then the third angel blew his trumpet, and a huge star burning like a torch fell from the sky; it landed on a third of the rivers and on the springs of water. (Now the name of the star is Wormwood.) So a third of the waters became wormwood, and many people died from these waters because they were poisoned. Then the fourth angel

blew his trumpet, and a third of the sun was struck,
and a third of the moon, and a third of the stars, so
that a third of them were darkened. And there was
no light for a third of the day and for a third of the
night likewise. (Revelation 8:7–12)

The Old Testament background of this picture comes from
Ezekiel 5. In Ezekiel 5:1–2, Ezekiel is told to shave off some of
his hair and beard. Then he is told to divide that hair into thirds.
He is told to burn one third, to hack one third to pieces with a
sword, and to scatter one third to the wind. Verse 12 explains that
these three dispositions are a visual representation of what will
happen to the Jews when Nebuchadnezzar besieges and destroys
Jerusalem in 586 BC. Many will die as a result of the famine and
sword, but some will be spared, albeit scattered.

The message of Ezekiel 5 is that God shows restraint when
he executes judgment. That is the same message as in the four
trumpets in Revelation 8.

Two

Two symbolizes testimony. There are two important aspects of
people acting in pairs. First, emissaries were often sent in pairs,
as is evident in Jesus's dealings with the twelve (Mark 6:6; 11:1–
2). Jesus sent the twelve out in pairs when he gave them jobs
to do, whether they were to evangelize the Jewish villages or
prepare for the last Passover he would observe with them. Second,
the Jewish law of evidence required two witnesses in order to
obtain a conviction (Deuteronomy 19:15). One witness's word was
not enough. That testimony had to be corroborated by at least one
other, or there could be no conviction.

The only significant usage of the number two is in Revelation 11.

And I will grant my two witnesses authority to
prophesy for 1,260 days, dressed in sackcloth. (These
are the two olive trees and the two lampstands that

stand before the Lord of the earth.) If anyone wants to harm them, fire comes out of their mouths and completely consumes their enemies. If anyone wants to harm them, they must be killed this way. These two have the power to close up the sky so that it does not rain during the time they are prophesying. They have power to turn the waters to blood and to strike the earth with every kind of plague whenever they want. When they have completed their testimony, the beast that comes up from the abyss will make war on them and conquer them and kill them. Their corpses will lie in the street of the great city that is symbolically called Sodom and Egypt, where their Lord was also crucified. For three and a half days those from every people, tribe, nation, and language will look at their corpses, because they will not permit them to be placed in a tomb. And those who live on the earth will rejoice over them and celebrate, even sending gifts to each other, because these two prophets had tormented those who live on the earth. But after three and a half days a breath of life from God entered them, and they stood on their feet, and tremendous fear seized those who were watching them. (Revelation 11:3–11)

The Old Testament background for this vignette is Zechariah 4.

He asked me, "What do you see?" I replied, "I see a menorah of pure gold with a receptacle at the top and seven lamps, with fourteen pipes going to the lamps. There are also two olive trees beside it, one on the right of the receptacle and the other on the left." (Zechariah 4:2–3)

Next I asked the messenger, "What are these two olive trees on the right and the left of the menorah?" Before he could reply I asked again, "What are these two extensions of the olive trees, which are emptying out the golden oil through the two golden pipes?" He replied, "Don't you know what these are?" And I said, "No, sir." So he said, "These are the two anointed ones who stand by the Lord of the whole earth." (Zechariah 4:11–14)

The word for "anointed ones" in Zechariah 4:14 can be translated literally as "sons of fresh oil." This is to maintain consistency with the imagery of olive trees in the vision. In the context, these two olive trees would be Joshua, the priest, and Zerubbabel, the governor. Only the high priest and king were anointed for office in the Old Testament, and these two were respectively the descendants of Aaron and David.

However, the two prophets in Revelation 11 are clearly Moses and Elijah, as representatives of the law and the prophets. That is clear from the things they did in the vision. Consuming their enemies with fire and preventing the rain (Revelation 11:5–6) are reminiscent of Elijah in his confrontation with Ahab (2 Kings 1:10; 1 Kings 17:1). Turning water to blood and striking the earth with plagues (Revelation 11:6) is a clear allusion to Moses's confrontation with Pharaoh (Exodus 7–12).

This is not the first time that Moses and Elijah have acted as a pair. You may recall that Jesus was visited by Moses and Elijah at the Transfiguration (Matthew 17:3). So it should be no surprise that in Revelation 11, these same two are sent to proclaim God's word.

Four

Four symbolizes the entire Creation. There are many backgrounds of this number: four compass points, four wind directions, and four seasons. In Babylonian mythology, four signs of the zodiac—Taurus, Leo, Scorpio, and Aquarius—were regarded as powerful figures who supported heaven by four corners, or as the beasts of burden of the four-wheeled heavenly chariot.

In Revelation 4:6–8, John saw four living creatures around God's throne, worshiping him. In Revelation 5:6–14, these same four living creatures worship the Lamb. Then, throughout the entire book of Revelation, these four living creatures worship and serve God (Revelation 7:11–12; 14:3; 15:7; 19:4).

The primary background for John's vision of four living creatures in Revelation 4 and 5 is Ezekiel 1:4–28, where the prophet describes four living beings that were a part of God's heavenly entourage. But it is by no means the only Old Testament use of the image of four servants of God.

In Zechariah 1:18–21, the prophet saw a vision of four nations being broken by four of God's servants The point of that text is this: wherever and whenever God decides to judge the enemies of his people, his servants are there to do the job. In Zechariah 6:1–8, the prophet saw four chariots depicting God's omnipresence and omniscience. The point is this: God's servants ride at his bidding to exercise his judgments—even to the farthest reaches of his creation.

These two visions are reprised in Revelation 6:1–8, when the four living creatures announce the arrival of four horsemen who are on a mission from God.

The Old Testament also mentions "the four winds" and "the four corners of the earth" as a depiction of the entirety of God's created world. For example, Isaiah 11:12 mentions the four corners of the earth from which God gathers his people. And Jeremiah 49:36 describes the four winds by which God scatters his enemies.

John picks up on these Old Testament figures in Revelation. Revelation 7:1 describes four angels standing at the four corners of the earth, holding back the wind of God's judgment until he releases them in Revelation 9:13–15. Moreover, since God's redemptive reach goes to the four corners of the earth, when Satan gets the chance, he travels to the four corners of the earth to deceive the nations and rally them against God (Revelation 20:7–8).

Ten

The number ten symbolizes limits. It likely comes from the basics of human anatomy—the ten fingers on the human hand. The significance of "ten" in the Bible is similar to a person counting to ten. Once a person has counted to ten, he's exhausted all his fingers and he's ready to say, "I've had enough!"

There are many places in the Bible where one counts to ten and then says, "Enough!" God promised Abram innumerable descendants (Genesis 13:6). But ten years later, he still had no child. Ten years was the limit of Abram's patience with God's promise. It was at that point when he and Sarai took matters into their own hands and he fathered Ishmael with Hagar (Genesis 16:3). Ten people was the limit of God's patience with wicked Sodom. Abraham bargained with God to spare Sodom, testing God's limits. If there had been ten righteous people, God would have spared the city, but that was the bottom limit (Genesis 18:32). Also, Jacob ran out of patience when his father-in-law, Laban, changed his terms of employment ten times (Genesis 31:41).

There are other more obvious uses of the number ten being used to set limits. The Ten Commandments set God's limits on Israel's conduct (Exodus 34:28). The ten plagues showed the limit of God's patience with Egypt. Egypt suffered for Pharaoh's stubborn refusal to let Israel go. In spite of plague after plague, Pharaoh continued to harden his heart. It was the tenth plague that resulted in judgment on Egypt and release for Israel. Additionally, ten rebellions exhausted God's patience with the Exodus generation. God said as much when the spies returned to Kadesh Barnea after spying out the Promised Land and voted ten to two against invasion. God said Israel had tempted him ten times and not obeyed him. As a result, the entire adult generation died in the desert (Numbers 14:20–23).

Incidentally, the later Jewish rabbis took this number literally. They counted the ten rebellions as follows: (1) the

Red Sea (Exodus 14:11–13), (2) Marah (Exodus 15:23–25), (3) the Wilderness of Sin (Exodus 16:2–4), (4) hoarding manna (Exodus 16:19–20), (5) gathering manna on the Sabbath (Exodus 16:27–29), (6) Rephidim (Exodus 17:1–7), (7) Horeb (Exodus 32:1–6), (8) Taberah (Numbers 11:1–3), (9) Kibroth Hattaavah (Numbers 11:4–20), and, finally, the last straw, (10) Kadesh Barnea (Numbers 14:1–24).

Ten is a significant number in Revelation. Jesus said that Christians in Pergamum would suffer ten days before God said, "Enough!" (Revelation 2:10). The point is that God sets limits on the devil. He can do only what God allows him to do.

The dragon and the sea beast each have ten horns (Revelation 12:3; 13:1). Yes, they have power (symbolized by their horns), but they have only the power God gives them (hence the number ten). It is God who sets the limits of their power.

The beast's ten horns are further described as ten kings (Revelation 17:7, 12). The point is that God sets limits on the beast's power.

One Thousand

One thousand symbolizes limitlessness. Perhaps the best Old Testament text to make this point is Psalm 50:10: "For every wild animal in the forest belongs to me, as well as the cattle that graze on a thousand hills." God is not exempting the livestock on other hills or the livestock in valleys. What he's saying is that all livestock everywhere belong to him.

Apply that reasoning to other Bible texts that use the number one thousand.

> So realize that the Lord your God is the true God,
> the faithful God who keeps covenant faithfully with
> those who love him and keep his commandments, to
> a thousand generations ... (Deuteronomy 7:9)

The message in the above verse is that God loves everyone who loves and obeys him.

> God has countless chariots; they number in the thousands. The Lord comes from Sinai in holy splendor. (Psalm 68:17)

The message in the above verse is that God has immeasurable power.

> Yes, in your eyes a thousand years are like yesterday that quickly passes, or like one of the divisions of the nighttime. (Psalm 90:4)

The message in the above verse is that time is insignificant to God. Man's eon is God's moment.

> Now, dear friends, do not let this one thing escape your notice, that a single day is like a thousand years with the Lord and a thousand years are like a single day. (2 Peter 3:8)

God's schedule is not to be judged by man's.

And, especially, remember the symbolic use of the number one thousand when we get to Revelation 20.

> He seized the dragon- the ancient serpent, who is the devil and Satan- and tied him up for a thousand years. The angel then threw him into the abyss and locked and sealed it so that he could not deceive the nations until the one thousand years were finished. (After these things he must be released for a brief period of time.) Then I saw thrones and seated on them were those who had been given authority to judge. I also saw the souls of those who had been beheaded because of the testimony about Jesus and because of the word of God. These had not worshiped

the beast or his image and had refused to receive his mark on their forehead or hand. They came to life and reigned with Christ for a thousand years. (The rest of the dead did not come to life until the thousand years were finished.) This is the first resurrection. Blessed and holy is the one who takes part in the first resurrection. The second death has no power over them, but they will be priests of God and of Christ, and they will reign with him for a thousand years. (Revelation 20:2–7)

The devil's power is limited; he has only ten horns. But God's dominion over the devil is unlimited; it lasts a thousand years!

Amen!

Hallelujah!

Chapter 5

THE OLD TESTAMENT BACKGROUND OF REVELATION

In the 404 verses of Revelation, there is not a single Old Testament quotation, yet there are hundreds of allusions to the Old Testament. Nearly 70 percent of the book—278 verses—alludes to Old Testament passages. *The Greek New Testament*, published by United Bible Societies (UBS), cross-references verses in Revelation to Old Testament passages more than five hundred times. By contrast, in all of Paul's letters, there are only ninety-five direct quotations and only about one hundred other allusions to the Old Testament.

Balaam and Balak, Jezebel, the throne in heaven, the four living creatures, the beast out of the sea, the song of Moses, the fall of Babylon, the new heaven and earth, the New Jerusalem, the Tree of Life, etc., all come right out of the pages of the Old Testament. It is a mistake to think that a reader can understand the visions in the book without a working knowledge of the Old Testament.

In Revelation 1, John saw a vision that included seven golden lampstands: "I turned to see whose voice was speaking to me, and when I did so, I saw seven golden lampstands …" (Revelation 1:12). This vision was reminiscent of the menorah in the tabernacle and temple (Exodus 25:31–40), as well as a similar menorah in a vision seen by the prophet Zechariah (Zechariah 4:2).

In John's vision, he saw "one like a son of man." He describes the one he saw in Revelation 1:13–16.

> and in the midst of the lampstands was one like a son of man. He was dressed in a robe extending down to his feet and he wore a wide golden belt around his chest. His head and hair were as white as wool, even as white as snow, and his eyes were like a fiery flame. His feet were like polished bronze refined in a furnace, and his voice was like the roar of many waters. He held seven stars in his right hand, and a sharp double- edged sword extended out of his mouth. His face shone like the sun shining at full strength. (Revelation 1:13–16)

The picture of "one like a son of man" comes from an Old Testament image of the Messiah in Daniel 7. In the middle of a judgment scene, in which the nations of the world are being judged, God sits on his throne. Into God's presence comes "one like a son of man" (Daniel 7:13). He is given eternal dominion and a kingdom that will never be destroyed.

A few chapters later, in Revelation 4, John sees even more of the scene from Daniel 7 re-enacted.

> Immediately I was in the Spirit, and a throne was standing in heaven with someone seated on it! And the one seated on it was like jasper and carnelian in appearance, and a rainbow looking like it was made of emerald encircled the throne. In a circle around the throne were twenty- four other thrones, and seated on those thrones were twenty- four elders. They were dressed in white clothing and had golden crowns on their heads. From the throne came out flashes of lightning and roaring and crashes of

thunder. Seven flaming torches, which are the seven spirits of God, were burning in front of the throne. (Revelation 4:2–5)

The vision in Revelation 4 actually imports aspects of the visions of several prophets. It is reminiscent of the visions Isaiah and Ezekiel saw at the beginnings of their ministries (Isaiah 6:1; Ezekiel 1:26–28). But the overall scene picks up on that same passage in Daniel 7, in which "one like a son of man" is first introduced. This time John's focus is God on his throne, which comes from Daniel 7:9–10.

In Revelation 4, John's attention is drawn to four living creatures around God's throne.

> and in front of the throne was something like a sea of glass, like crystal. In the middle of the throne and around the throne were four living creatures full of eyes in front and in back. The first living creature was like a lion, the second creature like an ox, the third creature had a face like a man's, and the fourth creature looked like an eagle flying. Each one of the four living creatures had six wings and was full of eyes all around and inside. (Revelation 4:6–8)

The above vision is reminiscent of Ezekiel's vision of God (Ezekiel 1:5–10). In that vision, Ezekiel also saw four living beings surrounding God and doing his bidding.

Revelation 6 begins with the opening of four seals and the announcement of four horsemen.

> I looked on when the Lamb opened one of the seven seals, and I heard one of the four living creatures saying with a thunderous voice, "Come!" So I looked, and here came a white horse! The one who rode it had a bow, and he was given a crown, and as a conqueror he rode out to conquer. Then when the Lamb opened

the second seal, I heard the second living creature saying, "Come!" And another horse, fiery red, came out, and the one who rode it was granted permission to take peace from the earth, so that people would butcher one another, and he was given a huge sword. Then when the Lamb opened the third seal I heard the third living creature saying, "Come!" So I looked, and here came a black horse! The one who rode it had a balance scale in his hand. Then I heard something like a voice from among the four living creatures saying, "A quart of wheat will cost a day's pay and three quarts of barley will cost a day's pay. But do not damage the olive oil and the wine!" Then when the Lamb opened the fourth seal I heard the voice of the fourth living creature saying, "Come!" So I looked and here came a pale green horse! The name of the one who rode it was Death, and Hades followed right behind. They were given authority over a fourth of the earth, to kill its population with the sword, famine, and disease, and by the wild animals of the earth. (Revelation 6:1–8)

The horses and riders are reminiscent of God's judgments in the Old Testament. In a similar vision, Zechariah saw four charioteers executing God's judgments (Zechariah 6:1–8). On another occasion, God described his "four terrible judgments" to Ezekiel (Ezekiel 14:21).

Later in chapter 6, there is an earthquake with consequences that shake the entire universe.

Then I looked when the Lamb opened the sixth seal, and a huge earthquake took place; the sun became as black as sackcloth made of hair, and the full moon became blood red; and the stars in the sky fell to the earth like a fig tree dropping its unripe figs when shaken by a fierce wind. The sky was split apart like a scroll being rolled up, and every mountain and island was moved from its place. Then the kings of the earth, the very important people, the generals, the rich, the powerful, and everyone, slave and free, hid themselves in the caves and among the rocks of the mountains. They said to the mountains and to the rocks, "Fall on us and hide us from the face of the one who is seated on the throne and from the wrath of the Lamb, because the great day of their wrath has come, and who is able to withstand it?" (Revelation 6:12–17)

These verses are reminiscent of other descriptions of God's judgments in the Old Testament—descriptions that include the same images: the sun being darkened, the moon turning to blood, the stars falling from the sky, and people trying to hide themselves in caves (Joel 2:30–31; Isaiah 34:4; Isaiah 2:19; Hosea 10:8).

In Revelation 7, John sees God's people being sealed with his seal of approval.

After this I saw four angels standing at the four corners of the earth, holding back the four winds of the earth so no wind could blow on the earth, on the sea, or on any tree. Then I saw another angel ascending from the east, who had the seal of the living God. He shouted out with a loud voice to the four angels who had been given permission to damage the earth and the sea: "Do not damage the earth or the sea or the trees until we have put a seal on the foreheads of the servants of our God." Now I heard the number of those who were marked with the seal, one hundred and forty- four thousand, sealed from all the tribes of the people of Israel: From the tribe of Judah, twelve thousand were sealed, from the tribe of Reuben, twelve thousand, from the tribe of Gad, twelve thousand, from the tribe of

> Asher, twelve thousand, from the tribe of Naphtali,
> twelve thousand, from the tribe of Manasseh, twelve
> thousand, from the tribe of Simeon, twelve thousand,
> from the tribe of Levi, twelve thousand, from the
> tribe of Issachar, twelve thousand, from the tribe of
> Zebulun, twelve thousand, from the tribe of Joseph,
> twelve thousand, from the tribe of Benjamin, twelve
> thousand were sealed. (Revelation 7:1–8)

Ezekiel saw something very similar in Ezekiel 9:1–6, when God's judgment of Jerusalem was delayed long enough to allow his faithful ones to receive his seal of approval.

In Revelation 8, John sees a vision in which God's coming judgments are announced by seven angels blowing seven trumpets.

> Now the seven angels holding the seven trumpets
> prepared to blow them. The first angel blew his
> trumpet, and there was hail and fire mixed with
> blood, and it was thrown at the earth so that a third
> of the earth was burned up, a third of the trees
> were burned up, and all the green grass was burned
> up. Then the second angel blew his trumpet, and
> something like a great mountain of burning fire was
> thrown into the sea. A third of the sea became blood,
> and a third of the creatures living in the sea died,
> and a third of the ships were completely destroyed.
> Then the third angel blew his trumpet, and a huge
> star burning like a torch fell from the sky; it landed
> on a third of the rivers and on the springs of water.
> (Now the name of the star is Wormwood.) So a third of
> the waters became wormwood, and many people died
> from these waters because they were poisoned. Then
> the fourth angel blew his trumpet, and a third of the
> sun was struck, and a third of the moon, and a third
> of the stars, so that a third of them were darkened.

And there was no light for a third of the day and for
a third of the night likewise. (Revelation 8:6–12)

The figure of trumpets announcing judgments comes from
"the day of the Lord" in Joel 2:1–3.

The rest of the picture, the judgments themselves, is reminiscent
of the plagues of Egypt. In particular, the judgments are reprises
of the plagues of hail (Exodus 9:23–26), water being turned into
blood (Exodus 7:19–21), and darkness (Exodus 10:21–23).

In Revelation 10, John is given a little book to eat.

> Then the voice I had heard from heaven began to
> speak to me again, "Go and take the open scroll in
> the hand of the angel who is standing on the sea and
> on the land." So I went to the angel and asked him to
> give me the little scroll. He said to me, "Take the scroll
> and eat it. It will make your stomach bitter, but it will
> be as sweet as honey in your mouth." So I took the
> little scroll from the angel's hand and ate it, and it did
> taste as sweet as honey in my mouth, but when I had
> eaten it, my stomach became bitter. Then they told
> me: "You must prophesy again about many peoples,
> nations, languages, and kings." (Revelation 10:8–11)

The prophet Ezekiel had a similar experience (Ezekiel 2:8–3:3).

In Revelation 11, John is given a measuring rod and told to
measure the temple and its environs.

> Then a measuring rod like a staff was given to me,
> and I was told, "Get up and measure the temple of
> God, and the altar, and the ones who worship there.
> But do not measure the outer courtyard of the temple;
> leave it out, because it has been given to the Gentiles,
> and they will trample on the holy city for forty- two
> months." (Revelation 11:1–2)

Zechariah similarly envisioned a man measuring Jerusalem (Zechariah 2:1–5).

In Revelation 11, John also saw two witnesses who were commissioned by God.

> And I will grant my two witnesses authority to prophesy for 1,260 days, dressed in sackcloth. (These are the two olive trees and the two lampstands that stand before the Lord of the earth.) If anyone wants to harm them, fire comes out of their mouths and completely consumes their enemies. If anyone wants to harm them, they must be killed this way. These two have the power to close up the sky so that it does not rain during the time they are prophesying. They have power to turn the waters to blood and to strike the earth with every kind of plague whenever they want. (Revelation 11:3–6)

This vision is very similar to one in Zechariah 4:11–14. In both visions, there are two individuals standing center stage. However, the two represent different individuals in each vision. In Zechariah's vision, the two are likely the priest, Joshua, and the governor, Zerubbabel, who were God's anointed to the people of Zechariah's day. But in Revelation 11, they are clearly Moses, who turned water into blood and inflicted plagues on Egypt (Exodus 7:19–21), and Elijah, who shut up the sky and prevented rain for more than three years (1 Kings 17:1).

In Revelation 12, John saw Satan being thrown down from heaven.

> Then war broke out in heaven: Michael and his angels fought against the dragon, and the dragon and his angels fought back. But the dragon was not strong enough to prevail, so there was no longer any place left in heaven for him and his angels. So that huge dragon- the ancient serpent, the one called the

devil and Satan, who deceives the whole world- was thrown down to the earth, and his angels along with him. (Revelation 12:7–9)

His description sounds remarkably like a similar description in Isaiah 14:12–15.

In Revelation 13, John sees a horrific beast coming up out of the sea. It has features of a leopard, a bear, and a lion, but it is not really like any of them.

> Then I saw a beast coming up out of the sea. It had ten horns and seven heads, and on its horns were ten diadem crowns, and on its heads a blasphemous name. Now the beast that I saw was like a leopard, but its feet were like a bear's, and its mouth was like a lion's mouth. The dragon gave the beast his power, his throne, and great authority to rule. (Revelation 13:1–2)

In a similar Old Testament passage, Daniel saw four beasts coming out of the sea (Daniel 7:1–7). The first three have features of a lion, a bear, and a leopard, respectively. But then a fourth horrific beast arises that is not like any of the others. Later, in verse 17, Daniel is told that these four beasts represent four kingdoms that were in the future, from his perspective. Today, as we shall see later, it is easy to recognize them as Babylon, Medo-Persia, Greece, and Rome.

In Revelation 14, God's judgment is seen as a matter of harvesting first grain and then grapes.

> Then I looked, and a white cloud appeared, and seated on the cloud was one like a son of man! He had a golden crown on his head and a sharp sickle in his hand. Then another angel came out of the temple, shouting in a loud voice to the one seated on the cloud, "Use your sickle and start to reap, because the time

to reap has come, since the earths harvest is ripe!" So the one seated on the cloud swung his sickle over the earth, and the earth was reaped. Then another angel came out of the temple in heaven, and he too had a sharp sickle. Another angel, who was in charge of the fire, came from the altar and called in a loud voice to the angel who had the sharp sickle, "Use your sharp sickle and gather the clusters of grapes off the vine of the earth, because its grapes are now ripe." So the angel swung his sickle over the earth and gathered the grapes from the vineyard of the earth and tossed them into the great winepress of the wrath of God. Then the winepress was stomped outside the city, and blood poured out of the winepress up to the height of horses' bridles for a distance of almost two hundred miles. (Revelation 14:14–20)

Harvesting was a figure depicting God's judgment in the Old Testament (Joel 3:12–14; Isaiah 63:1–6).

In Revelation 18, John hears the proclamation that "Babylon the great" has fallen.

After these things I saw another angel, who possessed great authority, coming down out of heaven, and the earth was lit up by his radiance. He shouted with a powerful voice: "Fallen, fallen, is Babylon the great! She has become a lair for demons, a haunt for every unclean spirit, a haunt for every unclean bird, a haunt for every unclean and detested beast. For all the nations have fallen from the wine of her immoral passion, and the kings of the earth have committed sexual immorality with her, and the merchants of the earth have gotten rich from the power of her sensual behavior." (Revelation 18:1–3)

Isaiah and Jeremiah had made similar proclamations centuries earlier (Isaiah 21:9; Jeremiah 51:7–8).

In Revelation 19, John hears that the bride of the Lamb has made herself ready for her wedding ceremony.

> Then a voice came from the throne, saying: "Praise our God all you his servants, and all you who fear Him, both the small and the great!" Then I heard what sounded like the voice of a vast throng, like the roar of many waters and like loud crashes of thunder. They were shouting: "Hallelujah! For the Lord our God, the All- Powerful, reigns! Let us rejoice and exult and give him glory, because the wedding celebration of the Lamb has come, and his bride has made herself ready. She was permitted to be dressed in bright, clean, fine linen" (for the fine linen is the righteous deeds of the saints). Then the angel said to me, "Write the following: Blessed are those who are invited to the banquet at the wedding celebration of the Lamb!" He also said to me, "These are the true words of God." (Revelation 19:5–9)

The Old Testament prophets spoke of Israel both as God's betrothed and as his wife (Hosea 2:19–20; Isaiah 54:1–8).

When the bridegroom arrives for his wedding, he comes as a conquering general riding a white horse.

> Then I saw heaven opened and here came a white horse! The one riding it was called "Faithful" and "True," and with justice he judges and goes to war. His eyes are like a fiery flame and there are many diadem crowns on his head. He has a name written that no one knows except himself. He is dressed in clothing dipped in blood, and he is called the Word of God. The armies that are in heaven, dressed in white, clean, fine linen, were following him on white horses. From his mouth extends a sharp sword, so that with it he can strike the nations. He will rule them with an iron rod, and he stomps the winepress of

the furious wrath of God, the All-Powerful. He has a
name written on his clothing and on his thigh: "King
of kings and Lord of lords." (Revelation 19:11–16)

This picture of the divine warrior is a montage of various Old
Testament passages (Isaiah 63:1–6; Isaiah 11:1–5; Psalm 2:9).

These are just a few of many examples of Old Testament
allusions in Revelation. In its pages, John alludes to passages
from Isaiah, Jeremiah, Ezekiel, Daniel, Psalms, Exodus, and
Deuteronomy. He often reinterprets Old Testament passages,
giving them new meanings that are not the same as their
meanings in their original contexts. These examples serve to
illustrate that in order to understand Revelation, you must be
conversant with the Old Testament.

Amen!

Hallelujah!

Chapter 6

THE HISTORICAL BACKGROUND
OF REVELATION

Israelite History

Six Major Middle Eastern Kingdoms

In Biblical history, Israel interacted with or was subject to six prominent Middle Eastern kingdoms: Egypt, Assyria, Babylon, Persia, Greece, and Rome. In the words of a modern theme park empire, these amounted to "Six Flags Over Israel." You can remember their sequence by using a slogan as a mnemonic aid: "Eat at Bob's, Pasadena's greatest restaurant."

Abraham and the Patriarchs

The Patriarchal period of the Old Testament is described in Genesis 12–36. It began when Abram (later Abraham) set out from the city of Ur, a city located within the modern country of Iraq, and headed west, at God's direction. After a stopover in Haran and a detour to Egypt, Abraham settled in Canaan, within the modern country of Israel. During the time of Abraham and his descendants, Egypt was the overlord of the territory.

Abraham had three sets of children. He was married to Sarai (later Sarah), but he fathered his oldest son, Ishmael, with her servant, Hagar. Modern Islam traces its origins back to Abraham through Ishmael. After Sarah died, he married Keturah and had an additional six sons, whose descendants also populate the Arab world today.

Abraham and Sarah had a special son, a son promised by God, in their old age. His name was Isaac. He and his wife, Rebekah, had twin sons, Esau and Jacob. The descendants of Jacob became the fathers of the tribes of Israel.

Israel in Egypt

Genesis 37 through 50 describes the events that led to Jacob and his entire family moving to Goshen, in Egypt's Nile delta, as a result of a severe famine. They remained there for about four hundred years. Jacob's family was welcome at first. However, as years passed and Egyptian dynasties came and went, they began to be viewed with suspicion as a threat to Egypt's security, and they were ultimately subjected to slavery. That was their plight when Moses came on the scene.

Moses and the Exodus Generation

Moses was born during a period of extreme barbarity when Egyptians were mandating infanticide of all Israelite sons. Exodus 1 and 2 tells how Moses was providentially spared so that he was raised by his Israelite mother (acting as a nursemaid) while living as the adopted son of Pharaoh's daughter and an heir apparent to the Egyptian throne. He was thus in a unique position to see the plight of the Israelites from both the Egyptian and Israelite perspectives.

The time came when Moses had to make a choice. In a dramatic turn of events, he sided with the oppressed against the oppressors, becoming a fugitive from Egyptian justice. After forty years in Egypt's palace, he lived a meager existence as a nomadic shepherd in the Sinai desert for the next forty years.

But God was not through with Moses. God called Moses in a

dramatic scene told in Exodus 3. He sent Moses back to Egypt, this time as a deliverer of the oppressed Israelites. After a show of God's power in ten plagues, the Israelites left Egypt for a trek across the Sinai Peninsula back to the land where Abraham had once settled. On the way, they stopped at Mount Sinai, where God established his covenant with them and set out his demands in the form of ten commandments and several hundred laws that built on that core.

The trip that could have been relatively short was delayed for forty years because of Israel's repeated rebellions against God. The books of Exodus, Leviticus, Numbers, and Deuteronomy give details about God's expectations and Israel's rebellions.

Joshua and the Judges

Israel finally arrived at the Jordan River. Moses died there, and his protégé, Joshua, took the reins of leadership. Joshua and the Israelites conquered and settled the region that today is known as Israel. The details are laid out in the book of Joshua.

The Israelites were not a unified nation. Rather, they were a loose confederation of tribes, each settled in its own discrete territory. Each tribe was made up of the descendants of one of Jacob's sons.

About once every generation, the Israelites would lose their focus on God and be drawn into the sinful conduct of the foreigners still living in the land. God would subject them to oppression by some outside force. They would return to God, who would raise up a charismatic military/political leader called a judge. The judge would lead the Israelites to throw off the yoke of their oppressors, and God would give the victory, leading to a period of renewed dedication to God. But before long, they would be at it again, and the cycle would repeat itself. In all, this cycle repeated itself more than a dozen times over a period of two hundred years. Details are given in the books of Judges and Ruth, and the first seven chapters of 1 Samuel.

The United Kingdom

The last of the judges was a man named Samuel. In about 1030 BC, representatives of Israel approached Samuel with the request that he appoint one king over all the tribes. Against his better judgment, but at God's direction, he did so. The first king was a man named Saul, from the tribe of Benjamin. However, because of Saul's faithlessness, God rejected him and removed him in favor of an obscure shepherd named David. During Saul's entire reign, Israel was engaged in continual conflict with the Philistines. Saul's reign—along with the rise of David—is described in 1 Samuel 8–31.

In about 1000 BC, after Saul's death, David assumed the throne of the United Kingdom. The book of 2 Samuel is devoted to his reign. David conquered the city of Jerusalem and made it his national capital. God made a promise to David, recorded in 2 Samuel 7, that his dynasty would endure. That promise was initially fulfilled in Solomon, but it was ultimately and eternally fulfilled in Jesus.

Solomon succeeded David as king. He built the first temple in about 970 BC, and the worship of all the Israelites became centralized in Jerusalem. The history of Solomon's reign is detailed in 1 Kings 1–11.

Solomon was succeeded by his son, Rehoboam, in about 930 BC. Almost immediately, a civil war erupted and ten of the twelve tribes seceded from the union. This resulted in two kingdoms. The Northern Kingdom, with its capital ultimately in Samaria, was called Israel. The Southern Kingdom, whose capital was in Jerusalem, became known as Judah. The rest of 1 Kings, beginning in chapter 12, and all of 2 Kings, gives the history of the divided kingdom.

The Divided Kingdom and the Assyrian Empire

The Northern Kingdom (Israel) lasted from 922 to 721 BC. It was ruled by a series of increasingly corrupt kings who introduced and promoted idol worship for its entire two hundred years of existence.

During that entire time, either Egypt, to the south, or Assyria, to the north, dominated the region, with the result that Israel found itself almost always in the center of conflict between those two powerful nations. In fact, one of the major crossroads where the power struggles of those two empires regularly took place was the Valley of Jezreel, near a hill called Megiddo, located within Israel. This ancient battleground is the background for one of the most famous vignettes in Revelation, the Battle of Armageddon.

Assyria ultimately won the power struggle with Egypt. They then invaded Israel and exiled most of its inhabitants. The Assyrians relocated other conquered peoples into the region. This was their way of watering down the bloodlines of indigenous peoples in the territories they conquered. The eventual result was that the remaining Israelites intermarried with the relocated peoples and created a group of people known in the Gospels as the Samaritans.

In the meantime, the Southern Kingdom (Judah) continued to be ruled by David's descendants. Some Judean kings were wicked, and others were righteous, but most were mediocre.

The Babylonian Conquest of Judah

About the time Israel was being overrun by Assyria, in the 720s BC, one of the great Judean kings, Hezekiah, resisted Assyria and led the Southern Kingdom in a national religious revival. As a result of their return to God, Judah was spared the fate that had befallen Israel, and the Assyrian threat retreated.

Hezekiah's revival was followed by almost sixty years of national immorality and idolatry under his son, Manasseh, and his grandson, Amon. Hezekiah's great-grandson, Josiah, led Judah's last great revival during his thirty-one-year reign. That return to God once again forestalled disaster, and Judah escaped Israel's fate for a while.

But trouble was brewing between Assyria and an increasingly powerful Babylon, such that the Assyrian threat that had destroyed Israel was replaced by a Babylonian threat to destroy Judah. Assyria enlisted the aid of its former nemesis, Egypt, to stave off the Babylonians, but to no avail. The Babylonians defeated the Assyrian-Egyptian coalition at the pivotal battle of Carchemish in 605 BC and then proceeded to annex Judah as a part of the Babylonian Empire.

The Babylonian conquest began civilly enough. In 605 BC, Nebuchadnezzar of Babylon had some of the promising young Jewish leaders taken to Babylon, where they were trained for service to Babylon. The prophet Daniel and his friends Hananiah, Mishael, and Azariah (otherwise known as Shadrach, Meshach, and Abednego) were among those who were pressed into the service of Nebuchadnezzar at that time.

Judah revolted against Nebuchadnezzar in 597 BC. Nebuchadnezzar put down the revolt and deported the ruling elite of Judah to concentration camps in Babylon. The prophet Ezekiel was among those deportees.

Finally Judah revolted one last time in 586 BC. By that time, Nebuchadnezzar had had his fill of rebellion. His army totally destroyed Jerusalem and the temple that had been built by Solomon. The prophet Jeremiah was in Jerusalem during that entire time. He survived the destruction of Jerusalem and later died in Egypt.

The Persian Period

In 539 BC, Persia conquered Babylon. Shortly thereafter, King Cyrus allowed the Jewish exiles to return to their homeland. Cyrus urged the Jews to rebuild Jerusalem and the temple. They completed the project in about 520 BC, but the finished product was not nearly as grand as Solomon's temple had been.

Between 458 and 445 BC, more exiles returned to repopulate Jerusalem and Judah. They were led by the priest Ezra and the governor Nehemiah.

The Hellenistic / Greek Period

Alexander the Great conquered Persia in 331 BC. He established Greek language, religion, culture, and government throughout the Greek Empire in a process known as Hellenization (from the Greek word for "Greek"). Even though Alexander pretty much conquered the known world as a young man in his twenties, he didn't live long enough to consolidate the empire. He died in 323 BC, at the age of thirty.

Alexander's generals fought a forty-year war over his empire. When the dust settled, the Hellenistic world was divided four ways.

Lysimachus established the Attalid dynasty in the region encompassing much of modern Turkey and a bit of Eastern Europe, including modern Bulgaria. His capital was Pergamum, which was later the location of one of the seven churches in Revelation. Cassander took control of the region of Macedonia that encompassed modern Greece. The remaining two of Alexander's generals, Ptolemy and Seleucus, are of note in intertestamental history because they took control of the regions that overlapped in the territory of Israel.

Ptolemy established the Ptolemaic dynasty in Egypt. He and his descendants controlled the territory of Israel from 323 to 198 BC. About 250 BC, during the time the Ptolemaic dynasty controlled Israel, the Hebrew Bible was translated into Greek in Alexandria, Egypt. The translation is known as the Septuagint (abbreviated LXX).

Seleucus established the Seleucid dynasty in Mesopotamia and Central Asia. His descendants wrested control of Israel from the Ptolemies in 198 BC and controlled it until 141 BC.

The Maccabean Revolt and the Hasmonean Period

In 167 BC, a particularly sinister Seleucid ruler, Antiochus IV Epiphanes, outlawed Jewish observances. As if that were not bad enough, he mandated worship of Zeus and even ordered that a statue of Zeus be erected in the Jerusalem temple. His outrageous actions sparked a revolt of the Jews led by Judas Maccabeus and his family. The revolt continued for six years, to 161 BC. The highlight for the Jews was when they recaptured the temple and rededicated it in December, 164 BC. They initiated an eight-day observance, Hanukkah, that observant Jews celebrate to this day.

After the success of the Maccabean revolt, a succession of Jewish kings known as the Hasmonean Dynasty governed during a relatively peaceful period from 141 to 63 BC.

Religious Movements during the Hasmonean Period

Three distinct religious groups arose among the Jews during the Hasmonean period. The Pharisees were a popular group composed mostly of laymen. They advocated strict observance of the Jewish laws and traditions. The Pharisees accepted as scripture all the books of the Tanakh (our Old Testament), and they developed a number of traditions with which Jesus took issue during his ministry.

The Sadducees were a smaller, more elite group consisting mostly of priests. They accepted only the Torah (Genesis through Deuteronomy) as scripture and rejected the traditions that were advocated by the Pharisees.

The Essenes were a very small group who lived a monastic lifestyle near the Dead Sea. Modern historians associate them with the preservation of the Dead Sea Scrolls.

The Roman Era

The Hasmonean Dynasty came to an end in 63 BC, when the Roman general Pompey occupied the Middle East. Later, in 40 BC, the Roman Senate installed Herod the Great as a client king in Judea. Herod's thirty-six-year reign was marked by huge building projects, including Roman-style cities and fortresses. He also expanded the complex surrounding the temple in Jerusalem. The walls and pavement of the temple mount today were originally laid by Herod the Great during his building frenzy.

Jesus was born during the final years of Herod's reign.

Herod died in 4 BC. The Romans divided his kingdom among his three sons Archelaus, Antipas, and Philip, and his sister Salome.

The First Roman Emperors (Full Imperial Titles Are in Parentheses)

The Julio-Claudian Dynasty

Augustus (Imperator Caesar Augustus)

Augustus was the founder of the Roman Empire. He reigned as the first emperor from 27 BC to AD 14. His given name was Octavius. He was the nephew of Julius Caesar. When Julius Caesar was assassinated, he adopted Octavius posthumously via his last will. Octavius inherited both Caesar's money and his name. He used both to raise an army and extort a consulship from the Senate.

Octavius coerced the Senate into declaring Julius a god, thus making himself the "son of a god." Octavius took control of the western part of the Roman republic, leaving Mark Antony the eastern part. Octavius defeated Antony and Cleopatra in 31 BC and emerged as the sole ruler of the Roman world.

As emperor, he adopted the throne name Augustus (meaning "exalted"), which had religious overtones. Rome gave him the title Pater Patriae (meaning "father of his country") in 2 BC, and on his death declared him to be a god ("Divus Augustus").

During his life, Augustus accepted deification in the Roman provinces, thus laying the foundation for the concilia, or emperor cult, that would play a part in the drama of Revelation.

Jesus was born during the reign of Augustus (Luke 2:1–5).

Tiberius (Tiberius Julius Caesar Augustus)

Tiberius was emperor from AD 14 to 37. He was the stepson of Augustus. Tiberius's reign was a political disaster. He allowed the Praetorian Guard to engage in a reign of terror under their leader, the prefect Sejanus. The Roman people despised Tiberius. He moved to the island of Capri in AD 26 and never returned to Rome.

Jesus's ministry and death occurred during Tiberius's reign of intimidation (Luke 3:1–3).

Caligula (Gaius Caesar Augustus Germanicus)

Caligula ruled as emperor from AD 37 to 41. He was the youngest son of Germanicus, the nephew and adopted son of Tiberius and Agrippina. He was brought up in an army camp and nicknamed Caligula because of the little boots (*caligae*) he wore around the camp. Caligula was extravagant, autocratic, vicious, and mentally unstable. He wreaked havoc with the state finances and terrorized those around him until he was assassinated after fewer than four years in power.

Caligula demanded that he be worshipped as a god. As a part of enforcing that demand in the provinces, he ordered that his statue be placed in the Jerusalem temple. However, he died before the order was carried out.

Likely because his reign was relatively short, he is not mentioned in the New Testament.

Claudius (Tiberius Claudius Caesar Augustus Germanicus)

Claudius reigned as emperor from AD 41 to 54. He was a nephew of Tiberius and an uncle to Caligula. For years Claudius was kept secluded by his family because of numerous physical disabilities. His knees were weak and gave way under him. His head shook. He stammered, and his speech was confused. When he was excited, he slobbered and his nose ran. Because of his disabilities, his family never considered him a political threat. As a result, he escaped the purges initiated by Tiberius and Caligula against their political enemies. However, after Caligula's assassination, he became emperor.

He was a capable and progressive administrator. He engaged in significant public works and economic and political reform. Ultimately, he was poisoned by his fourth wife, Agrippina, in order to secure the throne for her son, his stepson, Nero.

During his reign, Claudius expelled Jews from Rome (Acts 18:1–3).

Nero (Imperator Nero Claudius Caesar Augustus Germanicus)

Nero was emperor from AD 54 to 68. Agrippina urged her third husband, Claudius, to adopt her son, Nero. After he did, she poisoned her husband, making Nero the emperor. (She had previously killed her second husband, also by poisoning.)

Nero's early years as emperor were good, thanks to the controlling influence of his mother, Agrippina; his tutor, the Roman philosopher Seneca; and the Praetorian prefect Burrus. However, as time went on, Nero's dark side came out. According to Suetonius, Nero tried to kill his mother through a planned shipwreck. Unfortunately for Nero, Agrippina survived. Thereafter he had her executed in AD 59 and passed it off as a suicide.

After his mother's murder, real corruption set in. The people blamed him when Rome burned in AD 64, and he tried to shift the blame to the Christians. Rome endured four more years of tyranny before he was toppled by the army and forced to commit suicide in AD 68. His death brought an end to the Julio-Claudian Dynasty

When Paul appealed to Caesar in Acts 25:10–12, he was appealing to none other than Nero. When Peter urged Christians to "honor the king" (1 Peter 2:17), the king was none other than

Nero. Ultimately, and ironically, both Paul and Peter were martyred during Nero's reign.

Civil War and Three Minor Emperors

Galba (Servius Galba Imperator Caesar Augustus)

Galba was the first of three rogue emperors who rose and fell in rapid succession during the civil war that followed Nero's death. He served as emperor from June 9, AD 68, to January 15, AD 69. Galba had become a consul in AD 33, and he had administered Aquitania, Germany, Africa, and Spain with competence and integrity.

When the Gallic legions rose against Nero in June, AD 68, they proclaimed Galba emperor. However, he soon made himself unpopular with the very army that had put him in power by blatant favoritism, ill-timed severity, and greed. He was assassinated by the Praetorian Guard in Rome after only seven months as emperor.

Otho (Imperator Marcus Otho Caesar Augustus)

Otho was emperor from January 15 to April 17, AD 69. Otho had once been a friend of Nero. The friendship ended when Nero began an affair with Otho's wife, Poppaea Sabina, in AD 58. Once she had secured her place as Nero's mistress, she divorced Otho. Nero then removed Otho from the picture by sending him to govern Lusitania that same year. Otho joined Galba in his revolt against Nero in AD 68. A few months after Galba was in power, Otho put out a contract on Galba's life by paying the Praetorians to assassinate him.

Otho was recognized as emperor everywhere in the empire except in Germany, where the army wanted to proclaim its general, Aulus Vitellius, as emperor. Vitellius marched on Italy and defeated Otho's army, forcing Otho to commit suicide after only three months as emperor.

Vitellius (Imperator Aulus Vitellius Caesar Augustus Germaniums)

Vitellius was emperor from April 19 to December 20, AD 69. Galba had appointed Vitellius to command the legions on the Lower Rhine in AD 68. After Otho's duplicity and the assassination of Galba, Vitellius's army marched on Rome. He ended Otho's reign by the victory of Bedriacum. A scant eight months later, Vespasian was proclaimed emperor in Alexandria. Vespasian's soldiers dragged Vitellius through the streets of Rome and murdered him.

The Flavian Dynasty

Vespasian (Imperator Caesar Vespasianus Augustus)

Vespasian was emperor from AD 69 to 79. During the civil war in Rome, Vespasian and his son Titus were otherwise occupied with the First Jewish-Roman War, which lasted from AD 66 to 73. They had been sent by Nero to put down the Jewish rebellion.

When word arrived of Nero's death and the political turmoil that followed it, Vespasian's army declared him to be emperor. He marched on Rome and defeated Vitellius to take the throne. Vespasian put an end to the civil war. During his ten-year reign, he put Rome on a good financial footing and restored military discipline to the army. He began building the Flavian Amphitheater, which is better known today as the Colosseum.

Vespasian died of an infection on June 23, AD 79. His last words were "Puto deus fio" ("I think I'm becoming a god"). After his death, he was deified.

Revelation may have been written during his reign. That seems to be suggested, as will be seen later, in Revelation 17:9–11.

Titus (Imperator Titus Caesar Vespasianus Augustus)

Titus was emperor from AD 79 to 81. He was the elder son of Vespasian. Titus was popular for his generosity, charm, and military prowess. He was exceptionally good-looking, cultivated, refined, and friendly. Suetonius called him "the darling of the human race."

When Vespasian returned to take power in Rome, he left Titus in command of the army. In that capacity, Titus engineered the destruction of Jerusalem in AD 70 and suppressed the Jewish revolt. As emperor, Titus completed the construction of the Colosseum his father had begun.

After barely two years in power, Titus died an untimely death at age forty-one, reportedly in the same farmhouse where his father had died. His last reported words were "I have made but one mistake."

Historians still speculate about the circumstances of Titus's death and his odd last words. Popular suspicion held that his brother, Domitian, had poisoned him. Cassius Dio believed that the "mistake" Titus made was failing to have his brother executed when he learned that Domitian had been openly plotting against him.

Domitian (Imperator Caesar Domitianus Augustus Germanicus)

Domitian was emperor from AD 81 to 96. He was the younger son of Vespasian and the last of the Flavian Dynasty. Domitian was paranoid about opposition plots and intrigue—likely because he was a master of both. Consequently, he unleashed a reign of terror in Rome that lasted until his assassination. He demanded to be called Lord and God, and he initiated an extremely severe persecution directed at Christians.

Most writers believe that Revelation was written during his reign. Undoubtedly, whether it was written during his reign or before, it was written to prepare Christians for the persecution he was to unleash on them.

Amen!

Hallelujah!

Chapter 7

THE CIRCUMSTANCES OF REVELATION (1:4–5)

From John, to the seven churches that are in the province of Asia: Grace and peace to you from "he who is," and who was, and who is still to come, and from the seven spirits who are before his throne, and from Jesus Christ -- the faithful witness, the firstborn from among the dead, the ruler over the kings of the earth.

—Revelation 1:4–5

Revelation is a message to seven churches in first-century Asia Minor: "From John, to the seven churches that are in the province of Asia:" (Revelation 1:4). These seven churches are typical of the church as a whole. We can be certain of that because each letter ends with a word to all the churches: "The one who has an ear had better hear what the Spirit says to the churches." (Revelation 2:7, 11, 17, 29; 3:6, 13, 22).

The Writer

The author identifies himself as John four times (Revelation 1:1–2, 4, 9; 22:8). But who was this John? Justin Martyr, in the second century, believed it was the apostle John. We know the author was well versed in scripture because he alludes to Old Testament passages so frequently. Even though he never quotes the Old Testament, his letter is brimming with more Old Testament references than any other New Testament book. We can be certain that he was well known to the seven churches of Asia Minor, to whom he wrote. That is apparent because he had only to identify himself by name, without providing any pedigree to authenticate his authority. Moreover, he expected them to read, understand, and act upon the message that he was sending, so it appears that they were well known to him, and he to them.

The book reveals the author was ultimately an optimist. He was convinced, in spite of all the oppression Christians were facing—and the cruelty they would continue to face—ultimately the church would triumph over its enemies.

The only other serious contender as a possible author is a man called John the Presbyter. Dionysius, writing in the third century, suggested the author was this enigmatic man whose name appears elsewhere in ancient writings.

But as for myself, I believe the writer of Revelation was the apostle John.

The Date of the Book

Most commentators believe Revelation was written either during the reign of Nero (AD 54–68) or of Domitian (AD 81–96). I believe it was written between those dates. The text itself appears to support a date near the end of Vespasian's reign (AD 69–79). "(This requires a mind that has wisdom.) The seven heads are seven mountains the woman sits on. They are also seven kings: five have fallen; one is, and the other has not yet come, but whenever he does come, he must remain for only a brief time. The beast that was, and is not, is himself an eighth king and yet is one of the seven, and is going to destruction" (Revelation 17:9–11).

The first five heads were emperors of the Julio-Claudian Dynasty: Augustus, Tiberius, Caligula, Claudius, and Nero. They were the "five" that "have fallen."

The last three were the emperors of the Flavian Dynasty: Vespasian, Titus, and Domitian. Vespasian was the "one" who "is." Titus was "the other" who "has not yet come" and who "must remain for only a brief time." Domitian was the beast, who "is himself an eighth king and yet is one of the seven."

Following the above analysis, Revelation was likely written late in the reign of Vespasian, perhaps around AD 78.

Christians Were Already Facing Persecution

Roman authorities were beginning to enforce emperor worship throughout the empire. Christians were facing increasing hostility from the authorities. Jesus had a warning of increased persecution for the church in Smyrna (2:10) and a promise to spare the church in Philadelphia from extreme testing (3:10). Christians were already suffering for their faith. In Pergamum, Antipas had already given his life (2:13) and others had been martyred (6:9). John, himself, had been exiled to a penal colony on the Island of Patmos (1:9).

Some Christians were beginning to dabble in sin. Some Christians in Pergamum were advocating compromise (2:14–15). And Christians in Thyatira were tolerating immorality and idolatry (2:20).

John's Purpose in Writing Is Clear

John writes to encourage the faithful to resist the demands of emperor worship. He tells his readers that the final showdown between God and Satan is imminent. Satan will increase his persecution of believers, but they must be faithful, even if it means death. They are sealed against any spiritual harm, and they will be vindicated when God judges his enemies and rewards his people.

The Message of the Book Is Grace and Peace

"From John, to the seven churches that are in the province of Asia: Grace and peace to you from 'he who is,' and who was, and who is still to come, and from the seven spirits who are before his throne, and from Jesus Christ- the faithful witness, the firstborn from among the dead, the ruler over the kings of the earth" (Revelation 1:4–5). "Grace" refers to blessings we don't deserve. "Peace" refers to harmony with God in the middle of turmoil.

There is a good reason why biblical writers like Paul and John made use of the combined greeting "grace and peace." In the first century, Greek speakers greeted one another with the Greek word "*charis*," meaning "grace"; Jews greeted one another with the Hebrew word "*shalom*," meaning "peace." By using both greetings, the writers emphasized the inherent unity of Jew and Gentile in Christ.

But who is the author of this grace and peace?

Grace and Peace Come from the Eternal God

God is eternal. That is the significance of the description of God as "he who is, and who was and who is still to come." It is reminiscent of the way God identified himself to Moses at the burning bush (Exodus 3:14). In the Septuagint translation of Exodus 3:14, God is quoted as using exactly the same wording to identify himself as that which John uses here: "*ho oon*" (the existing one). This was also one way in which God identified himself to the nation of Israel (Isaiah 41:4).

The meaning of "Yahweh," the personal name by which God revealed himself in the Old Testament, is "the existing one."

It doesn't matter whether you are talking about the past, the present, or the future; God always is.

Grace and Peace Are Also Gifts from the Holy Spirit

"[T]he seven spirits who are before his throne" refers to the Holy Spirit. An NIV footnote suggests an alternate reading that may actually give us a better concept of what John is getting at: "the sevenfold Spirit."

Remember the use of numbers in Revelation? To say that the Spirit is "the sevenfold Spirit" is to say that the Holy Spirit is engaged in seeing that the whole work of God is accomplished. It is God's Spirit at work!

Grace and Peace Are the Gifts of Jesus Christ Himself

Jesus is described three ways in this text. First, he is "the faithful witness." Both of those words are used of Jesus elsewhere in Revelation. Jesus is called "the faithful and true witness" in Revelation 3:14 and simply "'Faithful' and 'True'" in 19:11.

The word "witness" is translated from the Greek "*martus*," which can also be translated as "martyr." The ideas of martyrdom and faithfulness are intimately connected. Jesus is the first martyr identified in Revelation, but others had followed him by the time John was writing, and others still would follow him as John's message unfolded (2:13; 6:9–10).

Second, Jesus is described as "the firstborn from among the dead." The idea of Jesus as the "firstborn" is reminiscent of the Davidic king (cf. Psalm 89:27). In the New Testament, Paul takes that word, "firstborn," and describes Jesus this way: "He is the head of the body, the church, as well as the beginning, the firstborn from among the dead, so that he himself may become first in all things" (Colossians 1:18). So just as Jesus was the first to die as a martyr, he was also the first to rise as vindicated.

Third, Jesus is "the ruler over the kings of the earth." This is reminiscent of the Old Testament descriptions of both the king and the Messiah (Psalm 89:27; cf. Revelation 19:16).

Three expressions in a single verse—Revelation 1:5—depict the essence of the gospel: Jesus's death, his resurrection, and his eternal dominion.

Amen!

Hallelujah!

Chapter 8

THE KEY QUESTION ANSWERED BY THE BOOK (1:5–8)

To the one who loves us and has set us free from our sins at the cost of his own blood and has appointed us as a kingdom, as priests serving his God and Father -- to him be the glory and the power for ever and ever! Amen. (Look! He is returning with the clouds, and every eye will see him, even those who pierced him, and all the tribes on the earth will mourn because of him. This will certainly come to pass! Amen.) "I am the Alpha and the Omega," says the Lord God -- the one who is, and who was, and who is still to come -- the All-Powerful!

—Revelation 1:5–8

Revelation answers the question, who rules? The Roman emperor thought he ruled the world. He was mistaken! Revelation has as its main theme "God rules!"

Doxology

At this point in the text, John erupts in spontaneous praise. He extols the wonderful works Jesus has done on our behalf: "To the one who loves us and has set us free from our sins at the cost of his own blood and has appointed us as a kingdom, as priests serving his God and Father- to him be the glory and the power for ever and ever! Amen" (Revelation 1:5b–6).

He begins with the words "To the one who loves us." "Loves" is a present, active participle. The KJV incorrectly renders it as a past tense—"loved." In Greek, when a word is in the present tense and active voice, it often conveys both (1) present action and (2) ongoing action. Thus the meaning is not just that Jesus loves us now but also that he never stops loving us. His love continues— past, present, and future. There is no end to Jesus's love for us!

John then says Jesus "has set us free from our sins at the cost of his own blood."

The KJV says he "washed" us from our sins, but most modern translations say he "loosed" us from our sins. Most modern Greek editions use "*lusanti*" ("loosed"), not "*lousanti*" ("washed"). The two words sound the same in Greek, but they are spelled slightly differently. But regardless of whether we read "loosed" or "washed," the meaning is not radically different for the Christian. It is the form of the word that is telling. The word is an aorist participle—a form in Greek that refers to a completed past action. In other words, Jesus has "loosed" us from our sins so that we are no longer bound to them, or he has "washed" us from our sins so that we are no longer sullied by them.

John continues to say Jesus has transformed us into something special—a kingdom of priests: "and has appointed us as a kingdom, as priests serving his God and Father- to him be the glory and the power for ever and ever! Amen" (Revelation 1:6).

This was God's plan for Israel (Exodus 19:6; Isaiah 61:6). Here John affirms the church, which is elsewhere called "the Israel of God" (Galatians 6:16), is "a kingdom" (not "kings," as in the KJV). He continues the theme of the church as "a kingdom" and Christians as "priests" within the kingdom later, in Revelation 5:9–10: "They were singing a new song: 'You are worthy to take the scroll and to open its seals because you were killed, and at the cost of your own blood you have purchased for

God persons from every tribe, language, people, and nation. You have appointed them as a kingdom and priests to serve our God, and they will reign on the earth' (Revelation 5:9–10).

So, as Peter says elsewhere, the church in the New Testament becomes the fulfillment of God's plan for Israel in the Old Testament—a royal priesthood (1 Peter 2:9).

The Coming of the Lord

"(Look! He is returning with the clouds, and every eye will see him, even those who pierced him, and all the tribes on the earth will mourn because of him. This will certainly come to pass! Amen.)" (Revelation 1:7). This text combines images from two great Old Testament texts. The image of Jesus coming in the clouds alludes to Daniel 7:13. The image of people gazing on the one they have pierced alludes to Zechariah 12:10.

The Bible says a lot about the "coming" of the Lord. When most people read of the "coming" of the Lord, they think of what is commonly called the Second Coming. But much of the time, when the Bible talks about the Lord "coming," it is not talking about the second coming at all. The Bible speaks of many times when the Lord has "come" historically. Indeed, the Old Testament prophets regularly used the idea of the Lord's "coming" to describe God's judgment on a nation or a people. Here are a few examples from the prophet Isaiah.

> Look, the Lord's day of judgment is coming; it is a day of cruelty and savage, raging anger, destroying the earth and annihilating its sinners. Indeed the stars in the sky and their constellations no longer give out their light; the sun is darkened as soon as it rises, and the moon does not shine. I will punish the world for its evil, and wicked people for their sin. I will put an end to the pride of the insolent, I will bring down the arrogance of tyrants. I will make human beings more scarce than pure gold, and people more scarce than

gold from Ophir. So I will shake the heavens, and the earth will shake loose from its foundation, because of the fury of the Lord who commands armies, in the day he vents his raging anger. (Isaiah 13:9–13)

Isaiah's description seems stylistically similar to scenes described in apocalyptic writings like Revelation. It sounds like the end of the world. But a close look at the context—in particular, Isaiah 13:1—shows that the prophet is not describing the end of the world as a whole. Rather, he is describing the end of *Babylon's* world: "This is a message about Babylon that God revealed to Isaiah son of Amoz" (Isaiah 13:1).

In other passages, the same motif of the Lord's coming occurs. In Isaiah 19:1, the Lord's "coming" spells doom for Egypt, and in Isaiah 30:30–31, it spells doom for Assyria. Isaiah 63 offers another example to show that this is a common theme of the prophet.

Who is this who comes from Edom, dressed in bright red, coming from Bozrah? Who is this one wearing royal attire, who marches confidently because of his great strength? "It is I, the one who announces vindication, and who is able to deliver!" Why are your clothes red? Why do you look like someone who has stomped on grapes in a vat? "I have stomped grapes in the winepress all by myself; no one from the nations joined me. I stomped on them in my anger; I trampled them down in my rage. Their juice splashed on my garments, and stained all my clothes. For I looked forward to the day of vengeance, and then payback time arrived. I looked, but there was no one to help; I was shocked because there was no one offering support. So my right arm accomplished deliverance; my raging anger drove me on. I trampled nations in my anger, I made them drunk in my rage, I splashed their blood on the ground." (Isaiah 63:1–6)

Isaiah's description is similar to Revelation 14: "So the angel swung his sickle over the earth and gathered the grapes from the vineyard of the earth and tossed them into the great winepress of the wrath of God. Then the winepress was stomped outside the city, and blood poured out of the winepress up to the height of horses' bridles for a distance of almost two hundred miles" (Revelation 14:19–20). But the context of Isaiah 63 shows that the prophet is describing God's judgment on Edom.

When you read those prophetic texts, a common theme emerges. The Coming of the Lord, or the Day of the Lord, refers to the day when the Lord judges a nation and punishes it for its sins. When John says the Lord is coming, we should view that threat from a first-century perspective. In the past, God had judged Babylon, Egypt, Assyria, and Edom with previous comings. Now John assures first-century Christians that he is going to judge Rome as well. As we shall see in our study, Rome is the empire against whom the Lord's coming is directed in Revelation. "(Look! He is returning with the clouds, and every eye will see him, even those who pierced him, and all the tribes on the earth will mourn because of him. This will certainly come to pass! Amen.)" (Revelation 1:7).

But the coming that brings judgment to some brings grace to others. This is reminiscent of Zechariah 12, where God's people are depicted as receiving God's grace to repent of their rebellion against him:

> I will pour out on the kingship of David and the population of Jerusalem a spirit of grace and supplication so that they will look to me, the one they have pierced. They will lament for him as one laments for an only son, and there will be a bitter cry for him like the bitter cry for a firstborn. On that day the lamentation in Jerusalem will be as great as the lamentation at Hadad- Rimmon in the plain of Megiddo. The land will mourn, clan by clan- the clan of the royal household of David by itself and their wives by themselves; the clan of the family of Nathan

by itself and their wives by themselves; the clan of
the descendants of Levi by itself and their wives by
themselves; and the clan of the Shimeites by itself and
their wives by themselves- all the clans that remain,
each separately with their wives. (Zechariah 12:10–14)

The "coming" of the Lord is always the day of reckoning for
God's enemies and the day of reward for his friends. Whether the
coming of the Lord is good news or bad news depends entirely
upon your relationship to him when he comes.

Trust God!

"'I am the Alpha and the Omega,' says the Lord God- the one
who is, and who was, and who is still to come- the All- Powerful!"
(Revelation 1:8). Revelation's message is simple: "Trust God."

God describes himself as "the Alpha and Omega." These were
the first and last letters of the Greek alphabet. That is like saying
he covers our needs from *A* to *Z*. There isn't anything he isn't
capable of dealing with. Some translations add "the Beginning
and the End." This does not appear to be a part of the original
text here. It appears to be an early attempt to harmonize this
verse with Revelation 21:6.

Moreover, God is the one "who is, and who was, and who is
still to come." This reminds us of his self-revelation to Moses at
Sinai (Exodus 3:14). The name Yahweh, rendered "Lord" in most
translations, signifies existence. God *is!* Others come and go.
In Egypt, there were many pharaohs and many dynasties. One
pharaoh in particular received a ten-lesson course on who rules;
we call it the ten plagues. He finally learned that pharaohs come
and go but God *is* and God *rules!*

Down through the Old Testament, others had to learn their
lessons the hard way. Nebuchadnezzar had a dream that led to him
being deposed. He was off the throne, and quite insane, until he
acknowledged God *is* and God *rules.* You can read the story in Daniel
4, but the bottom line was Nebuchadnezzar's final realization:

"But at the end of the appointed time I, Nebuchadnezzar, looked up toward heaven, and my sanity returned to me. I extolled the Most High, and I praised and glorified the one who lives forever. For his authority is an everlasting authority, and his kingdom extends from one generation to the next. All the inhabitants of the earth are regarded as nothing. He does as he wishes with the army of heaven and with those who inhabit the earth. No one slaps his hand and says to him, 'What have you done?'" (Daniel 4:34–35).

Revelation was written at a time when the church was facing more upstart kings. In first-century Rome, there was a group of fellows—the Roman emperors—who thought they ruled the world. Revelation is God's promise that the Roman emperors were going to learn the same lesson Egypt's Pharaoh and Babylon's Nebuchadnezzar had learned centuries before: kingdoms of the world come and go; God's kingdom remains. In other words, God *is* and God *rules!*

There is one last great word that John uses to describe God. It is the word *"pantokrator,"* a Greek word that means "the Almighty, All-Powerful, Omnipotent (One)." It is a word that is used only of God, and it is a word we are going to find in a number of contexts throughout Revelation.

Those around God's throne extol him as "the All-Powerful" (Revelation 4:6–8; 11:16–17). The "Song of the Lamb" (15:3) and the altar (16:7) both praise God as "the All-Powerful." There is a battle on "the great day of God, the All-Powerful" (16:13–14). When God judges Rome, the elders praise God as "the All-Powerful" (19:6). When Jesus leads heaven's army, he executes the wrath of God, "the All-Powerful" (19:15). And in the center of "the new Jerusalem" is none other than "the Lord God - the All-Powerful" (21:22).

Throughout Revelation, John never lets us forget God is "the All-Powerful." He doesn't want the reader to lose sight of who's really in control of world affairs. God *is* and God *rules!*

Amen!

Hallelujah!

The First Seven

---◆◆◆---

SEVEN LETTERS TO SEVEN CHURCHES (1:9–3:22)

Chapter 9

PRELUDE TO THE SEVEN LETTERS (1:9–20)

A Brother in Fellowship (Revelation 1:9–11)

"I, John, your brother and the one who shares with you in the persecution, kingdom, and endurance that are in Jesus, was on the island called Patmos because of the word of God and the testimony about Jesus. I was in the Spirit on the Lord's Day when I heard behind me a loud voice like a trumpet, saying: "Write in a book what you see and send it to the seven churches- to Ephesus, Smyrna, Pergamum, Thyatira, Sardis, Philadelphia, and Laodicea"

—Revelation 1:9–11

John identifies with his readers in three important ways. First, he identifies with them as a fellow-sufferer of persecution as a Christian. "Persecution" is translated from the Greek word "*thlipsei*," a word that describes intense pressure. It refers to the pressure exerted on a kernel of wheat in order to break the hull so the grain can be ground into flour. It is also the word used to refer to the trampling of grapes in order to extract their juice. In other words, it refers to the pressure that brings its objects closer to their intended use.

New Testament writers regularly made the point that the difficulties faced by Christians, as uncomfortable as they may be, can ultimately have beneficial results in Christians' lives (James 1:2–4; Romans 5:1–5).

John's second area of fellowship with his readers was the "kingdom." This is translated from the Greek word "*basileia*," which describes the spiritual realm in which God rules and Christians live. *We* are the kingdom of God (Revelation 1:5–6).

John's third area of fellowship with his readers was "endurance." This is translated from the Greek word "*hypomone*"—one of two New Testament words for "patience." The other Greek word, "*makrothymia*," is sometimes translated as "long-suffering." The difference between the two words can be summed up this way. "Makrothymia" is the patience one exercises in passively putting up with difficult circumstances (or difficult people) when one doesn't really have to. Hence the translation "long-suffering." On the other hand, "hypomone" refers to perseverance. It is active, not passive.

For example, James reminds us of the "patience" (*hypomone*) of Job in James 5:10–11. Anyone who has read the book of Job knows that Job was anything but patient, in the way we commonly use the word. Job defends his own righteousness and challenges God's sense of "fair play." He does this with such vehemence that the Lord finally tells him that he's had enough. That's hardly our concept of patience—but it is a good description of the tenacity at the heart of "*hypomone*."

John has more in common with his first readers than they can imagine. He is a prisoner on the island of Patmos, and he is there because of his preaching. Patmos was a prison island ten miles long, five miles wide, and forty miles off the coast of Asia Minor (modern Turkey). It was the Alcatraz of its day. Yet, even though he was on that rock island, John was still "in the Spirit on the Lord's Day." In other words, he was engaged in worship. The Lord's Day is a reference to Sunday, even in modern Greek. Early

Christians applied "the Lord's Day" to the first day of the week in honor of Jesus's resurrection on that day[3]. What had started out for John as worship had apparently made him especially receptive to Jesus appearing to him in a vision.

The High Priest among the Lampstands (Revelation 1:12–20)

> I turned to see whose voice was speaking to me, and when I did so, I saw seven golden lampstands, and in the midst of the lampstands was one like a son of man. He was dressed in a robe extending down to his feet and he wore a wide golden belt around his chest. His head and hair were as white as wool, even as white as snow, and his eyes were like a fiery flame. His feet were like polished bronze refined in a furnace, and his voice was like the roar of many waters. He held seven stars in his right hand, and a sharp double- edged sword extended out of his mouth. His face shone like the sun shining at full strength. When I saw him I fell down at his feet as though I were dead, but he placed his right hand on me and said: "Do not be afraid! I am the first and the last, and the one who lives! I was dead, but look, now I am alive- forever and ever- and I hold the keys of death and of Hades! Therefore write what you saw, what is, and what will be after these things. The mystery of the seven stars that you saw in my right hand and the seven golden lampstands is this: The seven stars are the angels of the seven churches and the seven lampstands are the seven churches.
>
> —Revelation 1:12–20

John looks to see who's talking, and then tells us what he sees. The things John sees and hears in this first vision tell a great deal about the one whom he sees.

In order to get a good understanding of the visions in Revelation, it is important that you get the overall picture before you focus on the details. If you look too closely at the details without getting the big picture first, you could easily end up like the proverbial person who "can't see the forest for the trees."

The overall picture is of God's messenger from the book of Daniel. Daniel was visited by a messenger from God in Daniel 10:5–6. He was given a glimpse of future events from shortly after the birth of the Persian Empire through the death of Alexander the Great. The vision showed how Alexander's generals would divide up his empire and how they and their descendants would be at odds for generations. The vision zeroed in on one particularly sinister character, Antiochus IV Epiphanes, who tried to destroy the Jews, and on the revolt against him by Judas Maccabaeus and his followers.

John's description of Jesus in Revelation 1 is almost identical to Daniel's description of the divine messenger in Daniel 10. Both are girded with gold, both have blazing eyes, and both have brass feet. Their voices are described similarly as being a multitude or many waters. A comparison of the two passages leads us to conclude the vision in Revelation 1 is rooted in the vision in Daniel 10. John sees a messenger from God not unlike the messenger God sent to Daniel. But some of the details are different, and it is those details that help us sort out who the individual in Revelation 1 actually is.

First is his location and attire. John sees a man in a robe walking among lampstands. The image is of the High Priest in the holy place, tending the lamps (Exodus 27:20–21). Who is this priest? He is "one like a son of man." This image comes from Daniel 7:13–14. Daniel 7 depicts God on the throne ready to judge. Into his presence comes "one like a son of man," who is given an everlasting dominion. The Jews saw the coming Messiah. We see Jesus. Daniel 7:13 is the most often quoted verse from Daniel in the New Testament.

In Daniel's vision, the "one like a son of man" appears before

God in the form of a human being, but he is clearly of heavenly origin because he comes to his coronation accompanied by the clouds of the sky.

Jesus repeatedly referred to himself as "the Son of Man," and he emphasized that his return to earth would be accompanied by "clouds." In fact, Jesus used Daniel 7:13 as the text for his coming in judgment (Matthew 24:29–30).

Jesus's listeners understood that he was claiming to be none other than Daniel's "Son of Man" (Matthew 26:63–65). And when Jesus ascended from his disciples' view, the heavenly messengers on the scene picked up the theme of Jesus coming in the clouds (Acts 1:9–11). Even John recalls this description of Jesus's return in the early verses of Revelation (1:7).

Other parts of John's description, harking back to Daniel 7:9 and other passages, show that John is in the presence of deity. "While I was watching, thrones were set up, and the Ancient of Days took his seat. His attire was white like snow; the hair of his head was like lamb's wool. His throne was ablaze with fire and its wheels were all aflame" (Daniel 7:9). His voice is "like the voice of many waters"—a description that comes from Ezekiel 43:2. He has "a sharp two-edged sword" coming out of his mouth—a description that comes from Isaiah 49:1–3.

Here, in Revelation 1, he is the High Priest. Later, in Revelation 19:11–16, he will be the Divine Warrior.

So God sent a herald to John as he did to Daniel. But unlike the unidentified messenger to Daniel, there are enough details for us to identify John's messenger. It is our High Priest, whom the writer of Hebrews identifies as Jesus (Hebrews 4:14). When John saw him, he fell at his feet as if he were dead. That was the way Moses, Isaiah, and Ezekiel all reacted when they found themselves in the presence of God.

"The First and the Last" is another clear claim of divinity (Isaiah 44:6; 48:12). This is none other than Jesus, our High Priest, and he claims to be God. The high priest is walking among lampstands, holding stars in his hand. Think of the stars as flames. Imagine he is lighting the lamps by placing a flame on each lamp as he comes to it. That's not far-fetched, because the lamps are the churches, and the stars are the angels (messengers) of the churches. So when the High Priest places a star on each lampstand, he is passing his message to the church through the messenger of that particular church.

What Christ Thinks of the Churches

The high priest is tending the lampstands, which represent the churches. As he does so, he reports on the condition of each church. Each church existed in its own community, with its unique culture and challenges. In that respect, they were not unlike churches today. As Jesus lights each lampstand, he tells what he thinks of each church.

Amen!

Hallelujah!

Chapter 10

THE FIRST LETTER—EPHESUS (2:1–7)

To the angel of the church in Ephesus, write the following: "This is the solemn pronouncement of the one who has a firm grasp on the seven stars in his right hand- the one who walks among the seven golden lampstands: I know your works as well as your labor and steadfast endurance, and that you cannot tolerate evil. You have even put to the test those who refer to themselves as apostles (but are not), and have discovered that they are false. I am also aware that you have persisted steadfastly, endured much for the sake of my name, and have not grown weary. But I have this against you: You have departed from your first love! Therefore, remember from what high state you have fallen and repent! Do the deeds you did at the first; if not, I will come to you and remove your lampstand from its place- that is, if you do not repent. But you do have this going for you: You hate what the Nicolaitans practice- practices I also hate. The one who has an ear had better hear what the Spirit says to the churches. To the one who conquers, I will permit him to eat from the tree of life that is in the paradise of God.

—Revelation 2:1–7

The City

Ephesus was the political capital of Asia Minor and a center of commerce for the Roman Empire. It was located three miles inland, along the Cayster River. There is no city on the site today, because the harbor has long since been silted in. The nearest modern city is Kusadasi, Turkey.

In the last half of the first century, the city boasted a population of approximately five hundred thousand, making it about half the size of the city of Rome. The only larger cities in the Roman Empire of the day, besides Rome, were Alexandria and Syrian Antioch. Ephesus was the leading seaport of Asia Minor, and it was the beginning of all major trade routes through that part of the world in the first century. As a result, Christianity spread rapidly throughout Asia Minor once the church was planted in Ephesus. Luke tells about Paul's work in Ephesus and the spread of the gospel in Acts 19:8–10.

Ephesus had been made a free city by the Roman government in 98 BC, which meant that anyone born in the city was automatically a Roman citizen. The exchange between Paul and the Roman commander in Acts 22:28 demonstrates the importance and value of that heritage in the first century. Paul himself was a citizen of Rome because he was born in another free city—Tarsus (Acts 21:39).

Ephesus was as important to religion as it was to commerce. It was the center of worship of the Greek goddess Artemis, known to the Romans as Diana. Her temple was one of the seven wonders of the ancient world.

It is said that about four hundred years earlier, Alexander the Great asked to have his name carved on one of the 127 pillars of the Artemis temple, but the Ephesians declined, saying, "If we put the name of another god on her temple, it will upset her." Even though he was the most powerful man in the world of his day, he could not buy the privilege of having his name carved on a pillar of the idol's temple.

During the earliest days of Christianity in Ephesus, a riot broke out. It was spearheaded by craftsmen who traded in Artemis memorabilia (Acts 19:23–28). The riot involved the entire populace. It took place in the largest venue in the city, the grand theater, which still stands today (Acts 19:29–34). The theater had a seating capacity of about twenty-five thousand, so it is clear that this was no small disturbance. The mayor, fearful of intervention by the brutal Roman authorities, stepped in to quell this riot before it got entirely out of hand (Acts 19:35–41).

What could cause such an uproar? The riot had its roots in religion. It reflected the essential conflict between the monotheism of Christians and the polytheism of the city. But the real problem was economics. Paul's preaching was cutting into the sales of Artemis paraphernalia, and the people who manufactured and sold Artemis souvenirs were losing money. Then, as now, many of the world's conflicts that appeared on the surface to be cloaked in principle were really only matters of economics.

The Messenger

> "To the angel of the church in Ephesus, write the following: 'This is the solemn pronouncement of the one who has a firm grasp on the seven stars in his right hand -- the one who walks among the seven golden lampstands:'" (Revelation 2:1).

The messenger is the individual John saw in Revelation 1:9–20. In most of the seven letters, John singles out one or two aspects of the description from Revelation 1. In this letter, he identifies the messenger as the one who "holds the seven stars ... and walks among the seven golden lampstands." In other words, he identifies him as the High Priest, Jesus.

Recall that the lampstands are identified as the churches and the stars are their messengers. So here the priest who trims the lamps in the tabernacle or temple reports on their condition as he sees them.

The Message

> I know your works as well as your labor and steadfast endurance, and that you cannot tolerate evil. You have even put to the test those who refer to themselves as apostles (but are not), and have discovered that they are false. I am also aware that you have persisted steadfastly, endured much for the sake of my name, and have not grown weary. But I have this against you: You have departed from your first love! Therefore, remember from what high state you have fallen and repent! Do the deeds you did at the first; if not, I will come to you and remove your lampstand from its place -- that is, if you do not repent. But you do have this going for you: You hate what the Nicolaitans practice -- practices I also hate. (Revelation 2:2–6)

We know more about the church in Ephesus than about the churches in any of the other cities in Revelation. Much of what we know comes from the New Testament itself. The church in Ephesus began when Paul left Priscilla and Aquila, a wife and husband, there as missionaries, as related in Acts 18:19. During its early days, the church in Ephesus heard the preaching of Apollos (Acts 18:24–25), Paul (Acts 19:1–10), and Timothy (1 Timothy 1:3). By the time Revelation was written, the church in Ephesus had already received one letter from Paul and two addressed to their preacher, Timothy. Also, when Paul was on his last trip to Jerusalem, he made a special stop en route to pray with the elders from Ephesus (Acts 20:17–38). Tradition holds that John spent his last years in Ephesus where he died.

The church in Ephesus began with an unsurpassed zeal. New Christians, just converted from the occult practices of their past, burned the relics of their former practices rather than letting them serve as a temptation to themselves or others (Acts 19:19). And this was no small sacrifice. It represented a substantial sum of money.

By the time we get to the letter in Revelation 2, the church has lost its fervor. It is still working hard and persevering in its faith. Its teaching is healthy, and it does not put up with doctrinal error. But even though the church is doctrinally correct, it is spiritually destitute. The message is that the church must recapture the zeal it once had—or else! Jesus threatens to eliminate it entirely if it doesn't repent.

Today there is no church in Ephesus. Even the city lies in ruins. Is this perhaps evidence that the church in Ephesus failed to heed Jesus's warning?

The Promise

> "The one who has an ear had better hear what the
> Spirit says to the churches. To the one who conquers,
> I will permit him to eat from the tree of life that is in
> the paradise of God" (Revelation 2:7).

As in each of the letters, there is here a promise to the overcomers—those who are faithful to the end. This is a significant promise. The Bible itself begins with man in fellowship with God at the Tree of Life (Genesis 2:8–9). When man sinned, God banished him from access to the Tree of Life (Genesis 3:22–24). Here Jesus promises the overcomers a bite of the Tree of Life! This is the same tree that we will see at the end of Revelation, when man's fellowship with God—broken by sin—is finally restored (Revelation 22:1–5).

But even the promise includes a warning: "The one who has an ear had better hear what the Spirit says to the churches." Though directed to a specific congregation in Ephesus, this letter carries a message to other churches in similar circumstances. The warning is also a reminder that Revelation was intended to be understood—and acted upon—by its first readers, just as John wrote in Revelation 1:3.

Amen!
Hallelujah!

Chapter 11

THE SECOND LETTER—SMYRNA (2:8–11)

To the angel of the church in Smyrna write the following: "This is the solemn pronouncement of the one who is the first and the last, the one who was dead, but came to life: I know the distress you are suffering and your poverty (but you are rich). I also know the slander against you by those who call themselves Jews and really are not, but are a synagogue of Satan. Do not be afraid of the things you are about to suffer. The devil is about to have some of you thrown into prison so you may be tested, and you will experience suffering for ten days. Remain faithful even to the point of death, and I will give you the crown that is life itself. The one who has an ear had better hear what the Spirit says to the churches. The one who conquers will in no way be harmed by the second death."

—Revelation 2:8–11

The City

Smyrna, the modern city of Izmir, was located thirty-five miles north of Ephesus. In the first century, it was a sizable harbor city of two hundred thousand inhabitants. It was an intellectual center with a wealthy academic community.

Known for its famous buildings, it boasted a temple to Tiberius, as well as a host of temples and other religious edifices around the summit of Mount Pagos. That "crown of porticoes," so called by Apollonius, may be the image behind Jesus's promise of a "crown of life" to the overcomers in Smyrna (Revelation 1:10).

The city was built along a grand thoroughfare, called a "street of gold," that had temples at each end. This is likely the image Jesus used when he described the New Jerusalem in Revelation 21:21.

The Messenger

> "To the angel of the church in Smyrna write the following: 'This is the solemn pronouncement of the one who is the first and the last, the one who was dead, but came to life:' (Revelation 2:8).

Once again, John takes his description of the messenger from the vision in Revelation 1:17–18. "The one who is the first and the last" is a description of deity. It is reminiscent of what God said of himself in texts like Isaiah 44:6 and 48:12. The messenger is also "the one who was dead, but came to life." These words will be especially meaningful to Christians in Smyrna, because the messenger is going to tell them they are about to face persecution that may lead to their own deaths, at the hands of the Jewish community. So the messenger reminds them he faced the same experience from the Jews in Jerusalem. They killed him, but he came to life again. He can encourage them to "remain faithful even to the point of death" (Revelation 2:10) because he, himself, has gone through death, and come out alive.

The Message

> "I know the distress you are suffering and your poverty (but you are rich). I also know the slander against you by those who call themselves Jews and really are not, but are a synagogue of Satan. Do

not be afraid of the things you are about to suffer. The devil is about to have some of you thrown into prison so you may be tested, and you will experience suffering for ten days. Remain faithful even to the point of death, and I will give you the crown that is life itself" (Revelation 2:9–10).

Smyrna was home to a large Jewish community that was antagonistic to Christians. The messenger tells the church that they are about to undergo persecution from those Jews. The good news was that the persecution would last only a short time—ten days. The bad news was that the persecution would end in death!

Recall that ten is the number that signifies when someone says "Enough!" For example, after Laban changed his wages ten times, Jacob said "Enough!" (Genesis 31:6–7). And Job complained that his friends had accused him ten times when he said "Enough!" (Job 19:3). We say "three strikes and you're out!" But with God, people get ten strikes.

In the book of Exodus, God gave Pharaoh ten chances to do the right thing by freeing the Israelites. Plague after plague turned up the heat on Egypt until, with the tenth plague, God finally said "Enough!" It is the tenth plague that results in the final and decisive judgment on the nation of Egypt.

Ten plagues and the Red Sea should have convinced Israel to trust God, but it didn't. Israel rebelled ten times before God barred that generation from Canaan (Numbers 14:20–24). God gave Israel ten opportunities to change its heart and obey him. Interestingly, though twelve spies were sent into the land, it was the unfavorable report of ten that brought about Israel's disobedience at Kadesh Barnea. That was the straw that broke the camel's back, as far as God was concerned, causing him to say, "Enough!"

"Ten days" is the promise that God will say "Enough!" and will intervene. He will not allow us to be overcome by testing that is too strong for us to endure (1 Corinthians 10:13). The meaning of the encouragement "Remain faithful even to the point of death" is

"Be faithful, even if it costs you your life." And faithfulness would cost the lives of Christians from Smyrna. About eighty years after John wrote these words, one of their own would be martyred.

On one Sabbath day—February 23, AD 155—Polycarp, a disciple of John and an elder of this church, was burned to death in the theater in Smyrna for refusing to renounce Jesus. The Romans threatened to execute him but ultimately decided not to do so. When the Romans declined to execute Polycarp, the Jews were so enraged that they gathered the wood and set the fire, in violation of their own Sabbath laws. But Jesus, the messenger, promises that those who are faithful to death will ultimately receive the crown of life.

The Promise

> "The one who has an ear had better hear what the Spirit says to the churches. The one who conquers will in no way be harmed by the second death" (Revelation 2:11).

Each of the promises to each of the churches is particularly suited to its original readers. In Smyrna, the Christians are facing persecution and death. So they are encouraged by the one who "was dead, but came to life." He assures them that "the one who conquers will in no way be harmed by the second death."

We'll see that second death later, in Revelation 20:14. But for now, this reminds us of Jesus's words: "I tell you, my friends, do not be afraid of those who kill the body, and after that have nothing more they can do. But I will warn you whom you should fear: Fear the one who, after the killing, has authority to throw you into hell. Yes, I tell you, fear him!" (Luke 12:4–5).

As with all the letters, this one ends with the reminder that it has something to be understood and taken to heart by Christians not just in Smyrna, but in all times and places: "The one who has an ear had better hear what the Spirit says to the churches."

Amen!

Hallelujah!

Chapter 12

THE THIRD LETTER— PERGAMUM (2:12–17)

To the angel of the church in Pergamum write the following: "This is the solemn pronouncement of the one who has the sharp double- edged sword: I know where you live- where Satan's throne is. Yet you continue to cling to my name and you have not denied your faith in me, even in the days of Antipas, my faithful witness, who was killed in your city where Satan lives. But I have a few things against you: You have some people there who follow the teaching of Balaam, who instructed Balak to put a stumbling block before the people of Israel so they would eat food sacrificed to idols and commit sexual immorality. In the same way, there are also some among you who follow the teaching of the Nicolaitans. Therefore, repent! If not, I will come against you quickly and make war against those people with the sword of my mouth. The one who has an ear had better hear what the Spirit says to the churches. To the one who conquers, I will give him some of the hidden manna, and I will give him a white stone, and on that stone will be written a new name that no one can understand except the one who receives it."

—Revelation 2:12–17

The City

Pergamum, today known as Bergama, was at one time the capital of Asia Minor, before the seat of political power was transferred to Ephesus early in the first century. It was located inland, about sixty-five miles north of Smyrna, along the Caicus River, and it was home to about two hundred thousand people. It had the second largest library in the world, with two hundred thousand volumes, second only to the library in Alexandria, Egypt.

At one time, the king of Pergamum reportedly tried to hire Aristophanes, the librarian from Alexandria. Ptolemy II, Philadelphus, the ruler of Egypt, was so enraged that he imprisoned Aristophanes and cut off the supply of papyrus to Pergamum. That embargo was devastating to an enterprise like a library. Prior to that time, papyrus had been the main writing material in the world, and it was produced only in, and exported only from, Alexandria.

But, as the people in Pergamum were to learn, necessity is the mother of invention. When Pergamum could no longer acquire papyrus from Alexandria, the king, Eumenes II, commanded that an alternative writing material be developed. The people discovered they could stretch and dry specially treated sheep or goat skins and use them as a writing material. They called the material "vellum," but the world came to refer to it by the Greek word *"pergamene"* (lit. "from Pergamum"), in honor of the city. The word *"pergamene"* later became our "parchment." It was a much more durable writing material than papyrus ever was.

The two main gods of Pergamum were Dionysus and Asclepius. Dionysus, the god of the kings, was represented by the bull. Asclepius, the god of healing, was symbolized by a serpent spiraling around a staff (the emblem of the medical profession even today).

Pergamum was also the official center in Asia Minor for the imperial cult. It had three temples to the emperors, including the first in Asia Minor dedicated to Augustus. On a crag above the city of Pergamum was a throne-like altar to Zeus. No wonder Jesus describes Pergamum as the place "where Satan's throne is!" (2:13).

The Messenger

> "To the angel of the church in Pergamum write the following: 'This is the solemn pronouncement of the one who has the sharp double-edged sword:'" (Revelation 2:12).

Jesus describes himself with another part of the description from Revelation 1:16: "the one who has the sharp double-edged sword."

The "sharp double-edged sword" (Greek: *"rhomphaia"*) is the long, heavy broadsword with which the barbarians were armed for battle. Here it symbolizes the irresistible power of divine judgment, and it portends that the messenger's judgment is about to fall on the church in Pergamum.

The Message

> I know where you live -- where Satan's throne is. Yet you continue to cling to my name and you have not denied your faith in me, even in the days of Antipas, my faithful witness, who was killed in your city where Satan lives. But I have a few things against you: You have some people there who follow the teaching of Balaam, who instructed Balak to put a stumbling block before the people of Israel so they would eat food sacrificed to idols and commit sexual immorality. In the same way, there are also some among you who follow the teaching of the Nicolaitans. Therefore, repent! If not, I will come against you quickly and make war against those people with the sword of my mouth. (Revelation 2:13–16)

The church, by and large, is faithful. At least one of their own, a brother named Antipas, has already been martyred for his faith. But some people in the congregation are compromising with the world, and they are the ones who may face the double-edged sword of divine judgment.

What is the teaching of Baalam and of the Nicolaitans, anyway? The background of Baalam is Numbers 22–24; 25:1–4; 31:16. Israel was en route to the Promised Land. Balak, of Midian, tried to hire a prophet, Baalam, to curse Israel. Baalam asked God for permission, but the Lord, at first, refused. Balak upped the ante by offering Balaam a lot of money and power, and Baalam asked again. This time God allowed Baalam to go, but he warned him that he could say only what the Lord would allow him to say. Baalam tried to curse Israel three times, but each time he opened his mouth to curse them, out came a blessing! Finally Balak had enough and sent him on his way.

The next event for Israel involved idolatry and immorality. It was the incident at Baal Peor recounted in Numbers 25:1–9. The Israelite men got involved in sexual immorality with the Moabite women and started participating in idol worship. A plague broke out—the result of the Lord's anger. Phinehas, the grandson of Aaron, killed one of the perpetrators, along with his Midianite mistress. But by the time the plague had ended, twenty-four thousand Israelites lay dead.

Several chapters later, In Numbers 31, we learn the backstory to the incident at Baal Peor. The Israelites defeat their enemies, but they keep some of the women and children alive. Moses is aghast! "Moses said to them, 'Have you allowed all the women to live? Look, these people through the counsel of Balaam caused the Israelites to act treacherously against the Lord in the matter of Peor- which resulted in the plague among the community of the Lord!'" (Numbers 31:15–16). Now it makes sense!

God turned Baalam's curses into blessings. So Baalam suggested to Balak a way to force God's hand into cursing Israel. All it would take would be to draw the people of God into compromising their faith with the world. If they were to dabble in sin, God would curse them! So Balak's people enticed the Israelites into immorality and idolatry until the Lord turned on them! Baalam was the mastermind behind Baal-Peor!

But what is the connection between Baalam and the Nicolaitans? The name Baalam is derived by joining two Hebrew words: "*Baal*," meaning "destroyer," and "*ammon*," meaning "people." "Nicolaitan" is derived by joining two Greek words: "*Nikon*," meaning "destroyer," and "*laos*," meaning "people." So both words have a common meaning: "destroyer of people."

Why does this letter use two words, one Hebrew and one Greek, with the same meaning? Possibly it is meant to reflect that within the church at Pergamum there are both Jewish and Gentile Christians engaging in and encouraging compromise with the world.

The Promise

> "The one who has an ear had better hear what the
> Spirit says to the churches. To the one who conquers,
> I will give him some of the hidden manna, and I
> will give him a white stone, and on that stone will
> be written a new name that no one can understand
> except the one who receives it." (Revelation 2:17).

First the overcomers are promised "some of the hidden manna." This certainly would remind the readers of the manna that sustained ancient Israel in the desert (Deuteronomy 8:3). But to Christians, it is even more a reminder of Jesus himself (John 6:48–51).

The second promise is "a white stone with a new name written on it." Readers in Pergamum would be familiar with two uses of white stones with inscribed names. Among the ruins of Pergamum, archaeologists have found white stone pillars bearing the inscribed names of prominent citizens. So this could be Jesus's way of saying something Paul said elsewhere: "However, God's solid foundation remains standing, bearing this seal: 'The Lord knows those who are his,' and 'Everyone who confesses the name of the Lord must turn away from evil.'" (2 Timothy 2:19).

Alternatively, it could be a reference to an invitation to a banquet. It may be that Jesus intends for readers to think of the "white stone" as his invitation to the wedding supper of the Lamb. "Then the angel said to me, 'Write the following: Blessed are those who are invited to the banquet at the wedding celebration of the Lamb!' He also said to me, 'These are the true words of God'" (Revelation 19:9).

The "new name" in this promise is a reminder to the Christians of God's promise to Israel in Isaiah 62: "Nations will see your vindication, and all kings your splendor. You will be called by a new name that the Lord himself will give you" (Isaiah 62:2). That promise, however, was also a not-so-veiled threat, because if, as history bore out, Israel didn't live up to the name God gave them, "Your names will live on in the curse formulas of my chosen ones. The sovereign Lord will kill you, but he will give his servants another name" (Isaiah 65:15).

By the time Revelation was written, God had bestowed a new name in place of the name "Israel." That new name, bestowed in keeping with his promise, was "Christian."

Amen!

Hallelujah!

Chapter 13

THE FOURTH LETTER— THYATIRA (2:18–29)

To the angel of the church in Thyatira write the following: "This is the solemn pronouncement of the Son of God, the one who has eyes like a fiery flame and whose feet are like polished bronze: I know your deeds: your love, faith, service, and steadfast endurance. In fact, your more recent deeds are greater than your earlier ones. But I have this against you: You tolerate that woman Jezebel, who calls herself a prophetess, and by her teaching deceives my servants to commit sexual immorality and to eat food sacrificed to idols. I have given her time to repent, but she is not willing to repent of her sexual immorality. Look! I am throwing her onto a bed of violent illness, and those who commit adultery with her into terrible suffering, unless they repent of her deeds. Furthermore, I will strike her followers with a deadly disease, and then all the churches will know that I am the one who searches minds and hearts. I will repay each one of you what your deeds deserve. But to the rest of you in Thyatira, all who do not hold to this teaching (who have not learned the so-called "deep secrets of Satan"), to you I say: I do not put any additional burden on you. However, hold on to what

you have until I come. And to the one who conquers
and who continues in my deeds until the end, I will
give him authority over the nations- he will rule them
with an iron rod and like clay jars he will break them
to pieces, just as I have received the right to rule from
my Father- and I will give him the morning star. The
one who has an ear had better hear what the Spirit
says to the churches.

—Revelation 2:18–29

The City

Thyatira, which is now the modern Akhisar, was about forty-five
miles east of Pergamum. It was a blue-collar city that produced
and sold wool, linen, clothing, and goods made from leather
and bronze. Thyatira was home to more trade guilds, similar to
modern labor unions, than any other city in Asia Minor. Each
guild had its own patron deity and religious festivities, which
included sexual excesses.

This provided a Catch-22 for Christians in the first century.
In order to be able to work, they had to maintain membership
in the trade guilds. But, as members of the guilds, they were
expected to compromise their principles by engaging in their
guilds' idolatry and sexual immorality.

You may remember that Paul's first convert in Philippi was
a Thyatiran merchant—a dealer in purple cloth named Lydia
(Acts 16:14). Archaeological excavations have revealed that a
guild of dyers existed in Thyatira. Lydia's trade may have been
associated with this guild. They brewed a red dye, the modern
Turkey red, from the madder root that grows abundantly in the
area. Lydia's presence in Macedonia, five hundred miles away,
suggests this commodity was an important export from Thyatira.

Yet in spite of plenty of reason and opportunity to compromise,
the church was basically faithful. Even so, Jesus said there was a
woman in the congregation, whom he identified as "Jezebel," who

was encouraging Christians to get involved in sexual immorality and idolatry—the very things the trade guilds promoted.

Jesus's concern with the church was not just that this Jezebel was present in the church but also that the church was tolerating her licentiousness. Like the church in Corinth, they were patting themselves on the back because of their tolerance of blatant sin (1 Corinthians 5:1–2). The problem with tolerating sin in the church is that it leads to more sin that can infect the entire church.

The Messenger

"To the angel of the church in Thyatira write the following: 'This is the solemn pronouncement of the Son of God, the one who has eyes like a fiery flame and whose feet are like polished bronze:" (Revelation 2:18).

Once again, drawing from the vision in Revelation 1:14–15, the messenger is "the one who has eyes like a fiery flame and whose feet are like polished bronze." But just in case there is any doubt about who he is, he is further described not as "one like a son of man" (1:12) but as none other than "the Son of God."

The image, with its fiery flame and polished bronze, would remind the readers in Thyatira of the furnaces of the metalworkers, whose guilds were a key part of their economy.

But the descriptions, at one and the same time, emphasize imminent divine judgment. It is a reminder of the divine messenger who had been sent to Daniel centuries before, who was described in similar terms (Daniel 10:5–6).

The Message

I know your deeds: your love, faith, service, and steadfast endurance. In fact, your more recent deeds are greater than your earlier ones. But I have this against you: You tolerate that woman Jezebel, who calls herself a prophetess, and by her teaching deceives my servants to commit sexual immorality and to eat food sacrificed to idols. I have given her time to repent, but she is not willing to repent of her sexual immorality. Look! I am throwing her onto a bed of violent illness, and those who commit adultery with her into terrible suffering, unless they repent of her deeds. Furthermore, I will strike her followers with a deadly disease, and then all the churches will know that I am the one who searches minds and hearts. I will repay each one of you what your deeds deserve. But to the rest of you in Thyatira, all who do not hold to this teaching (who have not learned the so-called "deep secrets of Satan"), to you I say: I do not put any additional burden on you. However, hold on to what you have until I come. (Revelation 2:19–25)

We cannot know for certain just who this woman was, but we can be reasonably certain that she wasn't *actually* named Jezebel. Some names are considered to be damaged goods after certain people wear them. That's the reason respectable people these days don't name their sons Adolph Hitler, Benedict Arnold, or Judas Iscariot. Jezebel was just such a disgraced name.

Jezebel was the wife of Ahab, a ninth-century BC king of Israel. Ahab owes his prominence in the Old Testament to the religious apostasy that occurred during his reign. Jezebel was the queen to Israel's most decadent king (1 Kings 16:30–31). In fact, Jezebel was the real driving force behind Ahab's apostasy (1 Kings 21:25–26). She was the one who introduced him to the idolatry of Baal and the orgies of Ashtoreth. What a fitting name to give a woman in Thyatira who was encouraging Christians to participate in the idolatry and immorality in the trade guilds! She was just like her namesake, Jezebel, trying to convince God's people that they could dabble in sin and still be saints!

But the one with piercing eyes saw through this woman and

her followers. And he said they had better repent. They could run from God, but they could not hide (Jeremiah 17:10)! For the rest, the Lord says only, "Hold on to what you have" (i.e., be faithful).

Tertullian, a second-century lawyer, was something of an unwelcome conscience to the church of his day. He wrote a series of essays on idolatry, including a piece on compromise. In that essay, he sets up a scenario that would have been familiar to Christians in first-century Thyatira. It went something like this: A Christian might confess Caesar as Lord, or engage in idolatry or immorality, and then might attempt to justify his compromise by saying, "I must live." In other words, he might plead economic necessity as a justification for compromising his principles. Tertullian's answer to such foolishness was his insistence that Christ does not require that we live but does require that we *be faithful*.

The Promise

> "And to the one who conquers and who continues in my deeds until the end, I will give him authority over the nations -- he will rule them with an iron rod and like clay jars he will break them to pieces, just as I have received the right to rule from my Father -- and I will give him the morning star. The one who has an ear had better hear what the Spirit says to the churches" (Revelation 2:26–29).

The first promise—the promise of "authority over the nations"—reminds us of the first of the royal psalms: "Ask me, and I will give you the nations as your inheritance, the ends of the earth as your personal property. You will break them with an iron scepter; you will smash them like a potter's jar!" (Psalm 2:8–9).

The second part of the promise is "I will give him the morning star." The "morning star" is the planet Venus, which appears in the east as the harbinger of the coming day. It appears as the darkness passes away; its arrival announces the coming of the sun. In simple terms, the morning star signifies the dawning of a new day or a new era. The symbolism of the star was sometimes used to signify dominion. For example, the Babylonian kingdom had started with so much promise, but it was later brought low. God, through the prophet Isaiah, described Babylon's fall in terms of a star that had fallen from the sky (Isaiah 14:12). And remember Balaam? During one of his attempts to curse Israel, he looked to the distant future and described the rise of the Messiah's star (Numbers 24:17). Centuries after Balaam, when Jesus was born, the thing that tipped the wise men off was the appearance of his star (Matthew 2:1–2). So, in simple terms, when Jesus promises "the morning star" to the overcomers in Thyatira, he is promising nothing less than himself, because he is the morning star, which signifies a new day.

"I, Jesus, have sent my angel to testify to you about these things for the churches. I am the root and the descendant of David, the bright morning star!" (Revelation 22:16). Jesus promises himself to his people, just as Peter said elsewhere. "Moreover, we possess the prophetic word as an altogether reliable thing. You do well if you pay attention to this as you would to a light shining in a murky place, until the day dawns and the morning star rises in your hearts" (2 Peter 1:19).

Amen!

Hallelujah!

Chapter 14

THE FIFTH LETTER—SARDIS (3:1–6)

To the angel of the church in Sardis write the following: "This is the solemn pronouncement of the one who holds the seven spirits of God and the seven stars: 'I know your deeds, that you have a reputation that you are alive, but in reality you are dead. Wake up then, and strengthen what remains that was about to die, because I have not found your deeds complete in the sight of my God. Therefore, remember what you received and heard, and obey it, and repent. If you do not wake up, I will come like a thief, and you will never know at what hour I will come against you. But you have a few individuals in Sardis who have not stained their clothes, and they will walk with me dressed in white, because they are worthy. The one who conquers will be dressed like them in white clothing, and I will never erase his name from the book of life, but will declare his name before my Father and before his angels. The one who has an ear had better hear what the Spirit says to the churches.'"

—Revelation 3:1–6.

The City

Sardis, now modern Bin Tepe, was located about thirty miles south of Thyatira. Over six centuries earlier, it had been the capital of Lydia, whose last ruler was a man named Croesus. You may have heard some wealthy person described as being "as rich as Croesus." That description comes from the legendary wealth of the king who reigned from 560 to 546 BC. Croesus's luck ran out when Cyrus the Great of Persia invaded Lydia. When it appeared that the invasion was imminent, Croesus consulted the oracle of Delphi. The oracle cryptically said, "If Croesus goes to war, he will destroy a great empire." Naturally, Croesus thought that meant he would prevail. So he went to war with Cyrus and suffered defeat—destroying his own great empire.

In very early times, Sardis was an important commercial city. Pliny says that the art of dyeing wool was invented there, and it was known for manufacture of dyed woolen tapestries, carpets, and clothing. Electrum, an alloy of gold and silver, was mined in the Pactolus River nearby. This led to Sardis's fame as a producer of jewelry, as well as Sardis being the first city to develop the necessary processes to mint silver and gold coins. The principal goddess of Sardis was Cybele. The massive ruins of her temple are still visible today.

Sardis sat fifteen hundred feet up on a ledge jutting out of the side of a mountain. It was considered impregnable because of its nearly vertical rock walls. Even so, it was captured twice, by stealth. Herodotus tells of Cyrus taking the city in 549 BC. A Persian soldier observed a Sardian descending the southern winding path to retrieve his helmet after dropping it over the side. The Persians then followed his path back up to the summit and took the city by surprise.

From the Persians it passed into the hands of Alexander the Great. For the next three hundred years, its history is obscure. Then, in 214 BC, it was taken by Antiochus III after a siege of two years. Antiochus had read Herodotus's account of the Persian invasion of Sardis. His army then invaded the city in the same way the Persians had, with the same result.

During the reign of Tiberius, Sardis was among a dozen cities destroyed by an earthquake. The calamity was followed by a plague that wiped out a large part of the population. Sardis boasted a necropolis—a Greek term meaning "city of the dead"— which was a burial site that was visible for seven miles before reaching the city. By the end of the first century, the name of Sardis had become synonymous with unjustified pretensions and unfulfilled promises.

Over a century ago, a ship launched with the promise it was unsinkable. That was before it was ripped open by an iceberg on its maiden voyage. The "unsinkable" *Titanic* has been sitting at the bottom of the Atlantic Ocean ever since.

Sardis, much like the Titanic, never lived up to its promises.

The Messenger

> "To the angel of the church in Sardis write the following: 'This is the solemn pronouncement of the one who holds the seven spirits of God and the seven stars: "I know your deeds, that you have a reputation that you are alive, but in reality you are dead."'" (Revelation 3:1)

The messenger holds the seven spirits of God. "The seven spirits of God" in this instance is an apparent reference to the Holy Spirit, who was introduced in Revelation 1:4–5. From the beginning of Revelation, the Holy Spirit is placed on a par with God and Christ. We'll see his presence later in the throne scene both as "seven flaming torches" of God (4:5) and "seven eyes" of the Lamb (5:6). The figure of the Holy Spirit as "seven eyes" comes from Zechariah 4:1–10.

The messenger further identifies himself as "the one who holds ... the seven stars." That is a clear reference to Revelation 1:16. And the mystery of the stars has already been revealed so that we know the seven stars are the angels of the seven churches (1:20)

The Message

> I know your deeds, that you have a reputation that
> you are alive, but in reality you are dead. Wake up
> then, and strengthen what remains that was about
> to die, because I have not found your deeds complete
> in the sight of my God. Therefore, remember what
> you received and heard, and obey it, and repent. If
> you do not wake up, I will come like a thief, and you
> will never know at what hour I will come against
> you. But you have a few individuals in Sardis who
> have not stained their clothes, and they will walk
> with me dressed in white, because they are worthy.
> (Revelation 3:1–4)

The church in Sardis, like the city itself, appeared to be resting on its reputation. It appeared to be alive, but Jesus said it was just as dead as the corpses inhabiting the city's world-famous necropolis. This was much like looking at well-dressed bodies in caskets at a funeral parlor and commenting on how natural they look. They may very well look natural, but they're still dead!

Jesus assured the church that he knew their deeds, but he also knew they had not finished what they had started. He put it this way: "I have not found your deeds complete in the sight of my God." Popular doctrine may say that our works don't really matter all that much. But the Bible says otherwise in places like James 2:14–26. Here Jesus tells the church in Sardis that if it doesn't wake up, he will, like Cyrus the Great and Antiochus III, execute his own sneak attack on the church.

The church was in trouble, but some individual Christians were still living up to their calling. Jesus said they were "worthy." They had "not stained their clothes," so he said they would walk with him "dressed in white." The Sardians could not miss the contrast between "stained" and "white" garments. The heart of their economy was the dyeing trade. They took white cloth and stained it with colors to make it anything but white. So Jesus promised that those who had not stained their garments with sin would walk with him dressed in white.

The Promise

> "The one who conquers will be dressed like them in white clothing, and I will never erase his name from the book of life, but will declare his name before my Father and before his angels. The one who has an ear had better hear what the Spirit says to the churches" (Revelation 3:5–6).

The promise in this letter is threefold. First, there is the promise of white garments for the overcomer. As stated above, the Sardians would understand this promise, given their commercial dyeing trade. Second, there is the promise that the overcomer's name will be indelibly printed in the Book of Life. Third, there is the promise that Jesus will acknowledge the overcomer before God.

This idea of God keeping a book of names runs through the Bible. There are references both in the Old Testament (Exodus 32:32–33; Daniel 12:1) and in the New Testament (Philippians 4:3; 2 Timothy 2:19).

In Revelation, everyone worships the beast except for those whose names are in the Book of Life (Revelation 13:7–8; 17:8). During the Day of Judgment, the key question on which a person's destiny rests is this: "Was his name in the Book of Life?" (20:11–15). Ultimately, the New Jerusalem is home only to those whose names are written in the Book of Life (21:26–27).

I want my name there! Don't you?

Amen!

Hallelujah!

Chapter 15

THE SIXTH LETTER— PHILADELPHIA (3:7–13)

To the angel of the church in Philadelphia write the following: "This is the solemn pronouncement of the Holy One, the True One, who holds the key of David, who opens doors no one can shut, and shuts doors no one can open: 'I know your deeds. (Look! I have put in front of you an open door that no one can shut.) I know that you have little strength, but you have obeyed my word and have not denied my name. Listen! I am going to make those people from the synagogue of Satan -- who say they are Jews yet are not, but are lying -- Look, I will make them come and bow down at your feet and acknowledge that I have loved you. Because you have kept my admonition to endure steadfastly, I will also keep you from the hour of testing that is about to come on the whole world to test those who live on the earth. I am coming soon. Hold on to what you have so that no one can take away your crown. The one who conquers I will make a pillar in the temple of my God, and he will never depart from it. I will write on him the name of my God and the name of the city of my God (the new Jerusalem that comes down out of heaven from my

God), and my new name as well. The one who has
an ear had better hear what the Spirit says to the
churches.'"

—Revelation 3:7–13

The City

Philadelphia, now modern Alasehir ("city of Allah"), was situated
twenty-eight miles southeast of Sardis. It was in the Hermus River
valley on the main highway connecting Smyrna to territories in
the East. It was also on the imperial post road from Rome via
Troas, Pergamum, and Sardis. The region was a fertile wine-
growing district. Its coins bore the head of Bacchus (also known
as Dionysus), the god of drink. The population included Jews,
Jewish Christians, and converts from heathenism.

The region was earthquake prone. In AD 17, an earthquake
destroyed Philadelphia. The emperor, Tiberius, paid to have
the city rebuilt. As a result, Philadelphia ultimately became
dependent on government aid to exist.

Jesus didn't have a single word of condemnation for the
church. They were being persecuted. The chief opposition to the
church came from the Jews. But they were assured that God
would protect them and that they would ultimately be crowned.
All they needed to do was hang on.

The Messenger

"To the angel of the church in Philadelphia write the
following: 'This is the solemn pronouncement of the
Holy One, the True One, who holds the key of David,
who opens doors no one can shut, and shuts doors no
one can open:'" (Revelation 3:7–13).

There are two major aspects to the messenger's self-designation
in this letter. First, he is "the Holy One, the True One." These

descriptions are used elsewhere in Revelation of God himself (4:6–8; 6:10). Jesus is called "the Holy One" elsewhere in the New Testament (Mark 1:23–23; John 6:67–69). "The True One" is a recognized title of the Messiah in Revelation (3:14; 19:11). Elsewhere in the New Testament, Jesus is called "the true" something or another. He is "the true light" (John 1:9), "the true bread from heaven (John 6:32), and "the true vine" (John 15:1).

Second, he "holds the key of David." The figure of the "key of David" comes from Isaiah 22: "At that time I will summon my servant Eliakim, son of Hilkiah. I will put your robe on him, tie your belt around him, and transfer your authority to him. He will become a protector of the residents of Jerusalem and of the people of Judah. I will place the key to the house of David on his shoulder. When he opens the door, no one can close it; when he closes the door, no one can open it." (Isaiah 22:20–22).

What Isaiah said of Eliakim is true of Jesus. What Jesus does, no man can undo. This is similar to what is said about God in Job 12: "If he tears down, it cannot be rebuilt; if he imprisons a person, there is no escape" (Job 12:14).

The Message

> I know your deeds. (Look! I have put in front of you an open door that no one can shut.) I know that you have little strength, but you have obeyed my word and have not denied my name. Listen! I am going to make those people from the synagogue of Satan- who say they are Jews yet are not, but are lying- Look, I will make them come and bow down at your feet and acknowledge that I have loved you. Because you have kept my admonition to endure steadfastly, I will also keep you from the hour of testing that is about to come on the whole world to test those who live on the earth. I am coming soon. Hold on to what you have so that no one can take away your crown. (Revelation 3:8–11)

The metaphor of the open door was a common one that would have been familiar to early Christians. Jesus had used it to describe how his sheep could access true safety and security in his fold (John 10:7–9). Early Christians would have been even more familiar with the concept of a door of opportunity for evangelism (Acts 14:27; 1 Corinthians 16:8–9; Colossians 4:2–3). We will see the metaphor of the door again in Revelation (3:20; 4:1). The "open door" here is opportunity in the midst of opposition. There is opportunity for evangelism in spite of Jewish hostility against Christians.

When Jesus said "you have little strength," he was alluding to the fact that the church had little influence in Philadelphia because Christians were likely from lower classes of society. That was often the case, as is seen elsewhere in the New Testament (1 Corinthians 1:26).

In Philadelphia, the church had remained faithful even during their crisis of trial. Jesus wanted people to obey his word, as he had told his disciples earlier (John 17:6). When Jesus praised the church in Philadelphia, it was because they had not denied his name. He was likely referring to some crisis during which unbelievers tried to compel the Christians to deny Jesus but they stood true to their faith.

As in Smyrna, this opposition had come from the Jewish community (Revelation 2:9). Yet in time the Jews would be forced to acknowledge that these Christians were truly loved by God (3:9). This is a reminder of similar promises to God's people in the Old Testament (Isaiah 45:14; 60:14).

Jesus went on to give assurances to the faithful within the church: "Because you have kept my admonition to endure steadfastly, I will also keep you from the hour of testing that is about to come on the whole world to test those who live on the earth." (Revelation 3:10). Since they had persevered, he promised to preserve them. This implies not keeping them *from* temptation, but keeping them *in* it, as a result of which they will be delivered *out of* its power. It is consistent with his earlier prayer for the disciples in John 17: "I am not asking you to take them out of the world, but that you keep them safe from the evil one" (John 17:15).

Here Jesus urged the Christians in Philadelphia to persevere in light of his "coming." What did he mean when he said, "I am coming?" God's "coming" meant judgment for his enemies and justification for his people. In these letters to the churches, his "coming" posed a threat of judgment.

> I am coming soon. Hold on to what you have so that no one can take away your crown. (Revelation 3:11)

> Therefore, repent! If not, I will come against you quickly and make war against those people with the sword of my mouth. (Revelation 2:16)

Later in Revelation, the promise of reward takes on more prominence than the threat of judgment.

> Look! I am coming soon! Blessed is the one who keeps the words of the prophecy expressed in this book. (Revelation 22:7)

> Look! I am coming soon, and my reward is with me to pay each one according to what he has done! (Revelation 22:12)

> The one who testifies to these things says, "Yes, I am coming soon!" Amen! Come, Lord Jesus! (Revelation 22:20)

The Lord's coming can bring either the threat of punishment or the promise of reward, depending on one's relationship to God at the time of his "coming." "Once saved, always saved" is popular doctrine, but Jesus knew nothing about any such teaching. He told Christians in Smyrna, "Do not be afraid of the things you are about to suffer. The devil is about to have some of you thrown into prison so you may be tested, and you will experience suffering for ten days. Remain faithful even to the point of death, and I will give you the crown that is life itself" Revelation 2:10).

Paul lived with the same hope: "I have competed well; I have finished the race; I have kept the faith! Finally the crown of righteousness is reserved for me. The Lord, the righteous Judge, will award it to me in that day- and not to me only, but also to all who have set their affection on his appearing" (2 Timothy 4:7–8).

Christians have a crown that Jesus describes as "your crown." But he also says their crown can be taken away if they do not persevere.

The Promise

> "The one who conquers I will make a pillar in the temple of my God, and he will never depart from it. I will write on him the name of my God and the name of the city of my God (the new Jerusalem that comes down out of heaven from my God), and my new name as well. The one who has an ear had better hear what the Spirit says to the churches" (Revelation 3:12–13).

First, Jesus promised stability. He contrasted the stability of a "pillar" in God's temple with the instability of Philadelphia, which suffered frequent earthquakes. Strabo, the ancient historian and geographer, described the city shortly after the earthquake of AD 17 with these words: "And Philadelphia has not even its walls unimpaired, but daily they are shaken in some way, and gaps are made in them. But the inhabitants continue to occupy the land notwithstanding their sufferings, and to build new houses." The instability of Philadelphia stands in stark contrast to the stability of God's eternal kingdom (Daniel 2:44).

Second, Jesus promised access. The High Priest wore the name of Yahweh on a golden plate on his forehead when performing his duties in the tabernacle (Exodus 28:36–38).

God's people are seen elsewhere in Revelation. There they

have God's name on their foreheads, showing that they are priests, protected by God and having access to God.

> Do not damage the earth or the sea or the trees until we have put a seal on the foreheads of the servants of our God. (Revelation 7:3)

> They were told not to damage the grass of the earth, or any green plant or tree, but only those people who did not have the seal of God on their forehead. (Revelation 9:4)

> Then I looked, and here was the Lamb standing on Mount Zion, and with him were one hundred and forty-four thousand, who had his name and his Father's name written on their foreheads. (Revelation 14:1)

> His servants will worship him, and they will see his face, and his name will be on their foreheads. (Revelation 22:3–4)

Third, Jesus promised a part in the "new Jerusalem." This harkens back to Ezekiel's description of the heavenly city (Ezekiel 48:35). There are a number of New Testament references to heaven describing it as a city (Revelation 21:10; Galatians 4:26; Hebrews 12:22). Even on earth, our citizenship is really in heaven (Philippians 3:20).

Amen!

Hallelujah!

Chapter 16

THE SEVENTH LETTER— LAODICEA (3:14–22)

To the angel of the church in Laodicea write the following: "This is the solemn pronouncement of the Amen, the faithful and true witness, the originator of God's creation: 'I know your deeds, that you are neither cold nor hot. I wish you were either cold or hot! So because you are lukewarm, and neither hot nor cold, I am going to vomit you out of my mouth! Because you say, "I am rich and have acquired great wealth, and need nothing," but do not realize that you are wretched, pitiful, poor, blind, and naked, take my advice and buy gold from me refined by fire so you can become rich! Buy from me white clothing so you can be clothed and your shameful nakedness will not be exposed, and buy eye salve to put on your eyes so you can see! All those I love, I rebuke and discipline. So be earnest and repent! Listen! I am standing at the door and knocking! If anyone hears my voice and opens the door I will come into his home and share a meal with him, and he with me. I will grant the one who conquers permission to sit with me on my throne, just as I too conquered and sat down with my Father on his throne. The one who has an ear had better hear what the Spirit says to the churches.'"

—Revelation 3:14–22

The City

Laodicea, now modern Eskisehir, was forty-five miles southeast of Philadelphia and one hundred miles east of Ephesus. It was located on a group of hills between the Asopus and Caprus Rivers, two tributaries of the Lycus. It sat on the great Roman road that stretched to the inland of Asia Minor from the coast at Ephesus. This made it an important center of trade and communication.

In the first century, Laodicea was one of the most flourishing cities of Asia Minor. Hiero had bequeathed his property to the people and adorned the city with costly gifts. The citizens had developed a taste for Greek art, and they were distinguished in science and literature.

Laodicea was the banking center of first-century Asia Minor. It was a fashion center with a far-ranging reputation for a fine quality of glossy black wool peculiar to the sheep of the area. The city also boasted a medical school known worldwide for an eye ointment called Phrygian powder, as well as specialty ear ointments.

It was the chief city of a Roman *conventus*, or political district. The proconsul of the province held court in Laodicea and it was the place where taxes from the area towns were collected. Cicero held his court and wrote many of his letters there. The *conventus* represented by Laodicea comprised at least twenty-five towns. Archaeologists have discovered inscriptions in the region that refer to Laodicea as "the metropolis."

Laodicea, like Philadelphia, was destroyed by the earthquake of AD 17. However, because of their vast wealth, the people refused imperial help. Unlike Philadelphia, they rebuilt the city entirely by themselves.

But Laodicea had no good water supply. Its water was tepid

and had a high mineral content that made it terrible for drinking. Hierapolis, six miles to the north, was known for its hot mineral springs that had been fashioned into luxurious spas. Wealthy people from all over the world visited the spas of Hierapolis for their therapeutic value. Colosse, six miles to the southeast, had cold, pure water that was good for drinking. Because its own water was hardly drinkable, the city of Laodicea built aqueducts to pipe in cold drinking water from Colosse. The ruins of these are still visible today. Anyone who ever lived in or visited Laodicea could hardly mistake the reference to their terrible water.

Paul's protégé Epaphras was from the region near Laodicea, and Paul wrote at least one letter to the church there (Colossians 4:12–16). Like the city, the church was cocky and self-assured. They didn't know that they were spiritually destitute, and they made Jesus want to throw up!

The Messenger

> "To the angel of the church in Laodicea write the following: 'This is the solemn pronouncement of the Amen, the faithful and true witness, the originator of God's creation:'" (Revelation 3:14).

When the messenger identified himself as "the Amen," he laid claim to being God's final word. When he called himself "the faithful and true witness," he identified himself as the leader of God's armies found later in the book (19:11). He also declared himself to be God's message (21:5; 22:6). Then he called himself "the originator of God's creation." Other translations say "the beginning of God's creation." The idea is seen elsewhere (Colossians 1:18; Hebrews 12:1–2).

The Message

> I know your deeds, that you are neither cold nor hot.
> I wish you were either cold or hot! So because you

are lukewarm, and neither hot nor cold, I am going to vomit you out of my mouth! Because you say, "I am rich and have acquired great wealth, and need nothing," but do not realize that you are wretched, pitiful, poor, blind, and naked, take my advice and buy gold from me refined by fire so you can become rich! Buy from me white clothing so you can be clothed and your shameful nakedness will not be exposed, and buy eye salve to put on your eyes so you can see! All those I love, I rebuke and discipline. So be earnest and repent! Listen! I am standing at the door and knocking! If anyone hears my voice and opens the door I will come into his home and share a meal with him, and he with me. (Revelation 3:15–20)

Jesus made references that would have been very familiar to the Laodiceans. For one thing, he said that they were neither hot nor cold but lukewarm. Most commentators suggest that "cold" denotes that there is no pretense of religion while "hot" denotes zealous devotion. They further assume that "lukewarm" refers to someone who professes to be religious but is really not. Following their reasoning, Jesus preferred the outright opposition of one who was "cold" to the indifference of an apathetic Christian. That is probably not Jesus's intent in referring to their "lukewarmness."

The description of lukewarm water would certainly resonate with the residents of Laodicea. A six-mile-long aqueduct brought Laodicea its supply of water from Colosse. But by the time the water arrived in the open aqueducts, it had become tepid and had picked up all sorts of sediment. The residents, as wealthy as they were, knew what drinking lukewarm water was all about.

When Jesus referred to their spiritual devotion using the description of "lukewarm" water, he probably meant something like this: "The hot water of Hierapolis is good for bathing, and the cold water of Colosse is good for drinking, but you are like lukewarm water that is not good for anything and is almost impossible to stomach!"

Then Jesus moved to more figures very familiar to the Laodiceans. Laodicea was a center of high finance and fashion. To say they were spiritually destitute and naked would speak volumes about their spiritual condition. It's hard to read this description without thinking of the old short story "The Emperor's New Clothes"—the story of a ruler who was convinced he was dressed in the height of fashion, while he was really naked. Jesus said the Laodiceans thought they were dressed in the height of fashion, but they were spiritually stark naked!

Laodicea housed the foremost medical school of its day, renowned for treatment of the eyes. Calling them "blind" would speak volumes to them.

Bankers could never miss the encouragement to buy "gold refined by fire." Clothiers could not miss the significance of buying "white garments" instead of their famous black wool. Doctors could not miss the meaning of Jesus's encouragement to obtain "eye salve" so they could see.

Here was a city that seemed to have everything going for it. But the church had absolutely nothing going for it. What a tragedy!

Jesus counseled them, and others like them, to make needed changes. He urged them to repent. His words were motivated by love, as were similar words from God in the Old Testament (Proverbs 3:12; cf. Hebrews 12:6). Then Jesus added a picture we are all familiar with—knocking at the door. Revelation 3:20 is the basis for Holman Hunt's great picture of Jesus knocking at the door. But it is not the only place where people are told he is right at the door.

Elsewhere, the picture of Jesus "at the door" is a warning of his "coming" in judgment (Matthew 24:33; James 5:9). His disciples are told to always be ready for his coming (Luke 12:35–36). People who are not ready may find themselves shut out when he comes (Luke 13:25). But here, as in John 14:23, Jesus offers fellowship to those who invite him in.

The Promise

> "I will grant the one who conquers permission to sit
> with me on my throne, just as I too conquered and
> sat down with my Father on his throne. The one who
> has an ear had better hear what the Spirit says to
> the churches" (Revelation 3:21–22).

This promise of sitting on thrones and judging is developed
elsewhere. Jesus made the promise during his ministry
(Matthew 19:28). Paul repeated it (1 Corinthians 6:2). And it is
expanded later in Revelation.

> Then the angel showed me the river of the water of
> life- water as clear as crystal- pouring out from the
> throne of God and of the Lamb, flowing down the
> middle of the city's main street. On each side of the
> river is the tree of life producing twelve kinds of fruit,
> yielding its fruit every month of the year. Its leaves
> are for the healing of the nations. And there will no
> longer be any curse, and the throne of God and the
> Lamb will be in the city. His servants will worship
> him, and they will see his face, and his name will be
> on their foreheads. Night will be no more, and they
> will not need the light of a lamp or the light of the
> sun, because the Lord God will shine on them, and
> they will reign forever and ever. (Revelation 22:1–5)

The proof of our ultimate victory is the fact that Jesus is
already victorious! (John 16:33; Hebrews 1:3; Colossians 3:1).
Amen!
Hallelujah!

Chapter 17

SEVEN LESSONS FROM SEVEN LETTERS

Each of the seven letters is a message from Christ and the Holy Spirit to the messenger of a single local congregation. So each letter has a special message that is suited to the particular needs of that congregation. In each case, a promise of blessing is extended to any Christian who overcomes the temptations of the world that would draw him or her away from faithfulness to Christ.

These letters show that Christ knows his people both individually as Christians and collectively as his church. In each letter, he lays bare the strengths and weaknesses of each individual and each congregation.

Looking at the letters as a whole presents us with a picture of Christ's relationship to the church, in the form of seven things he wants us to know and do.

1. Christ Knows Every Christian

Every letter emphasizes this tie. He walks among the lampstands and knows the good and bad, the strengths and weaknesses, and the fears, joys, triumphs, and dangers that affect every individual Christian. He knew that the Ephesian church was sliding downhill, that Antipas of Pergamum had been killed for being faithful, and that the Christians in Smyrna were materially poor but spiritually rich.

In the same way, Christ knows each of us today. This should be a comfort to us if we are faithful. But it should scare us to death if we are not. Jesus knows you. If that thought makes you uncomfortable, maybe there's something about you that needs to be changed.

2. Christ Wants Churches to Guard Their Teaching

In five of the seven letters, Christ indicates approval or disapproval of the teaching of the congregation. He praises Ephesus for their doctrinal purity, but he condemns Pergamum and Thyatira for allowing the teaching of compromise. He urges Christians at Sardis to remember what they received and keep it. He praises Philadelphia for keeping his word.

Since we eventually become what we are taught, we must maintain doctrinal purity in our congregations and keep on guard against false teaching.

3. Christ Wants Christians to Grow in Service

Christ comments to five of the churches on the trend of their work. Thyatira is doing more than it used to. Philadelphia has an open door of opportunity. Ephesus has left its first love and needs to repent. Laodicea is lukewarm, and their lukewarmness makes him ill. Sardis has a great reputation, but they're not living up to it.

Only working Christians please Christ. Every congregation and every individual Christian falls somewhere along the line from Thyatira to Sardis. When Jesus looks at you and me, where do we fall? We must bear fruit or risk being cut off. Jesus is interested in whether we are stronger or weaker today than yesterday. He knows whether we are doing more or less than we did in our past. He wants to see progress.

4. Christ Wants Christians to Live in Purity

Both Pergamum and Thyatira were weak in their moral stance; Christians were eating meat offered to idols, and they were practicing and tolerating sexual sin in their fellowship. They lived where temptations abounded, and they were not taking a strong stand against sin.

The standards of the world must never become the standards of Christians. We must take a stand against sin both in our personal lives and in our congregations.

5. Christ Wants Christians to Be Ready for Persecution

Five of the seven churches are commended for standing firm during persecution. Two are told things are going to get worse. The primary purpose of Revelation was to prepare first-century Christians for persecution. They had already suffered under Nero, but worse was coming under Domitian.

Our so-called "persecutions" are so puny compared to theirs. We fear peer pressure, ridicule from others, and loss of social status when we refuse to live like the world. But we've never felt the intensity of hostility and persecution that Christians knew in the first century. Will we let these lesser threats make us fall, while early Christians were not stopped even by threats against their lives?

6. Christ Wants Christians to Know They Can Be Lost

Just look at what Christ said to each of the seven churches if you doubt that Christians themselves can be lost if they are not faithful to Christ.

- Ephesus: "Therefore, remember from what high state you have fallen and repent! Do the deeds you did at the first; if not, I will come to you and remove your lampstand from its place- that is, if you do not repent" (Revelation 2:5).
- Smyrna: "Do not be afraid of the things you are about to suffer. The devil is about to have some of you thrown into prison so you may be tested, and you will experience suffering for ten days. Remain faithful even to the point of death, and I will give you the crown that is life itself" (Revelation 2:10).

- Pergamum: "Therefore, repent! If not, I will come against you quickly and make war against those people with the sword of my mouth" (Revelation 2:16).
- Thyatira: "Look! I am throwing her onto a bed of violent illness, and those who commit adultery with her into terrible suffering, unless they repent of her deeds" (Revelation 2:22).
- Sardis: "Therefore, remember what you received and heard, and obey it, and repent. If you do not wake up, I will come like a thief, and you will never know at what hour I will come against you" (Revelation 3:3).
- Philadelphia: "I am coming soon. Hold on to what you have so that no one can take away your crown" (Revelation 3:11)
- Laodicea: "I know your deeds, that you are neither cold nor hot. I wish you were either cold or hot! So because you are lukewarm, and neither hot nor cold, I am going to vomit you out of my mouth!" (Revelation 3:15–16).

The doctrine of "once saved, always saved" is not found in the letters to the seven churches.

7. Christ Will Reward Christians Who Overcome

Just as each letter holds out a warning, each also holds out the hope of a promise.

- Ephesus: "The one who has an ear had better hear what the Spirit says to the churches. To the one who conquers, I will permit him to eat from the tree of life that is in the paradise of God" (Revelation 2:7).
- Smyrna: "The one who has an ear had better hear what the Spirit says to the churches. The one who conquers will in no way be harmed by the second death" (Revelation 2:11).
- Pergamum: "The one who has an ear had better hear what the Spirit says to the churches. To the one who conquers, I will give him some of the hidden manna, and I will give him a white stone, and on that stone will be written a

new name that no one can understand except the one who receives it" (Revelation 2:17).

- Thyatira: "And to the one who conquers and who continues in my deeds until the end, I will give him authority over the nations- he will rule them with an iron rod and like clay jars he will break them to pieces, just as I have received the right to rule from my Father- and I will give him the morning star. The one who has an ear had better hear what the Spirit says to the churches" (Revelation 2:26–29).

- Sardis: "But you have a few individuals in Sardis who have not stained their clothes, and they will walk with me dressed in white, because they are worthy. The one who conquers will be dressed like them in white clothing, and I will never erase his name from the book of life, but will declare his name before my Father and before his angels. The one who has an ear had better hear what the Spirit says to the churches" (Revelation 3:4–6)

- Philadelphia: "I am coming soon. Hold on to what you have so that no one can take away your crown. The one who conquers I will make a pillar in the temple of my God, and he will never depart from it. I will write on him the name of my God and the name of the city of my God (the new Jerusalem that comes down out of heaven from my God), and my new name as well. The one who has an ear had better hear what the Spirit says to the churches" (Revelation 3:11–13).

- Laodicea: "I will grant the one who conquers permission to sit with me on my throne, just as I too conquered and sat down with my Father on his throne. The one who has an ear had better hear what the Spirit says to the churches" (Revelation 3:21–22).

In each of the seven letters, we see that Christ does not ultimately want us to be cowered by fear. He wants us to be people of hope!

Amen!

Hallelujah!

The Second Seven

SEVEN SEALS (4:1–7:17)

Chapter 18

THE THRONE AND THE ONE SEATED ON IT (4:1–3)

The Invitation to the Throne Room (4:1)

> "After these things I looked, and there was a door standing open in heaven! And the first voice I had heard speaking to me like a trumpet said: 'Come up here so that I can show you what must happen after these things'" (Revelation 4:1).

Revelation 4:1–11:19 contains John's second vision. The first vision (1:9–3:22) focuses on the Son of Man among the lampstands and his words to each of the seven churches. Now he describes his second vision. He begins with "after these things." That does not mean "these things occurred after those previous things," but rather "this vision came after that vision."

Once again, God steps into human history to give eternal insight to his people. This is very similar to Israel's experience at Mount Sinai. After they arrived at the mountain, God had them prepare themselves for three days before he gave them the law (Exodus 19:9–11). Only after three days of preparation did God call Moses to the top of the mountain (Exodus 19:20).

In a similar way, Jesus has prepared his people by the seven letters. Now John, like Moses, is invited up into heaven to receive the decrees of the Lord.

The One on the Throne (4:2–3)

> "Immediately I was in the Spirit, and a throne was standing in heaven with someone seated on it! And the one seated on it was like jasper and carnelian in appearance, and a rainbow looking like it was made of emerald encircled the throne." (Revelation 4:2–3).

The initial focus of the vision is "a throne standing in heaven with someone seated on it." That someone had an appearance John describes in three images.

The first image is "like jasper." Jasper is a clear semiprecious gemstone. John probably intends us to think of something like a diamond—crystal clear and with no impurities to mar its clarity. Who is on the throne? We get a clue to his identity in Revelation 21:10–11, where the New Jerusalem is described as possessing "the glory of God; its brilliance … like a precious jewel, like a stone of crystal-clear jasper." The glory of God and of the city are both described in the same terms. John wants the reader to know that it is God who is on the throne. Jasper symbolizes the absolute purity of God on the throne.

The second figure is "like … carnelian." The Greek word is *"sardion,"* which is the reason many translations render it "sardius," rather than "carnelian." The stone was called "sardius" because it was mined at Sardis. We know it as "carnelian." It is a blood-red stone that is equivalent to our ruby. Its color signifies the judgment of the one on the throne.

The third figure is "a rainbow looking like it was made of emerald" that encircled the throne. Ever since the flood, the rainbow has signified God's mercy (Genesis 9:13–16). But this is not a multicolored rainbow. The rainbow in Revelation 4:3 is emerald green, signifying peace.

These three stones were featured on the high priest's

breastplate (Exodus 28:15–21). On the breastplate, they represented three of Israel's tribes. The blood-red carnelian represented Reuben, Israel's eldest son by Leah, who was judged by his father for incest with his stepmother (Genesis 49:3–4). The crystal-clear jasper represented Benjamin, who was Jacob's favorite because he was the last child of Rachel (Genesis 35:18). The green emerald represented Judah, from whom Jesus came, bringing peace between God and man (Genesis 49:10). They are also three of the foundation stones of the heavenly city we see later in Revelation 21:19–20.

John turns from his description of the one on the throne to the worship he receives from his heavenly entourage (4:9–11). In broad strokes, the rest of Revelation unfolds this way.

The one on the throne is holding a sealed book in his right hand, but no one anywhere is worthy to open the book (5:1–3). Just when everyone despairs of ever seeing what is in the book, the Lamb of God enters and takes the book out of God's hand (5:6–7). When he takes the book, the universe erupts in praise (5:11–13). As the Lamb opens the seals, God's judgments fall on the ungodly. They try to hide from the one on the throne and from the Lamb (6:15–17). Then, when the judgments are ultimately finished, the godly once again worship the one on the throne (19:1–5). Finally, at the end of the book, the godly reside with the one on the throne (21:2–4).

By introducing the one on the throne, John tells us about God's nature. God is pure and precious, as signified by the diamond-like jasper. He is the source of judgment, as signified by the blood-red carnelian. But he is also the source of mercy, as signified by the emerald rainbow. Which of these a person—or a nation—receives depends on how he or she responds to God, who sits on the throne.

The Throne as a Symbol of God's Judgment

The Old Testament is rich with references to God on the throne as the ruler of the universe who judges ungodly kings and kingdoms.

The best place to begin is one of the psalms that emphasizes the rule of God over the rulers of the earth. "God reigns over the nations! God sits on his holy throne! The nobles of the nations assemble, along with the people of the God of Abraham, for God has authority over the rulers of the earth. He is highly exalted!" (Psalm 47:8–9).

The psalmists were not the only ones with such an exalted view of God's dominion over the mighty and powerful leaders of the world. The prophets had the same exalted view of God. On one occasion, a prophet named Micaiah said that God, on his throne, plotted the death of King Ahab (1 Kings 22:19–22).

Isaiah saw a vision of God, as the judge of King Uzziah, sitting on his throne (Isaiah 6:1–3). Uzziah began ruling Judah at the age of sixteen, and he reigned for fifty-two years. Twelve years before he died, he forced his way into the temple to offer incense, in violation of God's law. As a result, Uzziah became a leper. (2 Chronicles 26:16–21). When Isaiah placed his vision of God on his throne "in the year of King Uzziah's death," he was saying that God was Uzziah's judge. As far as the Bible is concerned, kings and kingdoms may come and go, but God sits on an eternal throne. God judges kings and nations.

Ezekiel, an exile in Babylon, had a vision of God on his throne (Ezekiel 1:26–28). His vision was similar to the visions of both Isaiah and John. And the messages of all three visions are essentially the same. No matter what it may look like from a human perspective, God is in control. God sits in judgment over Uzziah of Judah and over Nebuchadnezzar of Babylon. God *is*, and God *rules!*

Nebuchadnezzar learned that lesson when he went insane and was driven from human society (Daniel 4:24–25). But when he accepted that God is the real ruler of the universe, he was restored to his sanity and his throne (Daniel 4:34–35).

The throne scene in Revelation 4 carries the same message to the emperors of Rome that Daniel had conveyed to Nebuchadnezzar of Babylon almost seven hundred years earlier: no matter how mighty and powerful you may think you are, God *is* and God *rules!*

The Throne as a Symbol of God's Mercy

To God's enemies, his throne was the source of judgment. But to God's people, his throne was depicted as the atonement lid that sat atop the ark of the covenant. You may recognize it more readily by its more familiar name—"the mercy seat."

The overall image comes from the Old Testament tabernacle. The tabernacle was a large tent that was divided into two unequal sections. The larger section, commonly referred to as the holy place, was the place where priests ministered on a daily basis. It contained a table that held fresh bread, known as "the bread of the presence," a menorah, which was a seven-branched lampstand, and an incense altar.

The holy place was separated from the smaller holy of holies by a thick curtain. The only object inside the holy of holies was the ark of the covenant, known as "the testimony" in the NET Bible. The top of the ark was an "atonement lid," or "mercy seat," which was thought of as being God's throne among his people (Exodus 25:17–22). God's throne within the holy of holies was a reminder to Israel of his presence, protection, and provision.

All of this reinforces the imagery that began with John's first vision of the high priest among the lampstands. The lampstands were in the holy place; the ark of the testimony was in the holy of holies.

The book of Hebrews also draws on the imagery of the tabernacle and the high priest (Hebrews 8:1–5). Hebrews reveals Jesus is the real high priest of the true tabernacle. The writer goes on to say the earthly tabernacle is "a copy and shadow of the heavenly things." Later he comes back to this same idea that the tabernacle and its components were copies of the heavenly reality (Hebrews 9:23–26). In other words, the earthly tabernacle was a physical copy of the spiritual reality Moses saw on Sinai.

What John describes in Revelation 4 is what Moses saw on Sinai. So when we read of God's throne in Revelation 4, the image of the tabernacle should be in our minds. And what an appropriate image! The tabernacle was God's tent among Israel's tents. It was a constant reminder of God's presence with his people in the desert en route to their promised land. Inside that tent was God's mercy seat—his throne in Israel's camp.

And what is the story of Revelation? Isn't it the story of God's people in this world on their way to the real Promised Land? The overcomers are on their way to the New Jerusalem of Revelation 21–22. And God himself is right there with his people, seated on his throne.

For God's enemies, God's throne is the throne of judgment. But for his people, it is the throne of mercy.

God *is*, and God *rules*!

Amen!

Hallelujah!

Chapter 19

THE SCENE AROUND THE THRONE (4:4–11)

The Twenty-Four Elders (4:4–6)

"In a circle around the throne were twenty-four other thrones, and seated on those thrones were twenty-four elders. They were dressed in white clothing and had golden crowns on their heads. From the throne came out flashes of lightning and roaring and crashes of thunder. Seven flaming torches, which are the seven spirits of God, were burning in front of the throne and in front of the throne was something like a sea of glass, like crystal" (Revelation 4:4–6).

Who are these twenty-four elders whom John sees on twenty-four thrones in verse 4? Remember in Revelation 2 and 3, Jesus made some promises to the overcomers. Those promises included a throne (3:21), white clothing (3:5), and a crown (2:10). These twenty-four elders are sitting on thrones, they are dressed in white, and they are wearing crowns. So it is fairly obvious that they are among the "overcomers."

The word which describes their "crown" is noteworthy. It is the Greek "*stephanos*," not "*diademnos*." The *stephanos* was the victory crown given as a prize, to commemorate some success achieved or service rendered, like a medal or a plaque would be given today. The *diademnos*, on the other hand, was the crown worn by a ruler. It is important to notice that these individuals who are sitting on thrones are wearing the prize they have received. They are not wearing the crowns of kings, but those of victors.

From these points, it appears that the twenty-four elders represent the redeemed overcomers. But why twenty-four? Why not twelve? Remember that twelve is the number of God's people. It is likely that twenty-four results from adding the twelve patriarchs or tribes of the Old Testament to the twelve apostles of the New Testament so that twenty-four represents the redeemed overcomers under both covenants.

What is this thunder and lightning John sees and hears in verse 5? In Exodus 19:16–18, God showed his power on Sinai in just such a way. Undoubtedly Revelation 4:5 was designed to remind John's readers of God's "shock and awe campaign" at Sinai, which, in turn, was designed to impress on Israel the glory of God!

Later in Revelation, these same figures of lightning and thunder are going to be used when God executes his judgments on the ungodly. But each time, they seem to become more intense. For example, when God instructs his angel to execute his judgment in Revelation 8:5, there is thunder, lightning, and an earthquake. Thunder, lightning, and earthquake depict God's judgment. But in Revelation 11:19, the picture becomes more intense with the addition of a great hailstorm. And in Revelation 16, the earthquake is "unequaled since humanity has been on the earth" (16:18) and the hailstones are "gigantic ... weighing about a hundred pounds each" (16:21).

These figures—thunder, lightning, earthquakes, and hailstorm—are symbols in Revelation for God's glory, which is seen in his judgment of the ungodly. The judgment of the world by God is a continuation of an important theme that runs through the Old Testament prophets. For example, Isaiah 24:21–23 says that God will judge the world, including the "kings of the earth."

In other words, God will be glorified, either by the obedience of the nations or by their destruction.

What are these flaming torches John sees before the throne in verses 5 and 6? The background of this figure also comes from the menorah that burned continually in the holy place of the tabernacle, just outside the heavy curtain separating it from the holy of holies (Exodus 27:20–21).

These may not be the same lamps John saw in Revelation 1. There they were "lampstands" (Greek: "*luchnos*"). Here they are "lamps" (Greek: "*lampos*").

Why the difference? The key may be their respective locations. Remember the tabernacle was a physical copy of the throne scene Moses saw in heaven. Following that lead, it is easy to see the lampstands of Revelation 1 are in the tabernacle, while the lamps of Revelation 4 are in heaven.

The church, depicted by the lampstands, stands in the same relationship to the throne scene as the menorah in the tabernacle. Both are reminders of God's presence and work in the world.

Some suggest these lamps in Revelation 4 are angels. In doing so, they rely on the little we know about the role of angels in God's grand scheme of things (Hebrews 1:14). However, Revelation 4 showcases God seated on the throne and Revelation 5 has Christ as the Lamb coming into the throne room. But if the lamps are angels, where is the Holy Spirit in the picture? Additionally, recall that Revelation, in its entirety is "from 'he who is,' and who was, and who is still to come, and from the seven spirits who are before his throne, and from Jesus Christ ..." (Revelation 1:4–5). Considering these two things, it seems more likely that the lamps in Revelation 4 are the Holy Spirit.

Four Living Creatures and the Sea of Glass (4:6–8)

> and in front of the throne was something like a sea
> of glass, like crystal. In the middle of the throne and
> around the throne were four living creatures full of
> eyes in front and in back. The first living creature

was like a lion, the second creature like an ox, the
third creature had a face like a man's, and the fourth
creature looked like an eagle flying. Each one of the
four living creatures had six wings and was full of
eyes all around and inside. They never rest day or
night, saying: "Holy Holy Holy is the Lord God, the
All- Powerful, Who was and who is, and who is still
to come!" (Revelation 4:6–8)

This scene is similar to one described in Ezekiel 1:5–10. When
Ezekiel saw the vision, his impression was "it looked like the glory
of the Lord ..." (Ezekiel 1:28). Later he realized it was, in fact, the
God of Israel whom he had seen (Ezekiel 10:20–21).

The descriptions of God's throne by John and Ezekiel have a
lot in common. For example, both mention four creatures in God's
entourage. However, there are differences between the creatures
as they are described. Ezekiel describes four living creatures,
each having four faces and four wings. But John describes four
living creatures, each with a different face and each having six
wings. Yet the faces are the same in both visions: lion, ox, man,
and eagle.

Why the differences between the two visions? Perhaps it is
to show there is no collusion between Ezekiel and John. When
two witnesses describe the same scene, they invariably differ in
the way they describe some of the details. This appears to be the
case here.

One easy way to understand the differences is that Ezekiel
sees each of the living creatures from all sides and he therefore
knows that each living creature has four faces. This perspective
makes sense, since Ezekiel is earthbound and is looking at God's
entourage moving about in the sky. While Ezekiel is stationary,
God's entourage is moving about, allowing Ezekiel to see each
of the living creatures from several angles, in a kind of parallax
effect.

John, on the other hand, has entered into their presence in

the throne room. He looks at them from one angle only. Since neither he nor they are moving, he may have seen the four living creatures from only one angle, in which case he would see on each creature only the face that was looking in his direction. The difference really is a small matter, though, since the four faces are the same in both visions.

What is the significance of the four living creatures and their faces? The living creatures depict the standards of Israel camped around the tabernacle in the desert. Numbers 2:1–31 describes the layout of Israel's camp. Each tribe had its own unique banner, and each triad (group of three tribes) camped around a common standard.

Jewish tradition says the tribal banners corresponded in color to the twelve stones in the breastplate of the high priest (Exodus 28:15–21) and that the standard of each triad was depicted by one of four images. The lion was the standard of Judah. That would be easy to surmise from Jacob's blessing of Judah in Genesis 49:9. When Israel camped in the desert, Judah camped east of the tabernacle, joined by Issachar and Zebulun, forming the first triad. The ox was the standard of Ephraim. Ephraim camped to the west of the tabernacle, joined by Benjamin and Manasseh, forming the second triad. The man was the standard of Reuben. Reuben camped to the south of the tabernacle, joined by Gad and Simeon, forming the third triad. The eagle had become the standard of Dan. Their standard had originally been the serpent, but that changed fairly quickly. Jewish tradition holds that Ahiezer, the leader of the tribe of Dan during the Exodus (Numbers 2:25), changed the tribal standard from a serpent to an eagle with a serpent in its mouth during Israel's forty years in the desert. Dan camped to the north of the tabernacle, joined by Asher and Naphthali, forming the fourth triad.

This is the same order in which Ezekiel describes the faces of the living beings he saw in his vision: the face of a man looking straight on, the face of a lion on the right, the face of an ox on the left, and also the face of an eagle, apparently in back (Ezekiel 1:10). There really cannot be any doubt about the overall picture of the throne scene in Revelation 4.

If you were observing Israel's encampment from the south while they were en route to the Promised Land, you would see on the south the face of a man as the standard of Reuben's triad. To the east (your right) you would see the face of a lion as the standard of Judah's triad. To the west (your left) you would see the face of an ox as the standard of Ephraim's triad. Finally, to the north you would see the face of an eagle as the standard of Dan's triad.

The heavenly scene in Revelation 4 is designed to make John's readers think of God's people being cared for by God in a hostile environment while they are on the road to the Promised Land.

But what about the sea of glass? John saw "something like a sea of glass" before the throne; Ezekiel saw something similar above it (Ezekiel 1:22). The simple explanation is that it is a matter of perspective. Earthbound Ezekiel is looking up toward heaven, and he sees a ceiling that looks like ice stretched out over the heads of the living beings. John, on the other hand, has entered heaven and is looking at the throne from heaven. To him it looks like a sea of glass. In other words, earth's ceiling is heaven's floor!

Once again, the imagery comes from Moses's experience at Sinai (Exodus 24:9–10). But it may also be a reference to the basin in the tabernacle and the temple that was called "the sea" (1 Kings 7:23–35).

Revelation contains many other references to features of the tabernacle and temple. We've already seen the lamps that correspond to the Menorah (Revelation 4:5). In later passages, we'll see the altar of sacrifice (6:9), the altar of incense (8:3), and the ark of the covenant (11:19). We'll see this particular sea again in Revelation as well. Here it separates man from God. Later we'll see that the overcomers have crossed the sea and that they're standing on the other side (15:2–3). There the overcomers sing the "song of Moses ... and ... of the Lamb." The song of Moses comes from Exodus 15. It is the song Israel sang on the east shore of the Red Sea after they had walked through the sea on dry ground and the Egyptian army had drowned trying to follow them.

Israel's perspective was different on the two shores of the Red Sea. On the west, with Pharaoh's army bearing down on them, they despaired of life. But on the east, after God had delivered them and disposed of their enemies, they sang with joy. Their song was the song of Moses.

John wants his readers to see this imagery. He pictures the overcomers singing a song of deliverance after they've crossed over the sea. To have the overcomers standing by the sea and singing songs of deliverance indicates that God's enemy has been overthrown and God's people have been rescued.

That explains the song of Moses. But why the song of the Lamb? These are not really two songs; they are one. The song of Moses *is* the song of the Lamb. If it makes it easier to think of it this way, the first verse of the song rejoices over Israel's deliverance by God's hand through Moses, while the second—and final—verse rejoices in the overcomers' ultimate deliverance by God's hand through the Lamb. Once more, John's focus is on the redeemed of both covenants.

Later still John says "the sea existed no more" (21:1). Do you see the progression? In Revelation 4, the sea separates the overcomers from God. In Revelation 15, the overcomers have crossed over the sea and are singing the song of deliverance. Finally, in the New Jerusalem, there is no more sea. What had once separated them from God has been removed, and there is nothing to separate them from God any longer.

Heaven's Worship (4:9–11)

"And whenever the living creatures give glory, honor, and thanks to the one who sits on the throne, who lives forever and ever, the twenty-four elders throw themselves to the ground before the one who sits on the throne and worship the one who lives forever and ever, and they offer their crowns before his throne, saying: 'You are worthy, our Lord and God, to receive glory and honor and power, since you created all things, and because of your will they existed and were created!'" (Revelation 4:9–11).

The four living creatures lead the heavenly entourage in glorifying God. These are the creatures of Ezekiel 1. They are also the seraphs of Isaiah 6.

> "In the year of King Uzziah's death, I saw the sovereign master seated on a high, elevated throne. The hem of his robe filled the temple. Seraphs stood over him; each one had six wings. With two wings they covered their faces, with two they covered their feet, and they used the remaining two to fly. They called out to one another, 'Holy, holy, holy is the Lord who commands armies! His majestic splendor fills the entire earth!'" (Isaiah 6:1–3).

Isaiah doesn't describe their faces because they were covered in the presence of God. But they are singing a song similar to the one in Revelation 4—"Holy, holy, holy is the Lord God Almighty ..." They are "heaven's choir," and they are singing praises to God.

Putting the two pictures of Isaiah 6 and Revelation 4 together, the living creatures sing, "Holy, holy, holy." When the living creatures sing their song, the twenty-four elders take off their crowns and fall before the throne. Then they sing their song: "Worthy Art Thou!" At this point, they're only singing verse one, which is about God being worthy. But in the next chapter, they'll add a verse about the Lamb being worthy as well.

Amen!

Hallelujah!

Chapter 20

THE SEALED BOOK AND THE WORTHY LAMB (5:1–7)

The Sealed Book (5:1–4)

> "Then I saw in the right hand of the one who was seated on the throne a scroll written on the front and back and sealed with seven seals. And I saw a powerful angel proclaiming in a loud voice: 'Who is worthy to open the scroll and to break its seals?' But no one in heaven or on earth or under the earth was able to open the scroll or look into it. So I began weeping bitterly because no one was found who was worthy to open the scroll or to look into it" (Revelation 5:1–4).

John sees a book in the right hand of the one on the throne. The book consists of writing on both sides of every page. Literally, the Greek text says it contained writing "within and on the back." That was unusual, because first century manuscripts were written on one side only. But this manuscript had no space left for writing anywhere. It was full of words covering every square inch of space, and the words were full of significance. It contained the whole revelation of God on whatever subject it addressed. But what could that subject be?

Ezekiel had a similar experience in Ezekiel 2:9–10. There the scroll was filled with "laments, mourning, and woe." Revelation 5 uses the same imagery as Ezekiel 2, so it seems that the words on the scroll spell out bad news for someone. But whom could it be?

The book John sees is sealed with seven seals. To get the picture, you should not visualize a traditional "scroll." Rather, imagine a seven-page pamphlet with the pages bound together along one edge, like a small tract or booklet. Imagine this booklet rolled up, with each page sealed where its edge ends. By opening each seal, you open one page at a time without revealing the contents of the other pages.

Remember that the number seven speaks of the completion of God's purpose. So this scroll contains not only a message from God but the complete will, or purpose, of God. But John sees that it cannot be read, because the pages are sealed.

This is apparently an insurmountable problem. A mighty angel asks for a volunteer worthy to receive and open the book. But his request is met with silence. It seems that no one is worthy—either in heaven or on earth, or even under the earth—to open the seals, or even to look inside, and reveal the message from God on the throne.

The prophet Isaiah once described Israel as a people to whom God's word was sealed (Isaiah 29:11–14). Israel's sins had sealed God's word to their minds. No wonder John weeps! It appears that God's purpose has been thwarted.

The Worthy Lamb (5:5–7)

> Then one of the elders said to me, "Stop weeping! Look, the Lion of the tribe of Judah, the root of David, has conquered; thus he can open the scroll and its seven seals." Then I saw standing in the middle of the throne and of the four living creatures, and in the middle of the elders, a Lamb that appeared to have been killed. He had seven horns and seven eyes, which are the seven spirits of God sent out into all the earth. Then he came and took the scroll from the right hand of the one who was seated on the throne. (Revelation 5:5–7)

One of the elders tells John not to give up hope so quickly. There is one who is worthy, but it is not the one everyone expects. You see, the emperor declared himself to be a god, worthy of worship. That is the significance of the Greek word *"kaisarsebaston"* (literally "Caesar, worthy of worship"). Every one of the Roman emperors in the first century took some form of the throne name "Caesar Augustus," the Latin version of *"kaisarsebaston."*

But Revelation affirms that it is not Caesar on *his* throne, but God on *his*, who alone is worthy of worship. And when it comes time to receive and reveal the will of God, Caesar is not even in the running.

There is one, and only one, who is worthy. He is the "Lion of the Tribe of Judah." The "Lion of the tribe of Judah" comes from Jacob blessing his son Judah in Genesis 49:8–10.

This worthy one is further identified with another Old Testament figure—the "Root of David" from Isaiah 11:1–5. David was the son of Jesse, and Jesus is the pre-eminent son of David! As David surpassed his father, Jesse, so also Jesus surpassed his ancestor David (Jeremiah 23:5–6).

In 2 Samuel 7:12–16, the Lord promised an heir to David's throne. In the immediate future, he was talking about Solomon, but the Jews saw in that promise a future messiah, the ultimate son of David, to whom the Lord promised the throne in his eternal kingdom (Psalm 89:20–37). This is a staple of the apostolic preaching in the New Testament.

David wrote:

> I constantly trust in the Lord; because he is at my right hand, I will not be upended. So my heart rejoices and I am happy; My life is safe. You will not abandon me to Sheol; you will not allow your faithful follower to see the Pit. You lead me in the path of life; I experience absolute joy in your presence; you always give me sheer delight. (Psalm 16:8–11)

Peter quoted that passage from David but applied it to the resurrected Jesus.

> Brothers, I can speak confidently to you about our forefather David, that he both died and was buried, and his tomb is with us to this day. So then, because he was a prophet and knew that God had sworn to him with an oath to seat one of his descendants on his throne, David by foreseeing this spoke about the resurrection of the Christ, that he was neither abandoned to Hades, nor did his body experience decay. (Acts 2:29–31)

And Paul made the same connection.

> From Paul, a slave of Christ Jesus, called to be an apostle, set apart for the gospel of God. This gospel he promised beforehand through his prophets in the holy scriptures, concerning his Son who was a descendant of David with reference to the flesh, who was appointed the Son-of-God-in-power according to the Holy Spirit by the resurrection from the dead, Jesus Christ our Lord. (Romans 1:1–4)

The voice says the Lion of Judah and Root of David has "overcome." "Overcome" (Greek: "*nikaoo*") is the same word that is used repeatedly in Revelation 2–3 to describe Christian overcomers. But here Jesus is described as the first overcomer. As Paul puts it, Jesus met the powers of the universe on the cross and defeated them (Colossians 2:13–15). The Lion has overcome! He is able to take and open the scroll, so there is no more need for tears.

A lion is announced, so John expects to see a lion. Instead he sees a lamb advancing to the throne to take the scroll. But this is no ordinary lamb! It looks as if it has been slain. Many translations make this sound like a mere matter of appearance. The New English Bible does a good job conveying the sense of the text when it describes the lamb as having "the marks of slaughter upon him." The literal translation is "standing as one having been slain." These are Greek perfect participles. The idea is of something that actually happened in the past but that has abiding results in the present.

John sees a lamb. It is obvious the lamb has been slaughtered, but there it stands, alive! This is no matter of mere appearance. The Lamb was actually killed (Revelation 5:9–10). The Greek word *"sphazoo"* was the word for ritual sacrificial slaughter. So this is a sacrificial lamb that has been sacrificed but is alive nevertheless! Isaiah described the Messiah in terms similar to this (Isaiah 53:7), so there can be no doubt who this Lamb is.

We cannot help but think of John the Baptizer introducing Jesus to his disciples as "the Lamb of God" (John 1:29). It reminds us that Jesus is "our Passover lamb" (1 Corinthians 5:7). It also reminds us that we were redeemed not with silver or gold, but with the blood of the lamb (1 Peter 1:18–19).

This lamb in Revelation 5 has "seven horns and seven eyes." The number seven is a depiction of God's complete will. So what do seven horns and seven eyes signify? The horn in the Old Testament is a symbol of strength (Deuteronomy 33:17). To say that the lamb has seven horns is to say he has God's power. In other words, he is omnipotent! To say that he has seven eyes is an affirmation that he has God's vision (Proverbs 15:3). In other words, he is omniscient!

Then John saw the lamb do what no one else in creation was worthy to do. He walked up to the throne of God and took the book out of the hand of the Almighty. No wonder heaven erupts with praise of his worth! Our word "worship" comes from the Old English word "worth-ship." It is an affirmation of worth.

Revelation 4 declares that God on the throne is worthy of worship.

Revelation 5 adds a second verse, declaring that the Lamb is worthy of worship as well.

Amen!

Hallelujah!

Chapter 21

THE WORSHIP OF THE LAMB (5:7–14)

Then he came and took the scroll from the right hand of the one who was seated on the throne, and when he had taken the scroll, the four living creatures and the twenty-four elders threw themselves to the ground before the Lamb. Each of them had a harp and golden bowls full of incense (which are the prayers of the saints). They were singing a new song: "You are worthy to take the scroll and to open its seals because you were killed, and at the cost of your own blood you have purchased for God persons from every tribe, language, people, and nation. You have appointed them as a kingdom and priests to serve our God, and they will reign on the earth." Then I looked and heard the voice of many angels in a circle around the throne, as well as the living creatures and the elders. Their number was ten thousand times ten thousand- thousands times thousands- all of whom were singing in a loud voice: "Worthy is the lamb who was killed to receive power and wealth and wisdom and might and honor and glory and praise!" Then I heard every creature- in heaven, on earth, under the earth, in the sea, and all that is in them- singing: "To the one seated on the throne and to the Lamb be praise, honor, glory, and ruling power

forever and ever!" And the four living creatures were
saying "Amen," and the elders threw themselves to
the ground and worshiped.

—Revelation 5:7–14

In Revelation 4, all eyes are on the throne. Now, in Revelation 5,
all eyes are on the Lamb. The entire heavenly entourage, the four
creatures and the twenty-four elders, fall before the Lamb and
worship him. Their harps signify their worship, and John tells
his readers that their bowls of incense signify the prayers of the
saints (Psalm 141:2).

John's situation is unique vis-à-vis every human before or
since. He has the unique distinction of seeing the same moment
in celestial history from both earth's and heaven's perspectives.
John was with the few who saw Jesus ascend to heaven in Acts 1.
Now he sees the ascended Christ as he enters into heaven. And
when Jesus enters, all heaven erupts with praise.

The fact they sing a "new song" means only that it is new as
compared with the song in Revelation 4. There the song was a song
of praise to God on the throne that depicts God as worthy because of
his work in creation. Here the song is a song of praise to the Lamb
that depicts the Lamb as worthy because of his work in redemption.

This is the New Testament counterpart to the song of Moses.
Recall after Israel crossed the Red Sea and the Egyptian army
drowned in it, the Israelites sang the song of Moses, in which they
praised God for redeeming them and for vanquishing their enemies.

That is the way the concept of a "new song" is used in the
scriptures. It is a "new song" sung after God delivers his people.
Throughout the Old Testament, there are many mentions of a "new
song" sung after God acted decisively for his people (Psalms 33:3;
40:3; 96:1; 98:1; 144:9; 149:1). Isaiah also urges people to sing a
new song in light of God's deliverance (Isaiah 42:10).

In Revelation 14:2–3, we will read of God's people who have
been delivered. It should be no surprise they are on Mount Zion,

singing a new song that commemorates their redemption. Then, just a chapter later, in the context of God's judgments on the ungodly, the redeemed are once again singing a new song of deliverance (Revelation 15:3).

So what is it about this Lamb that is so special? The Lamb is worthy because of his death and because of what his death accomplished. Look at what his death did. His death purchased people from every possible group. The King James Version incorrectly says he purchased "us." That is not what the Greek text says. It says he purchased people—but not just any people, and not just people from a select group. Jesus's death made it possible for people to be purchased from every tribe (ethnic group), tongue (language group), people (racial group), and nation (national group).

No matter what it is that segregates people from one another, it has been abolished in the cross. As Paul put it, "There is neither Jew nor Greek, slave nor free, male nor female, for you are all one in Christ Jesus" (Galatians 3:28).

The days are past when one had to be a physical descendant of Abraham in order to be a part of God's people. Jesus opened the doors of heaven to everyone. His death made these people into a "kingdom" and "priests." In spite of their diversity of race, culture, and language, the Lamb's blood has made them into a "kingdom" (not "kings," as in some translations), in which God rules. In spite of the fact that their sins once separated them from God, the Lamb's blood has made them into "priests" with access to God!

The Old Testament prophets said it was God's intention to give his people access to his throne (Isaiah 61:6). No wonder the hosts of heaven sing praises to the Lamb with their own version of "Worthy art Thou!"

Revelation 5 Begins With A Question: "Who Is Worthy?"

Of course there is the foregone conclusion that God is worthy. That is why the singers sing the first stanza of "Worthy Art

Thou" in Revelation 4. There they ascribe to God the same kind of worthiness that the prophets ascribed to him centuries before (1 Chronicles 29:11).

But "who is worthy" to take the book out of God's hand and open it? They looked everywhere and no one could be found who was worthy. But, just when it seemed hopeless, there was found one—no more and no less—who was worthy! Now everyone who was involved in the search joins in the assent that he truly is worthy! Every created being joins in the act. They sing about the worthiness of the one on the throne—and of the Lamb as well (Revelation 5:13).

The singers are the ones described by Daniel as those who minister to and stand before God (Daniel 7:10). And when everyone and everything in creation agrees that God and the Lamb are worthy, there's just one thing for the elders and the four living creatures left to say—"Amen!"

The Old Testament background of this entire scene is Daniel 7:9–14

> While I was watching, thrones were set up, and the Ancient of Days took his seat. His attire was white like snow; the hair of his head was like lamb's wool. His throne was ablaze with fire and its wheels were all aflame. A river of fire was streaming forth and proceeding from his presence. Many thousands were ministering to him; Many tens of thousands stood ready to serve him. The court convened and the books were opened. Then I kept on watching because of the arrogant words of the horn that was speaking. I was watching until the beast was killed and its body destroyed and thrown into the flaming fire. As for the rest of the beasts, their ruling authority had already been removed, though they were permitted to go on living for a time and a season. I was watching in the night visions, And with the clouds of the sky one like a son of man was approaching. He went

up to the Ancient of Days and was escorted before him. To him was given ruling authority, honor, and sovereignty. All peoples, nations, and language groups were serving him. His authority is eternal and will not pass away. His kingdom will not be destroyed. (Daniel 7:9–14)

In that grand vision, God is seen on the throne, ready to judge. God's judgment is about to come upon one kingdom and a king who thought he was worthy of worship. Into that scene came "one like a son of man," who was led into his presence. He was given dominion over all peoples, nations, and languages. There is a final word about his rule: "his dominion is an everlasting dominion, which shall not pass away, and his kingdom that which shall not be destroyed." Ready or not, God's enemy is about to be judged!

We're going to see that the nation and the king who were facing judgment in Daniel 7 are the same as the enemies of God's people in Revelation. It is the Roman Empire and the Roman emperors—in particular, one emperor named Domitian.

The scene in Revelation 4 and 5 is this: God is on his throne. His court is assembled, and his judgments are ready to be pronounced. But there is no one worthy to pronounce God's judgments. Then the only worthy one in the universe comes to the throne. He takes the book, and it is time for God's judgments to begin. The judgments are the seals, trumpets, thunders, and bowls that we'll see in the rest of the book.

The Breakdown of the Seals, Trumpets, and Bowls

Revelation revolves around sets of seven. We've already seen seven letters to seven churches. Now we begin to see God's judgments unfold on his enemies in the form of seven seals, seven trumpets, and seven bowls.

Each set of seven is broken into three units. Each begins with four images that are similar to one another. Those four are followed by two images that are different from the first four. Then there is a break or interlude of some sort, followed by the seventh image. In the case of the seals and trumpets, the seventh image contains the next set of seven. So the seventh seal contains the seven trumpets, and the seventh trumpet contains seven unrecorded thunders.

In Revelation 6, the Lamb we saw in chapter 5—the only one in the universe who is worthy to do so—begins to open the seven seals on the document he retrieved from the hand of God on the throne.

Amen!

Hallelujah!

Chapter 22

THE FIRST FOUR SEALS (6:1–8)

I looked on when the Lamb opened one of the seven seals, and I heard one of the four living creatures saying with a thunderous voice, "Come!" So I looked, and here came a white horse! The one who rode it had a bow, and he was given a crown, and as a conqueror he rode out to conquer. Then when the Lamb opened the second seal, I heard the second living creature saying, "Come!" And another horse, fiery red, came out, and the one who rode it was granted permission to take peace from the earth, so that people would butcher one another, and he was given a huge sword. Then when the Lamb opened the third seal I heard the third living creature saying, "Come!" So I looked, and here came a black horse! The one who rode it had a balance scale in his hand. Then I heard something like a voice from among the four living creatures saying, "A quart of wheat will cost a day's pay and three quarts of barley will cost a day's pay. But do not damage the olive oil and the wine!" Then when the Lamb opened the fourth seal I heard the voice of the fourth living creature saying, "Come!" So I looked and here came a pale green horse! The name of the one who rode it was Death, and Hades followed right behind. They were given authority over a fourth of the earth, to kill its population with the sword, famine, and disease, and by the wild animals of the earth.

—Revelation 6:1–8

As Christ opens four seals, horsemen ride across the stage. The first rides a white horse, the second rides a red horse, the third rides a black horse, and the fourth rides a pale green horse. There are three possible approaches to understanding these horsemen. The most common approach—the one adopted by most commentators—begins by identifying the first rider as Christ. They point out that Christ rides a white horse later in Revelation (19:11–16). Following this identification, these writers assert that the remaining horsemen represent Satan's efforts to destroy Christ's work using bloodshed (symbolized by the red horse), economic oppression (symbolized by the black horse), and death (symbolized by the pale green horse).

Another approach views all four riders as the minions of Satan opposed to Christ. All four are seen as Satan's workers that he uses in his attempts to rout Christians and destroy the church. This seems to flow naturally from the fact that the fourth rider is identified as Death and Hades follows him. In addition, they point out that the fifth seal introduces the souls of dead saints, so the flow seems quite natural.

A third approach sees these riders as a parade of God's powers. In this view, each horseman is a weapon God uses on his enemies. Following this reasoning, the four riders in Revelation 6 may be the same as the four winds of the earth that are held back before their destructive power is unleashed in chapter 7:1–3.

Keep those three possibilities in mind as we look at the four seals and the four horsemen they contain.

The First Seal: The White Horse (6:1–2)

> "I looked on when the Lamb opened one of the seven
> seals, and I heard one of the four living creatures
> saying with a thunderous voice, 'Come!' So I looked,
> and here came a white horse! The one who rode it had
> a bow, and he was given a crown, and as a conqueror
> he rode out to conquer" (Revelation 6:1–2).

This is probably *not* the same as the rider John describes in
Revelation 19:11–16. The rider in Revelation 19 is clearly Christ.
We'll focus more closely on the points of identification when we
examine that passage. But for now, it is enough to note the rider
in Revelation 19 is called "Faithful and True," his name is "The
Word of God," the armies of heaven follow him, he judges and
makes war in righteousness, and he has the name "KING OF
KINGS, AND LORD OF LORDS" tattooed on him. So it is clear
John expects his readers to identify the rider in Revelation 19 as
Christ.

But is the rider in the first seal the same as the rider in
Revelation 19? Is the horseman in the first seal Christ? Proponents
of identifying the rider in the first seal as Christ point out that
both passages depict a rider on a white horse, and each rider is
wearing a crown (or crowns). But they overlook or minimize some
very important differences between the descriptions of the riders
in the two texts.

For one thing, the crowns worn by the riders in the two texts
are entirely different. The rider in the first seal is wearing a
single crown, but the rider in Revelation (19) is wearing many
crowns. Not only that, but the riders are wearing different *kinds*
of crowns. The rider in the first seal is wearing a *stephanos*—a
victor's crown, worn by a victorious general or by the winner of
an athletic competition. A *stephanos* is a wreath, similar to those
in pictures of Roman conquerors. But the rider in Revelation 19
is wearing many crowns of a different type. Each of those crowns
is a *diademnos*—a ruler's crown, not a victor's crown.

Moreover, the riders carry different weapons. The rider in the first seal carries a bow, while the rider in Revelation 19 wields a sword in his teeth! The sword was a favorite weapon of the Romans, but it was not the weapon for which their enemies were known. Their mortal enemies, the Parthians, historically used archers to hit their enemies from a distance while their foot soldiers approached for hand-to-hand combat.

But there is something more compelling. This rider appears to parallel the others. He is not distinct from them, as one would expect if he were Christ and the others were the agents of Satan trying to destroy his kingdom.

This group of four riders has its Old Testament roots in Zechariah 6:1–8. As in Zechariah 6, the riders in Revelation 6 are God's agents to discipline his enemies. Zechariah's vision conveys the message that the Lord is the one who controls history. He will conquer the nations who oppress Israel. Since his chariots claim victory in the north, total victory is certain. The chariots are vehicles of God's judgment. So, too, are the horsemen in Revelation 6. They are the executors of God's judgment on the enemies of his people.

In Revelation 7, these horsemen are seen in a different image as four winds God is going to use to discipline the Roman Empire. This, too, is consistent with the prophet's vision (Zechariah 6:4–5).

The horsemen in Revelation 6 are the same as the four winds in Revelation 7:1–3. The message they convey is one that is seen throughout the Bible: God controls the destinies of nations (Acts 17:26). This group of four riders suggests four ways God works to bring godless nations to their knees. He has brought other nations to their knees before—great and powerful nations like Assyria, Babylon, Edom, Egypt, and even Israel.

John's vision sequence begins with God parading four tools he has at his disposal to bring down nations at his will. The first rider rides a white horse. First-century readers would recognize this as the horse of the conquering Roman general, who rides it in his parade of triumph after he has been victorious over his enemies. Rome was used to having its way with its enemies by riding out into battle and conquering them in great military campaigns. The rider on the white horse is God's way of telling Rome that it would, itself, be conquered, in part by military invasion.

The Second Seal: The Fiery Red Horse (6:3–4)

> "Then when the Lamb opened the second seal, I heard the second living creature saying, 'Come!' And another horse, fiery red, came out, and the one who rode it was granted permission to take peace from the earth, so that people would butcher one another, and he was given a huge sword" (Revelation 6:3–4).

"Red" (Greek: "*purros*") comes from one word for "fire" (Greek: "*pur*"). Literally, the color is "flame-colored." But red is also the color of bloodshed. The second rider is given "power to take peace from the earth." That includes inciting men to slaughter. Hence the reference to men butchering one another.

Note these are humans engaging in the depicted butchery. It is not the horseman, nor the angels, slaughtering men. It is people butchering one another. The divine permission granted to this rider reminds us of Jesus's own words: "Do not think that I have come to bring peace to the earth. I have not come to bring peace but a sword" (Matthew 10:34).

Revelation uses the same word here for "sword" that Jesus used in Matthew 10:34. The Greek language had two words for "sword." The *rhomphaia* was the long, heavy battle sword. "*Rhomphaia*" is the word John uses to describe the "double-edged sword" that extends from Jesus's mouth throughout Revelation (Revelation 1:16; 2:12; 2:16; 19:15; 19:21). On the battlefield, the *rhomphaia* would be wielded with two hands by a very muscular soldier. But John describes Jesus as wielding that sword in his teeth!

In contrast, the rider on the red horse carries a different

sword entirely. He carries a sword designated by the Greek word "*machaira*." The *machaira* was a short sword that could be carried in a sheath at the girdle. It was the kind of sword Peter used in defending Jesus (John 18:10). The *machaira* was more like a knife than a sword. Herodotus used "*machaira*" to describe the close-combat dagger of Greek soldiers. Homer, in the Iliad, used "*machaira*" to describe a knife used to slaughter animals and a knife used by a surgeon to cut out an arrow from a wounded man. Aristophanes and Euripides used "*machaira*" of a knife used for cutting up meat. Plato used "*machaira*" of a pruning knife. In the Septuagint, "*machaira*" describes the knife wielded by Abraham when he was about to sacrifice Isaac (Genesis 22:6, 10). In the New Testament, "*machaira*" also describes the sword of governmental authority (Romans 13:3–4).

The rider on the red horse rides on the heels of the white horse. He represents bloodshed, which is essential to the military conquest that has already been figured in the rider on the white horse. He also may represent bloodshed as a part of civil unrest— or even civil war—among people who are subject to such a military conquest.

The Third Seal: The Black Horse (6:5–6)

> "Then when the Lamb opened the third seal I heard the third living creature saying, 'Come!' So I looked, and here came a black horse! The one who rode it had a balance scale in his hand. Then I heard something like a voice from among the four living creatures saying, 'A quart of wheat will cost a day's pay and three quarts of barley will cost a day's pay. But do not damage the olive oil and the wine!'" (Revelation 6:5–6).

Black is the biblical color of mourning. In the Old Testament, the word depicting "mourning" literally means "in black" (Jeremiah 4:28; 8:21; Malachi 3:14).

But it is not only the color of the horse that identifies the rider. The horseman carries in his hand a pair of scales, symbolizing a time when food is doled out by weight because of its scarcity, as would be the case during a siege (Leviticus 26:26). This horseman is carrying scales on which to weigh out foodstuffs.

A day's pay—literally, a denarius—will buy a quart of wheat or three quarts of barley. A denarius was a day's pay for a laborer (Matthew 20:2). Thus the announcement by the heavenly voice means that a man could buy one day's ration of wheat for a day's pay. But if he were a family man, he would have to make do with coarser cattle feed (barley) so he could make his money go as far as possible toward feeding his family. That left nothing for other necessities of life, such as clothing or shelter. And it certainly left nothing for such luxuries as oil and wine. Food was available, but only at black market prices.

The rider on the black horse depicts economic disaster in the wake of military conquest. It sounds like God's description of the siege conditions which took place in Jerusalem in 586 BC (Ezekiel 4:8–17).

The Fourth Seal: The Pale Green Horse (6:7–8)

> "Then when the Lamb opened the fourth seal I heard the voice of the fourth living creature saying, 'Come!' So I looked and here came a pale green horse! The name of the one who rode it was Death, and Hades followed right behind. They were given authority over a fourth of the earth, to kill its population with the sword, famine, and disease, and by the wild animals of the earth" (Revelation 6:7–8).

The words "pale green" are translated from the Greek word "*chlooros*," which was the yellowish green color of a corpse. The text tells us that the rider is Death, personified, and that Hades, the realm of the dead, is following along and picking up the corpses he leaves behind.

This is not just any kind of death. It is death by plague. The Greek word "*chlooros*," when used of a person, means "pale" or "pallid." Thucydides used it to describe the appearance of persons stricken with plague. Homer used it to describe a person who was pale from fear.

In the Septuagint, "*Thanatos*" ("death") sometimes suggests death by plague (Jeremiah 14:12; 21:7). In modern history, "death" has been used in a similar manner. For example, in the fourteenth century, a devastating plague was called "Black Death." So it is possible that we should read the name of the fourth rider as "Pestilence" or "Plague" rather than "Death."

Thus military conquest (the white horse) leads to bloodshed (the red horse). Bloodshed results in economic disaster (the black horse). And economic disaster gives rise to disease and death (the pale green horse).

The Four Horsemen Remind Us of the Scourges Described by the Prophets

These four horsemen represent the same four calamities that were often described by the Old Testament prophets (Jeremiah 14:11–12; 15:1–3; Ezekiel 5:11–17; 14:21; 33:27–29). All together, these four horsemen are God's agents.

In Revelation 6:8, some translations say power was given to "him" (Death), but the best texts say "they" (the four horsemen) were given it. "They were given authority over a fourth of the earth, to kill its population with the sword, famine, and disease, and by the wild animals of the earth" (Revelation 6:8). These are God's *agents*, but don't get the idea that they are *angels*, because later, we're going to see Death (the fourth rider) and his companion Hades cast into a lake of fire (20:14). This is nothing new. The Bible describes other times when God uses an agent and then punishes the very agent he used. He did it to Sargon and Sennacherib of Assyria centuries before. After using Assyria to destroy godless Israel, he then demolished Assyria (Isaiah 10:5–7, 12–13)

For now, these four agents of God—the four horsemen—wait to be released to do their work. These are the agents God uses to bring down any nation that becomes his enemy: military conquest, bloodshed, economic disaster, and disease leading to death.

Picture it this way. During our nation's expansion to the west, settlers and soldiers occasionally saw a handful of riders on a ridge watching them. They knew the riders they could see on the ridge were not the real threat. The real threat was the hundreds or thousands of riders they couldn't see on the other side of the ridge. These four riders in Revelation 6 are the ones John can see on the ridge. At the moment, they're doing nothing but waiting on God's command to attack his enemies.

But for now, the Lamb continues opening the seals.

Amen!

Hallelujah!

Chapter 23

THE FIFTH AND SIXTH SEALS (6:9–17)

The Fifth Seal (6:9–11)

> Now when the Lamb opened the fifth seal, I saw under the altar the souls of those who had been violently killed because of the word of God and because of the testimony they had given. They cried out with a loud voice, "How long, Sovereign Master, holy and true, before you judge those who live on the earth and avenge our blood?" Each of them was given a long white robe and they were told to rest for a little longer, until the full number was reached of both their fellow servants and their brothers who were going to be killed just as they had been. (Revelation 6:9–11).

The fifth seal is the key to understanding the rest of Revelation. When the Lamb opens the fifth seal, John sees the souls of the martyred saints. Notice that these souls are already under the altar in the heavenly scene of Revelation 4–5.

The question is, which altar are they under? Within the holy place inside the tabernacle was the altar of incense, on which the priests burned incense daily. Outside the tabernacle, yet within the courtyard, was the altar of sacrifice.

There is good reason to believe the altar in Revelation 6 could be the altar of sacrifice. Throughout the Bible, there is a connection between life and blood (Leviticus 17:11). And the blood of sacrificial animals was poured out at the base of that altar (Leviticus 4:7). So John's readers can hardly miss the sacrificial symbolism of the picture in the fifth seal.

Moreover, the one opening the seals is himself a sacrificial lamb who was slaughtered and yet lives (Revelation 5:6–14). These martyrs have followed the example of their Lord. Their blood has been poured out at the base of the altar because of their loyalty to the word of God and their testimony (Philippians 2:17; 2 Timothy 4:6).

But it is more likely that the altar in view in the fifth seal is the golden incense altar inside the holy place (Exodus 30:1–10). When the altar is mentioned elsewhere in Revelation, the reference is to the incense altar, not the sacrificial altar (Revelation 8:3–5; 9:13; 11:1; 14:18; 16:7).

The martyrs in the fifth seal are under the altar, praying for vindication. They remember God's promise to vindicate and avenge his people (Deuteronomy 32:43; 2 Kings 9:7; Psalm 79:10; Luke 18:7–8).

They present a compelling question. They want to know just how long God is going to put up with his enemies and how long it is going to be until he judges the earth and vindicates their blood. The judgment of the earth need not be taken literally. Their question has to do with the judgment of the godless Roman Empire that had made its mission the destruction of the church.

Each martyr in the picture was given a white robe. That identifies them for us. They are overcomers—faithful Christians who were promised a white robe in Revelation 3:5. They were also told to wait a while. Others will die before God brings the persecutor down. Their question is "How long?" God's answer is "wait a little longer." That is not a message we like to hear, but it is God's message, nevertheless.

The message to first-century Christians was that there has already been persecution and there is more to come. But take heart! God will act—that is certain—and the persecutor will be destroyed. God's name will be vindicated. God's people will be avenged.

We're going to see these people again in Revelation. We'll see them in Revelation 7:9–17, enjoying relief in the presence of God. We'll see them again in Revelation 14:1–5 standing with the Lamb on Mount Zion. We'll see them yet again in Revelation 15:2–4, having crossed over the sea. In Revelation 15, they are standing on the other side of the sea that had previously separated the elders from God in Revelation 4. There they stand in Revelation 15 singing the song of Moses and of the Lamb. That tells us they have at last been delivered from their enemy.

Remember the song of Moses was the song Israel sang in Exodus 15 after they had passed through the Red Sea and the Egyptian army had drowned in it. It was their song of deliverance. Likewise, the song of the Lamb in Revelation 15 is the song of deliverance by the Lamb.

We see them again in Revelation 19:1–6 rejoicing because God has avenged them, as promised. Finally, in Revelation 20:4–6, we see them enthroned with Christ.

Revelation is another Exodus, not unlike the Exodus of the Old Testament. In the Old Testament, God's people were delivered from their enemies by God's power. They were sustained through all sorts of hardships in the desert while they were on their way to the Promised Land. In Revelation, God's people are also delivered from their enemies. They, too, are sustained by God on their way to their ultimate reward in heaven.

The Sixth Seal (6:12–17)

> Then I looked when the Lamb opened the sixth seal, and a huge earthquake took place; the sun became as black as sackcloth made of hair, and the full moon became blood red; and the stars in the sky fell to the earth like a fig tree dropping its unripe figs when shaken by a fierce wind. The sky was split apart like a scroll being rolled up, and every mountain and

island was moved from its place. Then the kings of
the earth, the very important people, the generals,
the rich, the powerful, and everyone, slave and free,
hid themselves in the caves and among the rocks of
the mountains. They said to the mountains and to
the rocks, "Fall on us and hide us from the face of
the one who is seated on the throne and from the
wrath of the Lamb, because the great day of their
wrath has come, and who is able to withstand it?"
(Revelation 6:12–17)

The sixth seal describes cataclysmic events. It sounds like the end
of the world, but it's not!

The vision in the sixth seal has people fleeing and trying to
hide from God's wrath. But the Bible says that when the final
coming arrives, there will be "sudden destruction" and there will
be no time to hide in caves (1 Thessalonians 5:2–3). What is in
view is the "Day of the Lord" as described by the Old Testament
prophets. The prophets used descriptions like the images in the
sixth seal to portend the fall of a nation at God's hand. Several
prophets used this kind of language to describe the "Day of the
Lord" for wicked nations. Jesus even used similar language to
describe the "Day of the Lord" for Jerusalem. The "Day of the
Lord" is a day of terror when God punishes his enemy, even if that
enemy is Israel (Amos 5:18–20) or Judah (Zephaniah 1:14–15).

Isaiah 34:1–17 depicts Edom's "Day of the Lord" using
descriptive language very much like that used in the sixth seal.
Hosea 10:1–8 uses similar language to describe Samaria's "Day
of the Lord" at the hand of the Assyrians. Nahum 1:1–6 depicts
Assyria's "Day of the Lord" at the hand of the Babylonians.

Perhaps most surprising are the number of prophetic
descriptions of Judah's "Day of the Lord" at the hand of the
Babylonians in 586 BC (Isaiah 2:1–22; 22:1–25; Zephaniah 1:1–
18; Jeremiah 4:23–29).

Ezekiel 32:2–11 is Egypt's "Day of the Lord" administered by
the Babylonians. Isaiah 13:1–22 is Babylon's "Day of the Lord" at

the hand of Medo-Persia. Zechariah 14:1–21 describes the "Day of the Lord" for unbelieving nations. And in Matthew 24:1–51, Jesus uses the same language to describe Jerusalem's "Day of the Lord" at the hand of the Romans in AD 70. The "Day of the Lord" in the Bible is God's judgment on a godless nation. It may not be the end of the world, but it is always the end of someone's world (Joel 3:14–19).

The descriptions in the sixth seal come from Joel's description of a locust plague (Joel 1:1–2:31). Joel uses the description of a locust plague to describe Judah's "Day of the Lord." Imagine the earth quaking with the whirring of millions of locust wings. Picture the locusts as a spreading cloud darkening the sun and obscuring the stars. Imagine that the moon would look like blood through the millions of wings in the locust plague.

Revelation uses the same terms to describe the "Day of the Lord" for the enemy of God in the first century—the Roman Empire!

Amen!

Hallelujah!

Chapter 24

THE ONE HUNDRED FORTY-FOUR THOUSAND AND THE GREAT MULTITUDE (7:1–17)

The Sealing of One Hundred Forty-Four Thousand (7:1–8)

After this I saw four angels standing at the four corners of the earth, holding back the four winds of the earth so no wind could blow on the earth, on the sea, or on any tree. Then I saw another angel ascending from the east, who had the seal of the living God. He shouted out with a loud voice to the four angels who had been given permission to damage the earth and the sea: "Do not damage the earth or the sea or the trees until we have put a seal on the foreheads of the servants of our God." Now I heard the number of those who were marked with the seal, one hundred and forty- four thousand, sealed from all the tribes of the people of Israel: From the tribe of Judah, twelve thousand were sealed, from the tribe of Reuben, twelve thousand, from the tribe of Gad, twelve thousand, from the tribe of Asher, twelve thousand, from the tribe of Naphtali, twelve thousand, from the tribe of Manasseh, twelve thousand, from the tribe of Simeon, twelve thousand, from the tribe of Levi, twelve thousand, from the tribe of Issachar, twelve thousand, from the tribe of Zebulun, twelve thousand, from the tribe of Joseph, twelve thousand, from the tribe of Benjamin, twelve thousand were sealed. (Revelation 7:1–8)

This is an interlude between the sixth and seventh seals. It asks the question: "What will happen to God's people when he executes his judgment on his enemies?" The scene begins with four angels holding back the winds to delay God's judgment for a time. Old Testament prophets, in various places, painted word pictures using wind as God's agent of judgment. Jeremiah turned up the heat when he described God's judgment on Judah as a "scorching wind" (Jeremiah 4:11–12; 18:17). Wind also describes God's judgment of Elam (Jeremiah 49:34–38) and "the northland" (Zechariah 6:1–8).

John calls upon these Old Testament metaphors of wind as God's agent of judgment in Revelation 7; but, here God restrains the wind while the godly ones are marked with the seal of the living God. The primary Old Testament background for this image is found in Ezekiel 9:1–11. There the prophet saw armed guards taking stations at the temple. While they waited for God's command to strike, a scribe went throughout Jerusalem, placing marks on the foreheads of godly people who grieved because of the corruption of the people. When all the godly were marked, the guards were told to start at the temple and kill everyone who didn't have the mark on his or her forehead.

The vision in Ezekiel 9 was designed to assure the godly that they would be preserved when God hammered Jerusalem with the sword of Nebuchadnezzar in 586 BC. In Revelation 7, John sees a similar vision. The winds of judgment are restrained while God's seal of approval is placed on the foreheads of his people before he hammers his enemies. This assures us that God can and will take care of his own people while at the same time executing his judgment on his enemies. It is a reminder of Paul's confidence in 2 Timothy 2:19: "However, God's solid foundation remains standing, bearing this seal: 'The Lord knows those who are his,' and 'Everyone who confesses the name of the Lord must turn away from evil'" (2 Timothy 2:19).

But why are we told that one hundred forty-four thousand are sealed? Obviously this is intended to make us think of the numbers twelve and one thousand, because we are told that the one hundred forty-four thousand consists of twelve thousand from each of the twelve tribes. In other words, the one hundred forty-four thousand consists of 12 × 12 × 1000.

Remember that twelve and its multiples are used in the Bible to identify God's people. When we think of God's people in the Old Testament, we think of the twelve patriarchs and the twelve tribes. When we think of God's people in the New Testament, we think of the twelve apostles. We've already seen God's redeemed people depicted as twenty-four elders sitting on thrones around God's throne in heaven, and we identified them as the redeemed under the old and new covenants (Revelation 4:4).

What happens to God's people when he destroys his enemies? God knows those who are his, and he will preserve them. But the reader might wonder whether the godly might be overlooked and fall victim to God's judgment. The number one hundred forty-four thousand is intended to assure the godly that God doesn't make mistakes. How many of God's people are going to get sealed and protected? Every one of them! How many are going to slip through the cracks? Not a single one!

Numbers are important in apocalyptic literature. For example, one thousand signifies all of something. Psalm 50:9–11 uses the number one thousand to assert that all cattle in the world belong to God. When the Lord says "the cattle on 1,000 hills" belong to him, that is tantamount to saying all the cattle belong to him.

Numbers are significant to us, too. How many of us haven't said to a wayward child, "I've told you a thousand times" to do or not do something? And what about the number twelve? We seldom think about the fact that we use "a dozen" to describe a complete set of something, or that hotels often do not have a thirteenth floor. These are carryovers that remind us that numbers have a symbolic significance to us.

Twelve thousand each from twelve tribes means all of God's people were sealed. But why just seal individuals from Israel? And why not from all of the tribes? This use of numbers is a reminder that the number is figurative, not literal; it is not intended to be mathematically precise. You see, Israel actually had thirteen tribes, not twelve. We speak of twelve patriarchs because Jacob had twelve sons. We also know that there were twelve land divisions in the Promised Land. So we naturally know that there were twelve tribes, right? Wrong! The patriarchs are not the same as the tribes. Before Jacob died, he adopted Joseph's sons, Manasseh and Ephraim, in place of Joseph (Genesis 48:1–22). As a result, there was no tribe of Joseph. In the place of Joseph, there were two tribes of Manasseh and Ephraim. Thus, even though Jacob had twelve sons, Israel actually was divided into thirteen tribes. In the list in Revelation 7:8, the tribe of Joseph refers to Ephraim, since Manasseh is listed separately in verse 6. This is consistent with other Old Testament references.

Sometimes Old Testament references to a tribe of Joseph refer to one or both of his sons. In some passages a reference to a tribe of Joseph refers to both Ephraim and Manasseh (Joshua 18:11). In other texts it is a reference only to Ephraim (Psalm 78:67).

Yes, there were only twelve land divisions in the Promised Land. But remember there was no land division assigned to the tribe of Levi (Joshua 13:14, 33). So there were twelve patriarchs and twelve land divisions, but there were thirteen tribes.

In Revelation 7, you have to look closely to find that one of the tribes is missing. When John says there were twelve thousand from each of the twelve tribes, he lists Ephraim as Joseph and leaves Dan out of the list entirely. Why would that be? Is it because there is no one from the tribe of Dan who is godly? No, rather it is because the purpose of the numbers is not to mathematically quantify the godly.

Ancients were not as meticulous in their use of numbers as we are in our computer age. Here's an example of "creative numerology" from the gospel of Matthew. After Matthew lists the ancestors of Jesus in Matthew 1, he concludes as follows: "So all the generations from Abraham to David are fourteen generations, and from David to the deportation to Babylon, fourteen generations, and from the deportation to Babylon to Christ, fourteen generations" (Matthew 1:17).

As we've already seen, a close look at Matthew's genealogy and a comparison with the Old Testament narrative shows that Matthew left out names in order to list fourteen generations between Abraham and David, another fourteen between David and the Exile, and a third set of fourteen between the Exile and Jesus. He did this because there is something special about the number fourteen. As we saw earlier in our discussion of major symbolic numbers and their opposites in chapter 3, fourteen is the gematrical number that represents the name of David. Matthew wanted the reader to see the number fourteen and to identify Jesus as the son of David.

So don't take the number one hundred forty-four thousand literally, and don't look for a literal twelve thousand from each of twelve literal tribes. The point of the picture is simple: God knows his people, and he doesn't miss even one. He protects every godly saint!

But why do the one hundred forty-four thousand come only from Israel? Were there no godly Gentiles around? Yes, there were. But by the time of the writing of Revelation, Christian writers had taken to considering the church to be the real Israel of God (Galatians 6:15–16). Being a Jew or not being a Jew didn't matter anymore. All that mattered was being in Christ (Philippians 3:3–7). Even Jesus's brother, himself a Jewish Christian, described all Christians as "the twelve tribes dispersed abroad" (James 1:1).

Likewise, when John spoke of the one hundred forty-four

thousand as the tribes of Israel, that was not literal. He was speaking of Christians—Jew and Gentile—who were sealed for protection in the day of tribulation associated with God's judgments.

The Great Multitude (7:9–17)

> After these things I looked, and here was an enormous crowd that no one could count, made up of persons from every nation, tribe, people, and language, standing before the throne and before the Lamb dressed in long white robes, and with palm branches in their hands. They were shouting out in a loud voice, "Salvation belongs to our God, to the one seated on the throne, and to the Lamb!" And all the angels stood there in a circle around the throne and around the elders and the four living creatures, and they threw themselves down with their faces to the ground before the throne and worshiped God, saying, "Amen! Praise and glory, and wisdom and thanksgiving, and honor and power and strength be to our God for ever and ever. Amen!" Then one of the elders asked me, "These dressed in long white robes- who are they and where have they come from?" So I said to him, "My lord, you know the answer." Then he said to me, "These are the ones who have come out of the great tribulation. They have washed their robes and made them white in the blood of the Lamb! For this reason they are before the throne of God, and they serve him day and night in his temple, and the one seated on the throne will shelter them. They will never go hungry or be thirsty again, and the sun will not beat down on them, nor any burning heat, because the Lamb in the middle of the throne will shepherd them and lead them to springs of living water, and God will wipe away every tear from their eyes." (Revelation 7:9–17)

If the one hundred forty-four thousand is the church on earth, who is the great multitude of Revelation 7:9–17?

Some writers say the one hundred forty-four thousand represent the redeemed of the Jews and the great multitude represents the redeemed of the Gentiles. They point to the fact that the one hundred forty-four thousand come from the tribes of Israel and the great multitude comes from "every nation, tribe, people, and language."

There is a more compelling line of reasoning. The one hundred forty-four thousand are on earth; the great multitude is in heaven. The great multitude is "standing before the throne and before the Lamb dressed in long white robes," praising God and the Lamb. The one hundred forty-four thousand were sealed for protection while still on earth. They are the redeemed facing distress on earth. The great multitude is in heaven. They are the redeemed after the distress of the earth is behind them.

An elder asks, "who are they, and where have they come from?" John doesn't know the answer, so the elder gives it: they are the overcomers enjoying their reward (7:13–14). These are the same martyrs we saw under the altar in the fifth seal (6:9–11).

The one hundred forty-four thousand are on earth; the great multitude is in heaven. The one hundred forty-four thousand face persecution and are promised God's protection. The great multitude are saints who have gone on to their reward. Both may be the same group viewed from two perspectives. From earth's viewpoint, they are protected and preserved by God. From heaven's viewpoint, their reward is already secured. Even if they are not the same group at the moment John sees them, the one hundred forty-four thousand will become a part of the great multitude if they are faithful to death.

Shifting vantage points is a common feature of apocalyptic writings. It is seen in elsewhere in Revelation. Remember that John physically saw Jesus ascend to heaven in Acts 1, but in Revelation 5, he sees the same scene from heaven's viewpoint, as the Lamb enters the throne room of God.

In Revelation 1, John sees Jesus walking in heaven's tabernacle, inspecting the lampstands that he identifies as the churches. Then, in Revelation 2–3, he sends a message to each of the churches on earth in the seven cities. The vision is of Jesus walking among his churches, but the messages are sent from heaven to earth.

Later, in Revelation 12, we'll see this same shifting of perspective from earth to heaven and back to earth. First, the dragon (identified as Satan) seeks to devour the child of the woman. When he is unsuccessful, he chases the child into heaven. When he loses the conflict in heaven, he pursues her other children on earth.

Other apocalyptic passages refer to activities in heaven that have an effect on earth. Daniel 10 is a good example. In 537 BC, the third year after Persia conquered Babylon, Daniel's prayers were interrupted by an angel who told him that he had intended to come to set Daniel's mind at ease earlier but he had been detained by conflict with the prince of Persia. But another angel, Michael, showed up to take over the fight with the Persian prince so that this angel could make his trip to put Daniel's mind at ease. When he had done that, he left Daniel to join Michael in the fight against the prince of Persia. He goes on to say, "When I go, the prince of Greece will come." (Daniel 10:10–13, 20–21). The reference to the "prince of Greece" refers to Alexander the Great's conquest of Persia in 334–331 BC. So Daniel 10 covers two centuries of Persian dominance on the world stage.

The Persian kings thought they were fighting only the Egyptians and Greeks and, later, that pesky Macedonian, Alexander. They didn't know they were in the middle of a heavenly conflict, involving angels, that was designed to bring down Persia and to elevate Greece. This vignette fulfills the vision of a ram and a goat in Daniel 8:19–21.

Revelation 7 presents two perspectives of one common theme. The message is the same whether you look at it from the vantage point of godly people on earth (the one hundred forty-four thousand) or godly people who have gone on to their reward (the great multitude). The message is this: God is able to protect and preserve his people here, and he is able to provide for them hereafter.

Amen!

Hallelujah!

The Third Seven

——◆——

SEVEN TRUMPETS (8:1–11:19)

Chapter 25

THE FIRST FOUR TRUMPETS (8:1–13)

The Form of Sevens in Revelation

Revelation is developed around sets of seven. The seven seals, seven trumpets, and seven bowls are developed in a particular way. Each begins with four items that are similar, followed by two that are different from the first four. Then there is an interlude of some sort that is followed by the seventh item.

The seven seals follow that pattern. The first four seals introduce four horsemen. The fifth seal shows the martyrs asking "How long" before God would vindicate and avenge them. The sixth seal announces the "Day of the Lord" and the beginning of judgment. But before judgment begins in earnest, the interlude in Revelation 7 depicts God's people being marked for preservation and the dead enjoying their reward in heaven.

The Seventh Seal Contains Seven Trumpets

The trumpets follow the same pattern as the seals. The first four trumpets, described in Revelation 8, affect all the earth. The fifth and sixth trumpets in Revelation 9 are followed by an interlude in Revelation 10:1–11:14. The seventh trumpet is revealed in Revelation 11:15–19.

The Seventh Seal (8:1–5)

> Now when the Lamb opened the seventh seal there
> was silence in heaven for about half an hour. Then
> I saw the seven angels who stand before God, and
> seven trumpets were given to them. Another angel
> holding a golden censer came and was stationed at
> the altar. A large amount of incense was given to
> him to offer up, with the prayers of all the saints, on
> the golden altar that is before the throne. The smoke
> coming from the incense, along with the prayers of
> the saints, ascended before God from the angel's
> hand. Then the angel took the censer, filled it with
> fire from the altar, and threw it on the earth, and
> there were crashes of thunder, roaring, flashes of
> lightning, and an earthquake. (Revelation 8:1–5)

The seventh seal is judgment. When the Lamb opens the seventh
seal, there is silence in heaven. This is a dramatic pause designed
to get everyone's attention before God's judgment begins. It is like
the bailiff calling for order in the court when the judge takes the
bench to pronounce judgment. This is a familiar refrain from the
prophets (Habakkuk 2:20; Zephaniah 1:7).

The seventh seal contains seven angels with seven trumpets.
Trumpets are used in scripture in three ways. All three are
described in Numbers 10. First, they were used to gather the
assembly together (Numbers 10:1–8). Second, they were used
to sound an alarm (Numbers 10:9). Third, they were used as a
fanfare of joy (Numbers 10:10). The trumpets in Revelation 8 fall
into the second category. They are alarms warning Rome of God's
coming judgment. God is about to send the enemies of Rome to
execute his wrath. This is consistent with the use of trumpets in
the Old Testament Prophets as harbingers of God's judgment on
Judah (Joel 2:1–2; Zephaniah 1:14–18; Jeremiah 4:5–9).

The reason God's judgment is coming in Revelation 8 is
because of the prayers of the martyred saints in the fifth seal

(6:9–11) that go up before God along with the prayers of the living saints (8:3). The prayers of the martyrs who are under the altar in the fifth seal are commingled with the prayers of the living saints that go up from the altar. The incense that accompanies the prayers of the living saints likely represents intercession. That makes sense, because the word "intercede" means "enter in with," and the smoke of the incense is intermingled with the prayers of the saints. Intercession is an important concept for Christians. Christ intercedes for us (Romans 8:34), as does the Holy Spirit (Romans 8:26–27). Other Christians also intercede for us (1 Timothy 2:1–2).

Then, in response to the cries of the martyrs and the prayers of the saints, along with intercession, judgment erupts as an angel takes a censer filled with fire from the altar and hurls it to earth, with the result of thunder, lightning, and an earthquake (Revelation 8:5). The overall picture comes from Ezekiel 10:1–2 where the prophet sees almost exactly the same thing—a man filling his hands with burning coals and then scattering them over the city of Jerusalem.

In order to understand the judgment on Jerusalem in Ezekiel 10, it is necessary to recall the flow of Ezekiel's visions of the presence of God. In Ezekiel 1, the prophet, himself an exile, sees a vision of God among the exiles in Babylon (Ezekiel 1:28). That raises the question in his mind (as it should), why is God with the exiles in Babylon and not in Jerusalem in the temple?

Later, in Ezekiel 8, he has a vision of the corruption of the leaders in Jerusalem, which has gotten so bad that the Lord has determined to abandon Jerusalem and destroy it. But first, as we saw in Ezekiel 9, he has his mark put on his people to distinguish them from those he plans to destroy. Then he has the guards go through the city killing everyone who doesn't have his mark of approval. Finally, the glory of the Lord departs from the temple and heads east toward Babylon (Ezekiel 10:18). But before leaving the city, an angel throws coals of fire on Jerusalem from the very presence of God (Ezekiel 10:1–2).

Revelation 7–8 parallels Ezekiel 9–10. It's time for judgment to begin. First God's people are identified and sealed (Revelation 7), and then judgment comes from the altar (8:5).

The first four trumpets, like the four horsemen of the first four seals, need to be seen as a group. They depict natural calamities. Each is a judgment—but not an irrevocable judgment, since each trumpet damages only one-third of the thing it affects. So the four trumpets should be viewed as four warnings designed to call the wicked to repent. If repentance is forthcoming, there will be no need for future judgment. Unfortunately, as we shall see, repentance is the last thing on people's minds when they are affected by the four trumpets.

First Trumpet: Land Disaster (8:6–7)

> "Now the seven angels holding the seven trumpets prepared to blow them. The first angel blew his trumpet, and there was hail and fire mixed with blood, and it was thrown at the earth so that a third of the earth was burned up, a third of the trees were burned up, and all the green grass was burned up" (Revelation 8:6–7).

The first trumpet sounds like the seventh plague on Egypt— the plague of hail unlike anything Egypt had ever seen before (Exodus 9:24).

Second Trumpet: Maritime Disaster (8:8–9)

> "Then the second angel blew his trumpet, and something like a great mountain of burning fire was thrown into the sea. A third of the sea became blood, and a third of the creatures living in the sea died, and a third of the ships were completely destroyed" (Revelation 8:8–9).

The second trumpet sounds like the plagues against the Nile that affected Egypt's commerce (Exodus 7:14–21).

Third Trumpet: Freshwater Disaster (8:10–11)

> "Then the third angel blew his trumpet, and a huge star burning like a torch fell from the sky; it landed on a third of the rivers and on the springs of water. (Now the name of the star is Wormwood.) So a third of the waters became wormwood, and many people died from these waters because they were poisoned" (Revelation 8:10–11).

This trumpet, like the second, sounds like the plague on the Nile water, but this time it is on the fresh potable water—not the seawater of the maritime trade.

But this trumpet adds an additional element—a star called Wormwood. Wormwood is a poisonous plant. It is used in the Old Testament in relation to divine judgment (Jeremiah 9:12–15).

Fourth Trumpet: Cosmic Disaster (8:12–13)

> "Then the fourth angel blew his trumpet, and a third of the sun was struck, and a third of the moon, and a third of the stars, so that a third of them were darkened. And there was no light for a third of the day and for a third of the night likewise. Then I looked, and I heard an eagle flying directly overhead, proclaiming with a loud voice, 'Woe! Woe! Woe to those who live on the earth because of the remaining sounds of the trumpets of the three angels who are about to blow them!' (Revelation 8:12–13).

The fourth trumpet sounds like ninth plague—the plague of darkness (Exodus 10:21–23).

The Background of the First Four Trumpets

The plagues were designed to make Pharaoh repent and release the Israelites. Instead, he became more belligerent as the plagues intensified. Likewise, the enemies of God in Revelation become more belligerent as his judgments intensify, so God has to make his warnings increasingly severe.

An Eagle Announces Worse Woes Yet to Come (8:13)

> "Then I looked, and I heard an eagle flying directly overhead, proclaiming with a loud voice, 'Woe! Woe! Woe to those who live on the earth because of the remaining sounds of the trumpets of the three angels who are about to blow them!'" (Revelation 8:13).

The King James Version uses "angel," but the best Greek texts read "eagle." From our American heritage, we would tend to think of this as the noble symbol of our nation. But we need to remember to read this text, as well as the rest of Revelation, through first-century eyes. John's original readers would have thought of a bird of prey, or possibly a carrion-eating bird, such as a vulture. That is the meaning when the same Greek word for "eagle," "aetou," is used in Matthew 24:28. Jesus says "Wherever the corpse is, there the vultures will gather." But the King James Version takes the word literally and reads "there will the eagles be gathered."

The point of this eagle's message is that despite how bad the calamities pronounced by the first four trumpets have been, worse is yet to come in the remaining three.

Amen!

Hallelujah!

Chapter 26

THE FIFTH AND SIXTH TRUMPETS (9:1–21)

The Fifth Trumpet (First Woe):
Internal Decay (9:1–11)

Then the fifth angel blew his trumpet, and I saw a star that had fallen from the sky to the earth, and he was given the key to the shaft of the abyss. He opened the shaft of the abyss and smoke rose out of it like smoke from a giant furnace. The sun and the air were darkened with smoke from the shaft. Then out of the smoke came locusts onto the earth, and they were given power like that of the scorpions of the earth. They were told not to damage the grass of the earth, or any green plant or tree, but only those people who did not have the seal of God on their forehead. The locusts were not given permission to kill them, but only to torture them for five months, and their torture was like that of a scorpion when it stings a person. In those days people will seek death, but will not be able to find it; they will long to die, but death will flee from them. Now the locusts looked like horses equipped for battle. On their heads were something like crowns similar to gold, and their faces looked like men's faces. They had hair like women's hair, and their teeth were like lions' teeth. They had breastplates like iron breastplates, and the sound of their wings was like the noise of many horse-drawn chariots charging into battle. They have tails and stingers like scorpions, and their ability to injure people for five months is in their tails. They have as king over them the angel of the abyss, whose name in Hebrew is Abaddon, and in Greek, Apollyon.

—Revelation 9:1–11

Out of the abyss comes smoke and supercharged locusts. The Greek word *"abyssos"* comes from an adjective that means "bottomless" or "unfathomable." The abyss in Greek thought was the underworld—the realm of the dead. In the New Testament, this realm of the dead is depicted as a prison, smoldering with fires, where demons are held captive. In Revelation, it is where Satan and his minions are imprisoned, and from which they emerge to do their dastardly work. We will see the abyss again in Revelation (11:7; 17:8; 20:1–3).

The description of locusts in Revelation 9:7-9 is very similar to descriptions found in other ancient Eastern writings. It is also very similar to the prophetic description of a locust plague in Joel 1:4–2:10. The unique thing about these locusts is their stingers. They do not harm crops, which is the normal function of locusts. Instead they torment people—but not all people. They do not harm the people who have been marked with God's seal (Revelation 9:4–5). Those are the people we saw sealed for protection in Revelation 7:1–8.

The leader of these locusts is called Destroyer, but as we can see, there is a limit to the destruction he can wreak. The Bible is filled with references to the fact that the devil's power, as great as it might be, is always limited by God (Job 26:6; Proverbs 15:11; Proverbs 27:20). If the devil is powerful, the one who sets limits on his power is even more so!

Once more, the background of this picture is to be found in the plagues of Egypt. In particular, it reminds us of the eighth plague—the plague of locusts (Exodus 10:1–20).

It is significant that the plague of locusts came near the end, rather than the beginning, of the calamities that befell Egypt. Many people do not realize that the first three Egyptian plagues— the plague of water being turned to blood, and the following plagues of frogs and lice—affected the Israelites in Goshen as well as the Egyptians throughout the country. However, the last seven plagues affected only Egypt. Israel was exempt (Exodus 8:22). In the trumpets, as in the plagues, God makes a distinction between his people and the enemy. Those who were sealed in chapter 7 are protected from the locusts in chapter 9.

But why all these judgments? Even the Old Testament prophets proclaimed that if the people would repent, God would relent from the disaster he had sent upon them (Joel 1:14–15; 2:12–13). The problem is that people, even in the midst of God's judgment, are not inclined to repent. So the woes just keep on coming.

The Sixth Trumpet (Second Woe): External Enemies (9:13–19)

Then the sixth angel blew his trumpet, and I heard a single voice coming from the horns on the golden altar that is before God, saying to the sixth angel, the one holding the trumpet, "Set free the four angels who are bound at the great river Euphrates!" Then the four angels who had been prepared for this hour, day, month, and year were set free to kill a third of humanity. The number of soldiers on horseback was two hundred million; I heard their number. Now this is what the horses and their riders looked like in my vision: The riders had breastplates that were fiery red, dark blue, and sulfurous yellow in color. The heads of the horses looked like lions' heads, and

> fire, smoke, and sulfur came out of their mouths. A
> third of humanity was killed by these three plagues,
> that is, by the fire, the smoke, and the sulfur that
> came out of their mouths. For the power of the horses
> resides in their mouths and in their tails, because
> their tails are like snakes, having heads that inflict
> injuries. (Revelation 9:13–19)

We saw in Revelation 7:1 that the four winds were bound. And we saw that the four winds are the same as the horsemen in the first four seals (6:1–8). Now the winds are released, and we see a cavalry of two hundred million. The Greek literally translates to "twice ten thousand times ten thousand." We should not take this as a literal number. By way of comparison, the combined strength of all armies in World War II, Allied and Axis combined, was just over fifty million. Even that number was so huge as to be unimaginable in the first century.

The Roman army consisted of thirty legions of 5,000 soldiers each, for a total of about 150,000 men. Each legion had about 120 cavalry, so the ratio was 40 infantrymen for each cavalryman. A cavalry of 200 million would be part of an army of 8 billion—more people than live on the earth today. This is not a literal army! This army is on a mission from God. That is clear from the fact that it comes from the Euphrates River. Twice in the Old Testament an army came west across the Euphrates to execute God's discipline against his people. The Assyrians came across to discipline Israel in the late eighth century BC. The Babylonians crossed the Euphrates to defeat Assyria and Egypt at Carchemish and to subjugate Judah in the late seventh century BC (Jeremiah 46:1–28).

The weapons of this army are fire, smoke, and sulfur—ancient symbols of God's judgment on the wicked (Genesis 19:24–28; Ezekiel 38:18–23; Psalm 11:6; Luke 17:28–30). Their horses have lions' mouths and serpents' heads for tails (Revelation 9:19).

In other words, they get the enemy coming or going. This demonstrates the inescapable nature of God's judgment.

The Purpose of the Six Trumpets (9:20–21)

> "The rest of humanity, who had not been killed by these plagues, did not repent of the works of their hands, so that they did not stop worshiping demons and idols made of gold, silver, bronze, stone, and wood- idols that cannot see or hear or walk about. Furthermore, they did not repent of their murders, of their magic spells, of their sexual immorality, or of their stealing" (Revelation 9:20–21).

God wants people to repent and turn to him (2 Peter 3:9). But when God's warnings are persistently rejected, only judgment remains (Ephesians 5:5–6; Hebrews 10:26–31).

Yet, in spite of God's warnings, some people will not repent. Pharaoh refused to repent as God turned up the heat in each successive plague. The Jews refused to repent in light of Jesus's teaching and miracles. They goaded him to perform miracles so they would believe. But even when he did so, they attributed it to the power of the devil. They insisted that they would believe if he came down from the cross. He did them one better; he came out of the grave. And they still refused to believe!

Some people won't repent, no matter what.

The only thing left for God to do is finish the job he started.

Amen!

Hallelujah!

Chapter 27

THE INTERLUDE AND THE SEVENTH TRUMPET (10:1–11:19)

Up to this point, God has been holding back in his judgments. The first four trumpets affected only one-third of the earth, the sea, the fresh water, and the celestial bodies. But partial judgment hasn't brought about mankind's repentance. So he turned up the heat in the fifth and sixth trumpets with a plague of supercharged locusts and an army that was larger than the population of today's world. But mankind still didn't repent. The only thing left for God to do is finish the job with total, irrevocable judgment.

But first a word from our sponsor. Many of us grew up hearing those words on television shows after a brief teaser. Those words led into a commercial that announced who was responsible for financing the show we were about to see. In a real sense, that is what the interlude in Revelation 10 and 11 is. It is the announcement that everything that comes after, like everything before, is directly attributable to the God who sits on the throne. In the context of Revelation, it is a word of peace and comfort for the Christians, designed to assure them that, no matter how out of control things may appear, God is ultimately in control.

Four Things Discussed in the Interlude

The interlude contains four parts. First are the unrecorded thunders (10:1–7), which signify that they would receive no more warnings of coming judgments. No more signs, second chances, or any other form of "heads-up" from heaven. This time God means business! Second is the vignette about the little book (10:8–11), which tells John that he must continue to preach a bittersweet message that brings him pain. Third is the measuring of the temple (11:1–2), which assures the readers that God knows and protects his people even in the most trying of circumstances. Fourth are the two witnesses (11:3–13), which promise that the gospel will ultimately triumph over the evil in the world.

The Unrecorded Thunders—
No More Warning (10:1–7)

> Then I saw another powerful angel descending from heaven, wrapped in a cloud, with a rainbow above his head; his face was like the sun and his legs were like pillars of fire. He held in his hand a little scroll that was open, and he put his right foot on the sea and his left on the land. Then he shouted in a loud voice like a lion roaring, and when he shouted, the seven thunders sounded their voices. When the seven thunders spoke, I was preparing to write, but just then I heard a voice from heaven say, "Seal up what the seven thunders spoke and do not write it down." Then the angel I saw standing on the sea and on the land raised his right hand to heaven and swore by the one who lives forever and ever, who created heaven and what is in it, and the earth and what is in it, and the sea and what is in it, "There will be no more delay! But in the days when the seventh angel is about to blow his trumpet, the mystery of God is

> completed, just as he has proclaimed to his servants
> the prophets." (Revelation 10:1–7).

John sees a powerful angel, a reminder of God's covenant presence with his people. The angel's description provides all the evidence required. For one thing, he is wrapped in a cloud, a reminder of the Shekinah that symbolized God's presence with Israel in the desert (Exodus 13:21–22). A rainbow hovers over his head, symbolizing God's covenant with mankind dating back to the time of Noah (Genesis 9:12–16). This angel stands astride the earth like Colossus, an image familiar to first-century readers in Asia Minor. They would certainly have known of some famous ruins on the island of Rhodes, just eleven miles south of their own shores. In 282 BC, a huge statue called Colossus had been erected at the northernmost point of the Island of Rhodes, the nearest point to Asia Minor. Colossus was a 110-foot bronze statue of the sun god Helios. It was one of the seven wonders of the ancient world, but it didn't stand for long. An earthquake just fifty-six years later, in 226 BC, broke it at the knees.

In the first century, Colossus was a well-known ruin visited by people from all over the world. According to Pliny the Elder, few people could wrap their arms around the fallen thumb, and each of its fingers was larger than most statues. Colossus was the inspiration for Auguste Bartholdi's statue "Liberty Enlightening the World", which today stands in New York Harbor.

As John describes the scene, this angel that rises through the clouds is so tall that John sees a rainbow around his head and the sun for his face. He dwarfs Colossus, but unlike the famous statue, he never collapses.

Seven Thunders—Warning of the Coming Storm

When the angel spoke, seven thunders sounded. John was about to write down the message of the thunders, as he had been instructed (Revelation 1:10–11, 19). But a voice from heaven (not the angel) says, "Seal up what the seven thunders spoke and do not write it down."

The significance of sealing up the words of the seven thunders is that there will be no more delay. God's judgment is set to be given full force (10:5–7). This is the answer to the prayers of the martyrs from the fifth seal (6:9–11). They have been crying out for vindication and vengeance against their enemies. Now this voice from heaven says the time has come and there will be no more warning for the enemy. If six trumpets haven't brought repentance, six hundred won't. The time for judgment has come.

The Little Book—The Bittersweet Message (10:8–11)

> Then the voice I had heard from heaven began to speak to me again, "Go and take the open scroll in the hand of the angel who is standing on the sea and on the land." So I went to the angel and asked him to give me the little scroll. He said to me, "Take the scroll and eat it. It will make your stomach bitter, but it will be as sweet as honey in your mouth." So I took the little scroll from the angel's hand and ate it, and it did taste as sweet as honey in my mouth, but when I had eaten it, my stomach became bitter. Then they told me: "You must prophesy again about many peoples, nations, languages, and kings." (Revelation 10:8–11)

The angel has a "scroll" in his hand. Do not confuse this with the scroll that was received by the Lamb in chapter 5 and opened by him in chapter 6. There the Greek word was *"biblion"* ("book"); here it is *"biblaridion"* ("small book"). We should think of this as a booklet or tract.

The Old Testament background of this image comes from Ezekiel 2:1–3:14. There the prophet was given a book to eat. The book was as sweet as honey to him because it was the word of God. But it was a difficult message to stomach because it required him to preach a message of judgment to God's people, Judah. He ends by saying, "I went bitterly, my spirit full of fury" (Ezekiel 3:14).

John has a similar experience. The message is as sweet as honey to him because it contains the word of God. But it is a bitter message, full of bad news. The sweetness is in the message; the bitterness in the delivery.

In the rest of Revelation, John will be called upon to pronounce woes upon people who rejected God. He will be called to warn Christians of persecution that faces them and conflict among the church. Most of all, he will be called upon to pronounce God's judgment on the Roman Empire—the enemy of God and his people. Like Ezekiel of old, John will have to keep preaching, even if that preaching doesn't produce repentance.

Preaching sometimes produces no repentance where repentance should be expected (Ezekiel 3:4–9). But preaching sometimes produces repentance where repentance would not ordinarily be expected (Jonah 3:1–10). But whether preaching produces repentance or not, the preacher is still called upon to preach.

The Measuring of the Temple (11:1–2)

> "Then a measuring rod like a staff was given to me, and I was told, 'Get up and measure the temple of God, and the altar, and the ones who worship there. But do not measure the outer courtyard of the temple; leave it out, because it has been given to the Gentiles, and they will trample on the holy city for forty-two months'" (Revelation 11:1–2).

John is told to measure the temple of God, the altar, and the worshippers. It is important to note what is measured and what is not. The sanctuary itself (Greek: "*naos*") is measured, not the temple complex (Greek: "*hieron*").

Some commentators look at this text and conclude that Revelation was written before AD 70, while the Jerusalem temple was still standing. From an Old Testament prophetic context, it means the opposite—the temple had already fallen.

In 572 BC, Ezekiel saw a vision of a man measuring the temple (Ezekiel 40:1–5). That was fourteen years after it had been physically razed by the Babylonians in 586 BC (Ezekiel 40–48). Just as the measuring of the temple in Ezekiel's vision occurred long after the structure had been demolished, John is now told to measure the temple years after it had been physically destroyed by the Romans.

The purpose of this measuring is to separate the holy (those within the sanctuary) from the common (those outside the sanctuary). The Jerusalem temple sanctuary, prior to its destruction, had a relatively small footprint. It was about ninety feet long, thirty feet wide, and sixty feet high. It sat on a huge, almost square, thirty-seven-acre platform that was known as the "Court of the Gentiles." That platform stands today as the only remnant of the first-century temple complex. In Jesus's day, the courtyard was treated as something akin to a bazaar, with vendors selling souvenirs, sacrificial animals, and food, as well as currency exchangers. That was the background of the Gospel narratives of Jesus cleansing the temple (Matthew 21:12–17; Mark 11:15–19; Luke 19:45–48; John 2:13–16).

The point of John measuring the temple was to separate the holy from the common. That theme comes from the Old Testament. In the book of Leviticus, it is clear that, from God's perspective, everything and everyone is either holy or common. And everything and everyone that is common is either clean or unclean. In Leviticus, it is clear that sin draws everything from the holy to the common, and sin takes clean things and makes them unclean. On the other hand, the prescribed sacrifices and rituals make unclean things clean and restore common things to holiness. But what is God's sanctuary in Revelation 11? The Jerusalem temple was long gone. But Christians had taken to considering themselves, individually and collectively, as God's temple (1 Corinthians 3:16). So the temple John is called to measure is the church in the world.

As we saw in the seven letters, some of the churches were blurring distinctions between the holy and the profane. In doing that, they followed the lead of the Old Testament priests before them (Ezekiel 22:26; 44:23). But God knows who is holy and who is not (2 Timothy 2:19). Jesus has already examined the seven churches. He knows who is—and who isn't—holy. What John measures is the sanctuary, the *naos*, which represents the church. What he does *not* measure is the outer court—the court of the Gentiles—where secular Jews and Gentiles go about their daily business. Why doesn't he measure the outer court? Because there are no holy ones in the unmeasured world. All the holy ones are among the worshippers who are measured within the walls of the sanctuary.

John is told that the world will trample on the outer courtyard for forty-two months. What is the significance of that? Remember from the introductory chapters you have already read, that forty-two months is the same as three and one-half years and 1,260 days. The Jewish year consisted of 360 days. Every seven years, they added an intercalary month to realign their lunar calendar with the solar year.

Three and one-half years is half of seven years. As we saw in our introductory discussion of significant numbers and their opposites, it represents a time when Satan strives to thwart God's will, but during which God remains in control. So this image of the Gentiles trampling the courtyard underfoot is our introduction to the onslaught against the church by the Roman Empire.

The Two Witnesses (11:3–13)

> And I will grant my two witnesses authority to prophesy for 1,260 days, dressed in sackcloth. (These are the two olive trees and the two lampstands that stand before the Lord of the earth.) If anyone wants to harm them, fire comes out of their mouths and

completely consumes their enemies. If anyone wants
to harm them, they must be killed this way. These
two have the power to close up the sky so that it does
not rain during the time they are prophesying. They
have power to turn the waters to blood and to strike
the earth with every kind of plague whenever they
want. When they have completed their testimony,
the beast that comes up from the abyss will make
war on them and conquer them and kill them. Their
corpses will lie in the street of the great city that is
symbolically called Sodom and Egypt, where their
Lord was also crucified. For three and a half days
those from every people, tribe, nation, and language
will look at their corpses, because they will not
permit them to be placed in a tomb. And those who
live on the earth will rejoice over them and celebrate,
even sending gifts to each other, because these two
prophets had tormented those who live on the earth.
But after three and a half days a breath of life from
God entered them, and they stood on their feet, and
tremendous fear seized those who were watching
them. Then they heard a loud voice from heaven
saying to them: "Come up here!" So the two prophets
went up to heaven in a cloud while their enemies
stared at them. Just then a major earthquake took
place and a tenth of the city collapsed; seven thousand
people were killed in the earthquake, and the rest
were terrified and gave glory to the God of heaven.
(Revelation 11:3–13)

Forty-two months and 1,260 days in John's vision are two
pictures, from two different perspectives, of the three and one-
half years during which the Roman Empire besieged the church.
Keep in mind that this was not a literal three and one-half years.
Rather, the figurative time frame is designed to convey a message
unrelated to the actual length of time involved. The time during

which the church was besieged is depicted as forty-two months. The preaching of the witnesses, though it took place during the same time as the siege, is depicted as 1260 days. The significance of these two numbers comes from the fact that sieges are counted differently, depending upon whether you are conducting the siege or whether you are the people boxed in by it. Sieges are measured in months, but preaching is measured day by day.

John sees two witnesses depicted as olive trees and lampstands. This composite image comes from Zechariah 4:1–14. From the historical context in Zechariah 4, it is clear that the two anointed messengers were Joshua, the priest, and Zerubbabel, the governor, respectively the descendants of Aaron and David. This is important to Zechariah's context because they were anointed, and the only people anointed for office in the Old Testament were the priest and the king.

But the anointed ones John sees in Revelation 11 are entirely different people, as is evident from verses 5–6. The men in John's vision are clearly to be identified with Moses, as representative of the law, and Elijah, as representative of the prophets. When we read of fire consuming their enemies and the sky being closed up, we are intended to think of Elijah. In 2 Kings 1:1–18, Elijah called down fire on the two groups of soldiers sent by Ahaziah to arrest him. And in 1 Kings 17:1, the sky was shut up at his word so that it didn't rain for three and one-half years (James 5:17). When we read of water being turned to blood and plagues striking the earth, we are intended to think of Moses, who turned water to blood and brought the plagues on Egypt (Exodus 7–12). Moses and Elijah, as representatives of the law and the prophets, were sent to prepare Jesus for his own exodus at the Transfiguration (Luke 9:28–31). In fact, the word Luke uses for Jesus's departure in that passage is the Greek word "*exodus*," from which the Old Testament book derives its name.

John's vision falls into three phases of progress. First, the gospel is preached with considerable success (Revelation 11:5–6). Then the gospel expansion is seemingly crushed by opposition

(11:7–10). As was their Lord before them, the preachers are killed. Then John tells his readers that their corpses "lie in the street of the great city that is symbolically called Sodom and Egypt, where their Lord was also crucified (11:8).

Where is this city? And why is it designated by references to Sodom, Egypt, and Jerusalem? Consider Sodom. Most people who have read the Old Testament account of the destruction of Sodom (Genesis 19) equate the city with sexual sin. But there was more involved than just sexual sin. Their perversity was only the outward manifestation of their real spiritual disease. According to God's assessment of the wickedness of Sodom, their sin lay in the fact that they were so self-obsessed that they had no regard for the needy among them (Ezekiel 16:49–50). Then, of course, we can recognize the sin of Egypt oppressing the Jews. And who can miss the image of Jerusalem killing the Messiah.

What is not so apparent in the description by John is that the city in view is not literally any of the three locations he mentions—Sodom, Egypt, or Jerusalem. The figures are intended to symbolize the Roman Empire and its relentless oppression of Christians in the first century.

But try as it might, the Roman Empire could not keep the church down. That is the point of the fact that the messengers are not only resurrected to life but also snatched up to heaven (Revelation 11:11–13). Who can read that without thinking of Elijah being taken to heaven in a whirlwind (2 Kings 2) or Moses dying on Mount Nebo and entering heaven without ever passing through the Promised Land (Deuteronomy 34)? And, especially, who can read this without thinking of Jesus? The Jews and Romans conspired to kill him. They put his body in a grave and thought they were done with him. But God's response was "Oh no you don't!"

The resurrection and ascension of the two witnesses in John's vision is like the resurrection and ascension of Jesus. Their enemies saw them exalted—just before they saw their own end. God raised Jesus from the dead and brought down the Jews in the destruction of Jerusalem. Revelation continues that theme. God raises the church from the ashes of Roman persecution and dashes the Roman Empire into oblivion. The kingdom of God is established, and the empire of Rome destroyed.

The earthquake in John's vision depicts God's judgment on Rome. They wouldn't repent before (Revelation 9:20–21), but now they give him glory even as they are left in the dust of history (11:13). This is a recurring New Testament promise (1:7; Philippians 2:10–11). Jesus *will* be praised and God *will* be glorified. If people will not praise and glorify him voluntarily, they will do so under compulsion. But one way or another, God *will* be glorified!

The whole interlude is a message of divine retribution. There is to be no more delay. God's judgment is to be proclaimed, even if it is a bittersweet message. All the while, God knows who belongs to him—and who does not. And he protects and preserves his people. The gospel may appear to be crushed, but it will ultimately triumph. Other kingdoms come and go, but God's kingdom endures (Daniel 2:44)!

Seventh Trumpet—Third Woe—Final Judgment on Rome (11:15–19)

> Then the seventh angel blew his trumpet, and there were loud voices in heaven saying: "The kingdom of the world has become the kingdom of our Lord and of his Christ, and he will reign for ever and ever." Then the twenty- four elders who are seated on their thrones before God threw themselves down with their faces to the ground and worshiped God with these words: "We give you thanks, Lord God, the All-Powerful, the one who is and who was, because you have taken your great power and begun to reign. The nations were enraged, but your wrath has come, and the time has come for the dead to be judged, and the time has come to give to your servants, the prophets,

their reward, as well as to the saints and to those who
revere your name, both small and great, and the time
has come to destroy those who destroy the earth."
Then the temple of God in heaven was opened and
the ark of his covenant was visible within his temple.
And there were flashes of lightning, roaring, crashes
of thunder, an earthquake, and a great hailstorm.
(Revelation 11:15–19)

With the blowing of the seventh trumpet, John hears the exultant
praise of heaven saying, "The kingdom of the world has become
the kingdom of our Lord and of his Christ, and he will reign
forever and ever." This comes like a headline announcing the
end of a long, hard war. It is like the crowds of Times Square
erupting in praise when the word came that World War II was
over. Imagine a jumbotron in Times Square with a scrolling
headline that announces, "God's Kingdom Wins"!

Revelation 12–22 will detail how God's kingdom wins. Those
chapters will describe the battle and the spiritual struggle behind
the war. But for now, the twenty-four elders are singing God's
praises with these words: "We give you thanks, Lord God, the All-
Powerful, the one who is and who was, because you have taken
your great power and begun to reign" (Revelation 11:17). Notice
how verse 17 extols God as the one "who is and who was," but it
doesn't contain the words we would expect; there is no "who is
to come." In fact, the addition of those words in the King James
Version appears to be an attempt to add the words we would
expect to read. Why is there no reference to God as the one "who
is to come" here? The answer is quite simple. In this vision, he
has already come. He has taken his rightful place on the throne.

Now the time has come for judging the dead (i.e., those
who are dead in sin) and rewarding the righteous (i.e., the
overcomers). Notice that judgment is for the wicked but reward
is for the righteous. The Lord has come to both save and destroy
(2 Thessalonians 1:5–10). Judgment comes because God is true to

his word. He is faithful to his word whether we are or not. That is the nature of his covenant. It is the reason that judgment—in the form of lightning, thunder, earthquake, and hailstorm—proceeds from "the ark of his covenant" (Revelation 11:19; 2 Timothy 2:11–12).

Notice that each time judgment appears in Revelation, it is intensified. In Revelation 4:5, we saw lightning and thunder. In 8:5, there was the added touch of an earthquake. Now, in 11:19, a hailstorm is added to the mix. Later, in 16:18–21, we'll see that intensified as the earthquake becomes a mega earthquake and the hailstones become mega hailstones.

God just keeps increasing the power of his judgments until, at some point in time, mankind either bows down or is broken. In either case, God is glorified!

The seventh trumpet announces judgment and victory. It is a reminder that the kingdoms of men come and go but the kingdom of God will stand forever (11:15; Daniel 2:44).

Amen!

Hallelujah!

The Fourth Seven

SEVEN VISIONS OF THE ETERNAL STRUGGLE (12:1–14:20)

Chapter 28

THE WOMAN AND THE DRAGON (12:1–6)

Then a great sign appeared in heaven: a woman clothed with the sun, and with the moon under her feet, and on her head was a crown of twelve stars. She was pregnant and was screaming in labor pains, struggling to give birth. Then another sign appeared in heaven: a huge red dragon that had seven heads and ten horns, and on its heads were seven diadem crowns. Now the dragon's tail swept away a third of the stars in heaven and hurled them to the earth. Then the dragon stood before the woman who was about to give birth, so that he might devour her child as soon as it was born. So the woman gave birth to a son, a male child, who is going to rule over all the nations with an iron rod. Her child was suddenly caught up to God and to his throne, and she fled into the wilderness where a place had been prepared for her by God, so she could be taken care of for 1,260 days.

—Revelation 12:1–6

Our Earthly Conflict Is Part of an Eternal Struggle

The question the minds of all first-century Christians as they read Revelation the first time was, "Who really rules the world?"

There was one who sat on a throne in Rome who insisted, "I rule the world!" But there is another one who sits on a throne in heaven who differed with him and said, "You're mistaken. I rule the world." Remember Revelation 11:15: "Then the seventh angel blew his trumpet, and there were loud voices in heaven saying: 'The kingdom of the world has become the kingdom of our Lord and of his Christ, and he will reign for ever and ever.'"

Revelation 12 depicts the struggle between the kingdom of the world and the kingdom of God. Two visions in chapters 12 and 13 pull back the curtains to reveal an eternal struggle. The first vision in Revelation 12 shows that Christians suffer persecution because of Satan's hatred for the Messiah. But Satan's defeat in heaven guarantees his ultimate eternal defeat. When the dragon cannot kill the woman's son, who is clearly Jesus, he wages war against "the rest of her descendants" (i.e., Christians). They will suffer until the final victory of God and his Messiah. The second vision in Revelation 13 introduces Satan's agents in his war against the Messiah's followers.

G. R. Beasley-Murray says, "These chapters ... form the central section of the book. Not only do they come at the midpoint of the work, they provide an understanding of the nature of the conflict in which the Church is engaged, and into which John sees she is to be drawn to the limit. The struggle of the saints against the Caesars is here portrayed in the context of an age-long resistance to the God of heaven on the part of evil powers. That process is about to reach its climax in an all-out warfare against the Church of Christ. The raging of the powers of hell, however, terrible as it may be, is shown to be in vain, for in the victory of the crucified and ascended Christ they have been defeated, and their final overthrow is not far distant."[4]

The Woman Described (12:1–2)

> "Then a great sign appeared in heaven: a woman
> clothed with the sun, and with the moon under her

feet, and on her head was a crown of twelve stars. She was pregnant and was screaming in labor pains, struggling to give birth" (Revelation 12:1–2).

Revelation 12 begins with a vision of a radiant woman. She wears the sun as a garment, and the moon is under her feet. She wears a crown of twelve stars. This is the victor's crown, the *stephanos*, not the ruler's crown. The woman is pregnant and about to give birth. To a first century mind, the image of the sun, moon, and twelve stars was a description of God's covenant people that goes all the way back to a dream Joseph had of his father, mother, and brothers in Genesis 37:9–11.

The Dragon (12:3–4)

"Then another sign appeared in heaven: a huge red dragon that had seven heads and ten horns, and on its heads were seven diadem crowns. Now the dragon's tail swept away a third of the stars in heaven and hurled them to the earth. Then the dragon stood before the woman who was about to give birth, so that he might devour her child as soon as it was born" (Revelation 12:3–4).

The ancients thought of the dragon as a mysterious creature that lived in the depths of the ocean. It appears in the Old Testament under various names: the creature of the deep (Job 7:12), Leviathan (Psalm 74:14; Isaiah 27:1), and the Proud One (Psalm 89:10; Isaiah 51:9). To the ancients, this monster was a figure for the forces of destruction and chaos. Here John identifies it as Satan (Revelation 12:9). But John's description makes it abundantly clear that God is ultimately in control even over Satan.

This dragon has seven heads. That somehow seems odd. As you'll recall, seven is the number of God's completed work. To say that the dragon has seven heads is to say that he plays a part in God's plan. But what could that part be? The dragon also has ten horns. You'll remember that ten is the number of limits. To say that the dragon has ten horns is to say that his power is limited by God. By contrast, the Lamb has seven horns. That is to say that he exercises God's power. He is omnipotent. Here is a place where it is important to think of numbers like the apocalyptic writer, not like a twenty-first-century reader. We would think that ten beats seven. Not so in apocalyptic writing. Seven horns of omnipotence trump ten horns of limitation every time!

The dragon also wears seven crowns. These crowns are referred to by the Greek word *"diademnos."* The word *"diademnos"* designates the ruler's crown. The fact that the dragon wears ruling crowns shows that the power in view here is governmental power (Romans 13:1–7). And the message is that no one has any power unless God gives it to him. To whatever extent this dragon rules, he rules by God's permission (Daniel 4:34–35).

But there's something more here. The devil may be allowed to wear a *diademnos* (a ruler's crown) for a time, but after Calvary he can never wear a *stephanos* (a victor's crown)! Just as the Lamb's seven horns beat the dragon's ten, so also does the Lamb's *stephanos* beat the dragon's *diademnos*!

And this dragon is a demonstrative sort. He intends to devour the woman's son as soon as he is born. As if to emphasize the seriousness of his purpose, when he slaps his tail down, he brings down one-third of the stars (Revelation 12:4). Remember that one-third is the number of someone holding back. God held back with the trumpets that destroyed one-third of creation (8:7–12; 9:13–18). So now the devil is holding back too. He destroys one-third of the celestial bodies with the swipe of his tail.

The Woman Gives Birth (12:5)

> "So the woman gave birth to a son, a male child, who is going to rule over all the nations with an iron rod. Her child was suddenly caught up to God and to his throne," (Revelation 12:5).

As soon as the child is born, he is caught up to God. As we'll see later, the dragon pursues him to heaven but finds himself cast out. In the meantime, the woman flees into the desert, where she is cared for by God for 1,260 days.

Who are these characters? We know the dragon is the devil because Revelation 12:9 says as much. It is also obvious that he woman's son is Jesus. "Rule … with a rod of iron" means to rule with complete authority, defeating all enemies. That was promised to the Messiah in Psalm 2:9. It is reminiscent of Jesus's promise to the overcomers from Thyatira (Revelation 2:27). It is also part of a description of Jesus that we'll see in Revelation 19:15.

It appears that the woman is God's covenant people idealized in Mary. Hence she has twelve stars in her crown. Pregnant, she depicts Old Testament Israel (Galatians 3:23–24). Delivered, she is the New Testament church (Galatians 3:25–29). In the Old Testament, she is Israel in labor to bring forth the Messiah (Micah 4:8–10; 5:2). She gives birth first to Christ (Revelation 12:5) and then to Christians (12:17).

The picture in Genesis 12 is an idealized image of Genesis 3:15. From that point on, the message of the Bible is "saved by one," and it is the story of the deliverance of God's people by the Messiah, Jesus.

Amen!

Hallelujah!

Chapter 29

THE FIRST VISION (12:7–12)

Then war broke out in heaven: Michael and his angels fought against the dragon, and the dragon and his angels fought back. But the dragon was not strong enough to prevail, so there was no longer any place left in heaven for him and his angels. So that huge dragon- the ancient serpent, the one called the devil and Satan, who deceives the whole world- was thrown down to the earth, and his angels along with him. Then I heard a loud voice in heaven saying, "The salvation and the power and the kingdom of our God, and the ruling authority of his Christ, have now come, because the accuser of our brothers and sisters, the one who accuses them day and night before our God, has been thrown down. But they overcame him by the blood of the Lamb and by the word of their testimony, and they did not love their lives so much that they were afraid to die. Therefore you heavens rejoice, and all who reside in them! But woe to the earth and the sea because the devil has come down to you! He is filled with terrible anger, for he knows that he only has a little time!" (Revelation 12:7–12)

The devil refuses to give up! He goes to heaven to fight. He is not smart, but he is persistent! In verses 7–12, we see two generals and two armies. As in the old Westerns, the hero tells the villain, "This town is not big enough for both of us." Then there's a gunfight. When the dust settles, the hero in the white hat has won. In John's picture in verses 7–12, when this battle is over, the dragon has been cast down. It is here that John tells us who the dragon is.

> "So that huge dragon- the ancient serpent, the one called the devil and Satan, who deceives the whole world- was thrown down to the earth, and his angels along with him" (Revelation 12:9).

The names John uses tell us about this enemy. The word "dragon" itself reflects that he devours his enemies. "That ancient serpent" refers to the snake in the garden of Eden (Genesis 3.1–15), to which Paul referred in 2 Corinthians 11:3. The word "ancient" does not mean primarily that the devil is old, but that he goes back to ancient times—to the primeval days. The word "serpent" reminds us that he is the beguiler, the trickster, who conned Eve and then Adam into disobeying God. In Revelation, "serpent" always refers to the devil (Revelation 12:13–15; 20:2). He is also described as "devil," "Satan," and "deceiver."

"Devil" is from the Greek word "*diabolos*," meaning "slanderer" or "accuser." It reminds us that he is always accusing us before God. The name "Satan" is carried from Hebrew into the Greek word "*satanos*," meaning "adversary" or "opponent." It labels him as our ultimate enemy. This is not a double name. These are two separate names—the devil and Satan.

Finally, John tells us that he is "the deceiver of the whole world." "Deceiver" comes from the Greek word "*planaoo*," meaning "seduce," "deceive," or "beguile." This is a reminder that he leads people into sin, or into rebellion against God, by means of lies. And his sinister influence affects "the whole world." In other words, through his deception, he has "caused all the people on earth to sin."

This Scene Depicts the Victory of Good over Evil

A recurrent and often overlooked Old Testament theme depicts all earthly conflict as a heavenly struggle, a war in the sphere of the unseen. Daniel 10 provides a good example of this. Just when Daniel was fretting about the state of the world, an angel arrived to encourage him (Daniel 10:1–11).

I believe the messenger was Gabriel, because he is the one who talked to Daniel in 8:16. He said, in essence, "Sorry I was detained, but I've been fighting the prince of Persia. Then Michael came over to help me so I could come to encourage you. Now, if you'll excuse me, I've got unfinished business with the prince of Persia. And, oh, by the way, when I'm done with him, the prince of Greece will come" (Daniel 10:12–13, 20). From the world's perspective, this was a conflict between Persia and Greece. Little did the Persian kings know that they weren't just fighting human armies—they were fighting Gabriel and Michael and the armies of heaven too!

John tells us that the dragon fought Michael and his angels in heaven (Revelation 12:7). From the book of Daniel, we know Michael is the angel of God's people (Daniel 10:21; 12:1). So the picture is this: our angel and his troops defeat the devil and his troops. We may not fully understand it, but here's where faith comes in. As Paul said in Ephesians 6:12, "… our struggle is not against flesh and blood, but against the rulers, against the powers, against the world rulers of this darkness, against the spiritual forces of evil in the heavens." When the war is over, the heavenly voice gives the final word of defeat to the devil in Revelation 12:10–12.

"The accuser of our brothers and sisters" may infer that the speaker is one of the martyrs we saw in Revelation 6:9–12. Or it could be one of the great multitude of the redeemed before God's throne from Revelation 7:9–17. But it seems more likely that the speaker is an angel. Later we'll see an angel identifying himself as a "fellow servant" of Christians (19:10).

This vignette gives us several reasons to rejoice. All of them revolve around the fact that God's salvation, kingdom, and power have prevailed over Satan. God's salvation has come. This recalls the earlier chorus in Revelation 7:10. God's kingdom has come. This recalls the earlier proclamation in Revelation 11:15. God's power has come. This recalls the acclamation of the elders in Revelation 11:16–17.

And there is another reason to rejoice. "The ruling authority of his Christ" has come (12:10). This could well be translated as "and his Messiah will now exercise his authority over the world" or "and his chosen Savior will now use his authority." Remember Jesus's promise to the overcomers in Revelation 2:26–27. What he promised before has now become reality (11:15).

There is a final reason to rejoice. Our accuser has finally been discredited. The description of Satan as "our accuser" depicts the devil as a prosecuting attorney in the heavenly court. He has played that role before (Job 1:6–12; Zechariah 3:1–4; Jude 1:9). The accuser who used to accuse us of sin can't accuse us anymore. Why? Is it because we don't sin? No, rather it is because of the blood of the Lamb that takes away our sins. When the devil tries to accuse us, the Lord points to the blood.

How did these faithful ones overcome the devil? Verse 11 tells the story: "But they overcame him by the blood of the Lamb and by the word of their testimony, and they did not love their lives so much that they were afraid to die" (Revelation 12:11). Overcomers overcome by the blood of Christ. We have no merit of our own. The song says it well: "What can wash away my sins? Nothing but the blood of Jesus." The blood of the Lamb speaks of Calvary, where we were redeemed at the cost of his blood (1 Peter 1:18–20; Revelation 1:5; 5:9; 7:14). It also speaks of baptism, by which we come into contact with the cleansing blood (Acts 22:16; Romans 6:3–5). But it also speaks of a new way of living that brings us into daily contact with his blood (1 John 1:7).

These overcomers overcame by the blood of the Lamb, but that blood had an effect in their daily lives that is described as "the word of their testimony." The fact is that people—all people—talk about what they love. So it was as natural for the overcomers to talk about the Lamb and his blood as it is for us to talk about sports. We talk about what we love. Christianity spreads by shared testimony (Revelation 1:1–2, 9; 2 Timothy 2:2).

Moreover, "they did not love their lives so much that they were afraid to die." *The New Revised Standard Version* does a good job with this statement, rendering it, "they did not cling to life even in the face of death." They took Jesus's words to Smyrna to heart (Revelation 2:10). They were willing to face martyrdom in order to be faithful to Jesus. This is a bottom-line requirement for Jesus's disciples (Mark 8:35; John 12:25).

So heaven rejoices, but "Woe to earth" because the devil is earthbound and he's furious. He knows that he doesn't have much time to carry on his work of deceiving people (Revelation 12:12). That's why, even now, we must be on our guard. As Peter said in 1 Peter 5:8, "Be sober and alert. Your enemy the devil, like a roaring lion, is on the prowl looking for someone to devour." The devil may attack us, but he can never defeat us if we're washed in the blood of the Lamb!

Amen!

Hallelujah!

Chapter 30

THE SECOND VISION (12:13–18)

Now when the dragon realized that he had been thrown down to the earth, he pursued the woman who had given birth to the male child. But the woman was given the two wings of a giant eagle so that she could fly out into the wilderness, to the place God prepared for her, where she is taken care of- away from the presence of the serpent- for a time, times, and half a time. Then the serpent spouted water like a river out of his mouth after the woman in an attempt to sweep her away by a flood, but the earth came to her rescue; the ground opened up and swallowed the river that the dragon had spewed from his mouth. So the dragon became enraged at the woman and went away to make war on the rest of her children, those who keep God's commandments and hold to the testimony about Jesus. And the dragon stood on the sand of the seashore.

—Revelation 12:13–18

When the dragon realizes that his campaign to devour the woman's child has failed, he goes after the child's mother with a vengeance. But God has not abandoned her. He gives her the wings of an eagle so she can fly to a place prepared for her, where

God can preserve her and protect her. When the dragon's efforts are thwarted by God, he goes after her other children, leaving the dragon standing frustrated on the seashore.

The background of this picture comes from two passages—one from the law and one from the prophets. The passage from the law is Exodus 19. Israel, newly delivered from slavery in Egypt, has arrived at Mount Sinai, where they are about to receive the Ten Commandments from God. But before God gives Israel the law, he reminds them of what he has just done for them. "'You yourselves have seen what I did to Egypt and how I lifted you on eagles' wings and brought you to myself. And now, if you will diligently listen to me and keep my covenant, then you will be my special possession out of all the nations, for all the earth is mine, and you will be to me a kingdom of priests and a holy nation.' These are the words that you will speak to the Israelites" (Exodus 19:4–6).

A more familiar passage is from the prophet Isaiah. This one comes from a time when God's people had come to believe that God was tired of them and that he didn't care about them. Then the prophet told them about the eternal God who is always there for the weary and stumbling. Their problem was not that God had given up on them, but that they had given up on God. People who truly rely on God find God's inexhaustible strength to sustain them. "Do you not know? Have you not heard? The LORD is an eternal God, the creator of the whole earth. He does not get tired or weary; there is no limit to his wisdom. He gives strength to those who are tired; to the ones who lack power, he gives renewed energy. Even youths get tired and weary; even strong young men clumsily stumble. But those who wait for the LORD's help find renewed strength; they rise up as if they had eagles' wings, they run without growing weary, they walk without getting tired" (Isaiah 40:28–31).

Four Terms for the Same Time

In Revelation 11 and 12, we encounter four terms used of the same time period: three and one-half years, forty-two months, 1,260 days, and "a time, times, and half-a-time." These four figures depict the time when the devil goes after God's people. Each of the four descriptions tells us something about our struggle against the devil.

Forty-two months depicts the struggle as a time of persecution, during which the godless world persecutes the godly. "But do not measure the outer courtyard of the temple; leave it out, because it has been given to the Gentiles, and they will trample on the holy city for forty-two months" (Revelation 11:2).

But it is also 1,260 days. 1,260 days on a calendar is the same length of time as forty-two months. In Revelation, the 1,260 days is a time when God's witnesses are engaged in preaching (11:3). But it is also a time when God protects his people (12:6, 14). The figure comes from Elijah in 1 Kings 17:1–6. When the prophet decreed a drought in Israel, God directed him to a stream near the Jordan where he provided for him on a daily basis. From a stream in Israel, he went to the home of a Gentile widow, where God continued to provide for him on a day-by-day basis (1 Kings 17:7–16) for the rest of the three-and-one-half year drought.

The message of this time frame is that Satan can never win. But he keeps on trying. He tries to destroy Jesus and fails (Revelation 12:4–5). He tries to invade heaven and fails (12:7–9). He tries to destroy the church and fails (12:15–16). Satan tries to sweep the church away with a flood. This can be translated literally from the Greek as "to make her waterborne"—that is, to float her away.

Old Testament Background for Satan's Persecution as a Torrent

The Old Testament depicts Satan trying to destroy God's people by sending a torrent to overwhelm them (Psalm 124:1–8; Isaiah 8:5–8). But Satan can never destroy the church (Matthew 16:18). When Satan finds that he cannot destroy the church, he doubles down on his effort and works on individual Christians (Revelation 12:17).

That's what it means when John says that the dragon goes after the rest of the woman's children. These "other descendants" are faithful Christians who keep God's commandments and hold to the testimony of Jesus.

What Have We Seen in Revelation 12?

We saw a pregnant woman about to give birth to a son who will rule the nations with a rod of iron. That is the story of the Old Testament. We saw her child born and taken up into heaven. That is the story of the Gospels up to the ascension of Christ. Then we saw Satan's unsuccessful attempt to prevent the Messiah from taking his throne. When he was unsuccessful, he turned his efforts to destroying the church. That is the story of the book of Acts and the rest of the New Testament.

Amen!

Hallelujah!

Chapter 31

THE THIRD VISION (13:1–10)

The Devil's Three Allies

Over the next several chapters, John introduces his readers to the dragon's three allies. He introduces the sea beast in Revelation 13:1. Immediately after the sea beast, he introduces the earth beast in Revelation 13:11. The earth beast is also called the false prophet (19:20). John introduces the dragon's third ally, the great prostitute, in Revelation 17:1.

The Sea Beast (13:1–10)

> Then I saw a beast coming up out of the sea. It had ten horns and seven heads, and on its horns were ten diadem crowns, and on its heads a blasphemous name. Now the beast that I saw was like a leopard, but its feet were like a bear's, and its mouth was like a lion's mouth. The dragon gave the beast his power, his throne, and great authority to rule. One of the beast's heads appeared to have been killed, but the lethal wound had been healed. And the whole world followed the beast in amazement; they worshiped the dragon because he had given ruling authority to the beast, and they worshiped the beast too, saying: "Who is like the beast?" and "Who is able to make war

against him?" The beast was given a mouth speaking proud words and blasphemies, and he was permitted to exercise ruling authority for forty- two months. So the beast opened his mouth to blaspheme against God- to blaspheme both his name and his dwelling place, that is, those who dwell in heaven. The beast was permitted to go to war against the saints and conquer them. He was given ruling authority over every tribe, people, language, and nation, and all those who live on the earth will worship the beast, everyone whose name has not been written since the foundation of the world in the book of life belonging to the Lamb who was killed. If anyone has an ear, he had better listen! If anyone is meant for captivity, into captivity he will go. If anyone is to be killed by the sword, then by the sword he must be killed. This requires steadfast endurance and faith from the saints. (Revelation 13:1–10)

In Revelation 11:7, we saw a beast making war on God's two witnesses and killing them. There he was described as "the beast that comes up from the abyss." Later we will see a beast that "is about to come up from the abyss and then go to destruction (17:8). There we will see him in connection with the dragon's third ally, the great prostitute. The beast described in Revelation 13:1 is likely the same as the beast from the abyss, since "the abyss" was often used to refer to the depths of the ocean.

As John gives us his description of the sea beast, there are some telling identifiers that help us to understand just who this beast represents. For example, the sea beast, like the dragon, has seven heads and ten horns (12:3). This is one of those places where we need to recall the symbolic use of numbers in apocalyptic literature. As we have seen earlier, seven is the number of God doing his work. So when John says the sea beast has seven heads, that indicates that he rules by God's permission. The sea beast also has ten horns. Ten is the number of limitation. The presence of ten horns indicates that he has power but God sets limits on his power.

But unlike the dragon, who wore seven diadems, the sea beast has ten diadems. Recall that, unlike the way we use numbers, ten is not a greater number than seven. The presence of ten diadems indicates that God has set limits on his rule, just as he set limits on the beast's power.

On each of his seven heads, the sea beast wears a blasphemous name. It is noteworthy that some translations read, "blasphemous names," while others, like the NET Bible, read, "a blasphemous name." The reason for this is that some Greek texts use the plural *"onomata"* ("names"), while others use the singular *"onoma"* ("name"). The most reliable ancient manuscripts use the singular rather than the plural. So it seems that this is one name that is common to each of the seven heads—not seven different names.

Later John is going to tell us these seven heads represent seven rulers (17:9–10). Here we're told that each of these rulers wears "a blasphemous name." But what would that mean to a first century reader? "Blasphemous" means "insulting to God." In context in Revelation 13:1, it refers to a name or title that should be used only of God, such as "Lord," "God," "Almighty," "Divine," "Worshipful," etc. So it appears that each of these rulers wears a name that is an affront to God. They mock God by wearing a name that should be applied only to him. Who can read this without thinking of Herod's deification and death in Acts 12:20-23?

The best way to understand the sea beast is to compare him with his Old Testament counterpart in Daniel 7:1–8. John saw one beast. Daniel saw four. But in both cases, the beasts they saw emerged from the sea (Revelation 13:1; Daniel 7:3). Both had ten horns (Revelation 13:1; Daniel 7:7). Both descriptions include references to a leopard, a bear, and a lion (Revelation 13:2; Daniel 7:3–6). In both cases, the beast was boastful and blasphemous (Revelation 13:5; Daniel 7:8, 19–20, 25). Both made war against the saints (Revelation 13:7; Daniel 7:25) for the same length of time (Revelation 13:5;

Daniel 7:25). (Remember that forty-two months is the same as "a time, times and half-a-time" and that each represented three and one-half years.)

An angel told Daniel that the four beasts he saw represented four kingdoms that would arise from the earth (Daniel 7:17–18). He went on to tell him that in the days of the fourth kingdom, God would set up his eternal kingdom (Daniel 7:26–28). This follows the same line as Nebuchadnezzar's dream in Daniel 2. In that passage, Nebuchadnezzar had a dream of a statue composed of various materials. Daniel revealed to him that the statue represented four kingdoms and that God would establish his eternal kingdom in the days of the fourth kingdom (Daniel 2:37–45).

Both Nebuchadnezzar's dream and Daniel's vision of the four beasts tell the same story. It was a story that was just beginning to unfold in Daniel's time, but it was happening in real time during John's day. From our perspective today, it is recorded history. The four kingdoms were Babylon, Medo-Persia, Greece, and Rome. And, true to his word, God established his eternal kingdom in the days of the Roman Empire.

There are more important details from Daniel 7 that bear out this interpretation. For one thing, the fourth beast was killed, and its body was burned (Daniel 7:11–12). And the son of man was given an indestructible kingdom (Daniel 7:13–14). When Daniel expressed curiosity about the fourth beast (Daniel 7:19–20), he was told that the fourth beast was a fourth kingdom (Daniel 7:23). Historically, that fourth kingdom was the Roman Empire. Further, Daniel saw ten horns, identified as ten kings. Then he saw an eleventh king who would humiliate three of the earlier kings (Daniel 7:24).

The difference between the visions in Daniel and Revelation is a matter of historical perspective. Daniel looked forward through history, so he described the animals in this order: lion, bear, leopard. John, living in the time of Daniel's fourth beast, described Daniel's fourth beast with elements of the earlier three in reverse order: leopard, bear, and lion. The significance is that Daniel's fourth beast—the beast described by John, had characteristics of the earlier three. In other words, Rome incorporated and continued some characteristics of the earlier world empires of Greece, Medo-Persia, and Babylon, as one looks backward through history.

John was told that the seven heads of the sea beast are kings but that an eighth is coming (Revelation 17:9–11). Who are the seven kings? John was told that "five have fallen." These were the five kings of the Julio-Claudian Dynasty: Augustus, Tiberius, Caligula, Claudius, and Nero. He was told that one is. That would be Vespasian, the first of the three emperors of the Flavian Dynasty. He was then told that "one has not yet come." That would be Vespasian's elder son, Titus. Then John was told that the beast is an eighth king. That would be Domitian, Vespasian's younger son and Titus's brother. As an interesting note, this would place the writing of Revelation near the end of Vespasian's reign, around AD 78–79.

In each vision, Daniel and John described a particularly sinister king. In Daniel's vision, he was the eleventh king, who knocked off three earlier kings (Daniel 7:8, 24). But in Revelation, John says he is the eighth king. Again, this is a matter of perspective. Looking forward, Daniel saw ten kings, and then he saw an eleventh king who knocked off three, effectively making himself the eighth king. On the other hand, John didn't mention the three, because their reigns were merely a flash in the pan. The important kings were the first five and the last three.

Daniel's eleventh king—and John's eighth—was Domitian. But why was it important for Domitian to be regarded as the eighth king? Once again, this goes back to the apocalyptic use of numbers. Eight represents resurrection. Calling himself the eighth emperor was one of Domitian's ways of claiming deity.

Notice that John's sea beast appears to have something in common with the Lamb. The earlier description of the lamb included reference to the fact that he "appeared to have been killed" (Revelation 5:6). One of the sea beast's heads "appeared to have been killed, but the lethal wound had been healed" (13:3). But there's a difference between the two creatures. While the Lamb had actually been slain (5:9), the sea beast only "appeared to have been killed, but the lethal wound had been healed," (i.e., a scar showed how severe the wound had been).

The last of the Julio-Claudian emperors, Nero, engaged in a severe persecution of Christians in Rome during the last years of his reign. But his persecution died with him. When Nero committed suicide in AD 68, there was no one left in his family line to succeed him. Domitian thought he was perfectly positioned to fill the void and take Nero's place on the throne. His father and older brother were almost 1,500 miles away fighting the Jewish-Roman War. But Domitian didn't rise to power right away. Rome went through a brief civil war, with various factions of the army putting three kings, Galba, Otho, and Vitellius, on the throne in quick succession. There was such a rapid turnaround that AD 69 is referred to as "The Year of the Four Emperors." Galba was on the throne when the year began. During that year, Otho and Vitellius came and went. Historians believe that Domitian was involved in the intrigue that brought those three to their own swift ends. That would fit well with Daniel's vision, in which the eleventh king humiliates three of the earlier kings.

By the end of AD 69, Vespasian, Domitian's father, had returned from the Jewish-Roman War to take the throne, leaving his elder son, Titus, to finish the military campaign. Vespasian established the Flavian Dynasty. A decade later, he was succeeded by his elder son, Titus. When Titus died two years later, he was succeeded by his younger brother, Domitian. As emperor, Domitian fostered the myth that he was Nero reincarnated (i.e., Nero redivivus), and he revived the persecution of Christians. That would explain how one head of the sea beast "appeared to have been killed, but the lethal wound had been healed" (13:3).

In Revelation 13:2, John tells us that the dragon "gave the beast his power, his throne, and great authority to rule." From that point on, the beast became the dragon's deputy, with authority to speak and act in the name of the dragon. In verse 3 we're told that the whole world worshipped the beast—a reference to emperor worship, which was enforced throughout the Roman Empire near the end of the first century. The chorus in verse 4 is telling: "'Who is like the beast?' and 'Who is able to make war against him?'" Essentially, this is a psalm sung in praise of the sea beast. It flies in the face of the name of Michael, whose name means "Who is like God?"

The sea beast was given the power of speech. The passive verb points to God as the one who allows the beast to speak. In other words, God allowed the beast to speak. The Greek text says he spouted "great things and blasphemies," which means "outrageous blasphemies." Moreover, he uttered "proud words" insulting to God. The idea here is that the beast was claiming rights and authority that belong only to God.

The text also indicates that he was "allowed" to exercise authority. This again shows that God is in control. In other words, "God allowed the beast to have authority." Once again, note that the time period of the beast's authority is the same as the time in Revelation 11:2.

Finally John gives encouragement for Christians to hold fast to their faith (13:9–10). This is like the exhortation to the seven churches in chapters 2–3. It is the same idea is that expressed in Jeremiah 15:2. The *New Living Translation* does a good job with this text: "Anyone who is destined for prison will be taken to prison. Anyone destined to die by the sword will die by the sword. This means that God's holy people must endure persecution patiently and remain faithful" (Revelation 13:10 NLT).

In other words, Christians might be imprisoned or even killed for their faith. But even in the face of such persecution, Christians are called upon to endure, because their eternal reward will make it all worthwhile. In Revelation, the one who is ultimately destined for captivity and death is not the Christian but the beast!

Amen!

Hallelujah!

Chapter 32

THE FOURTH VISION (13:11–18)

Then I saw another beast coming up from the earth. He had two horns like a lamb, but was speaking like a dragon. He exercised all the ruling authority of the first beast on his behalf, and made the earth and those who inhabit it worship the first beast, the one whose lethal wound had been healed. He performed momentous signs, even making fire come down from heaven in front of people and, by the signs he was permitted to perform on behalf of the beast, he deceived those who live on the earth. He told those who live on the earth to make an image to the beast who had been wounded by the sword, but still lived. The second beast was empowered to give life to the image of the first beast so that it could speak, and could cause all those who did not worship the image of the beast to be killed. He also caused everyone (small and great, rich and poor, free and slave) to obtain a mark on their right hand or on their forehead. Thus no one was allowed to buy or sell things unless he bore the mark of the beast- that is, his name or his number. This calls for wisdom: Let the one who has insight calculate the beasts number, for it is man's number, and his number is 666.

—Revelation 13:11–18

Now John sees a second beast. This beast appears to be gentle. It looks like a lamb. A lamb almost always has a religious significance, so it appears that this beast has an outwardly religious appearance. It has two horns like a lamb; these horns are small and inoffensive and depict this beast as a gentle creature. But in reality, it exercises the power of the devil, because it has the voice of the dragon. John has already told us that the dragon is none other than the devil himself (Revelation 12:9).

This beast also has the authority of the first beast, who has the authority of the dragon (13:2). In first-century terms, this beast is backed by the power of Rome (the sea beast), which is backed by the power of the devil. This second beast (the earth beast) forces people to worship the first beast (the sea beast). Hence he is later going to be called "the false prophet" (19:20; 13:13).

"All these characteristics seem to identify the second beast as the 'commune' or 'concilia' set up in Asia Minor to enforce the state religion. This was an official body which had charge of the state religion and had as its duty to force all to do homage to the image of the emperor."[5] It is likely that this emperor cult was the very thing that Paul was warning early Christians against in 2 Thessalonians 2:1–12. Several references in Revelation 13:11–18 seem to fit the emperor cult and its stranglehold on people in the first century. For example, John mentions the creation of an image of the beast and the penalty of death for anyone who does not worship the image of the beast. By the end of the first century, temples had been erected to the Roman emperors throughout the empire. The agora, or marketplace, in each Roman city boasted a statue to the emperor. And everyone who traded in the agora was required to first pay homage to Caesar as "lord." So when John says that "no one was allowed to buy or sell things unless he bore the mark of the beast," that would have spoken volumes to early Christians. Without claiming allegiance to Caesar as "lord," Christians could not legally work or trade. That would have the effect of starving them out of the world's economy.

Don't get hung up on what this "mark of the beast" is. John's readers would have seen this as symbolic, as are all of the images in Revelation. This was no more a literal mark of the beast in this passage than there was a literal mark of God placed on the foreheads of God's servants in Revelation 7:3.

People have a tendency to go through Revelation "buffet style." They go past what doesn't fit their narrative, and go straight for whatever excites their taste buds. They happily take things figuratively until they get to something like "the mark of the beast" or "the thousand-year reign." Then they decide, for no discernible reason, to take those things literally. Hogwash! The fact is that by the end of the first century, one could not get work unless he belonged to one of the trade guilds. People could not buy and sell on the open market unless they claimed allegiance to Caesar as "lord." Otherwise they were forced out of work and into the black market.

Early in the Third Century, a convert named Tertullian challenged Christians who were involved in the trade guilds "head-on." Tertullian, the son of a Roman officer, was a lawyer. After his conversion, through some of his writings, he became something of an uninvited and unwelcome "conscience" to the church of his day, a real thorn in their flesh. He wrote, among other things, a series of essays on idolatry. The basic idea of one of his essays was this: A Christian might confess Caesar as Lord or engage in some pagan ritual, possibly involving idolatry or immorality, so that he might be able to continue in his trade. He might justify himself by glibly saying, "I must live." Tertullian asked that person some scathing questions: "But *must* you live?" "*Where* is it written that you must live?" Christ does not demand that we *must* live—he demands that we must *be faithful!*

So if this "mark of the beast" is figurative, what is the significance of the "number of the name?" John says that it is "man's number." It is not the number of "a man"; it is the number of "man." So what is this number, and what does it mean? Again, consider how numbers are used symbolically in apocalyptic literature. The number six falls short of seven every time. The more it tries to catch up, the further it falls behind. The number 6 is one short of 7, 66 is 11 short of 77, and 666 is 111 short of 777. See—it just gets further behind.

Six is the attempt of man to usurp God's place. It was mankind's sin when people decided they could just build a tower and climb their way to heaven (Genesis 11:1–9). John probably has a gematrical number in mind. The number 666 in Revelation 13:18 is clearly a gematria. It is likely that John had a specific name or word in mind when he wrote that sinister number, but what was it? Writers have come up with all sorts of creative suggestions that have included the pope, Hitler, Nero, and a host of others. Symbolically, 666 is rebellion, compounded and compounded again. It is man's attempt to usurp God's throne.

Undoubtedly, the number concealed a name that was well-known to John and to his original readers and hearers. But the name behind the number was quickly lost. Irenaeus, a second-century Christian, posed several possibilities, but even he did not know for certain the name behind the number.

There are three possible names that make sense in light of the historical setting. It may be one of them, or it may be something else entirely. The Greek word "*lateinos*" is translated as "Latin." It could be a reference to either the city of Rome or the Roman Empire. The numbers add up this way: 30 + 1 + 300 + 5 + 10 + 50 + 70 + 200 = 666.

The Greek word "*teitan*" is translated as "Titus." This was the name each of the three Flavian emperors—Vespasian, Titus, and Domitian—shared in common. As set out previously, it appears that Vespasian may have been the emperor at the time Revelation was written. Titus came to the throne shortly thereafter. Domitian began the first empire-wide persecution of Christians. The numbers add up this way: 300 + 5 + 10 + 300 + 1 + 50 = 666.

The Greek word "*kaisarsebaston*" is the Greek translation of the Latin "Caesar Augustus." The word, in both Latin and Greek, means "worshipful Caesar." This was a part of the imperial throne name that was adopted by every Roman emperor in the first century. The numbers add up this way: 20 + 1 + 10 + 200 + 1 + 100 + 200 + 5 + 2 + 1 + 6 + 70 + 50 = 666. (Note: this calculation of "kaisarsebaston" requires using the obsolete letter stigma, with a value of six, in the place of the letters sigma (two hundred) and tau (three hundred). I do not regard this as particularly objectionable, since the book was intended to be read aloud. The hearers would be used to associating the "st" sound with the value of six, even though they had long since stopped using stigma as a letter in spelling words.)

Why do I think *"kaisarsebaston"* ("Caesar Augustus") may be the name? First, remember that John equates the name of the sea beast with the number of the name (13:16–17). Second, recall that the first beast—the sea beast—had seven heads with a blasphemous name on each. Remember that the most reliable Greek texts suggest that this was one name that was shared in common by all the heads—not seven different names, as many translations suggest (13:1). Third, remember that the heads are elsewhere identified as kings (17:9–10).

There was a common name that was adopted by each and every Roman emperor in the first century. That name was Caesar Augustus. Here are the first century Roman emperors, in order. The common name, by which we recognize each, is underlined. But their entire Imperial names were as follows:

- Caesar <u>Augustus</u> (27 BC—AD 14)
- <u>Tiberius</u> Julius Caesar Augustus (AD 14—37)
- Gaius Caesar Augustus Germanicus (<u>Caligula</u>) (AD 37—41)
- Tiberius <u>Claudius</u> Caesar Augustus Germanicus (AD 41—54)
- <u>Nero</u> Claudius Caesar Augustus Germanicus (AD 54—68)
- Servius <u>Galba</u> Caesar Augustus (AD 68—69)
- Marcus <u>Otho</u> Caesar Augustus (AD 69)

- Aulus <u>Vitellius</u> Caesar Augustus Germanicus (AD 69)
- Caesar <u>Vespasianus</u> Augustus (AD 69—79)
- <u>Titus</u> Caesar Vespasianus Augustus (AD 79–81)
- Caesar <u>Domitianus</u> Augustus Germanicus (AD 81—96)

Every first-century Roman emperor took the name Caesar Augustus, which means "worshipful Caesar." Clearly this was a blasphemous name (13:1). The *Good News Translation* makes quite plain just what this blasphemy involved: "Then I saw a beast coming up out of the sea. It had ten horns and seven heads; on each of its horns there was a crown, and on each of its heads there was a name that was insulting to God" (13:1 GNT).

Remember from the earlier discussions of the use of numbers in apocalyptic literature that the numbers six, seven, and eight are singularly important. Seven is the number of God accomplishing his will. Six is man in rebellion against God's will. The number eight is not used in Revelation, but it is used in other apocalyptic literature. It was the number of resurrection. Early writers said that Christians met on "the eighth day of the week, which is also the first," because of Jesus's resurrection.

The second-century Sibylline Oracles say that Jesus is "888." This is another example of a gematria. The gematrical value of the name "Jesus" (Greek: *"Ieesous"*) is 888. The writer states that eight symbolizes resurrection, so Jesus is truly 888.

The one who is 666 can never measure up to the one who is, was, and always will be 888.

Amen!

Hallelujah!

Chapter 33

THE FIFTH, SIXTH, AND SEVENTH VISIONS (14:1–20)

The Fifth Vision: The Lamb and the 144,000 (14:1–5)

Then I looked, and here was the Lamb standing on Mount Zion, and with him were one hundred and forty-four thousand, who had his name and his Father's name written on their foreheads. I also heard a sound coming out of heaven like the sound of many waters and like the sound of loud thunder. Now the sound I heard was like that made by harpists playing their harps, and they were singing a new song before the throne and before the four living creatures and the elders. No one was able to learn the song except the one hundred and forty-four thousand who had been redeemed from the earth. These are the ones who have not defiled themselves with women, for they are virgins. These are the ones who follow the Lamb wherever he goes. These were redeemed from humanity as firstfruits to God and to the Lamb, and no lie was found on their lips; they are blameless. (Revelation 14:1–5)

John now sees the Lamb once again. This time he is accompanied by the one hundred forty-four thousand that John first saw in Revelation 7:2–3. He has just seen the worshippers of the sea beast—those who have the mark of the beast (likely his name) on their foreheads. By contrast, the one hundred forty-four thousand have the name of God on their foreheads. The one hundred forty-four thousand are now in the presence of the Lamb that he first saw in Revelation 5:6.

This group is standing on Mount Zion. A reading through the scriptures will show that Zion is not always a reference to a literal mountain in Jerusalem. Rather, it symbolizes God's throne. Wherever God sits on his throne is Zion. In that respect, it is much like the US president and Air Force One. The designation "Air Force One" does not refer to any particular airplane; it designates the airplane the president is on. So whatever airplane is flying the president from place to place is Air Force One. Likewise, whatever helicopter the president is on is Marine One.

Zion is used both figuratively and literally in the Bible. We first come across the designation of Zion when David captures Jerusalem in 2 Samuel 5:6–10. But Zion is also symbolic of Jerusalem in the psalms (Psalms 2:6; 48:1–2; 132:13–14). It is also a symbol of God's rule in the Prophets (Zechariah 8:1–3; Daniel 2:34–35; Isaiah 2:2–4). In the New Testament, Zion is a symbol of the church (Hebrews 12:22–24; 1 Corinthians 3:16; Ephesians 2:19–22). This Zion that John sees is in heaven (Revelation 14:2–3).

Who are these people who are with the Lamb? They are described in Revelation 14:4–5. He tells us that they are sexually pure (i.e., "they have not defiled themselves with women"). He further tells us that they "follow the Lamb" (i.e., they are obedient). But the most important things about these people are that they have been purchased from among men by the blood of Christ (5:8–10) and they are "firstfruits to God and to the Lamb" (see James 1:18).

Here is something important. Everyone in Revelation has a mark on his forehead. Each person wears either the name of God or the mark of the beast. The mark signifies to whom that person belongs. Look in the mirror. If you don't see the name of God figuratively tattooed on your forehead, then you're wearing the mark of the beast—and you need to do something to change your designation!

The Sixth Vision: Preview of Coming Attractions (14:6–13)

> Then I saw another angel flying directly overhead, and he had an eternal gospel to proclaim to those who live on the earth- to every nation, tribe, language, and people. He declared in a loud voice: "Fear God and give him glory, because the hour of his judgment has arrived, and worship the one who made heaven and earth, the sea and the springs of water!" A second angel followed the first, declaring: "Fallen, fallen is Babylon the great city! She made all the nations drink of the wine of her immoral passion." A third angel followed the first two, declaring in a loud voice: "If anyone worships the beast and his image, and takes the mark on his forehead or his hand, that person will also drink of the wine of Gods anger that has been mixed undiluted in the cup of his wrath, and he will be tortured with fire and sulfur in front of the holy angels and in front of the Lamb. And the smoke from their torture will go up forever and ever, and those who worship the beast and his image will have no rest day or night, along with anyone who receives the mark of his name." This requires the steadfast endurance of the saints- those who obey Gods commandments and hold to their faith in Jesus. Then I heard a voice from heaven say, "Write this: Blessed are the dead, those who die in the Lord from this moment on!" "Yes," says the Spirit, "so they can rest from their hard work, because their deeds will follow them." (Revelation 14:6–13)

The sixth vision consists of four angelic announcements. To get the picture, remember the last time you were checking out at your local grocery store. Recall the tabloids with their attention-grabbing headlines about things and people you otherwise wouldn't even be thinking about—everything from UFOs and extraterrestrials to celebrities and their dysfunctional lives. The headlines are designed for one purpose: to grab your attention so you'll pick up the tabloid and read the article that goes with the headline, which might read something like, "Elvis Lives (See page 10)." Or think of the video teasers you see every day on television and at the cinema. One television episode ends with a preview of the next episode. Or before you take in a movie, you sit through several trailers designed to bring you back to the theater for the next blockbuster. Even news programs use trailers to announce what's coming up at 6:00 or 10:00 p.m., or even what's coming after the next commercial break. In every case, the purpose is the same: to get you to watch what's coming later. That's the way you should read the four angelic announcements. Each is a headline or trailer that is described in greater detail in the remaining chapters of the book. In fact, the four headlines announce everything that is in the rest of Revelation.

The first headline (14:6–7) might read "God Judges Rome." The story line is developed in Revelation 14:14–16:21. The second headline (14:8) could be "Babylon the Great Falls." The story line is developed in Revelation 17–18. The third headline (14:9–12) might announce "Emperor Worshippers Judged; Saints Urged to be Faithful." The story line is developed in Revelation 19–20. The final headline (14:13) would proclaim "Dead Saints Live Forever." The story line is developed in Revelation 21–22.

The Seventh Vision: The Harvest of the Earth (Revelation 14:14–20)

> Then I looked, and a white cloud appeared, and seated on the cloud was one like a son of man! He had a golden crown on his head and a sharp sickle in his hand. Then another angel came out of the temple, shouting in a loud voice to the one seated on

the cloud, "Use your sickle and start to reap, because the time to reap has come, since the earth's harvest is ripe!" So the one seated on the cloud swung his sickle over the earth, and the earth was reaped. Then another angel came out of the temple in heaven, and he too had a sharp sickle. Another angel, who was in charge of the fire, came from the altar and called in a loud voice to the angel who had the sharp sickle, "Use your sharp sickle and gather the clusters of grapes off the vine of the earth, because its grapes are now ripe." So the angel swung his sickle over the earth and gathered the grapes from the vineyard of the earth and tossed them into the great winepress of the wrath of God. Then the winepress was stomped outside the city, and blood poured out of the winepress up to the height of horses' bridles for a distance of almost two hundred miles. (Revelation 14:14–20)

This is a two-part vision. The first part (14:14–16) describes a wheat harvest. This picture depicts judgment from the perspective of the righteous. Wheat is used in the gospels as a symbol of the righteous (Matthew 3:12; 13:30). The harvest of wheat conveys that, as far as the Christian is concerned, God's judgment is like being gathered into God's silo. The second part of the vision (Revelation 14:17–20) describes a harvest of grapes. This picture depicts judgment from the perspective of the wicked. The picture comes from Isaiah 63:1–6. Unlike wheat, which is gathered into a silo, grapes are put in a vat and their life blood is stomped out of them. In John's vision, the blood runs deep and far. It flows two hundred miles and as deep as a horse's bridle. This is yet another image in Revelation that is not intended to be taken literally, but figuratively. The point of this vision is that for the righteous, judgment is like being gathered to God, while for the wicked, it is like being stomped mercilessly by God.

Amen!

Hallelujah!

The Fifth Seven

SEVEN BOWLS (15:1–16:21)

Chapter 34

SEVEN ANGELS WITH SEVEN PLAGUES (15:1–8)

Then I saw another great and astounding sign in heaven: seven angels who have seven final plagues (they are final because in them God's anger is completed). Then I saw something like a sea of glass mixed with fire, and those who had conquered the beast and his image and the number of his name. They were standing by the sea of glass, holding harps given to them by God. They sang the song of Moses the servant of God and the song of the Lamb: "Great and astounding are your deeds, Lord God, the All-Powerful! Just and true are your ways, King over the nations! Who will not fear you, O Lord, and glorify your name, because you alone are holy? All nations will come and worship before you for your righteous acts have been revealed." After these things I looked, and the temple (the tent of the testimony) was opened in heaven, and the seven angels who had the seven plagues came out of the temple, dressed in clean bright linen, wearing wide golden belts around their chests. Then one of the four living creatures gave the seven angels seven golden bowls filled with the wrath of God who lives forever and ever, and the temple was filled with smoke from God's glory and from his power. Thus no one could enter the temple until the seven plagues from the seven angels were completed.

—Revelation 15:1–8

When the seven trumpets were blown in chapters 8 through 11, mercy was mixed with judgment. God was holding back so only one-third of the world was affected by the judgments of the trumpets. Why did God exercise such restraint? In order to give humanity the opportunity and incentive to repent. But that didn't work. Mankind refused to heed the warning and repent (9:20–21).

When the seven bowls are poured out on the earth, there will be no mercy; Rome will see that "Our God is a consuming fire" (Deuteronomy 4:23–24; Hebrews 12:28–29).

Saints Standing Beside the Sea (15:2–4)

Then I saw something like a sea of glass mixed with fire, and those who had conquered the beast and his image and the number of his name. They were standing by the sea of glass, holding harps given to them by God. They sang the song of Moses the servant of God and the song of the Lamb: "Great and astounding are your deeds, Lord God, the All-Powerful! Just and true are your ways, King over the nations! Who will not fear you, O Lord, and glorify your name, because you alone are holy? All nations will come and worship before you for your righteous acts have been revealed" (Revelation 15:2–4).

Before the bowls of judgment are poured out on the earth, John sees the saints standing beside a sea that looks like glass mixed with fire (15:2–4). This is the sea that separated God from his people earlier in the throne scene (4:6). Now the saints have crossed over to the other side of the sea. Later, even the sea will cease to exist when the redeemed are, at last, in fellowship with God (21:1).

Here John sees the saints standing by the sea, praising God and singing songs of deliverance. Once again we see the Exodus motif—God's people on the way out of bondage as they cross the Red Sea, and headed into the Promised Land as they cross the Jordan River. John's imagery calls to mind the Israelites singing the song of Moses after they've crossed the Red Sea and their pursuers have been destroyed (Exodus 15:1). This is the song of deliverance! It is important to John that we see God's people out of harm's way before God's judgments fall on the world that had attempted to destroy them.

God's Judgments Begin (15:5–8)

> After these things I looked, and the temple (the tent of the testimony) was opened in heaven, and the seven angels who had the seven plagues came out of the temple, dressed in clean bright linen, wearing wide golden belts around their chests. Then one of the four living creatures gave the seven angels seven golden bowls filled with the wrath of God who lives forever and ever, and the temple was filled with smoke from God's glory and from his power. Thus no one could enter the temple until the seven plagues from the seven angels were completed. (Revelation 15:5–8)

These judgments come from inside the temple and are delivered by seven angels. This is to show us that these are God's judgments on an ungodly world. But there's another touch here. The temple is filled with smoke so that no one can enter (15:8). What is that about? Simply put, there will be no more intercession allowed. God's judgment will be poured out without mercy!

This smoke is called "the smoke from God's glory and from his power." It is intended to remind us of the presence of God in the tabernacle and later in the temple (Exodus 40:34–35;

1 Kings 8:10–11). When the smoke of God's presence filled the sanctuary, the priests could not enter to perform their priestly duty of intercession. Now that God's presence fills the temple, there will be no more intercession. God's judgment is now irrevocable.

Amen!

Hallelujah!

Chapter 35

SEVEN BOWLS POURED OUT ON THE EARTH (16:1–21)

The Voice from the Temple (16:1)

"Then I heard a loud voice from the temple declaring to the seven angels: 'Go and pour out on the earth the seven bowls containing God's wrath'" (Revelation 16:1).

Whose is this loud voice from the temple? It must be God's voice, because as we've just seen, no one else could enter the temple. So God decrees that the seven bowls of his wrath be poured out on the earth (16:1).

As with the seals and trumpets before them, the seven bowls are broken into four that are similar, followed by two that are different. Then there is an interlude before the last bowl is poured out.

The First Four Bowls: Judgment on Rome's World (16:2–9)

So the first angel went and poured out his bowl on the earth. Then ugly and painful sores appeared on the people who had the mark of the beast and who worshiped his image. Next, the second angel poured out his bowl on the sea and it turned into blood, like that of a corpse, and every living creature that was in the sea died. Then the third angel poured out his bowl on the rivers and the springs of water, and they turned into blood. Now I heard the angel of the waters saying: "You are just- the one who is and who was, the Holy One- because you have passed these judgments, because they poured out the blood of your saints and prophets, so you have given them blood to drink. They got what they deserved!" Then I heard the altar reply, "Yes, Lord God, the All- Powerful, your judgments are true and just!" Then the fourth angel poured out his bowl on the sun, and it was permitted to scorch people with fire. Thus people were scorched by the terrible heat, yet they blasphemed the name of God, who has ruling authority over these plagues, and they would not repent and give him glory. (Revelation 16:2–9)

The first four bowls roughly parallel the first four trumpets of chapter 8. However, the first bowl is somewhat different. While the first trumpet affected the earth and its plant life, the first bowl affects people themselves. Each recalls one of the plagues of Egypt. The first trumpet recalls the seventh plague of hail (Exodus 9:13–35), but the first bowl emulates the sixth plague— the plague of boils (Exodus 9:8–12). While the plague of hail affected people indirectly by disrupting their food supply, the plague of boils was a more direct assault that inflicted pain on each individual who was affected.

The second, third, and fourth bowls more directly parallel their respective trumpets. The second hits the sea and kills everything in it. The third hits the fresh water and turns it to blood. The fourth hits the sun. While the fourth trumpet darkened the sun by one-third, the fourth bowl turns up the heat so that it scorches every living person.

God is praised because his judgments are true and just. His enemies are getting exactly what they deserve. Yet they are so hardened that they still refuse to repent of their misdeeds. So in the next bowl, God does not simply judge the entire Roman Empire; he turns his attention to its heart—Rome itself.

The Fifth Bowl: Judgment on the Throne of the Beast (16:10–11)

> "Then the fifth angel poured out his bowl on the throne of the beast so that darkness covered his kingdom, and people began to bite their tongues because of their pain. They blasphemed the God of heaven because of their sufferings and because of their sores, but nevertheless they still refused to repent of their deeds" (Revelation 16:10–11).

Don't lose sight of the ultimate conflict in Revelation. The one who sits on the throne in heaven in chapter 4 is directly attacking the usurper whose throne is on earth. Recall that the dragon, also known as the devil (12:9), attempted an assault on God's throne in chapter 12 but was defeated and cast down to earth. Recall also that the dragon gave his throne to the sea beast (13:2) and that the earth beast was his enforcer to coerce mankind into worshipping the sea beast, on pain of death (13:15).

In chapter 13, we saw that the earth beast was the concilia— the emperor cult—and that the Roman emperors claimed to be gods, even to the point of having temples erected in their honor throughout the Roman Empire. All the first-century Roman emperors took some variation of the name "Caesar Augustus" (Greek: *"kaisarsebaston"*) as a part of their imperial names.

With the pouring out of the fifth bowl, the one who is truly worthy of worship pours out his unmitigated wrath on the pretender who dares claim the designation that belongs only to God.

The Sixth Bowl: The Last Obstacle to Invasion Is Removed (16:12)

> "Then the sixth angel poured out his bowl on the great river Euphrates and dried up its water to prepare the way for the kings from the east" (Revelation 16:10–11).

The Euphrates River was considered to be the eastern border of the Roman Empire. It was the border an enemy had to cross in order to invade the empire. When the Euphrates dries up in this vision, that signifies that the last obstacle to the fall of Rome has been taken out of the way and that Rome's ultimate fall is certain.

The Interlude: Three Unclean Spirits (16:13–16)

> Then I saw three unclean spirits that looked like frogs coming out of the mouth of the dragon, out of the mouth of the beast, and out of the mouth of the false prophet. For they are the spirits of the demons performing signs who go out to the kings of the earth to bring them together for the battle that will take place on the great day of God, the All- Powerful. (Look! I will come like a thief! Blessed is the one who stays alert and does not lose his clothes so that he will not have to walk around naked and his shameful condition be seen.) Now the spirits gathered the kings and their armies to the place that is called Armageddon in Hebrew. (Revelation 16:13–16)

The drama heightens. The dragon and his cohorts, the beast (sea beast) and false prophet (earth beast), see that their plight has taken a serious turn. In response, they unite in the form of three unclean spirits that look like frogs to deceive Rome's allies. This becomes their last-ditch effort to repel a certain invasion by the forces of righteousness. The mention of frogs is possibly designed to remind us of yet another plague of the Exodus—the second plague of frogs (Exodus 8:1–15). Recall that the magicians of Egypt were able to copy the first two plagues—turning water to blood and producing frogs from the Nile—so that they were able to deceive Pharaoh and the Egyptians into believing that they could withstand God's deliverer, Moses. So too here, Rome is able to deceive its enemies into thinking they have a chance against God's invading army. So they line up for battle at Armageddon.

Armageddon is a literal place in Israel. The actual name is Har Megiddo, which means "hill of Megiddo." It refers to the Valley of Jezreel on the Plain of Megiddo, where many famous Old Testament battles were fought. Megiddo sat atop a narrow pass that strategically guarded the major roads between Assyria and Egypt. It is nowhere near the Euphrates River. At its nearest point, the Euphrates is over three hundred miles away as the crow flies. Hence the setting of this battle at Megiddo is not intended to be literal, any more than identifying Rome as Sodom, Egypt, or Jerusalem is intended to be literal elsewhere in Revelation (Revelation 11:8).

Armageddon was symbolic as the battlefield where God's enemies always met defeat. Megiddo is where Deborah defeated Sisera's army (Judges 5:19–20). It is where Jehu killed Ahaziah (2 Kings 9:27). Megiddo is where Josiah died at the hands of Pharaoh Necho (2 Chronicles 35:20–24).

The modern so-called prophets miss the point of Armageddon in Revelation. It is the battlefield where God's enemies meet their end. In context, it is a symbol for the final overthrow of Rome's evil forces. The name stands for an event, not a place. In Revelation 16, John describes the ultimate fall of Rome in terms early Christians would understand—the ultimate defeat of evil by the army of God at Megiddo.

The Seventh Bowl (16:17–21)

> Finally the seventh angel poured out his bowl into
> the air and a loud voice came out of the temple

from the throne, saying: "It is done!" Then there were flashes of lightning, roaring, and crashes of thunder, and there was a tremendous earthquake- an earthquake unequaled since humanity has been on the earth, so tremendous was that earthquake. The great city was split into three parts and the cities of the nations collapsed. So Babylon the great was remembered before God, and was given the cup filled with the wine made of God's furious wrath. Every island fled away and no mountains could be found. And gigantic hailstones, weighing about a hundred pounds each, fell from heaven on people, but they blasphemed God because of the plague of hail, since it was so horrendous. (Revelation 16:17–21 17)

Again, this is symbolic, not literal. It is a fanciful image to demonstrate the final and irrevocable fall of Rome and the effect of Rome's fall on the rest of its world. Historically, when the Roman Empire finally collapsed, there was greater worldwide panic and confusion than after the crash of the stock market in 1929. In fact, civilization itself collapsed for a time with the fall of Rome.

For all her faults, the Roman Empire was the repository of civilization from the first century BC to the fifth century AD. Roman military might had given the world two hundred years of relative peace. Roman laws had provided a degree of social stability to the empire, such as had never previously been known. The Roman Empire made transportation and communication possible on an unprecedented scale.

Civilization was set back for centuries when the empire collapsed. With the fall of the Roman Empire, the world plunged into a millennium known as the Dark Ages. The Goths entered Italy, captured Rome, and looted the city in AD 410. The Vandals plundered the city in AD 455. The Germans deposed the last emperor in AD 476.

What is the ultimate message of the bowls and their judgment on the Roman world? It is that sin is so pervasive that it can ruin not only individuals and families but even a whole civilization. God simply will not let rampant rebellion go unpunished.

Amen!

Hallelujah!

The Sixth Seven

SEVEN MESSAGES OF JUDGMENT (17:1–19:10)

Chapter 36

THE PROSTITUTE AND THE BEAST (17:1–18)

The First Angelic Message: Introduction to the Prostitute (17:1–6, 18)

Then one of the seven angels who had the seven bowls came and spoke to me. "Come," he said, "I will show you the condemnation and punishment of the great prostitute who sits on many waters, with whom the kings of the earth committed sexual immorality and the earth's inhabitants got drunk with the wine of her immorality." So he carried me away in the Spirit to a wilderness, and there I saw a woman sitting on a scarlet beast that was full of blasphemous names and had seven heads and ten horns. Now the woman was dressed in purple and scarlet clothing, and adorned with gold, precious stones, and pearls. She held in her hand a golden cup filled with detestable things and unclean things from her sexual immorality. On her forehead was written a name, a mystery: "Babylon the Great, the Mother of prostitutes and of the detestable things of the earth." I saw that the woman was drunk with the blood of the saints and

the blood of those who testified to Jesus. I was greatly
astounded when I saw her. (Revelation 17:1–6)

"As for the woman you saw, she is the great city
that has sovereignty over the kings of the earth."
(Revelation 17:18)

John sees a prostitute riding atop a beast. We may not know right
away just who the woman is, but we've seen the beast before. It has
seven heads and ten horns, and it is full of blasphemous names
(17:3). This is the sea beast John saw earlier in Revelation 13:1.
We've already identified the sea beast as the Roman Empire, with
its heads being the emperors themselves. We'll see the basis for
that identification in the second angelic message a few verses
from now.

But who is the woman? The angel identifies her for John. She
is "the great city that has sovereignty over the kings of the earth."
Only one city in the first-century world fits that bill. She is none
other than the city of Rome.

This vision actually predates John's vision in Revelation 16:19.
There she is destroyed; here she is riding high. How do we explain
that? Quite simply, that is the way history has always been
written. A historian will follow one thread of a story to a natural
stopping point, and then he will return to pick up another thread
and bring it along.

John now shows us the city in all her splendor. She is dressed
like a queen, in royal colors and wearing gaudy ornaments. He
calls her the "mother of prostitutes." She is drunk on the blood
of the saints she has killed (17:6). But why is she called Babylon
the Great? After all, Babylon had been defeated by the Persians
over five hundred years earlier!

Common apocalyptic technique was to call the current evil
empire by the name of a previous evil empire that had already
been overthrown by God. This was a technique used by New
Testament writers elsewhere. For example, Peter, writing to

Christians in the first century, referred to Rome as Babylon
(1 Peter 5:13). Peter was not writing from the Tigris River but
from the Tiber. In its day, Babylon had been the center of the
world's evil power. By the first century, that designation could
belong only to Rome.

The Second Angelic Message: Explanation
of the Sea Beast (17:7–17)

But the angel said to me, "Why are you astounded? I
will interpret for you the mystery of the woman and
of the beast with the seven heads and ten horns that
carries her. The beast you saw was, and is not, but
is about to come up from the abyss and then go to
destruction. The inhabitants of the earth- all those
whose names have not been written in the book of life
since the foundation of the world- will be astounded
when they see that the beast was, and is not, but is
to come. (This requires a mind that has wisdom.) The
seven heads are seven mountains the woman sits on.
They are also seven kings: five have fallen; one is,
and the other has not yet come, but whenever he does
come, he must remain for only a brief time. The beast
that was, and is not, is himself an eighth king and
yet is one of the seven, and is going to destruction.
The ten horns that you saw are ten kings who have
not yet received a kingdom, but will receive ruling
authority as kings with the beast for one hour. These
kings have a single intent, and they will give their
power and authority to the beast. They will make
war with the Lamb, but the Lamb will conquer
them, because he is Lord of lords and King of kings,
and those accompanying the Lamb are the called,
chosen, and faithful." Then the angel said to me,
"The waters you saw (where the prostitute is seated)
are peoples, multitudes, nations, and languages.

> The ten horns that you saw, and the beast- these
> will hate the prostitute and make her desolate and
> naked. They will consume her flesh and burn her up
> with fire. For God has put into their minds to carry
> out his purpose by making a decision to give their
> royal power to the beast until the words of God are
> fulfilled. (Revelation 17:7–17)

How do we know that the sea beast is Imperial Rome? One clue is the seven hills on which the woman sits (17:9). The city of Rome was famously built on seven hills. But a second clue is that the hills also represent kings (17:9–10). The angel mentions seven kings, followed by an eighth. The seven are the seven major emperors from Augustus through Titus. The eighth is Domitian. He says that five have fallen. These would be the five emperors of the Julio-Claudian Dynasty: Augustus, Tiberius, Caligula, Claudius, and Nero. The remaining three are the emperors of the Flavian Dynasty. The sixth emperor, of whom the angel says "one is" would be Vespasian, the father of the next two emperors. The seventh emperor, of whom the angel says he "has not yet come" and "he must remain only a brief time" would be Vespasian's elder son, Titus.

Then the angel says the beast himself is the eighth king. That would be Domitian, the younger son of Vespasian, who launched an empire-wide persecution of Christians near the end of the first century.

But Rome is not alone in its wickedness. The Roman Empire included a number of nations who were ultimately subject to the whims of Rome itself. Their rulers were "client" kings, who were nominally independent, but who were required to contribute money to Rome's coffers and troops to Rome's army. These client kings were free to handle day-to-day administration within their territories, under the watchful eyes of the governor, who was the Emperor's local representative, tasked with the job of making sure they didn't get too far out of line. An example from the book of Acts is the interrelation between the client king, Agrippa, and the Roman governors Felix and Festus (Acts 23-26). Client kings were subject to Roman governors, who were directly responsible to the emperor.

According to Revelation, Rome's client kings, as Rome would require and expect, would ally with her in an empire-wide onslaught against Christians (17:12). And, in the end, God would use the decadent emperors to bring about Rome's downfall (17:16–17).

Amen!

Hallelujah!

Chapter 37

ROME FALLS AND HEAVEN CELEBRATES (18:1–19:10)

The Third Angelic Message: The Announcement of Rome's Destruction (18:1–3)

> After these things I saw another angel, who possessed great authority, coming down out of heaven, and the earth was lit up by his radiance. He shouted with a powerful voice: "Fallen, fallen, is Babylon the great! She has become a lair for demons, a haunt for every unclean spirit, a haunt for every unclean bird, a haunt for every unclean and detested beast. For all the nations have fallen from the wine of her immoral passion, and the kings of the earth have committed sexual immorality with her, and the merchants of the earth have gotten rich from the power of her sensual behavior." (Revelation 18:1–3)

This announcement captures the imagery of the Old Testament prophets' description of the fall of ancient Babylon (Isaiah 13:20–22; Jeremiah 51:37–42). Even then the prophetic descriptions were not literally fulfilled. Rather, they were graphic descriptions of how a city at the height of civilization can be brought so low that it can never rise again. It has always been the same when pride lifts a ruler up. It was true of Nebuchadnezzar (Daniel 4:30–32) and his grandson, Belshazzar (Daniel 5:17–28), in the days of the Babylonian exile. And Daniel said it would be true of Alexander the Great (Daniel 8:8) and Antiochus IV Epiphanes (Daniel 8:25). God brings rulers to their knees when they exalt themselves above him.

The Fourth Angelic Message: The Effects of Rome's Judgment (18:4–20)

> Then I heard another voice from heaven saying, "Come out of her, my people, so you will not take part in her sins and so you will not receive her plagues, because her sins have piled up all the way to heaven and God has remembered her crimes. Repay her the same way she repaid others; pay her back double corresponding to her deeds. In the cup she mixed, mix double the amount for her. As much as she exalted herself and lived in sensual luxury, to this extent give her torment and grief because she said to herself, I rule as queen and am no widow; I will never experience grief! For this reason, she will experience her plagues in a single day: disease, mourning, and famine, and she will be burned down with fire, because the Lord God who judges her is powerful!" (Revelation 18:4–8)

This message begins with a call to God's people to stand aside so they will not be affected by the disaster that is about to overtake Rome (18:4–8). John is following the example of the Old Testament prophets who announced the fall of great nations like Babylon. Jeremiah, for example, had at first urged the exiles to settle down in Babylon (Jeremiah 29:4–10). But when God's judgment was announced on the doomed city, he urged them to get out to save their lives (Jeremiah 51:6, 45). Even Jesus urged the citizens of Jerusalem to run for their lives when they saw its end approaching in AD 70 (Matthew 24:15-20). As the exiled Jews were warned to flee the doomed Babylon, and the first century residents of Jerusalem were warned to flee their doomed city, so first century Christians are here warned to flee Rome before it is too late.

Fleeing the city had a twofold purpose. First, it would keep them from partaking in Rome's sins. Isaiah urged the exiles to get out of Babylon and not to touch anything unclean while they were leaving (Isaiah 52:11). Paul used Isaiah's words in 2 Corinthians 6:17 to urge Christians to avoid contamination by the world. Second, it would enable them to escape the coming judgment. As the angel describes it, God had been storing up vengeance as Rome's sins just kept piling up. This carries on an Old Testament theme that held that when God delayed judgment for one generation, it meant only that he was storing up even more judgment to be poured out on an even more wicked generation (Genesis 15:16; 2 Kings 2:20). Even Jesus said that because of his generation's refusal to heed God's servants, God would visit on his generation all the sins of the previous generations (Matthew 23:34–36). It's much like what we in California are told about earthquake faults. Unless there are small quakes along the way to release the pressure, the fault line just continues to build up pressure for an even more devastating earthquake in the future.

Rome had lived in decadent luxury at the expense of heavily taxed nations. It never entered the minds of the Romans that their future was anything less than totally secure (Revelation 18:7). But their end would come suddenly and unexpectedly (18:8). Revelation 18:7–8 is a reprise of what Babylon claimed of itself—and what God had to say about Babylon—in Isaiah 47:8–9. At its height, no nation could compare to ancient Babylon. But, as students of Old Testament history know, even that empire fell in a single night without so much as a battle (Daniel 5:30).

The angel goes on to describe, in graphic terms, the effect of Rome's fall on the rest of its world.

"Then the kings of the earth who committed immoral
acts with her and lived in sensual luxury with her
will weep and wail for her when they see the smoke
from the fire that burns her up. They will stand a
long way off because they are afraid of her torment,
and will say, 'Woe, woe, O great city, Babylon the
powerful city! For in a single hour your doom has
come!'" (Revelation 18:9–10).

This describes the effect on the client kings of Rome. Their
security had been so tied to Rome's patronage that when Rome
fell, it spelled their doom as well. But notice that none of the client
kings came to her aid. Perhaps that is meant to suggest that while
their first instinct is to mourn the benefits they had historically
had from Rome's patronage (18:9), their second instinct might
well be to distance themselves from Rome so as to curry favor
with the new power du jour.

Then the merchants of the earth will weep and mourn
for her because no one buys their cargo any longer-
cargo such as gold, silver, precious stones, pearls,
fine linen, purple cloth, silk, scarlet cloth, all sorts of
things made of citron wood, all sorts of objects made
of ivory, all sorts of things made of expensive wood,
bronze, iron and marble, cinnamon, spice, incense,
perfumed ointment, frankincense, wine, olive oil and
costly flour, wheat, cattle and sheep, horses and four-
wheeled carriages, slaves and human lives. (The ripe
fruit you greatly desired has gone from you, and all
your luxury and splendor have gone from you-they
will never ever be found again!) The merchants who
sold these things, who got rich from her, will stand a
long way off because they are afraid of her torment.
They will weep and mourn, saying, "Woe, woe, O
great city-dressed in fine linen, purple and scarlet
clothing, and adorned with gold, precious stones, and

pearls-because in a single hour such great wealth has been destroyed!" And every ship's captain, and all who sail along the coast- seamen, and all who make their living from the sea, stood a long way off and began to shout when they saw the smoke from the fire that burned her up, "Who is like the great city?" And they threw dust on their heads and were shouting with weeping and mourning, "Woe, Woe, O great city-in which all those who had ships on the sea got rich from her wealth-because in a single hour she has been destroyed!" (Revelation 18:11–19)

The Roman Empire was wrapped around the Mediterranean Sea, so shipping was done primarily by fleets of imperial and merchant ships. What is in view here is the impact of Rome's fall on worldwide commerce. The cargo listed in verses 12–13 includes the bare necessities of their day (e.g., olive oil, flour, wheat, cattle, and sheep), all needed for food throughout the empire. But it also includes luxury items, such as scented wood from North Africa, precious stones and pearls from India, silk and cinnamon from China, spices from China and Arabia, and slaves to provide labor so the decadent Romans don't have to do their own work. The luxury items listed in verse 16 highlight the decadence of the Romans.

The merchants had reason to mourn. The fall of Rome put them out of business, and they lost everything they had. In fact, it was a domino effect. When people stopped buying, merchants went out of business because there was no one left to purchase their goods. When merchants had no customers, shippers went out of business because there was no one left to ship their goods, and even if there had been, there was no one left to buy their cargos when they arrived at their destinations.

It is hard for us to imagine just how far-reaching the effects of Rome's fall were. Rome was the center of international trade, with shipping lanes throughout the Mediterranean. No merchant marine fleet like Rome's existed for a thousand years after the empire fell.

> "Rejoice over her, O heaven, and you saints and apostles and prophets, for God has pronounced judgment against her on your behalf!" (Revelation 18:20).

What was the effect of Rome's fall on the righteous? John described it in one word: "Rejoice!" The reason for rejoicing is that they have at last been vindicated. The city and empire that had tried to destroy them had itself been destroyed. As the angel puts it, "God has pronounced judgment against her on your behalf!" What they could not do for themselves God stepped in and did for them.

The Fifth Angelic Message: The Nature of Rome's Fall (18:21–22)

> "Then one powerful angel picked up a stone like a huge millstone, threw it into the sea, and said, 'With this kind of sudden violent force Babylon the great city will be thrown down and it will never be found again! And the sound of the harpists, musicians, flute players, and trumpeters will never be heard in you again. No craftsman who practices any trade will ever be found in you again; the noise of a mill will never be heard in you again'" (Revelation 18:21–22).

The background of this image is Jeremiah 51:63–64. Jeremiah had sent Seraiah to Babylon with a scroll that included prophecies against that city and its empire. He instructed Seraiah to read the scroll aloud in Babylon and then tie it to a stone and throw it into the Euphrates River. This was intended as a visual demonstration of God's determination to bring such severe judgments on Babylon that it would sink, never to rise again.

What God decreed against Babylon is multiplied many times

in this angelic message against Rome. While Seraiah threw a stone into the Euphrates, this angel threw a "stone like a huge millstone" into the sea. The sea, in this context, would be the Mediterranean, which was the lifeblood of the Roman Empire, just as the Euphrates had been the lifeblood of ancient Babylon. The "huge millstone" was the kind used in an ancient Roman water mill. Archaeologists have discovered many such water mills throughout the ruins of the Roman Empire. Some of the best-preserved millstones weighed over half a ton. If Seraiah's stone would never rise from the Euphrates, there is no doubt that this one would never rise from the depths of the Mediterranean.

There is no joy in the ruined city, as evidenced by the silence of harpists, musicians, flute players, and trumpeters. And notice that commercial enterprise ceased and that "the noise of a mill will never be heard … again." It's not hard to imagine that, with the millstone in the bottom of the Mediterranean Sea.

The Sixth Angelic Message: The Reason for Rome's Fall (18:23–24)

> "Even the light from a lamp will never shine in you again! The voices of the bridegroom and his bride will never be heard in you again. For your merchants were the tycoons of the world, because all the nations were deceived by your magic spells! The blood of the saints and prophets was found in her, along with the blood of all those who had been killed on the earth" (Revelation 18:23–24).

"The voices of the bridegroom and his bride" depicts joy, as do the musicians in verse 22. When the prophets decreed destruction of a city, one of the things they often said was that the sound of a bride and groom would not be heard there again (Jeremiah 16:9; 25:10). The devastation of Rome's fall would be so severe that there wouldn't even be the joy of a wedding for people to celebrate.

Why? Because Rome had intentionally set out to slaughter

God's people in the persecution under Nero, and they would continue to do the same, to an even greater extent, in the upcoming persecution under Domitian.

The Seventh Angelic Message: Praise over Rome's Fall (19:1–10)

> After these things I heard what sounded like the loud voice of a vast throng in heaven, saying, "Hallelujah! Salvation and glory and power belong to our God, because his judgments are true and just. For he has judged the great prostitute who corrupted the earth with her sexual immorality, and has avenged the blood of his servants poured out by her own hands!" Then a second time the crowd shouted, "Hallelujah!" The smoke rises from her forever and ever. The twenty- four elders and the four living creatures threw themselves to the ground and worshiped God, who was seated on the throne, saying: "Amen! Hallelujah!" Then a voice came from the throne, saying: "Praise our God all you his servants, and all you who fear Him, both the small and the great!" Then I heard what sounded like the voice of a vast throng, like the roar of many waters and like loud crashes of thunder. They were shouting: "Hallelujah! For the Lord our God, the All- Powerful, reigns! Let us rejoice and exult and give him glory, because the wedding celebration of the Lamb has come, and his bride has made herself ready. She was permitted to be dressed in bright, clean, fine linen" (for the fine linen is the righteous deeds of the saints). Then the angel said to me, "Write the following: Blessed are those who are invited to the banquet at the wedding celebration of the Lamb!" He also said to me, "These are the true words of God." So I threw myself down at his feet to worship him, but he said, "Do not do this! I am only a fellow servant with you and your

> brothers who hold to the testimony about Jesus.
> Worship God, for the testimony about Jesus is the
> spirit of prophecy." (Revelation 19:1–10)

The scene shifts from mourning on earth to rejoicing in heaven. One word predominates in heaven: "Hallelujah!" That word means "Praise the Lord," and it served as a call to worship in ancient times, when the Levite musicians would lead Jewish worshippers up the hill to the temple mount while singing the Hallel psalms (Psalms 113–118). Just as it functioned as a call to worship in the Jerusalem temple in years past, it now serves as a call to worship in heaven.

There are two verses to this "hallelujah chorus." The first (Revelation 19:1–5) praises God for judging the prostitute and avenging the blood of his servants. The prayers of the martyrs under the altar in the fifth seal have been answered (6:9–11). They have been avenged, and the Lord has been vindicated! At the end of that first round of hallelujahs, the entire heavenly entourage, including the four living creatures and the twenty-four elders from chapter 4, fall on their faces with a loud "Amen! Hallelujah!"

The second verse of this "hallelujah chorus" (19:6–8) announces the Wedding Supper of the Lamb. Isaiah 25 promises a similar banquet as the beginning of a new order of things. In Isaiah 25, after God "causes the song of tyrants to cease" (verse 5), he holds a banquet for his people (verses 6–7). That banquet includes the announcement that "The sovereign Lord will wipe away the tears from every face, and remove his people's disgrace from all the earth" (verse 8). And the people rejoice and celebrate his deliverance (verse 9). This angelic "hallelujah chorus" has the same features. The enemy has been vanquished, God has been vindicated, and his people have been avenged. It is time to celebrate!

We just saw that there is no cause for celebration in fallen Rome, but the opposite is true in heaven. The Wedding Supper of the Lamb has come, and we're preparing to meet the bride! The news is so good that John forgets himself and is about to worship the messenger. But the messenger stops him and redirects his worship to God.

Amen!

Hallelujah!

The Seventh Seven

SEVEN FINAL VISIONS
(19:11–22:5)

Chapter 38

SIX VISIONS OF VICTORY AND JUDGMENT (19:1–20:15)

The First Vision: The Rider on the White Horse (19:11–21)

Then I saw heaven opened and here came a white horse! The one riding it was called "Faithful" and "True," and with justice he judges and goes to war. His eyes are like a fiery flame and there are many diadem crowns on his head. He has a name written that no one knows except himself. He is dressed in clothing dipped in blood, and he is called the Word of God. The armies that are in heaven, dressed in white, clean, fine linen, were following him on white horses. From his mouth extends a sharp sword, so that with it he can strike the nations. He will rule them with an iron rod, and he stomps the winepress of the furious wrath of God, the All-Powerful. He has a name written on his clothing and on his thigh: "King of kings and Lord of lords." Then I saw one angel standing in the sun, and he shouted in a loud voice to all the birds flying high in the sky: "Come, gather around for the great banquet of God, to eat your fill of the flesh of kings, the flesh of generals, the flesh of powerful people, the flesh of horses and those who ride them, and the flesh of all people, both free and slave, and small and great!" Then I saw the beast and the kings of the earth and their armies assembled to do battle with the one who rode the horse and with his army. Now the beast was seized, and along with him the false prophet who had performed the signs on his behalf- signs by which he deceived those who had received the mark of the beast and those who worshiped his image. Both of them were thrown alive into the lake of fire burning with sulfur. The others were killed by the sword that extended from the mouth of the one who rode the horse, and all the birds gorged themselves with their flesh. (Revelation 19:11–21)

The groom rides home from victory to take his bride. The picture is of a victorious Roman general riding in his triumph through the streets of the city. He rides a white horse, which was the Roman symbol of victory. But who is this victorious general? It's not hard to figure out his identity. He is called "Faithful" and "True" (19:11). These are descriptions we've seen applied to Jesus himself earlier (1:5; 3:7).

In fact, several of our earlier glimpses of Christ come together in the description of this rider. He has blazing eyes and a double-edged sword coming out of his mouth (19:12, 15), so we know he is the high priest of chapter 1 (1:12–16). He rules with an iron rod (19:15), so we know he is the child born to the radiant woman in chapter 12 (12:5). He stomps the winepress of the furious wrath of God (19:15), so we know he is the one who exercised God's judgment against the ungodly in chapter 14 (14:19–20). Moreover, he wears many crowns. The Greek word *"diademata"* is used, which refers to rulers' crowns, not victory crowns (19:12). Up to this point, the only diadems in Revelation have been worn by his enemies (12:3; 13:1).

If you're curious as to where he picked up all these crowns, John discloses that as well. In this same vision, he hears an angel calling to the birds of the sky to feast on the flesh of dead kings and generals (19:18).

This general is unlike any other general and any other king you've ever read about. His robe is covered in blood (19:13), but the robes worn by his armies are all white and clean (19:14). In most armies, the soldiers do the fighting while the generals stay behind and direct their movements. In this army, the general does the killing. I want to be in his army! He is King of Kings and Lord of Lords!

Domitian *thought* he was king of kings and lord of lords. He was mistaken.

I love the way the historian Will Durant describes this drama of the showdown between Christ and Rome: "There is no greater drama in human record than the sight of a few Christians, scorned or oppressed by a succession of emperors, bearing all trials with a fierce tenacity, multiplying quietly, building order while their enemies generated chaos, fighting the sword with the word, brutality with hope, and at last defeating the strongest state that history has known. Caesar and Christ had met in the arena, and Christ had won."[6]

The Second Vision: The Great Banquet of God (19:17–18)

Following is the vision of two great feasts. First, there is the Wedding Supper of the Lamb, with the saints as his invited guests:

> "Then the angel said to me, 'Write the following: Blessed are those who are invited to the banquet at the wedding celebration of the Lamb!' He also said to me, 'These are the true words of God'" (Revelation 19:9).

Then there is the great supper of God, with his enemies as the entrée for carrion birds:

> "Then I saw one angel standing in the sun, and he shouted in a loud voice to all the birds flying high in the sky: 'Come, gather around for the great banquet of God, to eat your fill of the flesh of kings, the flesh of generals, the flesh of powerful people, the flesh of horses and those who ride them, and the flesh of all people, both free and slave, and small and great!'" (Revelation 19:17–18).

The difference between the two feasts is dramatic. The saints are granted *entry* to the wedding celebration of the Lamb, but the ungodly find themselves as the *entrée* at the great banquet of God. I'd much rather be a guest at the wedding celebration of the Lamb than the main course at the great supper of God!

The Third Vision: The Fall of the Two Beasts (19:19–21)

> Then I saw the beast and the kings of the earth and their armies assembled to do battle with the one who rode the horse and with his army. Now the beast was seized, and along with him the false prophet who had performed the signs on his behalf- signs by which he deceived those who had received the mark of the beast and those who worshiped his image. Both of them were thrown alive into the lake of fire burning with sulfur. The others were killed by the sword that extended from the mouth of the one who rode the horse, and all the birds gorged themselves with their flesh. (Revelation 19:19–21)

This is *the war*. We've waited a long time to see it, but in a moment it's all over. Here is something many writers overlook. For all the talk of the "Battle of Armageddon" (16:16), no battle is ever seen in Revelation! God's victory over his enemy is so certain that the battle is never even described.

The beast here is the sea beast from 13:1–10; the false prophet here is the earth beast from 13:11–18. The beast's number is 666 (13:18). He simply cannot win! Both beasts are taken and thrown into a fiery lake of burning sulfur. By way of reminder, burning sulfur is one Biblical description of God's judgment against sin, as at Sodom (Genesis 19:24).

The rest of the bodies on the battlefield are the ones killed by the rider on the white horse. Babylon, the great prostitute, has fallen. Now the beast and the false prophet have fallen, too. There is only one enemy left. I'll bet he's next—the dragon, Satan, himself!

The Fourth Vision: Binding of Satan (20:1–3)

> "Then I saw an angel descending from heaven, holding in his hand the key to the abyss and a huge chain. He seized the dragon- the ancient serpent, who is the devil and Satan- and tied him up for a thousand years. The angel then threw him into the abyss and locked and sealed it so that he could not deceive the nations until the one thousand years were finished. (After these things he must be released for a brief period of time.)" (Revelation 20:1–3).

Binding Satan is nothing new. He has been bound before. In the book of Job, Satan was limited so that he could do only what God allowed (Job 1:12; 2:6). During his ministry, Jesus bound Satan in order to cast out demons (Matthew 12:24–29). Jesus even said that he saw Satan fall when he discussed the work of the disciples he sent out (Luke 10:17–20). And on the cross, Christ triumphed over Satan and his minions (Colossians 2:15). God always has the upper hand over the devil.

But notice here that the binding of Satan in Revelation 20:1–3 is not absolute. Rather, it is a specific kind of binding. It is "so that he [cannot] deceive the nations." In other words, the purpose of this binding was to prevent Satan from using a worldwide empire to try to stamp out the church. He can still go after individual Christians, but he can't go after the church as a whole any more, as he did with Rome in the first century.

The Fifth Vision: The Thousand Years (20:4–6)

> Then I saw thrones and seated on them were those who had been given authority to judge. I also saw the souls of those who had been beheaded because of the testimony about Jesus and because of the word of God. These had not worshiped the beast or his image and had refused to receive his mark on their forehead or hand. They came to life and reigned with Christ for a thousand years. (The rest of the dead did not come to life until the thousand years were finished.) This is the first resurrection. Blessed and holy is the one who takes part in the first resurrection. The second death has no power over them, but they will be priests of God and of Christ, and they will reign with him for a thousand years. (Revelation 20:4–6)

Remember that Revelation is filled with symbols that were never intended to be taken literally. One of those symbols is "the thousand years." This is the only place it is mentioned in the Bible. Without these three verses, there would be no premillennialists, postmillennialists, or amillennialists. People who take the Bible seriously should avoid any doctrine that emphasizes something the Bible minimizes.

Everything we know about the so-called thousand-year reign comes from these three verses. Four questions can help clarify the meaning of Revelation 20:4–6.

The first question is, who reigns? The text itself answers the question. It is Christ and the Christian overcomers who reign.

We saw these overcomers under the altar in the fifth seal (6:9). We saw them in the great multitude (7:13–14). We saw them on Mount Zion (14:1–5). We saw them by the sea of glass (15:2–3). We saw them in heaven (19:1–2). We saw them following Christ, the Conqueror (19:14). Now we see them seated on thrones.

The second question is, why do they reign? The reign is spoken of in terms of *judging* not ruling. Those who were judged by Rome are now in the position to judge Rome (20:4). With the defeat of Rome and the emperor cult, they have at last been vindicated. Jesus promised them thrones (3:21), and they now sit on those thrones.

The third question is, where do they reign? Every time we see them, they're in heaven. Contrary to popular opinion among modern writers, there is *nothing* here about an earthly kingdom.

The fourth question is, when do they reign? The text tells us that their reign commences at the fall of Rome, when Satan is bound to prevent him from using a worldwide empire to try to destroy the church, and that it continues for a thousand years. The thousand years is no more literal than any of the other figures in the book. The point is that once Christ's kingdom defeats Satan's kingdom, that defeat is irrevocable. He may try another attack now and then (20:3, 7–8), but he will never succeed in destroying God's kingdom.

Satan's Doom (20:7–10)

> Now when the thousand years are finished, Satan will be released from his prison and will go out to deceive the nations at the four corners of the earth, Gog and Magog, to bring them together for the battle. They are as numerous as the grains of sand in the sea. They went up on the broad plain of the earth and encircled the camp of the saints and the beloved city, but fire came down from heaven and devoured them completely. And the devil who deceived them was thrown into the lake of fire and sulfur, where

> the beast and the false prophet are too, and they will
> be tormented there day and night forever and ever.
> (Revelation 20:7–10)

John presents his readers with a simple picture: Satan never gives up! He gets loose and tries it again. And God says, "No you don't" and throws him in the lake of burning sulfur. In the words of Jesus, "I will build my church, and the gates of Hades will not overpower it" (Matthew 16:18). John designed this snapshot to encourage those who hear and obey not to fret, but find encouragement. No matter what Satan tries, God always has the upper hand.

The Sixth Vision: The Dead Are Judged (20:11–15)

> Then I saw a large white throne and the one who was
> seated on it; the earth and the heaven fled from his
> presence, and no place was found for them. And I saw
> the dead, the great and the small, standing before
> the throne. Then books were opened, and another
> book was opened- the book of life. So the dead were
> judged by what was written in the books, according
> to their deeds. The sea gave up the dead that were in
> it, and Death and Hades gave up the dead that were
> in them, and each one was judged according to his
> deeds. Then Death and Hades were thrown into the
> lake of fire. This is the second death- the lake of fire.
> If anyone's name was not found written in the book
> of life, that person was thrown into the lake of fire.
> (Revelation 20:11–15)

There are two books by which each life is ultimately judged: the Book of Life, and the book of that person's life. Imagine the scene this way. When a person stands before the throne, God, the Judge, looks into the Book of Life to see if that person's name is recorded there. If that person's name is in the Book of Life, the

Judge looks no further. But if that person's name is not recorded in the Book of Life, then the Judge looks into the book of that individual's life to see why it is not there. It is as though the Judge, in an effort to find any and every way possible to extend mercy and grace, is looking to see whether there might have been some mistake or oversight involved. When he looks into the record of that individual's life, he finds that there is no mistake. That person, like everyone else, has sinned and falls short of the glory of God (Romans 3:23). The only people who survive the judgment unscathed are those whose names are in the Book of Life.

Amen!

Hallelujah!

Chapter 39

THE SEVENTH VISION: THE DESTINY OF THE REDEEMED (21:1–22:6)

Perfect Fellowship with God (21:1–8)

Then I saw a new heaven and a new earth, for the first heaven and earth had ceased to exist, and the sea existed no more. And I saw the holy city- the new Jerusalem- descending out of heaven from God, made ready like a bride adorned for her husband. And I heard a loud voice from the throne saying: "Look! The residence of God is among human beings. He will live among them, and they will be his people, and God himself will be with them. He will wipe away every tear from their eyes, and death will not exist any more- or mourning, or crying, or pain, for the former things have ceased to exist." And the one seated on the throne said: "Look! I am making all things new!" Then he said to me, "Write it down, because these words are reliable and true." He also said to me, "It is done! I am the Alpha and the Omega, the beginning and the end. To the one who is thirsty I will give water free of charge from the spring of the water of life. The one who conquers will inherit these things, and I will be his God and he will be my son. But to the cowards, unbelievers, detestable persons, murderers,

> the sexually immoral, and those who practice magic spells, idol worshipers, and all those who lie, their place will be in the lake that burns with fire and sulfur. That is the second death." (Revelation 21:1–8)

This is another of those places in Revelation that calls for the reader to take a macro view of the text before engaging in a micro view. In other words, the reader should back away from the text to look at the big picture first, before focusing on the minute details.

There are three major features in this text worth noting. First, there is a new heaven and a new earth (21:1). Don't think of these as two separate things but as a two-part description of one thing. Just as "the heavens and the earth" described creation in Genesis 1:1, so now "a new heaven and a new earth" describes a new creation.

There may be more here than meets the eye. In the ancient world, earthly temples were intended to be replicas of the temple of the deity in heaven. When Jews spoke of "heaven and earth," they did not always mean the physical universe. There are examples in biblical and extra-biblical writings showing that they referred to the Jerusalem temple as "heaven and earth."

For example, Psalm 78 is a temple hymn. In verse 60, the psalmist describes how God rejected Shiloh as the place for the tabernacle. In verses 67 and 68, he describes how the sanctuary was moved from the territory of Ephraim to Mount Zion in Jerusalem. Then, he likens God's temple to "heaven and earth," as follows: "He made his sanctuary as enduring as the heavens above; as secure as the earth, which he established permanently." (Psalm 78:69).

Josephus described the temple in terms of "heaven and earth." He distinguished between the parts that were accessible to man (the courtyard and the holy place, corresponding to the physical world) and the part that was inaccessible to man (the most holy place, corresponding to heaven). Heaven, the site of God's throne, was beyond this material world. It was behind the curtain and inaccessible to man.

You will recall that Moses received the "pattern" of the tabernacle as a revelation from God on Mount Sinai (Exodus 25:9, 40; 26:30), so it is not unusual that the temple would be considered a model of "heaven and earth." The writer of Hebrews looks back to the fact that the tabernacle and temple were models of the heavenly reality (Hebrews 8:5) to demonstrate that our heavenly sanctuary surpasses the old earthly sanctuary in Jerusalem. In other words, following Jewish thinking, the old "heaven and earth" had passed away, having been replaced by a "new heaven and earth."

So John may be juxtaposing the Jewish temple, which had long since been destroyed, with the permanency of God's true sanctuary in heaven. Or, he may be contrasting the physical world, which is temporary, with heaven, which is eternal. In either case, it is noteworthy that John describes the "newness" of this creation with the Greek word "*kainos*" rather than "*neos*." The difference between the two words is that "*neos*" refers to a newer model of the same old thing—what advertisers call "new and improved"— while "*kainos*" describes something that has been fundamentally transformed. We might think about this in terms of buying a new car. One person might buy this year's model of last year's Toyota (*neos*), while another person might buy something that uses totally new technology (*kainos*), like a Tesla. John describes this new creation as something that is fundamentally unlike anything that has gone before. He is not the first to see this new creation on the horizon. Isaiah looked forward to this new creation (Isaiah 65:17; 66:22). And the New Testament writers were still looking forward to it (2 Peter 3:12–13).

Second, there is no more sea (Revelation 21:1). Recall that in the throne scene in chapter 4, John saw "something like a sea of glass, like crystal" surrounding God's throne (4:6). That was similar to what Ezekiel saw in his vision of God (Ezekiel 1:22). It is also very similar to what Moses and his entourage saw when they ascended Sinai (Exodus 24:9–10).

When the tabernacle was built, the laver stood in front of the entrance to the holy place. Later, when Solomon built the first temple, the laver measured fifteen feet from rim to rim and had a circumference of forty-five feet. He called it "the sea." That was the barrier the priests had to pass in order to enter into God's presence. Revelation uses the same imagery, describing the sea as a barrier between God and man. In chapter 4, it stands between man and God (Revelation 4:6). But in chapter 15, the faithful have crossed over the sea (15:2–3). The picture there is of Israel standing on the eastern shore of the Red Sea after God delivered them from Egypt. In Exodus 15, the delivered people sang the song of Moses. But in Revelation 15, that song is also the song of the Lamb. Just as Moses had delivered Israel, so the Lamb has now delivered his people.

Now, at last, the sea is gone (21:1). There is no more separation from God. Indeed, there is no longer any need for man to be separated from God, because chapter 20 ended with Satan and everyone who had followed him being cast irrevocably into the lake of fire. The only people left are the redeemed, whose names had been found in the Book of Life, and there is no reason for them to be separated from God any longer.

Third, there is "the holy city - the new Jerusalem" (21:2). Jerusalem stands for both the place and its inhabitants. It is described as a "bride adorned for her husband" because its citizens are the bride of the Lamb (19:7). Just as a bride moves into her husband's house, so here God's people live with God himself (21:3).

The central feature of the "new heavens and new earth" envisioned by Isaiah was this New Jerusalem, in which there would be no suffering, no sorrow, and no death (Isaiah 65:17–25). That is the same as the description John gives of the New Jerusalem in Revelation 21:4.

In Revelation 21:1–4, Eden has been restored. God and man live together in peace. Everything that sin introduced into this world—pain, sorrow, and death—has "ceased to exist" (21:4). Those things that are the result of man's sin are "water under the bridge" and are long gone and forgotten. Then, in verses 5–8, God gives his personal assurance that this is the certain future for the overcomers. But he also gives his personal promise that his presence and his blessings are only for believers, not for the unbelievers (21:8) who have already been consigned to the lake of fire (20:15).

Perfect Protection by God (21:9–27)

> Then one of the seven angels who had the seven bowls full of the seven final plagues came and spoke to me, saying, "Come, I will show you the bride, the wife of the Lamb!" So he took me away in the Spirit to a huge, majestic mountain and showed me the holy city, Jerusalem, descending out of heaven from God. The city possesses the glory of God; its brilliance is like a precious jewel, like a stone of crystal- clear jasper. It has a massive, high wall with twelve gates, with twelve angels at the gates, and the names of the twelve tribes of the nation of Israel are written on the gates. There are three gates on the east side, three gates on the north side, three gates on the south side and three gates on the west side. The wall of the city has twelve foundations, and on them are the twelve names of the twelve apostles of the Lamb. The angel who spoke to me had a golden measuring rod with which to measure the city and its foundation stones and wall. Now the city is laid out as a square, its length and width the same. He measured the city with the measuring rod at fourteen hundred miles (its length and width and height are equal). He also measured its wall, one hundred forty- four cubits according to human measurement, which is also the angel's. The city's wall is made of jasper and the city is pure gold, like transparent glass. The foundations of the city's wall are decorated with every kind of precious stone. The first foundation

is jasper, the second sapphire, the third agate, the fourth emerald, the fifth onyx, the sixth carnelian, the seventh chrysolite, the eighth beryl, the ninth topaz, the tenth chrysoprase, the eleventh jacinth, and the twelfth amethyst. And the twelve gates are twelve pearls- each one of the gates is made from just one pearl! The main street of the city is pure gold, like transparent glass. Now I saw no temple in the city, because the Lord God- the All- Powerful- and the Lamb are its temple. The city does not need the sun or the moon to shine on it, because the glory of God lights it up, and its lamp is the Lamb. The nations will walk by its light and the kings of the earth will bring their grandeur into it. Its gates will never be closed during the day (and there will be no night there). They will bring the grandeur and the wealth of the nations into it, but nothing ritually unclean will ever enter into it, nor anyone who does what is detestable or practices falsehood, but only those whose names are written in the Lambs book of life. (Revelation 21:9–27)

This description is designed to contrast the heavenly city with the city of Rome in the first century. Note that The NET Bible, like the *New American Standard Bible*, has converted the dimensions in the Greek text to miles. Don't forget that the numbers are not intended to be taken literally. The dimensions in the Greek text are twelve thousand stadia on each side. The point, as we've seen before, is that there is enough room for all of God's people and no one will be cramped at all. However, the mileage measurements here are helpful to show us the contrast between God's city and Caesar's that the text intends to convey.

Caesar's city, Rome proper, occupied only about five square miles of land. But it commanded an empire that covered about 2.25 million square miles, and that held sway over the world. By contrast, God's city, the New Jerusalem described in Revelation

22, covers 2.25 million square miles—about the same area as the Roman Empire in the first century—and it rises fourteen hundred miles up in the air to boot! The message is simple: God's city is bigger than Caesar's empire.

The elderly Emperor Augustus was quoted as saying, "I found Rome a city of bricks and left it a city of marble." That is impressive. But Revelation 21 says that God made his city of precious stones, pearls, and gold. These materials, which we regard as precious, are what God uses as building materials.

Moreover, in God's city, there is no temple; and there is no need for the sun, because God and the Lamb are there. And there is no need to shut the city gates against any enemies, because there are no more enemies to fear. The only people there are those whose names are in the Book of Life.

Perfect Provision by God (Revelation 22:1–5)

> Then the angel showed me the river of the water of life- water as clear as crystal- pouring out from the throne of God and of the Lamb, flowing down the middle of the city's main street. On each side of the river is the tree of life producing twelve kinds of fruit, yielding its fruit every month of the year. Its leaves are for the healing of the nations. And there will no longer be any curse, and the throne of God and the Lamb will be in the city. His servants will worship him, and they will see his face, and his name will be on their foreheads. Night will be no more, and they will not need the light of a lamp or the light of the sun, because the Lord God will shine on them, and they will reign forever and ever. (Revelation 22:1–5)

This description of the New Jerusalem is similar to a vision in Ezekiel 47:1–12. In Ezekiel's vision, the water of life flows out from the temple. It begins as a trickle and ends as a flood. What river gets deeper as it goes without any tributaries? Only one that begins at God's temple.

The water in Ezekiel's vision flows eastward to the Dead Sea, where something amazing happens. Anyone who has visited Israel knows that any living fish in the Jordan River die within moments of entering the Dead Sea. In fact, it is called the Dead Sea because nothing can live in it. Yet when this flood from the temple reaches the Dead Sea, it turns the salt water to fresh water, and it turns the Dead Sea to a body of water teeming with life so that fishermen can fish for food along its shores. Moreover, the desert around the Dead Sea grows lush with vegetation so that there is never a lack of fruit for the people to eat.

John's vision of the New Jerusalem also features this living water pouring from the throne of God and of the Lamb and watering the Tree of Life. This is the very tree from which man was barred in Genesis 3:22–24, but now man has unlimited access to its fruit and medicinal leaves (Revelation 22:2). Its fruit is never out of season, and its leaves are available for healing. (In case you may be unaware of it, many of our modern medicines come from the leaves of plants in the rain forest.) So the Bible begins with man in fellowship with God around the Tree of Life, and it ends the same way.

In God's New Jerusalem, there is no curse of death any more, unlike man's experience in Eden (Genesis 3:14–19). In God's city, God and the Lamb share rule, following Paul's description in 1 Corinthians 15:20–28. In this city, God's people will worship him, see his face, and wear his name. This city is self-sufficient because its sufficiency is from God. Unlike any other city of the first century, it is not susceptible to siege. It is too big for any army to surround (fourteen hundred miles on any side). Its walls are too thick for any siege works to penetrate (144 cubits is about 216 feet thick). Its walls are too high for any catapult to overcome (fourteen hundred miles). It is built on twelve foundations, so no enemy can tunnel under the wall. Its water source cannot be cut off, because it originates within the city. No enemy can starve it out, because the Tree of Life yields fresh fruit year round.

This is the fulfillment of Nebuchadnezzar's dream in Daniel 2:31–44. He saw a succession of four empires, each of which was succeeded by the next. Then he saw a kingdom set up by God that destroyed those kingdoms and that would, unlike those human kingdoms, stand forever.

This is God's description of the church. Just as Jesus said, even the gates of Hades cannot and will not overpower it (Matthew 16:18).

Amen!

Hallelujah!

Epilogue (22:6–21)

Chapter 40

EPILOGUE (22:6–21)

Then the angel said to me, "These words are reliable and true. The Lord, the God of the spirits of the prophets, has sent his angel to show his servants what must happen soon." (Look! I am coming soon! Blessed is the one who keeps the words of the prophecy expressed in this book.) I, John, am the one who heard and saw these things, and when I heard and saw them, I threw myself down to worship at the feet of the angel who was showing them to me. But he said to me, "Do not do this! I am a fellow servant with you and with your brothers the prophets, and with those who obey the words of this book. Worship God!" Then he said to me, "Do not seal up the words of the prophecy contained in this book, because the time is near. The evildoer must continue to do evil, and the one who is morally filthy must continue to be filthy. The one who is righteous must continue to act righteously, and the one who is holy must continue to be holy." (Look! I am coming soon, and my reward is with me to pay each one according to what he has done! I am the Alpha and the Omega, the first and the last, the beginning and the end!) Blessed are those who wash their robes so they can have access to the tree of life and can enter into the city

by the gates. Outside are the dogs and the sorcerers
and the sexually immoral, and the murderers, and
the idolaters and everyone who loves and practices
falsehood! "I, Jesus, have sent my angel to testify
to you about these things for the churches. I am the
root and the descendant of David, the bright morning
star!" And the Spirit and the bride say, "Come!" And
let the one who hears say: "Come!" And let the one
who is thirsty come; let the one who wants it take the
water of life free of charge. I testify to the one who
hears the words of the prophecy contained in this
book: If anyone adds to them, God will add to him
the plagues described in this book. And if anyone
takes away from the words of this book of prophecy,
God will take away his share in the tree of life and in
the holy city that are described in this book. The one
who testifies to these things says, "Yes, I am coming
soon!" Amen! Come, Lord Jesus! The grace of the
Lord Jesus be with all.

—Revelation 22:6–21

Reliable and True (22:6–7)

John is assured that the words he has been given are "reliable
and true" and that they are revealed to show God's servants
"what must happen soon." This flies in the face of those who claim
Revelation is a mystery that is designed to bewilder and confuse
its readers. Quite the contrary, it was written to reveal—not
conceal—God's plan for his people.

Don't lose sight of the fact that the book was written in the
first-century world, by a first-century writer, for first-century
readers. And lest anyone miss the point that the book was
intended to be understood by those readers, it begins with the
word that became its title: "Revelation"—not "mystery."

The book begins with a proclamation of the coming of the Lord

(1:7). That can be a welcome promise to those who are faithful (3:11), but it is always a threat to those who oppose him (2:16). As we saw early on, the coming of the Lord is always associated in the Old Testament with the fall of a nation. This was true of Babylon (Isaiah 13:9–11), Egypt (Isaiah 19:1), Assyria (Isaiah 30:30–31), and Edom (Isaiah 63:1–6), just to name a few.

So what is the point of the coming of the Lord in Revelation? The first-century readers would certainly have understood it to mean that God was going to judge the Roman Empire and that he was going to establish his indestructible kingdom. That coming spelled certain doom to the world's most powerful empire, but it also offered a certain future for those who had been oppressed by that Roman juggernaut.

Worship God (22:8–9)

The news is just too good to be true. Which of us would not throw ourselves down at the feet of the messenger who just announced the end of our suffering and the beginning of our reward? Any believer might well be tempted to bow before one who brings such good news. We shouldn't be too critical here of John. Who of us has not had the experience of hearing a messenger of God who powerfully preaches the word of Christ, only to find ourselves inclined to give him more reverence than he is due? (1 Corinthians 3:5–9; Acts 14:8–18).

But the angel is quick to stop John's misguided obeisance, just as in Revelation 19:10. The revelation originates not with the angel but with God. Just as John is merely the messenger to the seven churches, so the angel is the messenger to John. God alone is worthy of worship; both the angel's message and John's revelation originate with God.

Do Not Seal Up the Words of the Prophecy (22:10–15)

John is told not to seal up the words of the prophecy in Revelation 22:10. By contrast, when Daniel received a similar prophecy, he was told to seal up those words (Daniel 12:4). Why the difference?

The prophecy in Daniel 10–12 covers six hundred years, beginning with the Persian Empire. The terminus of the prophecy is the destruction of Jerusalem in AD 70 (Daniel 12:7). Daniel was told to seal his vision because it had to do with the distant future—six hundred years from his day. On the other hand, John was told *not* to seal his vision because the time was near (Revelation 22:10). That means that the vision was to be fulfilled in the near future, from John's perspective. But he is also told that in the meantime, the wicked will get worse and the righteous will have to endure (22:11). But the promise for the believers and the threat for the unbelievers, though they be delayed, are nonetheless certain (22:12–15).

An Invitation and a Warning (22:16–19)

There is an invitation for those attuned to God's words (22:16–17) followed by a warning to those who distort his words (22:18–19). In light of the warning, what would John say to the modern writers who have taken it entirely out of its first-century context and tried to make it a book for the twenty-first century?

How to Recognize a False Prophet

Ancient Israel took the matter of false prophets seriously. God laid down the rule in Deuteronomy 18:20: "if any prophet presumes to speak anything in my name that I have not authorized him to speak ... that prophet must die." That led the people to ask, "How can we know?" God's answer is found in the next two verses. "Now if you say to yourselves, 'How can we tell that a message is not from the LORD?' -- whenever a prophet speaks in my name and the prediction is not fulfilled, then I have not spoken it; the prophet has presumed to speak it, so you need not fear him" (Deuteronomy 18:21–22).

Over the last several decades, writer after writer has taken

Revelation and used it to try to predict world events. Each has had to repeatedly rewrite and revise his predictions when the passage of time has proved them wrong. Yet their books continue to be best sellers.

Hal Lindsay, for example, wrote *The Late, Great Planet Earth* in 1970. He claimed that a forty-year countdown to Armageddon began on May 14, 1948, when David Ben-Gurion read the Declaration of Independence announcing the establishment of a Jewish nation—the state of Israel. "Obviously, in context, the generation that would see the signs -- chief among them the rebirth of Israel. A generation in the Bible is something like forty years. If this is a correct deduction, then within forty years or so of 1948, all these things could take place. Many scholars who have studied Bible prophecy all their lives believe that this is so."[7] In a later book, he wrote, "The decade of the 1980's could very well be the last decade of history as we know it."[8] Equating the Soviet Union with Gog and Magog, he wrote, "The current build-up of Russian ships in the Mediterranean serves as another significant sign of the possible nearness of Armageddon."[9]

Today, in 2016, we are sixty-eight years into his forty-year countdown—and there is no evidence that his prophecies are being fulfilled. When time proved him wrong, he equivocated: "I also said that '*if*' a generation was forty years and '*if*' the generation of the 'fig tree' *(Mat 24:32–34)* started with the foundation of the state of Israel, then Jesus '*might* come back by 1988.' But I put a lot of ifs and maybes in because I knew that no one could be absolutely certain."[10]

Lindsay once predicted that the Soviet Union would be the great enemy to the north that would swarm over Israel. But the Soviet Union collapsed on Christmas Day, 1991. When that happened, he sidestepped his false predictions and pretended to have known all along that, as he put it, "... world domination -- as Ezekiel makes clear -- *was never in the script for Russia!*"[11] So when the clock ticked past his forty-year countdown and the

Soviet Union collapsed, Lindsey sidestepped his false prediction by saying that the Soviet collapse was inevitable.

How many errors or mistakes must be shown before these so-called prophets and their followers finally admit that they are wrong in their attempts to predict future events?

A Promise and a Confident Assurance (Revelation 22:20–21)

> "The one who testifies to these things says, 'Yes, I am coming soon!' Amen! Come, Lord Jesus! The grace of the Lord Jesus be with all." (Revelation 22:20–21).

Revelation ends with a final promise by Jesus that he will come to vindicate his followers and avenge their enemies, just as promised in his answer to the martyrs under the altar in the fifth seal (6:9–11). John buys into that promise with a wholehearted "Amen! Come, Lord Jesus!"

The last words of the book are a closing benediction: "The grace of the Lord Jesus be with all." This is a common method used by the New Testament writers to end their letters. The point is that they desire that God's grace may enable the readers and hearers to understand and obey the contents of the letter. That was John's hope at the beginning of the book (1:3), and it is his prayer at the end.

Amen!

Hallelujah!

Endnotes

1. Hal Lindsay, *The 1980's: Countdown to Armageddon* (New York: Bantam Books, 1981), 8.
2. Hal Lindsay, *Planet Earth—2000 A.D.* (Palos Verdes, CA: Western Front, 1994), 3.
3. Didache 14, Ignatius to the Magnesians, 9:1.
4. G. R. Beasley-Murray, *The Book of Revelation*, revised (Eugene, Oregon: Wipf and Stock Publishers, 2010), 191.
5. Ray Summers, *Worthy is the Lamb* (Nashville, Tennessee: Broadman Press, 1951), 178.
6. Will Durant, chapter 30, part 1 in *The Story of Civilization*, vol. 3 (New York: Simon & Schuster, 1944) p 652.
7. Hal Lindsay, *The Late, Great Planet Earth* (Grand Rapids, Michigan: Zondervan Publishing House, 1970), 54.
8. Hal Lindsay, *The 1980's: Countdown to Armageddon*, 8.
9. Hal Lindsay, *The Late, Great Planet Earth*, 145–146.
10. Hal Lindsay, *Planet Earth—2000 A.D.*, 3.
11. Quoted by C. Marvin Pate and Calvin B. Haines Jr. in *Doomsday Delusions: What's Wrong with Predictions About the End of the World* (Downers Grove, Illinois: InterVarsity Press, 1995), 138.